CRUSADE TEXTS IN TRANSLATION

Volume 24

About the volume

Albert of Aachen's *History of the Journey to Jerusalem* presents the story of the First Crusade (1095–1099) and the early history of the crusader states (1099–1119). *Volume 1, The First Crusade*, is a long and richly detailed account of events well known from the reports of participants, such as Fulcher of Chartres, Raymond of Aguilers and the anonymous author of the *Gesta Francorum*, but told from a strikingly different perspective.

Albert did not go on crusade himself, but gathered reports and anecdotes from those who did, and wove them into narrative that foregrounds the activities of Peter the Hermit, Godfrey of Bouillon, Baldwin of Boulogne, and their followers. His *History* therefore offers a counter-balance, and sometimes a corrective, to the established view. Susan B. Edgington's English translation has been widely praised, following its first publication in the Oxford Medieval Texts series, and is here presented with a new introduction and updated notes and bibliography.

About the series

The crusading movement, which originated in the 11th century and lasted beyond the 16th, bequeathed to its future historians a legacy of sources which are unrivalled in their range and variety. These sources document in fascinating detail the motivations and viewpoints, military efforts and spiritual lives of the participants in the crusades. They also narrate the internal histories of the states and societies which crusaders established or supported in the many regions where they fought, as well as those of their opponents. Some of these sources have been translated in the past but the vast majority have been available only in their original language. The goal of this series is to provide a wide ranging corpus of texts, most of them translated for the first time, which will illuminate the history of the crusades and the crusader-states from every angle, including that of their principal adversaries, the Muslim powers of the Middle East.

About the translator

Susan B. Edgington is a Senior Research Fellow at Queen Mary, University of London, UK

For Hannah and Rebekah, Emma and Anne

ALBERT OF AACHEN'S *HISTORY OF THE JOURNEY TO JERUSALEM*

Crusade Texts in Translation

Titles in the series include

Mary Fisher
The Chronicle of Prussia by Nicolaus von Jeroschin
A History of the Teutonic Knights in Prussia, 1190–1331

Peter Lock
Marino Sanudo Torsello, The Book of the Secrets of the Faithful of the Cross
Liber Secretorum Fidelium Crucis

Susan B. Edgington and Carol Sweetenham
The *Chanson d'Antioche*
An Old French Account of the First Crusade

Denys Pringle
Pilgrimage to Jerusalem and the Holy Land, 1187–1291

Carol Sweetenham
Robert the Monk's History of the First Crusade
Historia Iherosolimitana

Damian J. Smith and Helena Buffery
The Book of Deeds of James I of Aragon
A Translation of the Medieval Catalan *Llibre dels Fets*

Albert of Aachen's *History of the Journey to Jerusalem*

Volume 1: Books 1-6. The First Crusade, 1095–1099

Translated by

SUSAN B. EDGINGTON
Queen Mary, University of London, UK

ASHGATE

Published by
Ashgate Publishing Limited
Wey Court East
Union Road
Farnham
Surrey, GU9 7PT
England

Ashgate Publishing Company
110 Cherry Street
Suite 3-1
Burlington, VT 05401-3818
USA

www.ashgate.com

British Library Cataloguing in Publication Data
Albert, of Aachen, 11th–12th cent.
Albert of Aachen's History of the Journey to Jerusalem. Volume 1. Books 1–6, The First Crusade, 1095-1099. – (Crusade Texts in Translation ; v. 24)
1. Crusades – First, 1096-–099 – Early works to 1800. I. Title II. Series
III. History of the journey to Jerusalem IV. Edgington, Susan.
940.1'8-dc23

Library of Congress Cataloging-in-Publication Data
Albert, of Aachen, 11th–12th cent.
[Historia Ierosolimitana. English]
Albert of Aachen's History of the Journey to Jerusalem / translated and edited by Susan B. Edgington.
pages cm. – (Crusade texts in Translation; 24, 25)
Translated from the Latin.
An earlier version of this work was published in one volume under the title Historia Ierosolimitana: history of the journey to Jerusalem by Clarendon Press in 2007. The current edition is presented with a new introduction and updated notes and bibliography. Includes bibliographical references and index.
1. Crusades--First, 1096–1099--Early works to 1800. 2. Jerusalem--History – Latin Kingdom, 1099–1244 – Early works to 1800. I. Edgington, Susan, translator, editor.
II. Title.
D161.A4313 2013
956'.014–dc23 2012044663

ISBN 9781409466529 (pbk)

Printed and bound in Great Britain
by MPG PRINTGROUP

Contents

Maps	vii
Abbreviations	ix
Preface	xi
Introduction	1
Book 1	15
Book 2	43
Book 3	79
Book 4	133
Book 5	177
Book 6	211
Appendix 1: People	251
Appendix 2: Places	265
Bibliography	273
Index	281

Maps

1	Routes across Europe, 1096	xii
2	The siege of Nicaea	xiii
3	The siege of Antioch, winter 1097–98	xiv
4	The march south, March–July 1099	xv
5	The capture of Jerusalem, 15 July 1099	xvi

Abbreviations

AA	Albert of Aachen, *Historia Ierosolimitana: History of the Journey to Jerusalem*, (ed. and trans.) Susan B. Edgington (Oxford: Oxford University Press, 2007)
AK	Anna Komnene, *The Alexiad*, (trans.) E. R. A. Sewter, rev. edn Peter Frankopan (London: Penguin, 2009)
BD	*Baldrici episcopi Dolensis Historia Jerosolimitana, RHC Occ* iv. 1–111
ChA	*The Chanson d'Antioche*, (trans.) Susan B. Edgington and Carol Sweetenham (Farnham: Ashgate, 2011)
Du Cange	C. Du Cange, *Glossarium mediae et infimae Latinitatis conditum a Carolo du Fresne, domino Du Cange; cum supplementis integris D. P. Carpenterii, Adelungii, aliorum, susque digessit G. A. L. Henschel* (10 vols, Niort: Favre, 1883–87)
EA	*Ekkehardi abbatis Uraugiensis Hierosolymita, RHC Occ* v: 1–40
FC	*Fulcheri Carnotensis Historia Hierosolymitana (1095–1127)*, (ed.) Heinrich Hagenmeyer (Heidelberg Carl Winters Universitätsbuchhandlung, 1913)
GN	Guibertus abbas S. Mariae Nogenti, *Dei gesta per Francos*, (ed.) Robert B. C. Huygens, *CCCM*, 127A (Turnhout: Brepols, 1996)
HL	*Lateinisches Hexameter-Lexikon: Dichterisches Formelgut von Ennius bis zum Archipoeta* (5 vols, Munich: Monumenta Germaniae Historica, 1979–89)
IA	Ibn al-Athir, *al Kāmil fī'l-ta'rīkh*, (trans.) D. S. Richards, vol. 1, 1097–1146 (Aldershot: Ashgate, 2006)
Kreuzzugsbriefe	H. Hagenmeyer (ed.), *Epistulae et chartae ad historiam primi belli sacrae spectantes: Die Kreuzzugsbriefe aus den Jahren 1088–1100* (Innsbruck: Verlag der Wagner'schen Universitäts-Buchhandlung, 1901)
ME	Ara E. Dostourian (trans.), *Armenia and the Crusades, Tenth to Twelfth Centuries: The Chronicle of Matthew of Edessa* (Lanham, NY: University Press of America, 1993)
MGH SS	*Monumenta Germaniae Historica, Scriptores*, (ed.) G. H. Pertz et al. (32 vols, Hanover, Weimar, Stuttgart and Cologne, 1826–1934)

OV	*The Ecclesiastical History of Orderic Vitalis*, (ed. and trans.) Marjorie Chibnall (6 vols, Oxford: Oxford University Press, 1969–80)
PL	*Patrologia cursus completus. Series Latina*, publ. J. P. Migne (221 vols, Paris, 1844–54)
PT	*Historia de Hierosolymitano itinere*, (ed.) John H. Hill and Laurita L. Hill, Documents relatifs à l'histoire des croisades, 12 (Paris: Paul Geuthner, 1977)
RA	*Le "Liber" de Raymond d'Aguilers*, (ed.) John H. Hill and Laurita L. Hill, Documents relatifs à l'histoire des croisades, 9 (Paris: Paul Geuthner, 1969)
RC	Ralph of Caen, (trans.) Bernard S. and David S. Bachrach, *The Gesta Tancredi of Ralph of Caen: A History of the Normans on the First Crusade* (Aldershot: Ashgate, 2005)
RHC	*Recueil des Historiens des Croisades*, (ed.) Academie des Inscriptions et Belles Lettres (Paris, 1841–1906)
RHC Arm	*RHC, Historiens Arméniens* (2 vols, Paris, 1869, 1906)
RHC Occ	*RHC, Historiens Occidenteaux* (5 vols, Paris, 1844–95)
RHC Or	*RHC, Historiens Orientaux* (5 vols, Paris 1872–1906)
RHGF	*Recueil des historiens des Gaules et de la France*, (ed.) Michel Bouquet et al. (24 vols, Paris, 1737–1904)
RM	Robert the Monk, *Historia Iherosolimitana*, (trans.) Carol Sweetenham, *Robert the Monk's History of the First Crusade* (Aldershot: Ashgate, 2005)
SSRH	*Scriptores rerum Hungaricarum tempore ducum regumque stirpis Arpadianae gestarum* (2 vols, Budapest, 1937–38)
Wisconsin History	*A History of the Crusades*, (ed.) Kenneth M. Setton et al. (6 vols, Madison, WI, 1969–89)
WT	William of Tyre, *Chronicon*, (ed.) Robert B. C. Huygens, *CCCM*, 63–63A (Turnhout: Brepols, 1986)

Preface

The publication of this paperback translation of Albert of Aachen's *History* is the culmination of a lifetime's work: I started to edit the *History* as my PhD thesis at the age of 21; I celebrated the publication of the edition and translation by Oxford Medieval Texts on my sixtieth birthday and now, six years later, I offer the translation, with updated introduction and notes, in a format which I hope will be accessible to students and all others who are interested in the First Crusade and the early years of the crusaders' settlement in the Latin East. Practical considerations have governed the decision to divide the work into two volumes and it does fall quite neatly into two parts. This volume, covering 1095–99, offers a different perspective on well known events, but the story does not stop with the battle of Ascalon, and Albert's account of events of the first twenty years of the Latin states (covered in volume 2) is yet more valuable, so I hope you will read that too.

I am especially grateful to Oxford University Press for granting permission to publish the translation in this format. I have previously acknowledged the numerous libraries and individuals who have assisted me along the way. For this version of the book I thank, in addition, John France for permission to use his maps as a basis for those in volume 1, and Chris Worthington for the hours of work he put into adapting and redrawing them. I also want to pay tribute to the very many colleagues and students whose insights and challenges have often led me to rethink my conclusions and assumptions, and whose company has been a pleasure along the way.

I have also been fortunate in good friends and in my family. I now have four granddaughters and I hope when they are older they will enjoy reading this book. So this is for Hannah and Rebekah, Emma and Anne.

SUSAN B. EDGINGTON
January 2013

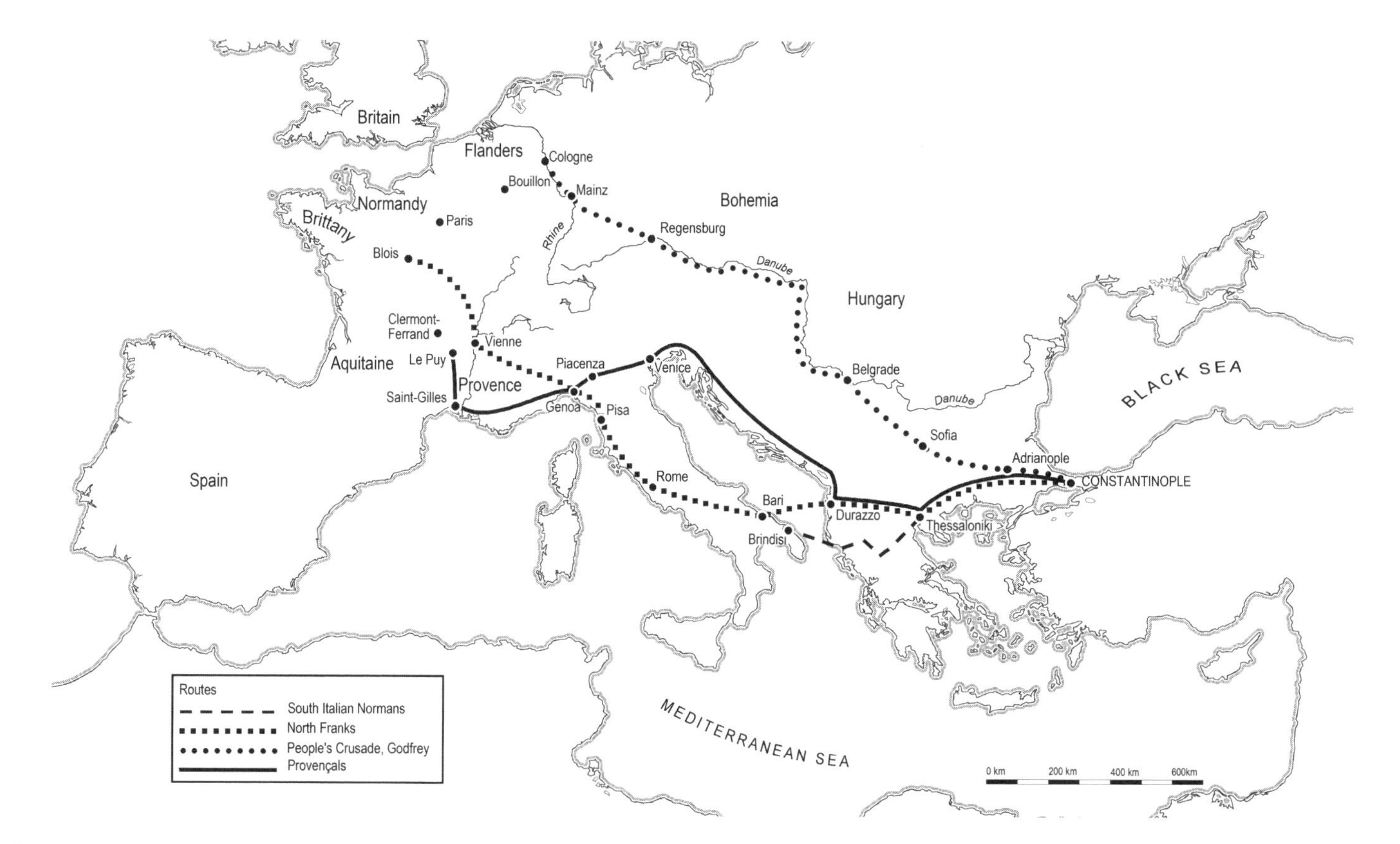

Map 1 Routes across Europe, 1096

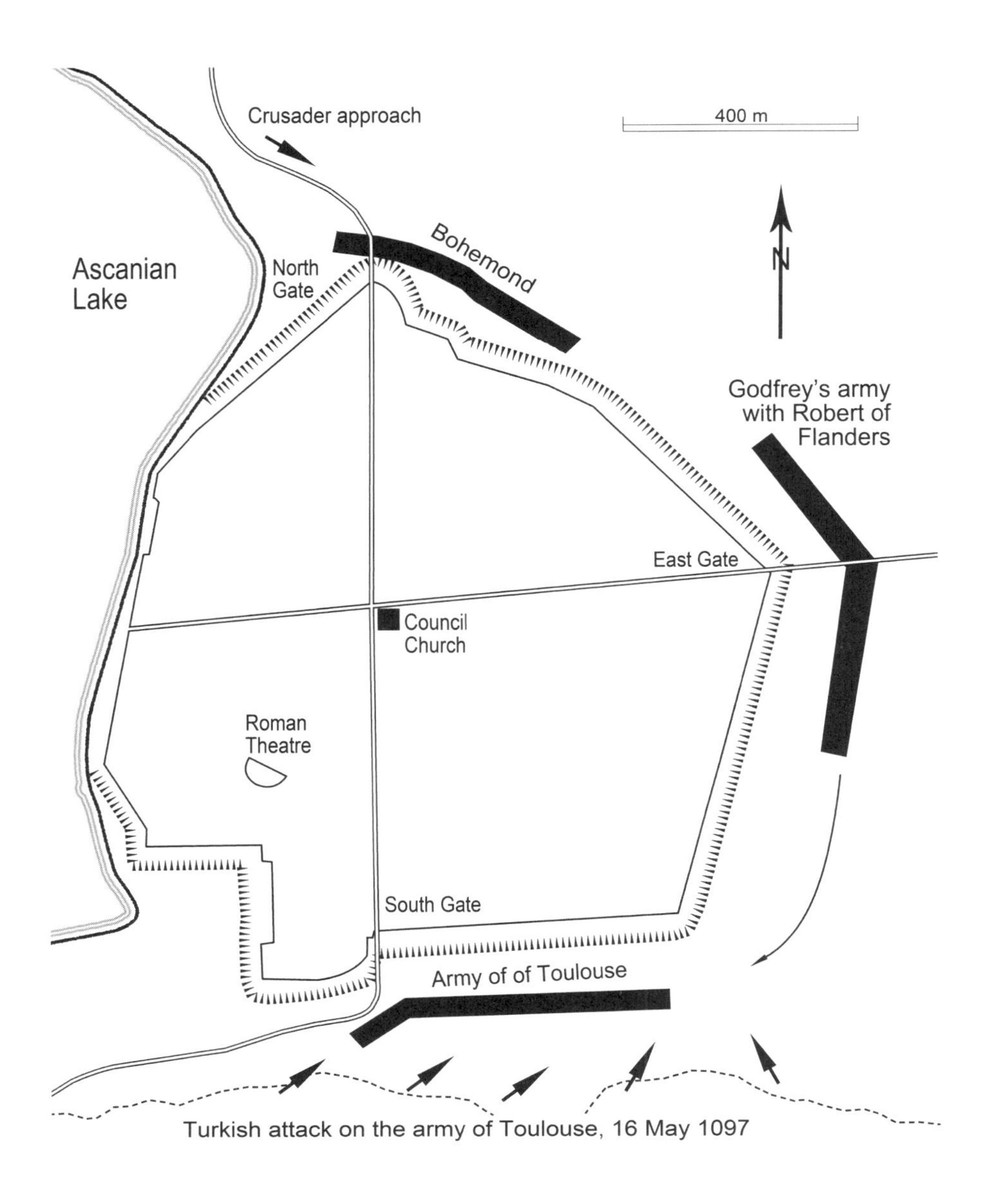

Map 2 The siege of Nicaea

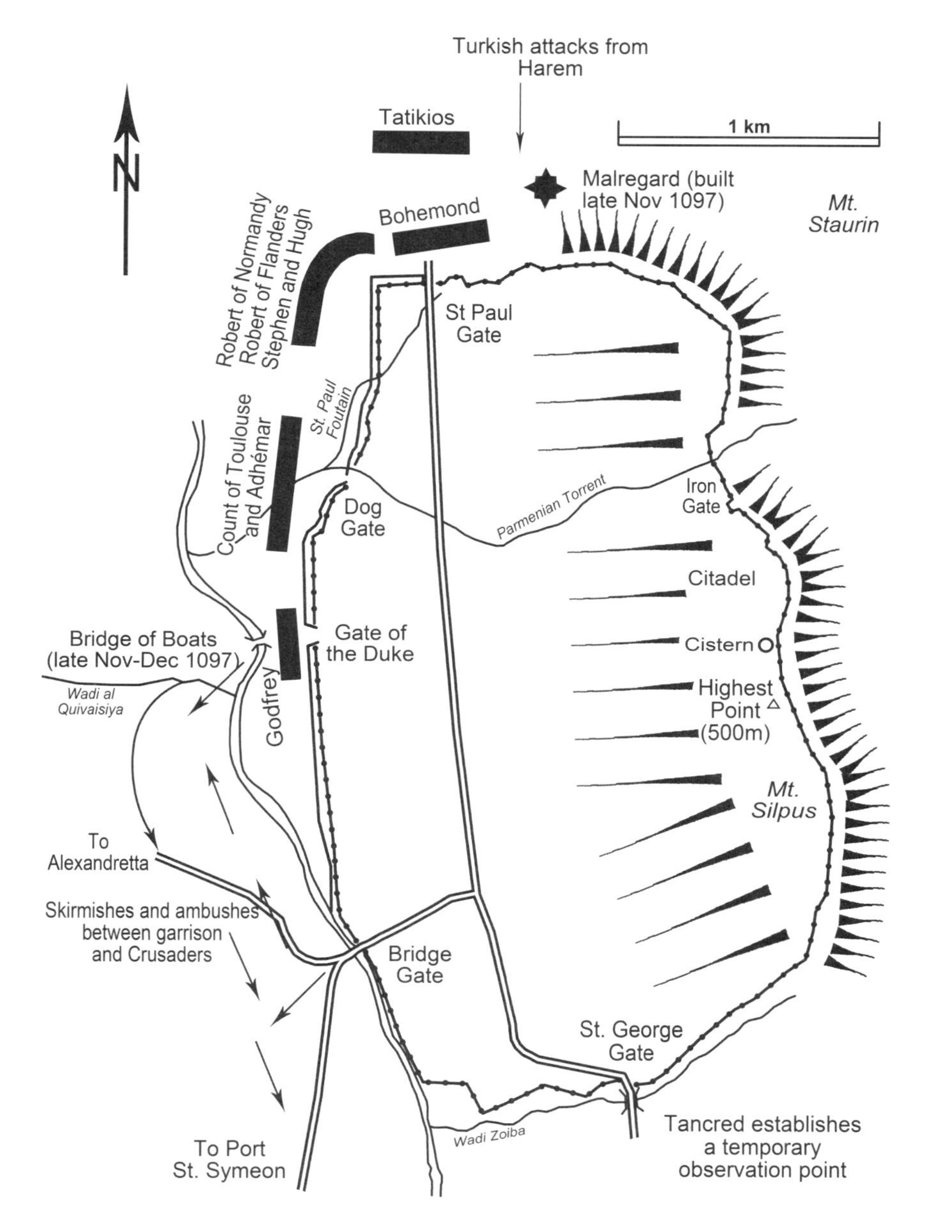

Map 3 The siege of Antioch, winter 1097–98

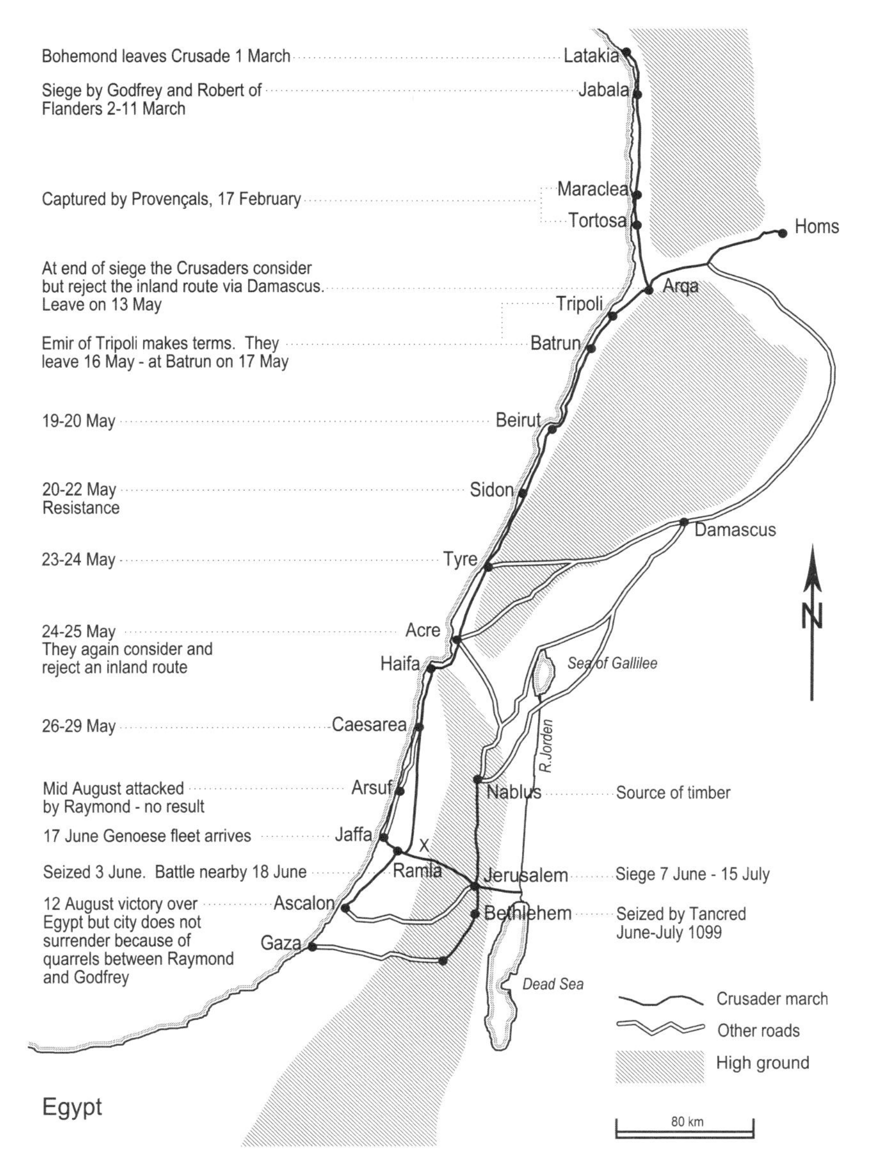

Map 4 The march south, March–July 1099

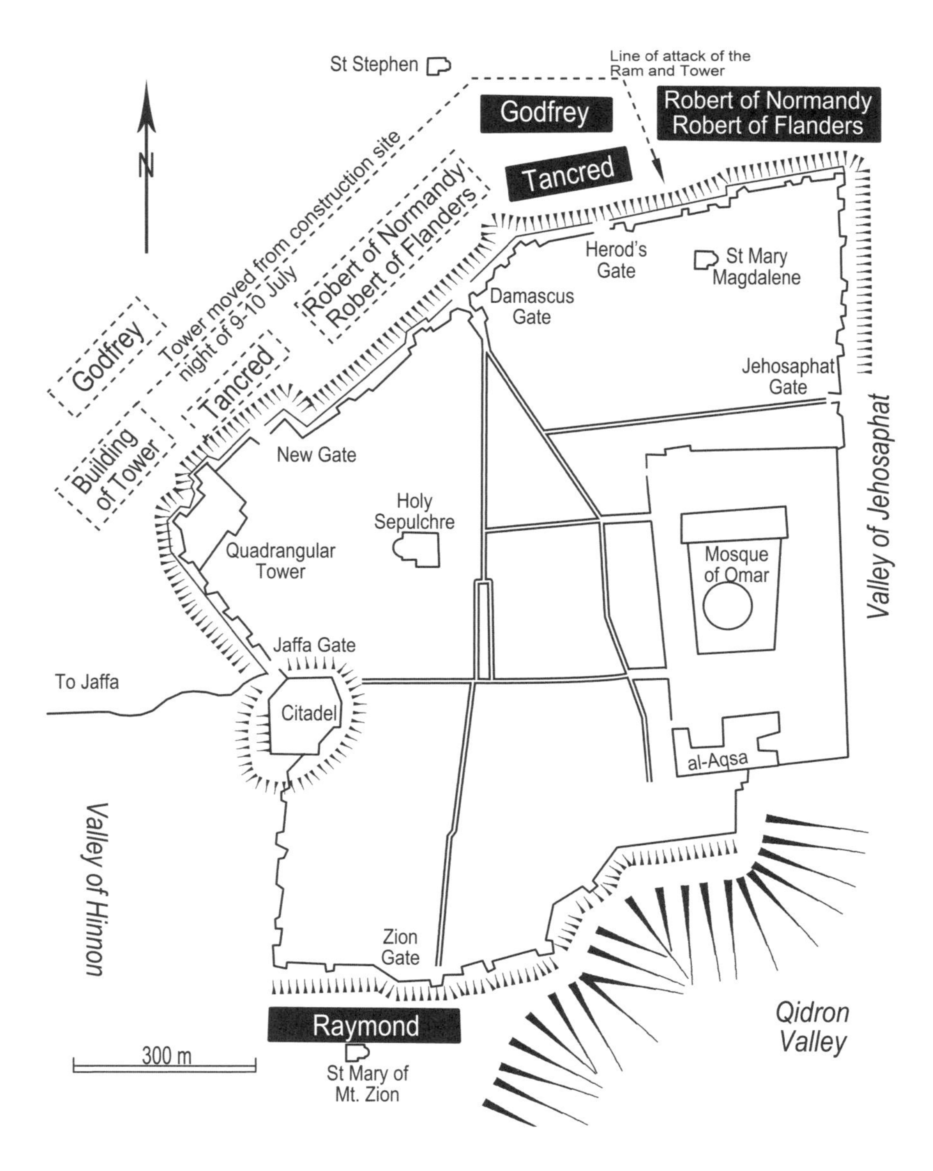

Map 5 The capture of Jerusalem, 15 July 1099

Introduction

The *Historia Ierosolimitana* and its Author

This first volume contains the first six books of Albert of Aachen's twelve-book *Historia Ierosolimitana*. The Latin title is difficult to translate in a few words: it is 'the story of people and things to do with Jerusalem'. More precisely, the *Historia* offers a narrative of the First Crusade (Books 1–6) and of the careers of the first generation of Latin settlers in Outremer (Books 7–12). It is a long and detailed account of events between 1095 and 1119, and the more important because its author apparently did not know the contemporary accounts written by Fulcher of Chartres, Raymond of Aguilers and the anonymous author of the *Gesta Francorum*.[1] Since these histories were to an extent interdependent, Albert's very different perspective on the same events is at the same time invaluable and – where his evidence differs from theirs – problematical.

We know very little about the author himself. The name 'Albert' (or 'Adalbert') is not found on the earliest manuscripts and seems to have emerged in the thirteenth century.[2] That the writer lived in or near Aachen in the Rhineland is not seriously in doubt. He has detailed knowledge of people and places in that region and a special interest in the crusaders whose homes were there. Also where we know the origins of the manuscripts they are from this area. However, we have no concrete evidence to help us identify 'our' Albert. The records from Aachen are patchy for the first decades of the twelfth century. They record an Adalbert as witness to a charter in 1134 and an Albert in 1158.[3] Both men were canons of St Mary's in Aachen which was probably Albert's church,[4] but the dates may be rather late, since the author Albert was probably born before 1080 (see below). Since there was a church dedicated to St Adalbert in Aachen, Albert (or Adalbert)

---

1 *Gesta Francorum et aliorum Hierosolimitanorum*, (ed.) R. Hill (London, 1962) [*GF*]; *Le "Liber" de Raymond d'Aguilers*, (ed.) J. H. and L. L. Hill (Paris, 1969) [RA]; Fulcher of Chartres, *Historia Hierosolymitana (1095–1127)*, (ed.) H. Hagenmeyer (Heidelberg, 1913) [FC].

2 The name is found in the first part of manuscript E and in its copies. Although E is the earliest extant copy of the *Historia*, the opening chapters are in a different hand (E_3) and are thought to have been written in the early part of the thirteenth century. More detail on this and other manuscript-related matters are to be found in the introduction to my edition: Albert of Aachen, *Historia Ierosolimitana: History of the Journey to Jerusalem*, (ed. and trans.) S. B. Edgington (Oxford, 2007) [AA].

3 P. Knoch, *Studien zu Albert von Aachen* (Stuttgart, 1966), p. 65; E. Meuthen, *Aachener Urkunden 1101–1250* (Bonn, 1972), pp. 175, 195.

4 It figures in a vision (6. 36).

was probably a popular name there. Although it is unsatisfactory to know so little about the author, it remains convenient to refer to him as Albert of Aachen.

There are a very few personal insights within the *Historia*, but in his first chapter or prologue Albert explains that he himself longed to go on crusade but was prevented from doing so, and therefore he decided to write an account instead. This suggests that Albert was of an age to join the expedition in 1096. He refers to hindrances ('impedimenta') and it is possible that he was, like other religious, forbidden by his superior to go.[5] He was born, by inference, no later than *c.*1080. As a canon of St Mary's, the cathedral church of Aachen, he will have received a monastic education, and he wrote serviceable Latin. He shows a rather superficial knowledge of classical literature, perhaps from reading anthologies ('florilegia') in the schoolroom. Predictably, he had a wider and deeper knowledge of the Old and New Testaments, though he never quoted at any length. It is impossible to guess, or deduce, whether Albert's native language was a form of French or German, but he was apparently able to gather oral testimony from returning crusaders and therefore probably had some facility in different vernacular dialects of northern France, Flanders and the Rhineland.

Dating

It is likely, and logical, that Albert wrote his prologue soon after the work was compiled, and hence it provides some clues to the date at which it was compiled. Albert says at the outset that the history concerns the journey and expedition to Jerusalem, that is, the First Crusade. He refers to the success of the campaign in opening the way to pilgrims, but he does not mention settlement, nor later expeditions, nor even the reign of Baldwin I (1100–18), all of which he is to chronicle in the second part of the *Historia* (Books 7–12).[6] This strongly suggests that Albert's original intention was to write the history of the crusade, culminating in the liberation of the Holy Places, an aim he achieved in Books 1–6. Whether there was ever a first redaction (covering 1095–99) in circulation cannot now be established, though its existence would satisfactorily explain why in his first eight books William of Tyre shares so much information uniquely with Albert, but there is no shared information after 1099.

The first six books of the *Historia*, according to the evidence of the prologue, were written soon after the events they describe. Book 6 was produced in its final form after 1102: this can be deduced from chapters 26 and 27, 36 and 37. Each pair of chapters describes a prophetic dream, and in each case the interpretation of the dream demonstrates its truth by reference to a later death: chapter 27 the

[5] See Pope Urban II's letter dated 19 Sept. 1096: H. Hagenmeyer (ed.), *Die Kreuzzugsbriefe aus den Jahren 1088–1100* (Innsbruck, 1901), pp. 137–8.

[6] More on the dating and other aspects of Books 7–12 will be found in volume 2 of this translation.

death of Stabelo the chamberlain, which took place in May 1102; chapter 37 the death of Duke Godfrey (July 1100). Albert may have intended to end his story at chapter 54, after the victory at Ascalon when many of the leaders set out for home. The first sentence has a fine valedictory ring to it: 'And so, with so many battles won, so many endeavours never before imaginable brought to victory and a good conclusion …'. Whether or not this was Albert's intention, he became caught up in the story again and Book 6 ends, less artistically, with the machinations of Bohemond and Raymond. Thus it may be inferred that Books 1–6, translated in this volume, were completed in the first years of the twelfth century. The prologue suggests this strongly and there is nothing in the text to indicate a later date.

Sources

A composition date in the first decade of the twelfth century is consistent with Albert's having used the tales of participants as his main source of information. He may have used written sources but, as observed above, there is no evidence that Albert was familiar with any of the extant written accounts. In the nineteenth century, it was suggested that Albert used a 'lost Lotharingian chronicle', a theory that allowed historians to use Albert's text in a selective fashion: information of which they approved came from Albert's written source; material they rejected was legendary. As late as the 1960s Knoch advanced a variation on the theory: that both Albert and William of Tyre used the same lost written source, accounting for the similarity of their narratives for the years 1095–99.[7] The difficulty is that no extrinsic trace of such a source survives, and, since we can therefore have no idea of its putative content, we still have to evaluate Albert's information by comparison with other sources which do survive. A further argument against the 'lost Lotharingian chronicle' is that it has been proposed only as a source for the First Crusade. Albert's *Historia* continues until 1119, and many events after 1099 are described with different levels of detail and apparent accuracy.[8] More than one lost written source is even more unlikely.

Albert himself says that he compiled his *Historia* 'ex auditu at relatione' ('by listening to those who had been there and from their reports'), implying that he used oral sources.[9] This helps to explain certain features of the text which may be accounted either strengths or weaknesses. Firstly, the informants were self-selected:

[7] For a resumé of the debate and a critique see Knoch, pp. 29–63; S. B. Edgington, 'The *Historia Iherosolimitana* of Albert of Aachen: A Critical Edition', Ph. D. thesis (University of London, 1991), pp. 17–25.

[8] See volume 2 of this translation, and C. Cahen, *La Syrie du nord* (Paris, 1940), p. 16: '… surtout pour les années postérieures à la croisade, la comparaison minutieuse avec les sources syriennes de toutes langues ne peut pas ne pas remplir d'admiration celui qui s'y livre devant l'étendue et l'exactitude de la plupart des informations d'Albert.'

[9] See 1. 1 (preface); 1. 24, 25; 2. 33, 65; 4. 53, 55; 6. 24.

they survived to tell the tale and they made the journey back to the Rhineland, and this had implications for the type of stories they would tell. Furthermore, oral evidence is likely to be shaky on perceptions of number, of distance and of time, and vagaries of memory may lead to inaccuracies. Because personal and place names have only been heard, not seen written down, they have to be recorded phonetically. More insidiously, people yield to the temptation to make a good story, to show themselves in a flattering light, to exaggerate the hardships, perhaps, and to minimize their own weaknesses. They are prone to hero-worship and susceptible to prejudice. Add to this the consideration that Albert was dealing not with a single informant but with a multiplicity of them, and so their sometimes contradictory reports had to be recorded side by side, or else reconciled. All these characteristics of oral evidence are present in Albert's *Historia*.[10] They demand caution, but they also account for the *Historia*'s vivid readability.

There is a demonstrable but complex relationship between Albert's *Historia* and certain poetic sources. Chief among these is the *Chanson d'Antioche*, an epic account of the First Crusade, culminating in the battle of Antioch, 1098. This *chanson*, unlike its companion pieces the *Les Chétifs* and the *Chanson de Jérusalem*,[11] incorporates authentic historical material, from which it is has been hypothesized that it was based upon a 'primitive *chanson*' dating from soon after the events it describes. However, the *Chanson d'Antioche* survives only in a version written down early in the thirteenth century, and thus it is impossible to recapture its original wording. The correspondence between some passages in the *Historia* and the *Chanson d'Antioche* will be apparent in the notes to the translation below, but it cannot be determined which of the two has primacy. It is probable that both incorporate early poetic material which originated in the camps of the crusaders.[12]

Albert did not use any known and extant written source when he wrote the *Historia*. Furthermore, his work is independent of the three accounts of the First Crusade written by participants: the anonymous author of *Gesta Francorum*, Raymond of Aguilers, and Fulcher of Chartres. These narratives were inter-related and also share an approach that may be characterized as 'French'. This became the accepted interpretation through the work of three writers in the first decade of the twelfth century: Robert of Reims, Guibert of Nogent, and Baudri of Dol all reworked the *Gesta Francorum* and they emphasized both the 'Frenchness' of the

10 H. von Sybel subjected the *Historia* to a damning critique, identifying Albert's errors and contradictions: *Geschichte des ersten Kreuzzugs* (Leipzig, 1841); trans. as *The History and Literature of the Crusades* (London, 1861), pp. 159–96.

11 The most recent editions of these two *chansons* are vols 5 and 6 in The Old French Crusade Cycle: *Les Chétifs*, (ed.) G. M. Myers (Tuscaloosa, AL, 1981) and *La Chanson de Jérusalem*, (ed.) N. R. Thorp (Tuscaloosa, AL, 1992).

12 *La Chanson d'Antioche*, (ed.) S. Duparc-Quioc (2 vols, Paris, 1977); trans. as *The Chanson d'Antioche*, by S. B. Edgington and C. Sweetenham (Farnham, 2011). See the introduction to the translation for latest thinking on the relationship with Albert of Aachen's *Historia*.

participants and the central role of the pope as instigator of the First Crusade.[13] Albert of Aachen, writing around the same time, preserved a different tradition about the origins of the crusade, stressing the role of Peter the Hermit. He also centred his account on the activities of Godfrey of Bouillon and his followers and, perhaps because Godfrey had been active in support of the German emperor Henry IV and against the papacy, he minimized the importance of the pope. Although William of Tyre, writing after the middle of the twelfth century, adopted Albert's perspective, this 'imperial' historiographical strand has been neglected in favour of the 'French' tradition.

Single Authorship

The above observations on dating and sources assume that the same person ('Albert') wrote the entire work as we have it now. An examination of the writing style leaves little room for doubt that the *Historia* is the work of a single author.[14] Albert's attitude to his subject matter also seems to be consistent throughout the twelve books. For example, he recounts battles with enthusiasm from beginning to end; he has a slightly prurient attitude towards women (the renegade nun, 2. 37; the fate of women on the 1101 expeditions, 8. 19–20); his use of biblical and classical allusions and quotations shows no significant variation over the length of the work. The main discernible change in subject matter is between the incorporation of legendary, *chanson*-style material into the first six books and the more sober narrative of Books 7–12. This surely reflects the material available to Albert: settlement is more prosaic than crusade. Albert's materials were more copious for the earlier period, 1095–99, presented in this volume. The numbers involved in the crusading expeditions and returning from them were greater, and letters and stories of survivors were correspondingly more common. There is a reflection of this in Albert's uniquely detailed account of the 1101 expeditions (Books 8 and 9), which must likewise have drawn on survivors' accounts. That he continued to depend on similar sources explains the comparative sparseness of information for the last decade (*c*.1110–19), and the confused chronology in Book 12.

---

[13] Texts of the three accounts are to be found in *RHC Occ*. as follows: Robert, iii, 717–880; Guibert, iv. 113–262; Baudri, iv. 1–110. (A new edn. of Guibert's *Dei gesta per Francos* by R. B. C. Huygens, *CCCM* cxxvii, is used in the notes; references to Robert [RM] are to the translation: C. Sweetenham (trans.), *Robert the Monk's History of the First Crusade* [Aldershot, 2005]). They are discussed by J. Riley-Smith, *The First Crusade and the Idea of Crusading* (London, 1986), pp. 135–52; S. B. Edgington, 'The First Crusade: reviewing the evidence', *The First Crusade: Origins and Impact*, (ed.) J. Phillips (Manchester, 1997), pp. 57–77, at 59–60.

[14] For discussion and examples, see AA, pp. xxviii–xxix.

Albert's Attitude to:

Crusaders

Received opinion has long been that Albert wrote the *Historia* as a panegyric of Godfrey of Bouillon. Aubé, for example, Godfrey's biographer, asserted that this was 'le but avoué' of Albert's work, and quoted in support 'la phrase liminaire' of the *Historia*: 'super passagio Godefridi de Bullione, et aliorum principum'.[15] However, these words appear for the first time in a manuscript dated 1390. The simplified view that the *Historia* is a deliberately slanted account of Godfrey and the house of Bouillon is not borne out by an objective reading. Similarly, we should reject the opinion of Knoch, that Albert was not only writing a 'hagiography' of Godfrey, but was deliberately overstating the part played by the Germans in the First Crusade.[16]

Albert's close interest in Godfrey and his family and followers is only to be expected since he lived in Godfrey's home territory and seems to have gained his information from Godfrey's followers. Book 2 of the *Historia* is a detailed account of Godfrey's expedition across Europe, information found nowhere else. In Book 3 and later books Godfrey's brother Baldwin's career in Edessa is recounted, again with much circumstantial detail. The focus away from the pope as instigator of the crusade, and from Adhémar as its spiritual leader, differs from the eye-witness accounts and it is too easy to give Raymond, Fulcher, and the *Gesta* author credence because 'they were there', while imputing distortion to Albert because 'he was not there'. In reality, we should bear in mind the politics of Christendom: Godfrey had fought with the emperor and against the pope, and Albert continued to be a staunch supporter of Henry IV.[17] Albert's bias should be accepted as no more and no less than that of other writers of his time. He disliked Raymond of Saint-Gilles, accusing him of avarice (e.g. 6. 28) and of being a source of discord (Book 6 *passim*). Albert expressed reasonable doubts about the Holy Lance, but avoided both the uncritical advocacy of Raymond of Aguilers and the hysterical anti-Provençal tone of Radulf of Caen.[18] When doubts arose as to the relic's authenticity, Albert was again remarkably even-handed in his reporting (5. 32). In

---

15 P. Aubé, *Godefroy de Bouillon* (Paris, 1985), p. 357; P. Rousset, *Les origines et les caractères de la première croisade* (Neuchatel, 1945), p. 23: 'Albert d'Aix écrit un panégyrique de Godefroid de Bouillon'; J. H. and L. L. Hill, *Raymond IV de Saint-Gilles 1041 (ou 1042)–1105* (Toulouse, 1959), p. 142: 'Parmi les écrivains contemporains (ou presque) Albert a fait l'éloge du pur et inactif Godefroy.'

16 Knoch, pp. 116–19, 125.

17 This is illustrated in 11. 48 (vol. 2).

18 RA pp. 68–75; Ralph of Caen [RC], trans. Bernard S. and David S. Bachrach, *The Gesta Tancredi of Ralph of Caen: A History of the Normans on the First Crusade* (Aldershot, 2005), pp. 118–21; AA 4. 43.

reporting such conflicts between crusaders Albert's point of view counter-balances the shared bias of other contemporary accounts.

Byzantines

Albert's treatment of the Byzantines shows less prejudice than the eyewitnesses'.[19] For example he describes the emperor Alexios Komnenos in very positive terms (1. 13; 1. 15). He emphasizes the emperor's liberality and supportiveness towards Walter Sansavoir and Peter the Hermit (1. 15); his hospitality towards the nobler leaders, especially Raymond (2. 18–20). Even where Godfrey's troops fought the emperor's, Albert makes it clear that the blame was not all on one side (2. 11), and at the end of it all Alexios showered the pilgrims with gifts.[20] Alexios also welcomed Svend of Denmark in 1097 (3. 57) and, in 1101, a stream of visitors.[21] Knoch claimed that Albert's attitude towards the Byzantines changed after Book 1, but there is little evidence of this.[22]

Albert's portrayal of the emperor may be contrasted with that in the anonymous *Gesta Francorum*. After the capture of Nicaea, Albert represents the emperor's behaviour as notably generous, while in the *Gesta* he is depicted as devious and calculating.[23] The *Historia*'s treatment of the incident when Stephen of Blois and other renegades from the siege of Antioch dissuaded the emperor from coming to the crusaders' assistance also shows Alexios in a different light from that cast by the *Gesta*.[24]

The worst epithet which Albert applies to the Greeks as a people is 'effeminati': this occurs in a speech by 'Suleyman' (the Turkish leader Qilij Arslan: 4. 6). This is not an unusual prejudice among western writers. When Albert censures an act of treason against Svend, he makes it clear that this was the work of a defined group of people: 'certain wicked Christians, that is to say Greeks'.[25] On two occasions Albert records unfavourable opinions of the emperor: where Godfrey was warned against him by some Franks (2. 10), and where Bohemond hesitated to take the oath, 'because he was regarded as a crafty and sly man' (2. 18). In both cases Albert is reporting the opinion of others, not necessarily giving his own. Overall, there is little evidence that Albert was as anti-Byzantine as his contemporary

---

[19] See B. Ebels-Hoving, *Byzantium in westerse ogen 1096–1204* (Assen, 1971), pp. 84–9. She refers to Albert's 'simple and objective' rendering of the facts, and his 'exceptionally independent and impartial mindset'.

[20] Although Albert had earlier pointed out, with a rare touch of irony, that the emperor did not lose by his generosity, as the money returned to him as payment for supplies (2. 16).

[21] See volume 2.

[22] Knoch, p. 57.

[23] AA 2. 28: *GF* p. 17.

[24] AA 4. 40: *GF* pp. 63–4.

[25] AA 3. 54. See Ebels-Hoving, p. 88: 'Generalizations are not Albert's style.'

authors – of course, this may just reflect his distance from events, but this is in itself interesting.

Other Eastern Christians

Albert's attitude to Christians of other rites than the Latin is surprisingly ecumenical. He never mentions doctrinal differences and treats all as 'fellow Christians'. This is true of the Greeks (see above); the Armenians (e.g. 3. 17), and the Syrians. All three groups are identified as assisting in the capture of Antioch – and as victims of the massacre which followed, when 'the earth was covered with blood and the corpses of the slaughtered, many of them also the killed and lifeless bodies of Christians, Gauls as well as Greeks, Syrians and Armenians mixed together' (4. 23). Co-operation seems to have been the norm: for example, a Syrian Christian was useful as an envoy (5. 7). During the siege of Jerusalem, 'native fellow Christians' aided the crusaders by showing them where to find timbers for siege engines and how to extinguish a form of Greek fire (6. 2; 6. 18), and 'a certain faithful Christian native of the city, fully instructed in Christ's law,' revealed a fragment of the True Cross he had concealed for safety during the Muslim occupation (6. 38). The Christian inhabitants of Bethlehem welcomed the crusaders into their city (5. 44). Whether Albert was truly unaware of doctrinal tensions between groups of Christians, or if he was deliberately underplaying them, just as he did the political differences between pope and emperor in western Europe, is a matter of speculation.

Muslims

Towards the Muslim enemy, Albert is no less remarkably impartial.[26] He usually refers to them simply as Turks or Saracens, and distinguishes between the two. He has an accurate idea of the Turks as former nomadic warriors, recent invaders of Byzantine lands and now the ruling elite over a large area. Their homeland, and the Saljūq Turkish Empire as a whole, he refers to as Khurasan; he uses 'Romania' (Rūm) for Turkish Asia Minor, formerly Byzantine ('Roman'). Saracens is always used for the Egyptians, and also for the indigenous Muslim population of Syria and Palestine. Less frequently, Albert refers to both peoples as 'gentiles'. He has some understanding of Islam and does not, like some other Christian writers, accuse the Muslims of idolatry. When the Christians captured the Turkish camp, they found a large number of books – not images (4. 56). Albert even spares some sympathy for the defeated enemy (e.g. 6. 30; 6. 47). He uses admiring adjectives when referring to the Muslim leaders (e.g. 3. 35; 4. 3, 5, 6, 7, 44, 45).[27] Albert

---

[26] H. Szklenar, *Studien zum Bild des Orients in vorhöfischen deutschen Epen* (Göttingen, 1966), pp. 193–5.

[27] R. C. Schwinges, *Kreuzzugsideologie und Toleranz* (Stuttgart, 1977), pp. 158–65.

even goes so far as to say that the 'king of Egypt' ruled justly and tolerantly in Jerusalem, 1098–99 (6. 32).[28]

Jews

It could be argued that Albert's objectivity with regard to the Byzantines and the Muslims was the outcome of his distance from the events he describes; that the eye-witness accounts were prejudiced as a result of their authors' experiences. Yet Albert also shows a remarkable sympathy with the Rhineland Jews, and expresses condemnation of their Christian attackers (1. 26–9). He particularly says that forced conversion has no value (1. 29). Albert is unique among Christian writers in his criticism of the crusaders' murder and enforced baptism of the Jews, and his sense of outrage is matched only by the Hebrew writers.[29]

Women

Unexpectedly, Albert even shows some empathetic understanding of women. Norman Daniel remarked on this: 'Albert had a genuine, imaginative understanding of the sorrows of the bereaved women "carried off by stern enemies to an unknown and alien land"' (e.g. 3. 46).[30] Furthermore, Albert did not stereotype; he knew that the captive women were not necessarily unhappy, for example the renegade nun (2. 37), and the knight's widow who married her Turkish captor (5. 5). He was aware that captivity was not a 'fate worse than death' to some young women, and shows them dressing up in order to appeal to their captors' better natures (2. 39). Movingly, he describes women forced into premature labour and childbirth during the agonies of thirst suffered in Anatolia (3. 2).

Evaluation

Albert's empathy is only one remarkable feature of the *Historia*. The work is notably secular in outlook. There are comparatively few biblical, patristic or liturgical citations, and these are usually found in speeches made by the leaders. Albert's prose style is unsophisticated, but it is vividly descriptive. All of these features should be viewed as deliberate on Albert's part. There is no reason to doubt that he saw himself as inventing a new type of literature to match a new

[28] R. M. Hill, 'The Christian view of the Muslims at the time of the First Crusade', *The Eastern Mediterranean Lands in the Period of the Crusades*, (ed.) P. M. Holt (Warminster, 1977), pp. 1–8.

[29] B. Z. Kedar, *Crusade and Mission* (Princeton, NJ, 1984), p. 62; L. Poliakov, *The History of Anti-Semitism* (4 vols, London, 1974–84), vol. 1, p. 44.

[30] N. Daniel, *The Arabs and Medieval Europe* (2nd edn, London, 1979), p. 201.

kind of enterprise, as he indicates in his own preface. What sort of audience he envisaged is hard to gauge.

Albert was apparently unaware of other narratives emerging from the same expedition. His *Historia* achieved a modest circulation within the Rhineland area. At some point that part dealing with the First Crusade (Books 1–6) was used by William of Tyre as one of the sources for his chronicle, and it was in this form that Albert influenced mainstream historiography of the First Crusade thereafter. Although the second part of the *Historia*, Books 7–12, contains much unique and important information, it was (and still is) widely disregarded. Manuscript copies of the *Historia* continued to be made until the sixteenth century and the first printed edition appeared in 1584, but during these centuries the work seems to have been little read. Although interest revived in the nineteenth century, the work was dismissed as too problematical to be useful to historians, and it is only in the last half-century that the value of its unique, independent and vividly detailed narrative has been recognized.

Manuscripts

Albert's original manuscript does not survive, but there are eleven manuscripts extant which contain complete, or almost complete, copies of the *Historia*.[31] In addition there is one which has lost significant portions (M), and another that survives only as fragments (J). They are as follows:

A Oxford, Bodleian Library, MS Laud Misc. 561 and 562 (Eberbach, s. xii)
B Paris, Bibliothèque Nationale, MS latin 5128 (Noyon?, s. xii^{ex})
C Vatican City, Biblioteca Apostolica Vaticana, MS Reg. lat. 509 (Utrecht, 1158)
D Vatican City, Biblioteca Apostolica Vaticana, MS Vat. lat. 1999 (s. xiii)
E Darmstadt, Hessische Landes- und Hochschulbibliothek, MS 102 (Liège, s. xii^{med})
[**F** and **G** were assigned to the early editions, see below.]
H Berlin, Staatsbibliothek zu Berlin Preussischer Kulturbesitz, MS lat. fol. 677 (Gladbach, s. xii^{med})
J Hanover, Niedersächsische Landesbibliothek, MS xxxvii, 1808 (s. xii^{ex})
K Vatican City, Biblioteca Apostolica Vaticana, MS Ottob. lat. 631 (s. xii^{ex})
L Vatican City, Biblioteca Apostolica Vaticana, MS Vat. lat. 7317 (s. xv)
M Nuremberg, Stadtbibliothek, MS Cent. II. 100 (s. xv)
N Trier, Stadtbibliothek, MS 1974/641 (Trier, s. xv)
O London, British Library, Additional MS 25440 (Liège, 1390)
P Florence, Biblioteca Medicea Laurenziana, MS Plut. 66 No 33 (1517)

[31] The manuscripts and their relationships are fully described in the edition: AA, pp. xxxvii–liv.

The modern edition, translated here, took ms E as its base and recorded variant readings from C, H, N, and A.

Previous Editions

1. Reinerus Reineccius, *Chronicon Hierosolymitanum* (Helmstedt, 1584). It was subtitled: 'De bello sacro historia, exposita libris xii, et nunc primum in lucem edita'. In the preface Reineck explained that the codex had been given to him by Christian Distelmeyer (1552–1612), counsellor to the elector of Brandenburg. It was written on parchment, and there was no author's name.
2. J. Bongars, *Gesta Dei per Francos* (2 vols, Hanover, 1611), i. 184–381. This was essentially a reprint of Reineck's edition, but Bongars was able to add the author's name. He owed this to David Hoeschel, who printed Albert's name in the preface to his *Alexiad*, having discovered it from J. Gretzer. The superscription on the manuscript in question read: 'Historia Hierosolymitanae expeditionis, edita ab Alberto, canonico et custode Aquensis Ecclesiae, super Passagio Godefridi de Bullione et aliorum principum.'
3. J. P. Migne, in vol. 166 of the *Patrologia Latina* (1854), used Bongars' edition verbatim.
4. Paul Meyer (ed.), *Liber Christianae expeditionis pro ereptione, emundatione, restitutione sanctae Hierosolymitanae ecclesiae,* in *Recueil des historiens des Croisades: historiens occidentaux* (5 vols, Paris, 1841–1906), iv. 267–713. This was the first critical edition, but based on an unscientific selection of manuscripts available outside Germany, that is, disregarding three of the earliest and/or best ones.
5. Bernhard Kugler did not produce an edition of the *Historia*, although it is believed that he planned to do so.[32] However in two books, *Eine neue Handschrift der Chronik Alberts von Aachen* (Tübingen, 1893) and *Die Deutschen Codices Alberts von Aachen* (Tübingen, 1894), he did the groundwork for a new edition using the German manuscripts.

Translations

F. P. G. Guizot used the Bongars reimpression of Reineck's edition for his French translation, which appeared in two volumes as *Histoire des faits et gestes dans les régions d'Outre-mer*, volumes xx and xxi in *La Collection des mémoires relatifs à l'histoire de France* (Paris, 1824). J. F. Michaud published long extracts from the *Historia*, translated into French, in his *Bibliothèque des croisades* (4 vols,

[32] H. Hagenmeyer, preface to FC, p. 81 note 2.

Paris, 1829), i. 43–81. The translated passages were linked by summaries and paraphrases. H. Hefele, *Geschichte des Ersten Kreuzzuges* (2 vols, Jena, 1923), used Meyer's *Recueil* edition for his German translation. He added very few historical notes, and although there were sixteen illustrations none was from an Albert manuscript. Albert is frequently quoted, particularly on the subject of the 'People's Crusade' of 1096, for which he has eye-witness status, but the first complete translation of the *Historia* into English accompanied my edition (Oxford Medieval Texts, 2007).

This Translation

The translation offered here is essentially the same as the one that accompanied the edition. An addition is the incorporation of chapter titles: these were not part of the first redaction of Albert's *Historia* and so were relegated to an appendix in the edition. The footnotes have been reduced by the removal of biographical and topographical detail and references to *Appendix 1: People* and *Appendix 2: Places* respectively.

My aim was to provide a translation which is both accurate and readable. Sometimes this has entailed breaking up or rearranging Albert's very long sentences, or rendering active as passive or vice versa. Albert rather frequently uses a singular (collective) noun with a plural verb; this has been silently amended except on a very few occasions where the change would be unreasonably pedantic.

A particular problem has been the rendering of names of people and places. For western European people, I have generally used the English equivalent for well known characters, e.g. Peter the Hermit (not Pierre or Pieter); for lesser known people I have not tried to be consistent, for example, Odo (not Eudes or Otto), but Rainald or Reinhard (depending on provenance) rather than Reginald. They are identified in*Appendix 1*. Greek characters have their modern transliterations, e.g. Alexios, Tatikios, Anna Komnene. Arabic and Turkish names are usually given in a form close to the one used by Albert in the text of the translation, and identified in Appendix 1 with a transliteration of Arabic names. (However, Arab historians' names are customarily used without diacritics.) Place names are even more problematical. Certain well known places have accepted 'crusader' names; for example, for Nicaea and Antioch it would not be sensible to insist on İznik and Antakya. Having made this decision, it seemed more faithful to the text to keep medieval renderings of less well known places: Philippopolis and Adrianople, rather than Plovdiv and Edirne, for instance. However, sometimes an obscure place has a modern name similar to its medieval name, so, for example, Semlin has become Zemun. In two cases a modern term has been adopted to avoid confusion: the medieval 'Romania' represented Turkish lands conquered from the Greeks in Asia Minor and has been translated as Rūm; Albert's 'Babylonia' has been rendered as Egypt. Modern identifications of places are in *Appendix 2*.

The historical notes correct dates and other matters of factual detail. They also provide references to other sources for the same events, which sometimes corroborate and sometimes conflict with Albert's account. They are intended to complete the rehabilitation of Albert as an indispensable resource for historians of the First Crusade and the first generation of settlement in the Latin East

Book 1

1. Preface to the following work

CONCERNING THE WAY AND EXPEDITION TO JERUSALEM, UNHEARD OF UNTIL THESE DAYS AND GREATLY TO BE WONDERED AT. Many times I was fired with longing for that same expedition and for offering prayer there. Since I was so inspired, but could not go because of various hindrances to the carrying out of my intention, with rash daring I decided to commend to posterity at least some of the things which were made known to me by listening to those who had been there and from their reports, so that even thus I would take great pains, not in idleness, but as if I were a companion in the journey, if not with my body then with all my heart and soul.[1] And therefore I have ventured to write with my poor mental powers and my childish and heedless style about their hardship and misfortunes and the way their faith was strengthened, and the good concord of the strong princes and the rest of the men in the love of Christ; how they left their homeland, kinsmen, wives, sons and daughters, castles, cities, lands, estates, and all the sweetness of this world, left settled things for unsettled, and sought exile in the name of Jesus; how they made the journey to Jerusalem with a strong hand[2] and a lusty army and their triumphant legions killed a thousand times a thousand Turks and Saracens in a bold attack; how they laid open the entrance and approach to the Holy Sepulchre of our Lord Jesus Christ and completely remitted the taxes and tributes of pilgrims wishing to enter there.

2. How Peter was the first originator of the expedition to Jerusalem and how he approached the patriarch

A certain priest, Peter by name, once a hermit, who was born in the city of Amiens which is in the west of the kingdom of the Franks, was the first to urge

---

1 It is possible that Albert [AA] was forbidden by his bishop to join the expedition: compare Robert the Monk [RM], p. 82 and Urban II's letter to Bologna: *Kreuzzugsbriefe*, pp. 137–8.

2 Exod. 13: passim. D. H. Green, *The Millstätter Exodus* (Cambridge, 1966) examines this vernacular version of the Bible story as 'a crusading epic' (his sub-title) and AA's use of the phrase 'in manu forti' at the outset of his narrative appears to be a conscious reference to the biblical parallel.

steadfastness in this journey with all the inspiration he could.[3] In Berry, a region of the aforesaid kingdom, he became a preacher of the utmost persuasiveness and oratory. In response to his constant urging and calling firstly bishops, abbots, clerics, monks; then the most noble laymen, princes of different domains, and all the common people, as many sinful as pious men, adulterers, murderers, thieves, perjurers, robbers: that is to say every sort of people of Christian faith, indeed even the female sex, led by repentance, all flocked joyfully to this journey. How it happened, and why the hermit preached this same journey and was its first instigator, this present book will tell. In fact some years before the beginning of this journey the priest set out to Jerusalem in order to pray, and there in the Temple of Our Lord's Sepulchre, alas, some unlawful and wicked things were seen, and he suffered them with a grieving heart, and groaned in the spirit,[4] calling on God himself as avenger of the wrongs he had seen. At length, disturbed by the wicked deeds, he sought out the patriarch of the holy church of Jerusalem.[5] He asked why the patriarch allowed gentiles and wicked men to defile the holy places, and let the offerings of the faithful be carried off, churches be used as stables, Christians beaten up, holy pilgrims robbed by excessive fees and distressed by the many violent acts of the infidels.

3. What the patriarch replied to Peter and how he asked for help from the Christians

The patriarch and venerable priest of Our Lord's Sepulchre heard what Peter had to say and uttered a holy and tearful reply: 'O most faithful of Christians, why do you reproach me about these things and make things difficult for our fatherly care, when our strength and power may not be reckoned more than a poor ant's against the tyranny of so many? The fact is, either we have to ransom our life by constant payments, or it will be cut short by fatal executions, and we expect the dangers to be greater from one day to the next unless there should be aid from the Christians, which we summon with you as our envoy.' Peter replied to him in this way: 'Reverend father, I have learnt enough and now I understand and see how inadequate is the band of Christians living here with you, and how many acts of oppression you are subject to from the gentiles. Because of this, for the love of God and for your liberation, and for the cleansing of the holy places, with God beside me and as long as life is vouchsafed to me, I shall return and seek out first of all the pope, then all the leaders of Christian peoples, kings, dukes, counts, and those holding the chief places in the kingdom, and I shall make known to them all the wretchedness of your servitude and the unendurable nature of your difficulties.

---

3 Peter 'the Hermit'. For identifications of people, biographical information and references, see Appendix 1: People

4 John 11: 33.

5 Symeon II.

Meanwhile it is right that all these things of which we have spoken should be seen so that they may be dealt with.'

4. How the majesty of Lord Jesus appeared to Peter in a dream and spoke to him

Meanwhile, as darkness was falling in the sky all around, Peter went back to the Holy Sepulchre to pray. There, since he was exhausted by prayers and vigils, he was overtaken by sleep. And the majesty of Lord Jesus was shown to him in a vision, deigning thus to address the frail and mortal man: 'Peter, most beloved son of the Christians, you will arise and go to see our patriarch and get from him a letter of our mission with the seal of the holy cross, and you will hasten as quickly as possible your journey to the land of your people;[6] you will disclose the malicious acts and injustices inflicted on our people and our holy place, and stir the hearts of the faithful to the cleansing of the holy places in Jerusalem, and to the restoring of the ceremonies of the holy places. For through dangers and diverse temptations the gates of paradise will now be opened to those called and chosen.'[7]

5. How Peter came to Rome and reported the patriarch's commission; and concerning an earthquake

With this wonderful revelation, worthy of God, the apparition withdrew and Peter was roused from his sleep. And in the first grey light of day he came forth from the entrance of the Temple and sought out the patriarch. He disclosed the divine vision to him just as it had happened and asked for a letter of holy mission with the seal of the holy cross. The patriarch did not refuse these to him, but rather complied with expressions of thanks. Peter received the licence from him, and in obedience to his mission returned to his native shores. He crossed the sea again with considerable anxiety and sailed back to the city of Bari, and when he was back on dry land he set out for Rome without delay. There he found the pope and revealed to him the mission he had heard and received from God and the patriarch, about the defiling by the gentiles and the outrages against the holy places and the pilgrims. Indeed, as soon as the pope had heard these things with a willing and attentive ear, he promised to obey in all things the commands and entreaties of

6 Cf. Acts 7: 3.

7 This passage (1. 2–4) bears close resemblance to the *Chanson d'Antioche* [*ChA*], pp. 109–11. The patriarchal letter became a charter ('cartula') fallen from heaven in the Rosenfeld Annals (*MGH SS* xvi. 101) and other north German annals based on these. See E. O. Blake and C. Morris, 'A hermit goes to war: Peter and the origins of the first crusade', *Studies in Church History*, 22 (1985), pp. 79–107 at 93–4.

the saints. Stirred into action because of this, he came to the city of *Verzellaus*,[8] crossing the Alps, and decreed that there should be a meeting of all the west of the Frankish kingdom, and a council at Le Puy, the city of St Mary.[9] Then he set out for Clermont in the Auvergne. When they had heard the divine mission and the pope's recommendation, the bishops of all the Frankish kingdom, the dukes and counts and great princes, of whatever class and rank, promised to God an expedition at their own expense to the Holy Sepulchre itself. And as a matter of fact, in that very spacious kingdom a holy concord and alliance for this journey originated among the most powerful, who pledged their right hands to it. And in confirmation of these things a great earthquake occurred, predicting nothing other than the mobilization of armies of different kingdoms: from the kingdom of the Franks as well as from Lotharingia, and at the same time from the land of German peoples and of the English and from the kingdom of the Danes.

6. Concerning a certain Walter going to Jerusalem, what he did or what he endured

In the year of our Lord's incarnation 1096, the fourth indiction, when Henry was the fourth king and the third august emperor of the Romans, in the forty-third year of his reign and the thirteenth of his imperial rule,[10] Urban II (who was also Odard) being pope,[11] the eighth day of March,[12] Walter, nicknamed 'Sansavoir', an outstanding warrior, entered the kingdom of Hungary with a great fellowship of Frankish foot soldiers and only eight knights who were starting on the journey to Jerusalem in response to the urging of the said Peter the Hermit. Once his purpose was heard and understood, and the reason the journey had been undertaken, he was graciously received there by Lord Coloman, the very Christian king of the Hungarians, who granted to him in peace passage through all the lands of his kingdom and a licence to buy food. And so, without any misfortune or assault upon them whatsoever, they advanced right to Belgrade, the city of the Bulgars, passing through Zemun where the territories of the Hungarians end. There they

---

8 Probably Vercelli (Italy). For closer identifications and comments on places, see Appendix 2: Places.

9 The spectacular volcanic landscape of Le Puy is dominated by the cathedral dedicated to the Virgin Mary, Notre-Dame du Puy.

10 AA's numbering of the German emperors and his arithmetic here with regard to dates are hard to understand or explain.

11 Urban II (1088–99) was formerly Odo or Eudes.

12 Probably a mistake for 8 May. William of Tyre [WT] also gives 8 Mar. as the date Walter set out, but quickly passes on to his entry into Hungary (p. 140). Orderic Vitalis [OV] says Walter and his companions were in Cologne on Easter Saturday (12 Apr.) and for Holy Week, but moved into Hungary ahead of Peter, which agrees with a May date for their arrival there (vol. 5, p. 29).

peacefully crossed the river Sava[13] in boats, but in that same place, Zemun, sixteen of the fellowship stayed behind to buy arms unknown to Walter, who had by then crossed the river long before. In fact, certain Hungarians with evil minds, seeing from afar that Walter and his army were absent, fell upon that band of sixteen and stripped them of their arms, clothes, gold and silver, then they let them go, naked and empty-handed. So they were lamenting their lack of possessions and arms all the way to the said Belgrade where Walter and all his band had pitched tents outside the walls to stay for a while. There they reported to him all the misfortune that had afflicted them, but he listened to them calmly, because going back to exact vengeance would have been wearisome. Then the same night that the naked and empty-handed comrades were taken in, Walter asked the prince of the Bulgars and the city magistracy for a licence to buy the necessities of life. The officials considered the damage and the people spying on their land, and they forbade all sales to them.[14] Because of this Walter and all his company were seriously troubled in their minds, and they began forcibly to seize and to lead away the Bulgars' herds of cattle and sheep which had been let out into the fields to graze and were wandering here and there. It came to the point where a serious quarrel began to develop between the pilgrims and the Bulgars who were driving off their herds, and arms were joined, until at length when the strength of the Bulgars was prevailing some hundred and forty of the pilgrims were cut off from the great number of their fellowship and, fleeing, they came to a certain chapel. The Bulgars were increasing in strength, while Walter was losing heart and taking flight with all his company, and they besieged the chapel where they burnt sixty of the men shut up in it and inflicted severe wounds on very many more of the rest who only just managed to slip away from the enemy and from the chapel to save their lives. After this disaster and weakening of his men Walter abandoned his comrades who were fleeing all around, and he passed through the Bulgarian woods in eight days and withdrew to a very rich city in the middle of the Bulgarian kingdom, called Niš, where he found the leader and prince of the country and reported to him all the outrage and the damage inflicted upon himself and he easily obtained justice from him with regard to all these things. Indeed that same lord of the country bestowed both arms and money on him in reconciliation, and gave him a safe-conduct through the Bulgarian towns of Sofiya, Philippopolis and Adrianople, and a licence to buy, and Walter marched down with all his band as far as the imperial city of Constantinople, which is the capital of all the empire of the Greeks. Moreover, as he marched down he entreated the lord emperor himself, with all possible urgency in a most humble petition, that he might peacefully take a breathing-space in his kingdom, with licence to buy the necessities of life, until

---

[13] Latin has river Morava. See Appendix 2: Places [Sava].

[14] This is the first of many incidents where provisioning the armies caused problems. The question is discussed in K. Leyser, 'Money and supplies on the first crusade', in T. Reuter (ed.), *Communications and Power in Medieval Europe: The Gregorian Revolution and Beyond* (London, 1994), pp. 77–95.

he had Peter the Hermit as comrade-in-arms, at whose instigation and inspiration he had started the journey, and with their thousands of men joined together they would cross the Straits of St George in boats and thus be able more safely to oppose the Turks and all the battle formations of the gentiles. All this was carried out, and the lord emperor, Alexios by name, graciously responded and granted everything he sought.

7. How Peter was making for Jerusalem with a numerous army; and he took revenge for his comrades in Hungary

Not long after all this the aforementioned Peter with his great army, as innumerable as the sand of the sea,[15] which had assembled and joined him from the different kingdoms, that is to say Franks, Swabians, Bavarians, Lotharingians, was carrying on in the same way the journey to Jerusalem. He marched down into the kingdom of Hungary on his journey and pitched his tents in front of the gate of Sopron with all the army of Christians he had led. When their tents were in place he sent messages right away to the ruler of Hungary, asking him to open the way into and through the middle of his kingdom to Peter and his comrades. This was granted to him, but on one condition, that he would not seize any plunder in the king's lands but would keep peacefully on his journey while, indeed, all the things the army needed might be procured at a price, without brawling and dispute. Therefore Peter rejoiced when he heard the king's kindness towards him and his men, and travelled through the kingdom of Hungary peacefully, giving and obtaining everything necessary for their use in quantity, justice, and fair measure,[16] and thus he and all his troops proceeded without disturbance as far as Zemun. But as he approached the boundaries of the said place, a rumour came to his ears and to those of his men, that a count of that region, Guz by name, one of the Hungarian king's nobles, corrupted by greed, had assembled a band of armed soldiers and had entered into a very wicked plot with the said duke, who was called Nichita,[17] prince of the Bulgars and ruler of the city of Belgrade, that the duke, having brought together the strength of his accomplices, would vanquish and kill the vanguard of Peter's army, while Guz would pursue and behead the men at the rear of Peter's soldiers, so that they might thus snatch and share between themselves all the spoils of

---

15 2 Kgs. (2 Sam.) 17: 11.

16 Cf. Wisd. 11: 21.

17 This 'duke' was evidently a Byzantine: apart from his name (Niketas), later (1. 13) he is in communication with the emperor. Duncalf calls him the Byzantine governor of Bulgaria (*Wisconsin History*, vol. 1, p. 259); J. Kalić suggests he was a Byzantine border commander ('Les données d'Albert d'Aix sur l'histoire des relations Byzantino-Hongroises vers la fin du XIe siècle'[in Serbo-Croat], *Recueil de travaux de la Faculté de philosophie*, 10 [1968], pp. 189–90). If his title was officially 'Dux' then he was probably general of the Bulgarian theme.

such a great army in horses, gold and silver, and clothes. Hearing this, because the Hungarians and Bulgars were fellow Christians, Peter refused altogether to believe them capable of so great a crime, until, as they approached Zemun, his companions caught sight of the weapons and spoils hanging on the ramparts and walls which had belonged to Walter's sixteen associates whom the Hungarians had delayed a little while before and had dared to rob by a trick. Then Peter, when he learnt of the outrage against his fellow countrymen, and saw their weapons and spoils, urged his companions to vengeance. At the signal from the trumpeters they shouted out bravely and ran together to the ramparts with standards held aloft, they attacked the walls with a hail of arrows which they shot at the eyes of those standing on the ramparts with such incessant and extraordinary density that the Hungarians could not withstand the strength of the attacking Gauls at all, and they turned away from the wall in the hope that they would be able to last out within the city in the face of the enemy troops. At this a certain Godfrey, who had the surname Burel and was born in the city of Etampes, commander and standard-bearer of two hundred infantry and likewise a foot soldier himself, vigorous in strength, as he watched the flight of the Hungarians at a distance from the walls, rapidly crossed the ramparts with a ladder, which he found by chance there. Reinold of the castle of Broyes, a distinguished cavalryman, who was wearing helmet and hauberk for protection, likewise climbed the walls after Godfrey until everyone, cavalry as well as infantry, was striving to enter. The Hungarians saw that their lives were in difficulty and danger threatened, and up to seven thousand of them massed together for the defence; they came out through another gate, which looked to the east, and took up a position on the top of a very high rock past which flowed the Danube, and from that direction their defence could not be overcome. The majority of them, who were unable to flee quickly through the gate because of the narrow approach, fell by the edge of the sword[18] before that very gate. Some who were hoping to find freedom on top of the slope were slaughtered by the pursuing pilgrims. Others, who rushed headlong from the peak of the mountain, were swallowed up in the waves of the Danube itself, but more slipped away in boats. About four thousand Hungarians died in that place; as few as a hundred of the pilgrims, apart from those wounded, were killed in the same place. After achieving this victory Peter stayed five days with all his men in the same fortress of Zemun because of the abundance of food which he found there in grain and flocks of sheep and herds of cattle and a plentiful supply of drink, and an infinite number of horses.

---

[18] Ecclus. 28: 22.

8. How they crossed with difficulty the river Sava

The aforesaid Duke Nichita learnt of this victory and the bloody massacre[19] of the Hungarians, and saw their bodies which had been cut to pieces by weapons, most of them destroyed by hideous wounds, which the Danube carried with its turbulent waves to Belgrade where the river bed turns and continues its journey and course a mile distant from Zemun. He called together his men and took advice from all of them, then because he was shaken by fear he refused to wait for Peter any longer in Belgrade but instead arranged to move to Niš, taking with him the entire treasure of Belgrade, in the hope of a defence against the forces of the French, Romans, and Germans, because this fortified city was enclosed by the strength of walls. Indeed, he put his fellow citizens to flight through the forests and the mountainous and uninhabited places with their herds, until the help of the imperial army of Constantinople had been summoned whereby he might oppose Peter's companions and avenge the Hungarians on account of the friendship and treaty which he had concluded with Guz, the count and prince of Zemun. Six days had passed after these events when a messenger was swiftly sent to Peter from a town of people unknown to the Franks, to make sure he was aware of the threats, saying: 'The king of Hungary has assembled an army from all his realm to avenge his men and is about to go into battle against you and not even one of your men is sure to escape his weapons. For grief and lamentation for the dead have roused the king and all his their kinsmen and friends. Therefore cross the river Sava[20] as quickly as possible, and hasten your journey away from here.' Peter realized the anger of the king and the great seriousness of the alliance against him, so he left Zemun with all his companions (taking with them, however, all their spoils and herds and booty of horses) and set out to cross the Sava. But he found few ships – only a hundred and fifty in number on the whole riverbank – in which such a great number could immediately cross and escape through fear of the king who was in hot pursuit. Because of this, as many as possible of those for whom there were no ships tried their best to cross using timbers joined together and fastened with osiers. But while they were tossing about on that same raft of joined timbers and osiers, with no way of steering and meanwhile separated from their companions, most of them perished, shot by the arrows of the Pechenegs, who inhabited Bulgaria.[21] Now Peter, seeing that his men were dying and drowning, ordered the Bavarians, Swabians and the rest of the Germans to help their Frankish brothers in accordance with their promise of obedience. They immediately brought in seven rafts and sank the seven little boats of the Pechenegs along with those who were on them,

19 'caede cruenta' is a phrase common in classical literature: *HL*, vol. 1, pp. 224–5.

20 As above and in the chapter title, AA has 'Maroa'.

21 The Pechenegs had settled in the Niš region in the middle of the eleventh century: *Chronicon S. Andreae*, *MGH SS*, vol. 7, p. 535; *Chronicon pictum Vindobonense* c.104 (*SSRH*, vol. 1, pp. 369–71); Michael Psellus, *Fourteen Byzantine Rulers*, tr. E. R. A. Sewter (Harmondsworth, 1966), pp. 317–20; Matthew of Edessa [ME], pp. 80, 90.

taking only seven people alive, whom they brought into Peter's presence and slaughtered on his orders. After he had thus avenged his men and the river Sava had been crossed, Peter entered the huge and very extensive forests of the Bulgars with his carts of food supplies and all his equipment and booty from Belgrade. And after spending eight days in the vast woodland he and his men approached the town of Niš with its heavily fortified walls. There they crossed a river by way of a stone bridge in front of the city, and by pitching their tents they took possession of a meadow, delightful in its greenness and wide extent, and the bank of the river.

9. How hostages were given to the duke of the Bulgars and, after they were received, a serious dispute with the Bulgars arose

Therefore the great host of pilgrims was quartered there and, in accordance with Peter's foresight and the decision of the majority, representatives were sent to Duke Nichita, prince of the Bulgars, who was then in that same city in person, to obtain permission to buy food. He graciously assented, but on one condition, that hostages would be given to him so that no injustice or act of violence, such as had happened at Belgrade, should be done by so great a number. Walter, son of Waleran of the castle of Breteuil which is near Beauvais, and Godfrey Burel of Etampes were selected and given to the duke as hostages. After they had been sent and received by the duke, the pilgrims were granted enough of all things to buy everywhere, and for those who had no means of buying a very great distribution of alms was collected by the city. After that night had been passed in complete quiet, therefore, and when the hostages had been faithfully restored to Peter by the prince, a hundred men of the Swabians[22] withdrew for a short time from the rear of Peter's army on account of a most vile dispute with a certain Bulgar which came about in the evening while selling and buying. They set fire to seven mills which were situated in the river below the aforesaid bridge, and reduced them to ashes.[23] They even set on fire some houses which were outside the town with a similar conflagration to satisfy their rage. But the citizens, seeing that their buildings were being consumed by fire, approached their Duke Nichita as an unanimous assembly, declaring that Peter and all his followers were false Christians and nothing more than robbers, and not peaceful men, who had killed the duke of Belgrade's Pechenegs and very many Hungarians of Zemun, and now had dared to start this fire, a wicked repayment for their kindness.

---

22 AA's 'Alemanni'; WT calls them 'Theutonici' (p. 145).

23 Probably river-mills of the type common in south-eastern Europe even today, which are fixed to the bank but sit above the river to harness the current.

10. How the duke, in pursuit of the army, seized much plunder and took many captive

When the duke heard of these outrages and the complaints of his men, he ordered that they should all take up arms eagerly, with the entire cavalry which he had brought together in that place, knowing about the attack on Zemun, and they should pursue the pilgrims without delay, so bringing on their heads all the evils which had been visited on themselves. Thereupon, following this order from the duke, the Bulgars, the Cumans, many Hungarians, with the Pechenegs, who had come together as an assembly of men determined on the defence of the city, snatched up bows of horn and bone,[24] put on hauberks and, having attached their standards each to a spear, they pursued Peter, who was proceeding unsuspectingly with his men, and without mercy they beheaded and stabbed those who were slow and at the tail end of the army, and they seized the carts and the waggons which were following behind in their sluggish way, carrying off women, girls, young boys (who have been found as exiles and prisoners in the land of Bulgaria right up to the present day), along with all their possessions and herds. Directly upon this sudden destruction and slaughter of pilgrims, a certain man, Lambert by name, who escaped by the speed of his horse, approached Peter and, as he knew nothing about this affair, reported it to him, and all that had happened, and how the beginnings of the evils and deceptions were the work of the Swabians because of the fire they had made. But Peter, a mile distant, knew nothing of all these things. He was seriously troubled at the words of the man who brought the information, and he called together the more prudent and intelligent men from the army, and spoke to them thus, saying:

11. How, after Peter had returned with his army to meet the duke and make peace, very many of the youth were destroyed

'A serious and severe misfortune threatens us, arising from the rage of the senseless Germans. Very many indeed of our men have been slain with those same Swabians by Duke Nichita and his guard, killed by bow and sword, in vengeance for the fire which was utterly unknown to me. However, all our waggons have been held back with our riches and herds. I see nothing more useful we may do about these things than to turn back to the duke and to make peace with him, because our men have acted unjustly towards him, when his citizens had peacefully supplied us with everything we needed.' When it heard Peter's speech and judgment the army turned round and retraced its journey to that same city of Niš, and pitched its tents

---

[24] These will have been the powerful composite bows used by these horse-archers and other nomadic peoples, including the Turks, rather than the shortbow common in the west. See D. Nicolle, *Arms and Armour of the Crusading Era, 1050–1350* (2 vols, New York, 1988), e.g. pp. 5, 6, 632 (illus. 10).

again in the same meadow as before so that Peter might make his apologies and those of the whole great army which had gone before, and thus appease the duke so that the army might recover its prisoners and waggons. While Peter, therefore, along with the more prudent of his men, was fully occupied with this project and plan and was composing his apology with careful words, a thousand foolish men, headstrong[25] youngsters of excessive irresponsibility, a wild and undisciplined set of people with neither cause nor reason, advanced in a great assault over the aforesaid stone bridge to the walls and gate of the city. Another thousand similarly frivolous youths, rushing together across the ford and the bridge with loud shouting and rage, joined them in support, refusing to listen to Peter their leader who, along with all sensible men, was forbidding what they were doing and ordering peace to be made. In this most serious disagreement of the quarrelling troops the whole army, except those two thousand men, stayed back with Peter, who was forbidding this mutiny, and it gave absolutely no assistance to them. The Bulgars, seeing this division among the people and that these two thousand could easily be overcome, burst out from two gates, risking arrows and lances and serious injury, and thus they checked them with great force and they put them all to flight. Fifty of them fell from the bridge and sank beneath the waters and were drowned. Three hundred on the other side of the bridge began to flee towards unfamiliar shallows; some of them were killed by weapons, others by water. At last those who had been held back from this madness and who had stayed with Peter in a plantation of trees on the other side of the river saw that their comrades were being massacred in such a savage martyrdom, and they could no longer keep themselves from helping them: they put on hauberks and swords, and, whether Peter was willing or not, they ran together to the bridge. At this point fighting broke out in a cruel manner on this side and that, with arrows, swords and lances. But as the Bulgars were in front of the ford and the bridge the pilgrims could not cross over by any means, but were vigorously put to flight. Peter, when he saw the destruction and flight of his men, sent a message to the duke through a certain Bulgar who had resolved to go with him on the road to Jerusalem, asking that he might deign to have a conference with Peter for a short time, and that they might arrange peace on both sides in the name of God. This was done.

12. The manner in which the army was for the most part scattered, and some thirty thousand were brought together again

When news of the peace talks had been spread among Peter's people and the storm had subsided to the point that everything might return to a state of harmony, the rebellious and incorrigible crowd on foot were retrieving and loading the carts and

[25] Literally 'stiff necked': Exod. 32: 9; Deut. 9: 13 etc.

waggons and pressing to continue the journey. Peter, Folcher,[26] and Reinold were forbidding them to do this until they could see if the conference would result in peace, but they were altogether unable to prevent the rebellious and foolish men from their undertaking. The citizens, though, seeing that Peter and the more adult part of his army were blocking the way of those who were going and were in the way of the waggons and carts, decided that they had prepared for flight with the rabble. Because of this they rushed out of the gate of the town with the duke's soldiers and pursued them with vigour, and for up to two miles these men inflicted great slaughter and took many captives from the army that had been held back. Also a waggon on which was Peter's chest full of countless gold and silver was captured and held, and was taken back to Niš at the same time as the prisoners and put in the duke's treasury, while the rest of the booty was divided among the soldiers. Men without number were killed, boys carried off with their mothers, women married and unmarried, of whom the number is not known. Peter, indeed, and all his band who were able to escape did so, through very thick and extensive woodland, some scattering over the steep slopes of the mountains and wilderness; they all scattered, as sheep hasten from wolves.[27] At length, after this escape, Peter, Reinold of Broyes, Walter son of Waleran of Breteuil, Godfrey Burel, Folcher of Orléans – all of these, with only fifty men, met by chance on the top of a certain mountain, and no more than these few of the forty thousand seemed to have survived. Then indeed Peter, contemplating the serious weakening of his people and his army, was reflecting anxiously on different things and lamenting with loud sighs the scattered legions and the thousands of his men who had fallen, while moreover only one of the Bulgars had died, and he wondered if any one of the forty thousand who had fled and been scattered was still alive. So he spoke and gave instructions, and accordingly those fugitives who had halted with him on top of the mountain made a great noise with signals and horns so that the pilgrims, wherever they were scattered over the mountains and forests and wilderness, might hear the signal from Peter and their fellows and turn back to be collected into one, to continue the journey they had undertaken. Nor had the day sunk to a close before about seven thousand heard the signal and assembled. Brought together thus, and turned back from their scattered ways, they set about their journey once more. They approached a certain city which had been evacuated by its citizens, where they pitched camp and devoted themselves to their comrades who had fled and been scattered. But they were able to find or search out very little food in the wilderness and suffered a very great famine there, because they had lost over two thousand waggons and carts which were carrying corn, barley and meat for food, and they found no one selling or offering anything. It was in the month of July that these misfortunes had befallen them, when in this region the corn and ripe crops had already turned golden for the harvest. Since the people were distressed by

[26] This Folcher is called Folcher of Orléans below, but Folcher of Chartres at his last appearance, his death in Asia Minor (1. 21).

[27] Vergil, *Aen*. i. 137.

hunger it seemed a good idea to the most prudent counsellors that the ripe crops found on the plains around the deserted and empty city might be roasted with fire and the roasted grains shaken out to sustain the hungry people. And indeed the people lived for three days on this small sustenance of corn, until those who had fled and been scattered were gathered together again to the number of thirty thousand, all except the ten thousand who had died.

13. How the emperor sent envoys to Peter to ensure he came to Constantinople

Meanwhile Duke Nichita's messengers had gone on ahead to the lord emperor of Constantinople and they reported to him all the evil facts concerning the deeds and misfortunes of Peter: the way he had killed the Hungarians at Zemun and how, arriving at the city of Niš, he had returned evil deeds for the kindness of the citizens, not, however, without reprisals. When the emperor heard these things, he sent envoys direct to Peter. They discovered that he had left the empty and deserted city and set out with all his company for the town of Sofiya, and they carried these messages to him in accordance with the emperor's orders: 'Peter, very serious complaints concerning you and your men have been brought to the lord emperor, because your army has pillaged and made discord in his territory. Therefore it is his imperial decree that you may not stay more than three days in any town of his empire until you enter the city of Constantinople. However, we are instructing all the cities through which you will pass that they should sell all things peacefully to you and your men on the emperor's orders, and because you are a Christian and your companions are Christians they should hinder your journey no further. And however much your followers have offended by their pride and rage against Duke Nichita, the emperor forgives you straight away, for he knows that you have paid heavy penalties for this wrongdoing.' When Peter heard this peaceful message from the lord emperor he was not a little glad and, weeping with joy, he gave thanks to God who, after so great and severe reproach, not undeserved, had now given him and his men grace in the eyes of so magnificent and renowned an emperor.

14. How Peter received a second message from the emperor, commanding him to hasten his journey

Therefore, willingly obeying the emperor's instructions, Peter went on from the town of Sofiya and withdrew to the city of Philippopolis with his whole company. There, for all the Greek citizens to hear, he told the story of his adventures and misfortunes, and he received very many gifts of bezants, silver, horses and mules, in the name of Jesus and in the fear of God, because all were moved by pity for him. Then, after the third dawn, departing cheerfully and rejoicing in the largesse of provisions, he withdrew to Adrianople. There he stayed only two days in quarters outside the walls of the city, and moved on at the third dawn. For a second message from the emperor asked him to hasten his journey to Constantinople because the emperor eagerly desired to see this same Peter, because of the news he had heard about him. However, as Peter's army arrived in Constantinople it was ordered to lodge far from the town, and a licence to buy was granted fully.

15. How Peter and his army were kindly received by the emperor; and then they crossed the sea

So Peter, who was insignificant in stature but great in speech and heart, was brought into the emperor's presence by his envoys, accompanied only by Folcher, so that the emperor might see if he was as the rumours about him claimed. Peter entered and greeted the emperor confidently in the name of Lord Jesus Christ, and he related in detail how he had left his homeland in the love and service of that same Christ, and he reminded the emperor in a few words of the misfortunes he had already endured. He announced that very powerful men would be following a short way behind him: counts and very noble dukes who, like him, had decided to make the journey to Jerusalem, fired by desire to see the Lord's Sepulchre. Moreover, when the emperor had seen Peter, and knew from his words the purpose he had in mind, he asked what he wanted, or what he desired of him. Peter begged that he might receive alms from the emperor's merciful hand, so that he and his men would have something to sustain life, and he declared how many and what an immeasurable quantity of goods he had lost because of the folly and rebelliousness of his men. The emperor was moved by pity when he heard Peter's humility, and ordered two hundred golden bezants to be given to him; indeed he paid out a measure of money to Peter's army from his coinage called the tartaron.[28] After this Peter returned from his conference and the emperor's palace, having been graciously approved by him, and he stayed only five days on the plains and estates of Constantinople. Walter Sansavoir had pitched his tents there at the same time and they became allies from that same day, and from then on their resources were pooled, weapons and all the things necessary for their use. Then at the end of the fifth day they took down their tents and crossed the Straits of St George with the vessels and support of the emperor, and, entering the lands of Cappadocia, they went in through the mountains to Nicomedia,[29] spending the night in that place. And after this they pitched camp at

---

[28] The 'tetartaron' was a small flat coin made of copper introduced by Alexios I Komnenos as part of his currency reform of 1092. The recency of its introduction explains why both AA and Fulcher of Chartres [FC] (p. 189) find it necessary to describe it: P. Grierson, *Byzantine Coins* (London, 1982), pp. 11, 219.

[29] AA's geography is faulty: Bithynia is the area between Constantinople and Nicomedia. Cappadocia is in central Asia Minor and AA appears to use the name generally for Asia Minor or Anatolia.

the port which is called Civitot. In accordance with the emperor's orders, merchants busily brought ships loaded with provisions, plenty of wine, corn, oil and barley and cheeses, selling everything to the pilgrims fairly and in good measure. While they were rejoicing in the abundance of victuals and caring for their exhausted bodies,[30] messengers of the most Christian emperor arrived who forbade Peter and all his army to travel towards the mountainous regions of the city of Nicaea, because of ambushes and attacks from the Turks, until their numbers were greater, swollen by the addition of the Christians who were coming. Peter listened to them and agreed with the messages and advice of the emperor, as did the whole body of Christians. And they delayed there, enjoying themselves in peace and joy for two months, sleeping in safety from any enemy attack.

16. How youths carried out raids in the lands around the city of Nicaea, and captured a certain castle belonging to Suleyman

Therefore after two months, made licentious and unruly by inactivity and the immeasurable supplies of food, they did not listen to Peter's voice, but against his will they went in through the mountainous regions to the land of the city of Nicaea and the territory of Suleyman, the duke of the Turks.[31] They plundered the herds of cattle, oxen, and sheep, flocks of goats which belonged to Greek subjects of the Turks, and carried them back to their comrades. Peter perceived these things with a sad heart, knowing that they would not plunder without retaliation. And so he often warned them not to seize any more of this booty, according to the emperor's advice. But he spoke to his foolish and rebellious people in vain. While these things were going well for them, and they did not yet fear that their spoils would be wrested away from them, it seemed a good idea to the spirited and conceited young men to form a detachment of the army and to find out how far they could go in seizing and carrying off booty in the meadows and pastures before the walls of the town of Nicaea in full view of the Turks. So about seven thousand foot soldiers gathered together, with as many as three hundred armoured horsemen and set out with a raising of their banners and excessive tumult, and carried off seven hundred oxen with the other herds from the meadows of Nicaea, and returned to Peter's tents, where they made a great and rich banquet. Indeed they sold the greater part of the cattle to the Greeks and to sailors who served the emperor. Moreover, seeing that the affair succeeded well for the French and the Romans and that they returned so many times with their booty without any hindrance, the Germans were themselves fired with greed for pillage; they gathered together about three thousand foot soldiers, but only two hundred horsemen, and with purple and red standards they followed a footpath through those same mountains

---

30 Cf. Vergil, *Aen*. viii. 607 and *Geo*. iv. 187.

31 Qilij Arslan I, sultan of Rūm, was the son of Suleyman (i.e. 'ibn Sulaymān') and so was called 'Solomon' by the westerners.

and arrived at a certain castle belonging to Suleyman – who was a powerful man, duke and prince of the Turks – situated where the mountains and forest come to an end, three miles away from Nicaea. They attacked this castle with all strength of arms and a warlike noise until they had overcome its inhabitants and put them to the sword, sparing only the Greek Christians. All the rest who were found in that same fortification were either slain or cast out. Thus the fortress was overcome and its inhabitants driven out, and the pilgrims were happy with the plentiful supply of food found there. Rejoicing in this victory, one after another they gave their advice, that if they remained in this fortress they would easily use their forces to take the lands of Suleyman and his chiefs, they would bring together spoils and food from all around, and safely wage war on Suleyman until the expected army of the great princes could approach.

17. How Duke Suleyman assembled his Turks and stormed the aforesaid castle; he took some captive and killed the rest

However, when Suleyman, the duke and prince of the Turks, heard about the arrival of the Christians and indeed the plundering and looting of his property, he assembled fifteen thousand Turks from all Rūm and the kingdom of Khurasan, men of war who were very experienced with the horn and bone bow and were very mobile archers. When these were assembled, two days after the victory of the Germans, he returned to the city of Nicaea from his distant land with a very strong united force. In Nicaea both his grief and his anger, already great, were increased by the news about the Swabians and their attack on the fortress which he had lost, and the slaughter and casting out of his men. Thereupon, after sunrise on the third day Suleyman, who had pitched camp with all his company, approached from Nicaea the fortress which the Germans had attacked. His standard-bearers, boldly attacking the fortress with the strength of the archers, cruelly shot arrows at the Germans who were resisting fiercely on the walls, and harassed them until they were no longer able to stand up and defend and they were thrust back from the wall and ramparts by an immeasurable hail of arrows, naked and unarmed, seeking protection from the darts within the fortification. The Turks, however, seeing that they had pushed back the Swabians from the walls and ramparts, made ready to climb across the walls and ramparts. But the Swabians who were inside the fortification, anxious and eager to stay alive, were holding their spears before them against those who wished to enter; others were resisting to their faces with swords and battleaxes until they dared no longer ascend. The Turks, therefore, found they were not strong enough to frighten the Swabians away by this assault and such a hail of arrows, so they brought together all kinds of wood to the fortress's very gate. These burned when the fire was put under them, and so did many buildings which were in the castle, until the flames and heat grew strong, and some were burnt up; others, hoping for safety,[32] leapt down from the walls. But the Turks who were outside were cutting down with swords those who were coming out and running away; about two hundred others who were beautiful in face and in youthful body they took away as prisoners; all the rest were destroyed by swords[33] and arrows.

18. How the army waited a week for Peter; and how the Turks beheaded some of the army

After this very severe vengeance Suleyman retreated with his men and with his Swabian prisoners, and news of the most cruel slaughter of Germans was carried into Peter's camp, whereupon the souls and hearts of all were violently overwhelmed by grief for the destruction of their comrades. Being troubled by this misfortune of their fellows, they held frequent conferences among themselves, debating whether they should rise up immediately to avenge them or wait for Peter. For before these days Peter had moved to Constantinople to see the emperor on behalf of his army and to ask him to make easier the sale of necessities to his men. However, while they were holding a council among themselves Walter Sansavoir forbade them utterly to go in vengeance of their brothers until the outcome of the affair was more fully known, and Peter was present in person, whose advice they would take about all things. The people were quietened by this advice from Walter for eight days while they waited for Peter to arrive. But he could not as yet in any way obtain from the emperor permission to return. On the eighth day after this some Turks, military men and famed in the art of war, a hundred in number, marched out from the city of Nicaea and went right through the area and the cities situated in the mountain regions, wishing to learn and find out about the spoils and plunder which the Gauls had taken. There on the same day they are said to have beheaded several pilgrims who were wandering here and there in scattered places, sometimes ten, sometimes fifteen, or more than that. When this rumour was set about in Peter's camp, that is, that the Turks were at hand and had beheaded some of their fellows who were wandering about, the pilgrims utterly refused to believe that the Turks had come down so far from Nicaea. But nevertheless some gave their advice that they should pursue them, to see if they could still be found in that territory.

19. How the Christians took up arms to avenge their comrades, and Suleyman brought a great army to meet them in battle

Meanwhile, when the truth came out, a tumult arose among the people, and the foot soldiers unanimously addressed Reinold of Broyes, Walter Sansavoir, the

[32] 'salutem sperantes' is a phrase common in classical literature: *HL*, vol. 5, p. 234.
[33] Jer. 16: 4 etc.

other Walter (of Breteuil) and Folcher of Orléans, who were foremost in Peter's army, demanding to rise against the insolence of the Turks to avenge their brothers. But the leaders refused to set out directly, until they had Peter's presence and advice. However Godfrey Burel, master of the foot soldiers, heard their replies and claimed that these distinguished knights were cowards and very little good in war; he persistently taunted with bitter speech the men who forbade the rest of the company to pursue the Turks to avenge their brothers. In opposition, the leaders of the great army could not hold out against the insults and taunts of that man and his followers, and, being greatly stirred by anger and indignation, they vowed to set out against the forces of the Turks and their ambushes, even if it was their fate to die in battle. Without delay, at the first sign of daybreak on the Wednesday, throughout the whole camp the knights and foot soldiers were ordered to arm and the trumpeters to sound the signal blasts, and all to gather together for war. Only those without weapons and the sick were left behind in the camp, with countless of the female sex. Armed, then, and all assembled, as many as twenty-five thousand foot soldiers and five hundred knights in armour set out on the way to the town of Nicaea in order to provoke Duke Suleyman and the rest of the Turks to war[34] and to join battle with them to avenge their brother soldiers. Therefore, when they were divided and organized into six divisions and assigned to different banners, they marched on right and left. With Peter absent and knowing nothing about all this, they had scarcely gone three miles from the port and post of Civitot, through the aforesaid forest and mountainous regions, boasting and shouting in a clamour and mighty tumult, when there, suddenly, was Suleyman with all his irresistible company: he had entered the same wood from the other side, coming down from the town of Nicaea, so that he would meet the Gauls in their camp with a sudden attack and put them all to the sword,[35] unknowing and unprepared as they were, and annihilate them. Suleyman, who had heard the approach and mighty noise of the Christians, wondered a great deal what this clamour meant, for everything the Christians had decided upon was unknown to him. Immediately he realized the pilgrims were there, he spoke thus to his men: 'Behold, the Franks against whom we were advancing are at hand. Moreover, you can be sure of one thing, that they come to fight against us. But let us retreat as quickly as possible from the forest and the mountainous regions onto the open and level plain, where we may freely join battle with them and they will not be able to find any place of refuge.' This was all carried out without delay as Suleyman had said, and in complete silence they left the forest and mountainous regions.

---

[34] Vergil, *Aen*. xi. 842.

[35] Biblical, e.g. Exod. 17: 13.

20. How the Turks fought fiercely with the Christians

The French, however, knowing nothing about Suleyman's arrival, were marching from the forests and mountainous regions with a clamour and loud shouting. Then for the first time they saw Suleyman's battle array in the middle of the plains and waiting for battle. When they saw them they began to comfort each other in the name of the Lord, and they sent forward two divisions which contained the five hundred knights. Suleyman saw the two divisions advancing and without waiting he loosened his horse's reins and his men did the same, and with an unbelievable and indescribable shout they astounded and stupefied the Christian soldiers. Thereupon, with a hail of arrows the Turks attacked the middle of the divisions,[36] which were seriously weakened and scattered and were cut off from the mass of people following. When they heard this clashing of weapons and the cruel pursuit of the shouting Turks, those at the rear of the army, who had not yet come out of the forest, gathered all together on the narrow path by which they had come, to stand firm and bar the narrow part of the path through the mountainous regions. But the divisions mentioned above, through whose divided ranks the Turks had made a concerted attack, had no way of returning to the forest and mountainous regions, so they seized upon the road towards Nicaea. They quickly turned back from this, shouting loudly, and rushed back through the middle of the Turks and, with horsemen and foot soldiers alike encouraging one another, they destroyed two hundred Turkish soldiers in a moment. The Turks, however, seeing that the strength of the cavalry was prevailing to the grief of their own men, had wounded their horses by shooting them with arrows, and in this way they reduced Christ's strong champions to fighting on foot.

21. How the Turks killed a countless multitude of Christians

There died Walter Sansavoir, pierced by seven arrows through his hauberk and breast. Reinold of Broyes and Folcher of Orléans,[37] who were very famous men in their own lands, died, destroyed in the same martyrdom, but not without a great massacre of Turks. But Walter of Breteuil, son of Waleran, and Godfrey Burel, the chief of foot soldiers, had slipped away in flight among the thornbushes and thickets and they returned along a narrow path, where they found all the troop which had withdrawn from the battle gathered together. When the soldiers knew of the flight of these two and their desertion, they all turned and fled, hurrying towards Civitot on the road by which they had come, and not protecting themselves adequately from the enemy. The Turks, therefore, rejoicing at the favourable outcome of their victory, slaughtered the wretched band of pilgrims, and they pursued them for a distance of three miles, to Peter's encampment, to kill them. Going into the pilgrim

---

[36] Cf. Vergil, *Geo*. iv. 84 etc.

[37] AA has 'Carnotensis' here, but see above, 1. 12. WT has 'Aurelianensis' (p. 152).

camp they found those who were there, the feeble and crippled, clerics, monks, aged women, boys at the breast, and put them all to the sword, regardless of age. They took away only young girls and nuns, whose faces and figures seemed to be pleasing to their eyes, and beardless and attractive young men. They carried off to Nicaea money, garments, mules, horses and anything of any value, even the tents themselves. There is, however, upon the seashore, near the aforesaid Civitot, a certain ancient and abandoned fortress; three thousand of the fleeing pilgrims took flight and entered the ruins in the hope of defending themselves. But they found it had no gates or barriers, so, such was their desperation and despair of aid, they used their shields in place of gates, with an enormous pile of rocks rolled in the entrance, defending their very lives manfully from the enemy only with spears and wooden bows, and by throwing rocks. The Turks, seeing that the slaughter of the men inside was not proceeding very well, surrounded the fortress on all sides, and as it had no roof they shot arrows high in the air so that they turned and fell onto the heads and bodies of those inside and killed the poor wretches; the others who saw this were forced to surrender. Many were brought back there who had thus been wounded and killed, but fearing cruel punishment by the infidels they could not be compelled to go out, either by arms or for fear of their lives.

22. How three thousand of the Christians, who had escaped from the Turks only to be besieged by them, were delivered by the assistance of the emperor

Already the sun had passed midday when these three thousand who had gone into the fortress were besieged by the Turks. They were defending their lives bravely, and they could be dislodged from this stronghold by no stratagem, not even in the shadow of night itself, until a messenger, who was a loyal Greek and a Christian, sailed across the sea by night and sought out Peter in the royal city, and reported to him all the dangers these men were in, and the ill fortune and destruction of the rest. Peter, having heard of the danger to his men and the tragedy of the slain, mourning and grieving, begged the emperor humbly in the name of Jesus Christ to help the few poor pilgrims who were left out of so many thousands, and not to allow them to be destroyed, deserted and desperate, by so many executioners. When the emperor heard Peter's account of the calamity and the siege of his men, he was moved by pity, and he summoned his Turcopoles[38] from all around, and all the nations

[38] The Turcopoles were imperial auxiliary cavalry troops, presumably originally ethnic Turks, which may explain why AA is prejudiced against them (see also 8. 32). Both he and Raymond of Aguilers [RA] (p. 55) describe them as offspring of Christian mothers and Turkish fathers, brought up among Turks (see 5. 3). There is a discussion by A. G. C. Savvides, 'Late Byzantine and western historiographers on Turkish mercenaries in Greek and Latin armies: the Turcoples/Tourkopoloi', in R. Beaton and C. Roueché (eds), *The Making of Byzantine History: Studies dedicated to Donald M. Nicol*, (Aldershot, 1993), pp. 122–36.

under his rule, and ordered them to go with all haste across the straits to assist the Christians who had fled and were besieged, and there to overcome and put to flight the Turks from the siege. However, knowledge of the emperor's command came to the Turks, and in the middle of the night they moved away from the fortress, taking with them the Christians they had captured and a great deal of booty, and thus the imprisoned and besieged pilgrim soldiers were freed from the infidels.

23. How a certain Gottschalk brought together a great army for that same expedition

Not long after Peter's crossing a certain priest called Gottschalk,[39] German by birth and an inhabitant of the Rhineland, was inspired by love and desire for the same journey to Jerusalem because of a sermon of Peter's. With his oratory he aroused the hearts of many from different nations to press forward on the road together, and he drew together over fifteen thousand from different regions of Lotharingia, eastern France, Bavaria, and Swabia, a crowd with as many knights as common foot soldiers who, as they had collected an indescribable quantity of money and other necessary supplies, were allowed to continue their journey peacefully into the kingdom of Hungary. Indeed, they were brought with honour to the gate of Mosony, and by King Coloman's favour to his fortress. They were even granted a licence to buy and sell necessary supplies and peace was proclaimed on both sides according to the king's instructions, lest a dispute might arise from such a large army. But when they were delayed there for some days, they began to wander, and the Bavarians and Swabians, a bold race, and the rest of the soldiers foolishly drank too much; they violated the proclaimed peace, little by little stealing wine, barley, and other necessities from the Hungarians, finally seizing sheep and cattle in the fields and killing them; they destroyed those who stood up to them and wanted to drive them out. The others committed several crimes, all of which we cannot report, like a people foolish in their boorish habits, unruly and wild. For, as those say who were present, they stabbed a certain young Hungarian in the market street with a stake through his private parts, because of a most contemptible dispute. A complaint about this affair and the other outrages was carried to the ears of the king and his princes.

24. The way in which Gottschalk's army behaved insolently in Hungary and was destroyed

The king was disturbed by this scandal, and all his household was thrown into confusion, so he ordered that his attendants should arm themselves and that the

---

[39] Ekkehard of Aura [EA] calls Gottschalk a 'false servant of God' (*Hierosolymita,* p. 20), but his more hostile account is essentially in agreement with AA's.

signal should be given to the whole of Hungary to stir to battle in vengeance of this crime and the other insults, and not one of the pilgrims was to be spared because they had carried out this vile deed. Gottschalk's army soon found out about the king's savage edict that they be slaughtered, and they sounded signals throughout all their company and gathered together on the plain of Belgrade beside St Martin's oratory.[40] Without delay the royal forces of the whole kingdom of Hungary were armed to destroy the assembled peoples. But they found that the Germans were fighting back strongly with spears, swords and arrows, as if they were desperate and fighting for their lives. Because of this the royal troops were no more keen than they were to advance. Since they saw that the affair was a matter of life and death for the Gauls and they would not be able to join battle without incalculable losses, they spoke flatteringly to them as a trick, in this way: 'A complaint was made to our lord king about the outrages which you have committed in his kingdom. But he thinks you are not all guilty of this crime, because there are some sensible ones among you, and the violated treaty and vile outrages have troubled you no less than the lord king himself and his men. Therefore, if you want to make amends to the lord king and placate the princes of this country, it is necessary and unavoidable that you give up all your weapons into the hands of the lord king, and show that you mean peace in accordance with our advice; if, indeed, you surrender to the king with all the money you possess you may calm his anger and thus find favour in his eyes.[41] However if you do otherwise, not a single one of you will be able to stand before him and his men or continue to live, because you have insulted him and broken faith so badly in his kingdom.' Gottschalk, therefore, and the other sensible men, who heard this and believed the words were spoken in good faith, and because the Hungarians were professed Christians, gave their advice to the whole assembly that in accordance with the speech they should give up their weapons to make amends to the king and thus all things would return to a state of peace and goodwill. Everyone agreed to this advice and gave up hauberks, helmets, all their weapons, and the whole of the money (that is, their means of support on the journey to Jerusalem) into the hands of the king's officials, and, humble and shaking with fear, they bowed their heads before the king, certain of gaining the king's complete mercy and kindness. The king's ministers and soldiers brought all the weapons into a room in the king's palace; the money and other

[40] The reference to Belgrade must be a mistake. The battle was almost certainly fought at Pannonhalma, where the Benedictines had built their first abbey in Hungary, dedicated to St Martin, just a hundred years before these events (G. Kriszt, *Medieval Churches of Hungary* [Budapest, 1990], p. 14). WT does not mention the chapel of St Martin, but places the battle at 'Bellagrava' 'in the heart of the kingdom' ('in umbilico', p. 154). It has been suggested that the 'campus' here and the 'planicies' below refer to the town square, but it is hard to believe that the king would allow the Germans into the town at this point or that the sort of fight described could have been accommodated in town: B. Kugler, 'Peter der Eremite und Albert von Aachen', *Historische Zeitschrift*, 44 (1880), pp. 22–42, at 31.

[41] Gen. 18: 3; 33: 10; Num. 11: 15.

valuables, as much as the army had accumulated, they put into the royal treasury. When everyone's weapons had been stowed away thus in the room, all the good faith and mercy which the Hungarians had promised the king would have for the people turned out to have been lies: quite the opposite, they rushed upon them in a cruel massacre, decapitating them, naked and weaponless as they were; they inflicted a most savage slaughter upon them, so much so – and those who were present and escaped with difficulty swear this is true – that the whole plain of Belgrade was covered with dead and slaughtered bodies and blood, and few were spared this martyrdom.

25. How a great number of people came together from different realms for that same expedition

The same year, at the beginning of summer, after Peter and Gottschalk had led the way with the army they had assembled, presently another such host was flocking together in bands from different kingdoms and lands, including, of course, France, England, Flanders, and Lotharingia, a great and countless host of Christians, burning with the fire of divine love and having taken the sign of the cross, carrying all their household utensils and worldly goods and articles of weaponry which they needed on the journey to Jerusalem. Crowds of them had been gathered into one from the different kingdoms and states, but as they did not in any way turn from fornication and unlawful relationships there was excessive revelling, continual delight with women and girls who had set out for the very purpose of frivolity, and boasting most rashly about the opportunity offered by this journey.

26. About the massacre of the Jews in Cologne

I do not know if it was because of a judgment of God or because of some delusion in their minds, but the pilgrims rose in a spirit of cruelty against the Jews who were scattered throughout all the cities, and they inflicted a most cruel slaughter on them, especially in the kingdom of Lotharingia, claiming that this was the beginning of their crusade and service against the enemies of Christianity.[42] This massacre of the

[42] The attacks on the Rhineland Jews are passed over by WT in a couple of sentences (p. 156). Frutolf's account is brief and unsympathetic to the Jews but agrees in essentials with AA's (Frutolf and Ekkehard, *Frutolfs und Ekkehards Chroniken und die anonyme Kaiserchronik*, (ed.) and trans. F.-J. Schmale and I. Schmale-Ott [Darmstadt, 1972], p. 108). For considerably more detail one must turn to the Hebrew accounts. A full discussion of these and of the situation of the Jews in general, may be found in R. Chazan, *European Jewry and the First Crusade* (London, 1987). Chazan prints as an appendix (pp. 223–97) translations of the two original Hebrew chronicles: the shorter (S) and longer (L). These are the source of many of the notes which follow. See also J. Cohen, 'The Hebrew crusade

Jews was first carried out in the city of Cologne by the citizens.[43] They suddenly attacked a small band of Jews, they decapitated many and inflicted serious wounds, they overthrew their homes and synagogues, dividing a substantial sum of money among themselves. When the Jews saw this cruelty, about two hundred started to flee by boat to Neuss at dead of night.[44] The pilgrims and crusaders[45] discovered these men and did not leave a single one alive, but after they had been punished with the same sort of massacre they robbed them of all their possessions.[46]

27. About a similar massacre carried out at Mainz

Not long after these events the pilgrims were continuing their journey, as they had vowed, and they arrived in a great crowd at the city of Mainz.[47] Here Count Emicho, a noble man and very powerful in this region, was waiting with a very great band of Germans for the arrival of the pilgrims who were coming together there by the royal road from different parts. The Jews of this city, hearing about the slaughter of their brothers and realizing that they could not escape the hands of so many, took refuge with the bishop, Ruthard, in the hope of safety, placing priceless treasures in his care and his trust, and putting great faith in his protection because he was the bishop of that same city.[48] He, moreover, as the most important priest in the city, put away carefully the incredible quantity of money which he received from them, and he settled the Jews in the very large hall of his home, out of sight of Count Emicho and his followers, so that they might remain there safe and sound in a totally secure and well fortified dwelling place. But Emicho and the rest of his troop consulted together, and at daybreak they attacked the Jews in the palace with arrows and spears, broke bolts and doors and overcame and killed about seven hundred of the Jews as they tried in vain to withstand the strength and attack of so many thousands. They slaughtered the women in just the same way, and cut

chronicles in their Christian cultural context', in A. Haverkamp (ed.), *Juden und Christen zur Zeit der Kreuzzüge* (Sigmaringen, 1999), pp. 17–34.

43 According to the Hebrew account L (p. 273) attacks had already taken place at Speyer, Worms and Mainz. S says letters of warning were received from French communities (p. 225). L gives the date: May 29, 1096.

44 A classical phrase, e.g. Caesar, *De bell. Gall.* 7: 26.

45 This appears to be the first recorded use of 'crucesignatus' as a noun: although there are one or two equally early uses in an adjectival sense, the substantive term only became widespread at the end of the twelfth century.

46 According to L the killing at Neuss was on June 24 (p. 275).

47 The Hebrew accounts offer a more detailed chronology: Speyer May 3 (S p. 227, L p. 244); Worms May 5 (S pp. 228–32, L p. 245), then Mainz (S pp. 232–3, L p. 245). They are not necessarily more trustworthy, though: L names Godfrey as one of the leaders of the oppressors (p. 247).

48 Archbishop Ruthard's good faith is attested also by the Jewish writer of L (pp. 90–93).

down with their swords young children, whatever their age and sex. The Jews, indeed, seeing how the Christian enemy were rising up against them and their little children and were sparing none of any age, even turned upon themselves and their companions, on children, women, mothers and sisters, and they all killed each other. Mothers with children at the breast – how horrible to relate – would cut their throats with knives, would stab others, preferring that they should die thus at their hands, rather than be killed by the weapons of the uncircumcised.[49]

28. How the army was refused passage and fought with the Hungarians

After this very cruel massacre of the Jews had taken place, and a few had escaped, and a few had been baptized rather through fear of death than for love of the Christian religion,[50] Count Emicho, Clarembald, Thomas, and all that irresistible association of men and women continued the journey to Jerusalem with a large amount of booty, going in the direction of the kingdom of Hungary, where the royal highway was normally open to all pilgrims. But when they came to the king's fortress at Mosony, which is defended by the river Danube and the Leitha with its marshes, they found the bridge and gate of the fortress closed on the orders of the king of Hungary, because a great fear had possessed all the Hungarians on account of the slaughter which they had inflicted on their brothers. And when their great army followed close behind, the corpses of those killed were still stinking. There were two hundred thousand foot soldiers and cavalry, but the cavalry numbered hardly three thousand. Since, therefore, the gate was closed, and passage through the kingdom was denied to them all, they set up camp all over the level ground of the plains, and when they sent envoys to the king and asked for peace their prayers and promises were not heard.[51] For this reason Emicho, Thomas, and Clarembald, men who were distinguished for soldierly deeds, came to a decision with the more careful of their companions, that they should lay waste the king's lands which adjoined this region, and should not withdraw from here until a bridge could be placed across the marsh and the river Leitha, over which they would penetrate, approaching the wall of the fortress by some artifice, so that even thus the way across Hungary would be opened up by the strength of their army. They stayed in front of the fortress for many days after the middle of June and put a bridge together, and they used often to fight with those they were besieging. The defenders of the fortress fought back bravely, hurling javelins from this point and that and

---

[49] The attacks did not end here. L also refers to Trier, Metz, Regensburg and Prague (p. 287).

[50] The forcible baptism of the Jews is described by Cosmas of Prague: *Die Chronik der Böhmen des Cosmas von Prague*, (ed.) B. Bretholz (Berlin, 1923), pp. 164–6. Cosmas stresses that it was against canon law.

[51] The Hebrew chronicle L has a confused account of the king of Hungary's attack on Emicho (pp. 296–7).

inflicting considerable losses on both sides. Now and then the defenders burst out from the stronghold and by the strength of their armed men they would force the Gauls back violently across the river and bridge; now and then the Gauls would prevail and would send the Hungarians back into the fortress, battle-weary and wounded. However, one evening at about the ninth hour, Thomas, Clarembald, and William, with three hundred men clad in hauberks and helmets who were skilled cavalrymen, went down to a vantage point where the Hungarians very frequently passed by in boats to keep a watch on the lie of the land, to see if they could perhaps come to blows with them, and in case an opportunity offered to wage war, or herds of their cattle might be found to carry off. As those men were going down with this in mind they were met by seven hundred knights of the king who were reconnoitring the army of the Christians on horseback and fully armed. The Hungarians, seeing that they could in no way flee from them, suddenly attacked the troops of Gauls. And, joining battle, they were overcome and wounded and seriously diminished, taking flight through places well known to them and returning by boat to their own land, sorrowing and grieving. In this conflict William beheaded the chief of the Hungarian army, who was a member of the king's council, a distinguished man with dazzling snow-white hair. Because of this victory all the legions spent the whole of that night in rejoicing, and they had many of the Hungarians as prisoners.

29. The way in which the army was routed by a sudden attack and a countless multitude perished

After many such encounters and daily massacres over a long period of time the army was overcome by weariness and weakened by lack of food. On an agreed day some men in armour engaged in battle across the bridge they had constructed, others who were scattered through the marshes boldly attacked the fortress of Mosony. After they had positioned siege engines they penetrated the walls in two places, they pressed the Hungarians very hard, until entry was opened up for nearly all if only they could persist until the following day. However, King Coloman and all his company mounted their horses promptly, ready to flee towards the kingdom of Russia if they saw the very great force of the Gauls invading their land after taking the fortress. For they had repaired some bridges which had been demolished a very long time before, and by way of these they would be able to cross the marshes and rivers into the land of Russia if they were forced by necessity. But though almost everything had turned out favourably for the Christians and they had broken through the walls causing a great breach, I do not know by what chance or misfortune, a great fear took possession of the entire army so that they were put to flight in the same way, and they were scattered and alarmed like sheep when attacked by wolves,[52] seeking refuge this way and that way and forgetting

---

[52] John 10: 12.

their comrades. The Hungarians, seeing the bold champions deserting so suddenly and making haste to flee, sallied forth in great strength from the gates with their king; without wasting any time they pursued the fleeing Gauls hotly, inflicting very many deaths and capturing very many, and spending most of the night in revenge. There was so great a massacre of the crowd who were on foot, of both sexes, that the waters of the Danube and Leitha were changed into blood-red torrents. Many, indeed, an uncountable number, who were hoping because of their fear of impending slaughter to escape by taking to the water, were carried forward by the waves of the Danube in their blind attempt, and were choked by the violent waters. It is amazing to relate:[53] so many of the fugitives were drowned that the waters of that very wide river could not be seen for a considerable time because there were so many thousands of bodies. Emicho, however, Thomas, Clarembald, William, and a few of the others whose horses were fit to run the distance had escaped unharmed, along with some who had hidden in the grass and bushes of the marshes, or who had been able to flee in the darkness of night. Emicho and certain of his men made for the return road to escape by the way they had come; Thomas, Clarembald, and several of their men slipped away in flight towards Carinthia and Italy. In this the hand of God is believed to have been against the pilgrims, who had sinned in his eyes by excessive impurities and fornicating unions, and they had punished the exiled Jews (who are admittedly hostile to Christ) with a great massacre, rather from greed for their money than for divine justice, since God is a just judge and commands no one to come to the yoke of the Catholic faith against his will or under compulsion.

30. Concerning ridiculous belief in a goose and a goat

There was also another abominable wickedness in this gathering of people on foot, who were stupid and insanely irresponsible, which, it cannot be doubted, is hateful to God and unbelievable to all the faithful. They claimed that a certain goose was inspired by the Holy Ghost, and a she-goat filled no less with the same, and they had made these their leaders for this holy journey to Jerusalem; they even worshipped them excessively, and as the beasts directed their courses for them in their animal way many of the troops believed wholeheartedly, claiming it was the truth.[54] For never let the hearts of the faithful believe that the Lord Jesus is willing for the tomb of his most holy body to be visited by stupid and irrational animals,

---

[53] 'Mirabile dictu!' was a phrase much used in classical literature: *HL*, vol. 3, pp. 367–8.

[54] The story of the goose is reported more fully by Guibert of Nogent [GN], who says the goose accompanied a little woman and even approached the altar at the church in Cambrai. The woman died in Lotharingia: GN says she would have done better to have feasted on the goose before she set out (p. 331). The tale is confirmed by the Jewish chronicles S and L (pp. 233 and 249).

and for these to be the leaders of Christian souls, those souls which he had rescued, which he had deigned to ransom with his own precious blood from the filthiness of idols; since when he was ascending into the heavens he appointed as leaders, guides, and teachers of his people men who were very holy and worthy of God, rather than stupid and irrational animals. But what wonder if in these modern times such abominations and such foul sins are found in so many thousands among some peoples: for these were the Lord's repayment to them, when wickedness was discovered in the midst of the just in the times of Moses and Joshua and of the other servants of God,and from him who is the God of vengeance[55] the rod of his majesty is swift and purifying?

---

55 Ps. 93 (94): 1.

Book 2

1. With whom and at what time Duke Godfrey set out on the second expedition

Therefore after Peter the Hermit's departure and the very great disaster which befell his army; and then a short while after the cruel massacre of the army led by Gottschalk the priest; indeed, after the misfortune of Hartmann a count from Swabia, of Emicho and the other brave men and princes from the land of Gaul, namely Drogo of Nesle, Clarembald of Vendeuil; after the obliteration of his army which was cruelly carried out in the kingdom of Hungary at the gate of Mosony: after all this, Godfrey duke of the realm of Lotharingia,[1] a most noble man, and his brother Baldwin, who shared the same mother,[2] Warner of Grez a relative of that same duke, Baldwin of Bourcq likewise, Rainald count of Toul, Peter his brother also, Dodo of Cons, Henry of Esch and his brother Godfrey, very brave knights and very illustrious princes, were making the journey by the direct route to Jerusalem in the middle of August of the same year.[3] They stayed in quarters near the city of Tulln in the land of Austria, where the river Leitha marks the boundary and divides the kingdom of Gaul. They stayed for three weeks of September, so that they might listen and find out for what reason or how the insurrection had arisen in which, a little while before, the army of pilgrims had been destroyed and was turned aside from its plan of going to Jerusalem with its princes and leaders, and was now coming back towards them in despair.

2. The princes demanded of the king of Pannonia, by way of intermediaries, why he had destroyed the Lord's people

At last, after a lot of destructive talk as to what they should do first, and what would be a safe and wise way to investigate the truth of the affair and the cruelty the Hungarians had shown towards their fellow Christians when they had dealt with them on many occasions, it seemed to everyone a sensible plan that they

---

[1] Godfrey, the future ruler of Jerusalem, is the hero of AA's narrative. See Appendix 1: People for further details of Godfrey and his companions.

[2] The eldest brother, Eustace III, travelled with Robert of Flanders and Robert of Normandy. Baldwin departed with Godfrey, accompanied by his wife and household.

[3] Pope Urban himself had set the date for departure, the Feast of the Assumption of the Blessed Virgin Mary, 15 Aug. 1096: see his letter to the faithful of Flanders, *Kreuzzugsbriefe*, pp. 136–7.

should not send in advance any of the most renowned and chief men for an enquiry into the abominable murder and wickedness, except Godfrey of Esch, because he was known to Coloman, the king of the country, having been sent a long while before this journey on an embassy from Duke Godfrey to this same king of Hungary. They sent along with him twelve others chosen from the duke's household, Baldric, Stabelo and others whose names are not known, to disclose the mission of so many nobles in this way: 'To King Coloman of Hungary, Godfrey, duke of Lotharingia, and the other nobles of Gaul send greetings and every token of goodwill in Christ. Our lords and princes wonder why, since you are of the Christian faith, you have destroyed the army of the living God with such a cruel martyrdom, and you have in fact forbidden them to pass through your land and kingdom, and have afflicted them with various false accusations. Because of this they are now shaken by fear and doubt, and they have decided to delay at Tulln until they learn from the mouth of the king why so cruel a deed was perpetrated by Christians persecuting Christians.'[4]

3. The king's reply; and how he summoned the duke

The king replied with all his assembled men listening, 'We are not persecutors of Christians, but whatever cruelty we have displayed towards them, or death we have inflicted on them, we carried out because we were compelled by an overwhelming necessity. For in the first place when we prepared all good things for your army which Peter the Hermit assembled, a licence was granted to buy goods in fair weight and measure, and we organized a peaceful passage for them through the land of Hungary. They returned evil to us for good;[5] not only stealing gold and silver, horses and mules and herds from our territory, but even destroying our cities and castles and killing about four thousand of our men; they plundered possessions and clothes. After Peter's company unjustly committed these quite intolerable outrages against us, Gottschalk's army followed, and the one that was destroyed, which was put to flight and which you met, laid siege to the castle and fortification of our realm at Mosony, wanting in their pride and in the tyranny of their strength[6] to enter our domain to punish and drive us out, from whom with God's help we were only just protected.' However, while the king was replying these things, he ordered those same envoys of the duke to be entertained with honour in his own palace in a place called Pannonhalma,[7] where everything they

[4] This letter is reproduced (from the *RHC Occ* edition of AA) in *Diplomata Hungariae Antiquissima*, (ed.) G. Györffy, 2 vols (Budapest, 1992), vol. 1, p. 319, where it is characterized as 'fictum', although it may have been based on knowledge of a real letter.

[5] Biblical, e.g. Gen. 44: 4.

[6] Eph. 6: 10.

[7] 'Pannonia' may refer to the whole of Hungary at this time, but here probably the religious centre Pannonhalma.

needed was served to them lavishly at the king's very table for eight days. After those eight days the king, who had taken counsel with his nobles about the duke's embassy, sent back the envoys with envoys from his own court to carry the king's replies to the duke and the army commanders in this manner: 'King Coloman sends greetings and unfeigned love[8] to Duke Godfrey and all his fellow Christians. We have heard this about you: that you are a powerful man and prince in your land, and found to be trustworthy by all who have known you, and because you are always careful of your good reputation I have now chosen to see and acknowledge you, and accordingly I have come to a decision, that you may come down to us at our castle of Sopron with no thought of any danger, and if we stay on either side of the marsh we may safely hold a conference about all the things you have asked us about, and of which you suppose us guilty.'[9]

4. How honourably the duke was received when he entered Pannonia; and what happened between him and the nobles of the realm

After he had heard this message from the king the duke left all his assembled company, in accordance with the advice of his senior colleagues and, taking with him only three hundred soldiers,[10] he set out to see the king in the place that had been indicated, and, leaving his company of men on both sides here and there, the duke summoned only Warner of Grez, a very noble man, and his kinsman Rainald of Toul and Peter to go up with him across the bridge over the marsh. He found the king there and greeted him in a friendly way and kissed him with humble devotion. Then they held various conversations between them about friendship and the reconciliation of Christians, until this consideration of peace and love made such good progress that the duke was convinced of the king's good faith, and he took twelve from the three hundred with whom he had come into Pannonhalma and the land of Hungary to see the king; in fact he appointed his brother Baldwin, who had been left at Tulln, to rule and look after the people when the army of three hundred had been sent back. Therefore the duke entered Pannonhalma, and he was received with honour by the king himself and his nobles. Everything necessary was served to them with goodwill and in quantity from the court and table of the king, as was fitting for such an illustrious prince. Then for eight days the king held many meetings of his men, who had also flocked to see such a very renowned

---

8 Rom. 12: 9.

9 Györffy also describes this letter (correctly, no doubt) as 'fictum', and he reproduces WT's version, which is couched in less direct, more diplomatic terms (*Diplomata*, vol. 1, pp. 320–21; WT pp. 163–4).

10 There is no way of knowing whether this figure is accurate or whether AA made it up. Godfrey may have selected 300 or AA reported that number, because it was the number selected by God for Gideon to lead against the Midianites (Judg. 7). In general AA's numbers are no more reliable than any other medieval writer's.

prince, seeking to find a plan by which such an innumerable army, heavily armed, could be allowed in trust and confidence into his country, and yet his kingdom and his people's possessions be safe. At last a plan was devised and was announced to the duke, that unless eminent men and leaders of the army were given as hostages, no passage would be granted to him and his men, so that the king would not lose his lands and kingdom, if some pretext arose, to the strength of such an infinite mass of people. When he heard this the duke acceded to the wishes of the king in all things, and did not refuse to give the hostages he sought, making the condition, however, that after this the army of pilgrims – in future as well as now – might pass through his land without any hindrance and obtain peacefully the necessities of life. Without delay, the king sealed a treaty with the duke, all the nobles of his kingdom sealed it also with a sworn oath not to harm the pilgrims further as they passed through. So, with all these matters settled thus on both sides in good faith, the king, on the advice of his men, asked that Baldwin, the duke's own brother, should be a hostage, and his wife as well,[11] and all his household. Without any argument the duke agreed to satisfy this condition. And at once, eight days after the embassy was sent, the duke ordered the whole army to hasten to the castle of Sopron, and their tents to be pitched on this other bank of the river and marsh.

5. Where the army pitched camp on the duke's orders

Then at the arrival of the duke's embassy his army began to be exceedingly cheerful, and they all rejoiced who were formerly uncertain because of the duke's long absence, thinking that he had been betrayed in mistaken trust and killed. But now they arose as if they were awoken from a deep sleep, and in accordance with the duke's command they came to the bank of the river and marsh and set up camp. When the tents were pitched, therefore, the duke returned from the kingdom of Hungary and was restored to his men, reporting how much care and honour the king had displayed towards him, and all the things he had agreed with the king and his nobles, and that his brother Baldwin had been requested by the king as hostage along with his wife and household, until the people had passed right through the land in quiet and peace; otherwise they would not be given permission to cross. And after a little he reminded his brother Baldwin at once that he was to be hostage for the people as had been decreed. But Baldwin began to resist and argue violently until the duke, worried by his irresolution, decided that Baldwin should assume the care of God's army, and he himself would not hesitate to become hostage in his brother's place. At last Baldwin put all the wavering out of his mind and consented to become a hostage and to be sent across into exile for the safety of his brothers.

[11] Baldwin's wife was called Godechilde, or Godevere.

6. In what manner the army crossed Hungary, after hostages were given

Therefore, now that so illustrious a prince had become a hostage and the king had returned with him into Pannonhalma, all the army were allowed in over the bridge across the marsh in accordance with the command and consent of the king, and they set up camp on the river Hantax. When the camp had been established, and everyone settled down in their quarters, Duke Godfrey appointed heralds to announce throughout each and every household and tent that no one, under pain of death, should touch anything, or carry off anything by violence in the kingdom of Hungary, or cause any insurrection, but should purchase everything at a fair price. In the same way the king also ordered it to be announced throughout the whole kingdom that the army might procure a plentiful supply of necessities: bread, wine, corn and barley, beasts of the field, birds of the sky.[12] And it was ordained, on pain of death, that the Hungarians should not burden the army by selling at an unjust price, or upset them, but rather they should offer all things for sale to them on lenient terms. So it was that the duke and the people crossed the kingdom of Hungary, every day in peace and quiet, buying in fair and just measure, and they arrived at the river Drava, where they made a heap of wood and joined together many reeds and got across the river, with the king continually marching on their left side with a strong troop of cavalry, together with Baldwin and the other hostages, until they arrived at the place which is called Francavilla. They stayed there for three days, and purchased the necessities of life and what the army needed at a fair price, then they went on down to Zemun with the whole army, spending five nights on the bank of the Sava.[13] There it became known to the duke and the other leaders of the army that the irresistible might of the imperial army of Constantinople was present to deny the pilgrims the way through the kingdom of Bulgaria. Because of this the duke and everyone formed a plan, that they should send a part of the army in advance across the river bearing arms, to keep back the enemy soldiers of the emperor until the people were clear. For no more than three ships were discovered there, in which a thousand armoured soldiers were sent across the take possession of the bank. The remaining multitude crossed over the river bed by joining together wood and vines.

7. Where the king restores the hostages; and the way in which the king of Greece addressed the duke through messengers

Scarcely had the people and their princes got clear, when they saw the king in all his state, with the duke's brother Baldwin and his wife and all the hostages, which he restored to the duke in that same place, and then he returned into his own kingdom, having commended the duke and his brother with very great

[12] Jer. 16: 4.

[13] This is the correct name for the river AA called the Morava in Book 1.

love, which he showed by many gifts and the kiss of peace. The duke and all his company settled on the other bank and stayed all night in the Bulgarian town of Belgrade, which Peter and his army had plundered and burnt not long before. When morning came, however, the duke and his army rose and entered the vast and strange forests of the Bulgarian kingdom, where legates of the emperor met them, bringing messages in these words: 'Alexios, the emperor of Constantinople in the kingdom of Greece, sends his entire love to Duke Godfrey and his followers. I ask you, most Christian duke, not to allow your people to lay waste and plunder my kingdom and territories which you have entered, but to obtain a licence to buy necessities, and then everything will be provided from our empire for your men to buy and sell in sufficient quantity.' When the duke learnt of the emperor's goodwill, he promised to obey the emperor's commands in all things. Therefore it was proclaimed to all that they should not seize anything at all by unjust force, unless it was fodder for the horses. So in fact they crossed through peacefully in accordance with the emperor's request, and arrived at his own fortress of Niš, where a wonderful abundance of food was offered as the emperor's gift to the duke: corn, barley, wine and oil, and many game animals; to the rest a licence to buy and sell was granted. The army rested there for four days in great plenty and enjoyment. After this the duke set out with all his army for Sofiya, where he was satisfied by no less a wealth of gifts from the emperor. Then after some days he left and went down to Philippopolis, a splendid city, and there in the same way for eight days he had a plentiful supply of all necessities as a gift from the emperor. Messages were brought to him there that the emperor held Hugh the Great, the king of France's brother, and Drogo and Clarembald in prison and in chains.[14]

8. What the duke demanded of the king when he greeted him in return; and what he did for the princes who were being held

When the duke heard this he sent an embassy to the emperor, requesting him to restore to freedom these princes of his land whom the emperor was holding prisoner, otherwise he would forfeit the duke's trust and friendship. Baldwin,

---

[14] Cf. Vergil, *Aen.* i. 54. It is unlikely that Hugh was literally under such restraint and the messages or rumours which reached Godfrey may well have exaggerated his plight. According to the *GF* Hugh had been detained by the governor of Dyrachium (Dürres, Albania) and was sent 'caute' (which Hill, p. 6, translates as 'under guard') to the emperor in Constantinople; while FC says he was detained 'non omnino liber' ('not altogether free', p. 155). Anna Komnene [AK] has a circumstantial and unflattering description of Hugh's arrogant behaviour; according to her he was shipwrecked on the Dalmatian coast, received in Dyrachium and entertained there, although 'he was not granted complete freedom'. He was then escorted to Constantinople where he swore to become the emperor's man (pp. 279–81).

count of Hainaut,[15] and Henry of Esch, knowing the duke's embassy which was intended for the emperor, set out in advance of it at first light on the road to Constantinople, without the duke's knowledge, so that they would arrive before the envoys and would get more gifts from the emperor. The duke received this news with displeasure, but yet, concealing his anger, he set out for Adrianople where, after they had crossed a certain river by swimming their horses, and pitched their tents, he spent the night. Then a bridge which stretches across the river through the middle of the city was barred to him and his men by the inhabitants. So they moved on quickly to Salabria and pitched their tents in delightful places in meadowland. Here the duke's messengers came back from the emperor; they reported that he had not yet made any move to give up the captive princes. This made the duke and all his company furiously angry, and they refused to give the emperor trust and friendship any longer. And at once the duke instructed that all the land was to be handed over for the pilgrims and foreign soldiers to plunder; they delayed there for eight days and devastated all this region.

9. How the king of Greece set free the captive princes and, consulting the interests of his kingdom, at the same time he summoned the duke

When the emperor heard that the region had been severely devastated, he sent to the duke Rodolph Peeldelau and Roger son of Dagobert, men who were very eloquent and of the country and race of the Franks, asking that the army should cease from looting his kingdom and laying it waste, and should return without delay the prisoners he was asking for. The duke, indeed, having formed a plan with the rest of the leaders, agreed to the imperial legation; he forbade looting and moved camp, withdrawing to the city of Constantinople itself with the whole company of pilgrims: there they pitched tents, lodging in a strong and irresistible band, armed with hauberks and every weapon of war. And there they found Hugh, Drogo, William the Carpenter, and Clarembald, who had been freed by the emperor and came to meet the duke, rejoicing at his arrival and that of his large company, and falling with many kisses into the embraces of the duke and the rest. In the same way, too, the aforesaid imperial legates hurried to the duke, asking him to enter the emperor's palace with some of the foremost in his army, to hear the word of the king; the rest of the multitude should stay outside the city walls.

[15] Baldwin II of Mons. Baldwin and his successors claimed Flanders, which may explain why he preferred to travel with Godfrey rather than his neighbour Robert of Flanders.

10. After some ill feeling on both sides, the duke eventually makes peace with the emperor

Hardly had the duke received this legation when certain strangers from the land of the Franks arrived secretly in the duke's camp, and they warned him very seriously to beware the tricks and poisoned garments of the emperor, and his deceitful words, and under no circumstances to go into his presence, no matter what coaxing promises he gave, but to sit outside the walls and, in safety, mistrust everything he offered to them. The duke, therefore, warned by the strangers in this way and well schooled in the Greeks' deceptions, did not go into the emperor's presence at all. On this account the emperor felt a violent indignation against the duke and all his army, and forbade them a licence to buy and sell. When Baldwin, the duke's brother, became aware of the emperor's indignation and saw the people in need and the very great lack of supplies, he proposed to the duke and the rest of the nobles in the army that they should once again start looting through the region and land of the Greeks, carrying off food, until the emperor was forced by these acts of malice to grant again the licence to buy and sell. The emperor, therefore, seeing the looting of the lands of his empire and the evils that assailed them, renewed for them all the licence to buy and sell. For it was Christmas.[16] That is why, in this solemn time and these days of peace and rejoicing, it seemed good and praiseworthy to all parties, and fitting in the presence of God, for friendship to be renewed on both sides, between the emperor's household and the duke and all the powerful men in the army. And so peace was made; they restrained themselves from all looting and outrage. And for these four holy days they settled in complete peace and enjoyment before the city walls of Constantinople.

11. Because of the emperor the duke changes the position of his camp; he send messages of goodwill to him, and when he is asked he pretends he will come

After the four days a legation from the emperor presented itself to the duke, asking him to move his camp, for the emperor's sake and at his wishes, and he would be quartered with his army within the palaces which were situated on the shore of the straits, because of the common chills of snow and wintry weather which were a problem in the rainy season, and so that their tents would not become soaked and worn out, and perish. At length the duke and the rest of his fellow nobles

[16] AA and AK are irreconcilable on the point of dating, for Anna says this took place at Easter. Thus one has to choose whether to believe the Byzantine princess, who was there at the time but wrote only some forty years later, or the Rhineland historian, writing close to the time but at second hand. Various ingenious solutions to the problem have been proposed, including that AA intended the Lord's incarnation, i.e. the feast of the Annunciation, 25 Mar. (AK, p. 286). Modern Byzantinists accept AA's dating; see H. E. Mayer, *The Crusades* (2nd edn, Oxford, 1988), p. 45 and n. 23.

yielded to the will of the emperor, and after the tents were moved to the palaces and turreted dwellings, which stretched for a distance of thirty miles along the sea-shore, they were quartered with the whole army of Christians. From that day onwards they procured and bought every abundance of rations and vital provisions. A short while afterwards an imperial legation once more arrived with the duke, which advised him to come to the emperor and listen to what he had to say. The duke altogether refused to do this, having been warned by the strangers about the emperor's cunning, but he sent distinguished men to him as messengers – Cono, count of Montaigu, Baldwin of Bourcq, Godfrey of Esch – to make his excuses and to speak in this way: 'Duke Godfrey sends loyalty and obedience to the great emperor. Freely and by choice I would come to you and contemplate the honours and riches of your court, but I am afraid because of many evil things I have heard about you: nevertheless, I do not know if these things have been invented and broadcast because of envy or hatred towards you.' When the emperor heard this he absolved himself from most of the charges, saying that the duke (or indeed any of his company) should never fear him or believe any lie about him, but he should serve and honour him and his men as if he were a son and a friend. The duke's messengers returned and recounted all that they had heard the emperor promise for their advantage, solemnly and faithfully from his own lips. But actually the duke still did not believe the emperor's honeyed promises: he absolutely refused to converse with him, and thus between these messages going to and fro fifteen days passed.

12. The emperor removes food from sale; the army invades parts of Greece

The emperor, therefore, recognizing that the duke was obdurate, and that he could not summon him to his presence, received the news with renewed annoyance, and removed barley and fish from sale, then bread to eat, so that the duke would be forced in this way to agree to see the emperor. But not so: one day, while the emperor was still trying to soften the duke's resistance, five hundred Turcopoles, at the instigation of the emperor himself, sailed in through the straits early in the morning armed with bows and quivers, and they shot the duke's soldiers with arrows. Some were killed and some were wounded, and they were kept away from the seashore so that they might not be permitted to buy food there as they were accustomed to do. Immediately this cruel news was carried to the duke's court. He instantly ordered trumpets to sound, the whole people to arm and to return before the city of Constantinople itself and pitch tents again. Upon this order from the duke the trumpeters gave the signal and everyone burst out to take up weapons, and they laid waste some of the palaces and towers – in which they had stayed as guests – with fire, others they smashed to pieces, bringing about irreparable damage to the people of Constantinople.

13. The duke's brother riskily leads his people across; the duke divides the task between them

Then presently a rumour started in the palace about this violent fire and destruction. The duke was terrified, fearing lest the emperor's soldiers and archers, having noticed the flames of the buildings and the sound of the army on the move, might suddenly seize with a strong army the bridge over which they had crossed from the city of Constantinople to the palace buildings. And for this reason he sent his brother Baldwin in advance with five hundred armoured knights to occupy the bridge, so that no imperial force which hurried on before would break it up and in that way prevent the pilgrims from crossing and returning beyond it. Baldwin, therefore, had scarcely taken up his position in the middle of the bridge, when Turcopole soldiers of the emperor appeared, sailing in from right and left, and, as they crossed, the Turcopoles attacked with arrows and fought bravely on every side. Baldwin did not have the force to withstand them from the bridge, so he made haste to flee their arrows, and having passed over the crown of the bridge, he quickly took himself to the other part of the bridge on dry land, so that he occupied it and kept watch towards the walls of the lordly and masterful city until the whole army could be transported across the bridge. The duke kept guard to the rear with his men. Meanwhile an endless band of Turcopoles and of all sorts of soldiers burst out from the gates of the city in the direction of St Argent,[17] using arrows and different weapons with the object of conquering Baldwin and the entire company of Christian peoples. But Baldwin stood fast in the agreed place, immovable and unconquerable in the face of their every attack, until from dawn until dusk the people had been taken back across the bridge in front of the city walls, and those who were rescued were lodged in the camp that had been pitched. He bravely attacked those same Turcopoles with his five hundred armed men as they came out of the gates and boldly fought the people and on all sides battle was fought violently; many fell on both sides; many of the Franks' horses died of arrow wounds. But in the end Baldwin prevailed; he sent these imperial soldiers back inside the gates, oppressed and put to flight and he gained the plain and the victory convincingly. Truly the Turcopoles and imperial soldiers, who were angry at being defeated in war and put to flight, sallied forth from the gates again and again and in ever greater numbers to challenge and overcome the army, until the duke arrived, and because it was night he reconciled everyone in peace, reminding his brother to return to the camp with everyone else and to restrain the troops and weapons from this battle in the darkness of night. In the same way the emperor himself, fearing any longer and in greater strength to press on with this storm of war, and that his

[17] The *Historia belli sacri* (*RHC Occ* iii.178) is the only other Latin source to refer to this place: the author says that Bohemond was quartered by the emperor 'extra civitatem in Sancto Argenteo'. AK refers to a Silver Lake ('Arguron Limnen', p. 285), which would seem to be the same place, and hence this incident took place near the palace of the Blachernae.

men were deserting and dying in the dusk, was glad that the duke wanted to keep his men from warfare, and he also ordered that there should be peace.

14. The emperor summons the duke to him, promising hostages; and what the duke himself replied to Bohemond's envoys

At sunrise the next day the crowd rose up on the duke's orders and went right through the lands and kingdom of the emperor, plundering it severely for six days, so that in this way at least the arrogance of the emperor and his men should be seen to be brought low. When the emperor heard what was happening he began to be sad and to lament because his land and kingdom was thus being destroyed. He took counsel at once, then sent a legation to the duke asking that he forbid the plunder and arson and give him satisfaction in all matters, speaking in this way: 'Let the hostilities cease between us and you, and the duke come into my presence, receiving from me, with no misgivings, hostages and my assurance that he shall come and return unharmed, certain of all the honour and glory we can bestow on him and his men.' The duke graciously assented to this, on condition that hostages should be given who were men in whom he would be able to have confidence concerning his own life and safety, and thus he would go down without hesitation and speak to the emperor willingly with his own voice and face to face. Very soon after the duke made this reply, the emperor's legates returned, and certain other legates, who came to that same court from Bohemond's direction,[18] greeted the duke, speaking in this way: 'Bohemond, most wealthy prince of Sicily and Calabria, asks you not to return to friendship with the emperor in any way, but to withdraw into the Bulgarian cities of Adrianople and Philippopolis and to spend the winter months there, confident that at the beginning of March Bohemond himself will be there with all his forces to help you overcome this emperor and invade his domain.' When he had heard this legation from Bohemond the duke put off making any reply to it until the next sunrise when, after taking counsel with his men, he replied that he had not left his homeland and family for the sake of profit or for the destruction of Christians, but had embarked on the journey to Jerusalem in the name of Christ, and he wished to complete the journey and to fulfil the intentions of the emperor, if he could recover and keep his favour and goodwill. Bohemond's messengers understood the duke's meaning and his reply, and they were courteously commended by him, so then they returned to the land of Apulia to report everything just as they had learnt it from the lips of the duke.

---

[18] Bohemond was the eldest son of Robert Guiscard, duke of Apulia and Calabria 1059–85. In the early 1080s they waged war on Alexios along the Dalmatian coast with considerable success, which explains why Alexios was extremely suspicious of Bohemond. The envoys mentioned here by AA are not in any other source, but the incident is not at all out of character for Bohemond.

15. Once he has received the emperor's son as hostage, the duke enters the court

But the emperor found out about this new legation from Bohemond and his suggestion, and he urged the duke and his comrades the more concerning a peace, saying that if he wished to please him and cross his land peacefully the duke should indeed present himself face to face in discussions; he, the emperor, would give his own very beloved son, John by name, as hostage, and would grant to the duke and his men all necessary supplies, with a permit to buy. When the duke learnt that this promise of the emperor had been decreed and affirmed, after consulting his men he moved his camp away from the city wall and once again withdrew across the bridge in order to take up quarters on the straits in walled buildings, warning all his army to be peaceable and to buy supplies without quarrelling. At daybreak the next day he ordered Cono, count of Montaigu, and Baldwin of Bourcq, very noble men and experienced in every language, to come into his presence, and he instructed them to take into their protection fearlessly the emperor's son as hostage. This was done. Therefore the hostage, the emperor's son, was now brought to the camp and put with loyal care into the guardianship of the duke and his men, and the duke sailed without delay across the straits to Constantinople. Taking with him the illustrious men Warner of Grez, Peter of Dampierre, and the rest of the nobles, he entered boldly into the emperor's court and he stood face to face with him, so that he would hear his words and make a speech to him in reply about all the things he asked of him or he was annoyed about. Baldwin, however, did not enter the palace at all, but stayed on the shore with the rest of the great army.

16. How splendidly the duke was received by the emperor and was put on show, and what happened between them

The emperor, moreover, when he saw the duke who was so honourable and his followers, in splendour and adorned with expensive clothing, lavishly fringed with both purple and gold, snow-white ermine, and grey and variegated marten fur, which the princes of Gaul use in particular, he wondered greatly at their beauty and ornament, and first he received the duke courteously with a kiss, then he was prompt to honour all the nobles and those the duke had brought with him with the same kiss of peace. However, the emperor was seated, as was his custom, looking powerful on the throne of his sovereignty, and he did not get up to offer kisses to the duke nor to anyone, but the duke bowed down with bended knee, and his men also bowed down to kiss the exceedingly glorious and powerful emperor. Then when everyone had been kissed according to rank he spoke to the duke in these words: 'I have heard about you that you are a very powerful knight and prince in your land, and a very wise man and completely honest. Because of this I am taking you as my adopted son, and I am putting everything I possess in your power, so that my empire and land can be freed and saved through you from the present and future multitudes.' The duke was pleased and beguiled by the emperor's peaceful and affectionate words, and he not only gave himself to him as a son, as is the custom of that land, but even as a vassal with hands joined, along with all the nobles who were there then, and those who followed afterwards.[19] And without any delay priceless gifts were taken from the emperor's treasury for the duke and all who had gathered there, as much in gold as in silver and in purple of many kinds, in mules and horses, and everything which was valuable. Thus indeed the emperor and duke were fastened together by an unbreakable chain of complete trust and friendship, and from the time of the Lord's Nativity,[20] when this peace came about, until a few days before Pentecost, every week four men were sent from the emperor's palace to the duke, laden with gold bezants,[21] with ten measures of tetartaron coinage, with which the duke's soldiers could be maintained. It was a remarkable thing, though: everything which the duke distributed to the soldiers out of the emperor's gift went back straight away to the royal treasury in buying food, and not only this, but even the money which the army had collected there from the whole world. No wonder, for as with wine and oil, so with corn and barley and all the food in the whole kingdom, it was sold to no one's advantage except the emperor's, and that is why the royal treasury was perpetually overflowing with money and could not be emptied by the presentation of gifts.

17. At the emperor's command the Lord's people move to Cappadocia; the duke often importunes the emperor for supplies

When peace and friendship had been established between the emperor and duke on these terms, as we have told, and the duke had returned to lodge in the buildings on the straits, he sent back the emperor's son, until then held as hostage, in an honourable way, further assured of the trust and friendship he had received from the emperor. Then the next day it was proclaimed on the duke's orders throughout the whole assembly of the Christian army that from then on peace and honour should be shown to the emperor and all his men, and justice should be observed in all matters of buying and selling. Similarly throughout his whole realm the emperor forbade anyone, on pain of death, to harm or cheat any of the army, but

---

19 The nature of the oaths demanded by Alexios of the crusader leaders has been the subject of much debate. AA's understanding is unequivocal and, even though he does not refer here to the conquest of territory, it is clear from later statements that Godfrey undertook to restore any conquests to the emperor. J. H. Pryor argues that the crusader leaders swore oaths of fealty but did not pay homage, so they did not become the emperor's vassals ('The oath of the leaders of the first crusade to Emperor Alexius I Comnenus', *Parergon*, n.s., 2 [1984], pp. 111–41).

20 Evidently the season of Christmas broadly interpreted.

21 'Bezant' was the westerners' name for a Byzantine gold coin, the hyperpyron: P. Grierson, *Byzantine Coins* (London, 1982), p. 341.

said everything should be sold to the pilgrims in fair weight and measure, indeed the price should be lowered. After this, at the beginning of Lent, the emperor summoned the duke to come into his presence, entreating him pressingly by their friendship and pledged trust and beseeching him to cross the straits and to set up his tents in the land of Cappadocia, because of the buildings that his incorrigible people were destroying. The duke graciously agreed to this, and when they had crossed the river he and all the people pitched camp and stayed on the other shore on the plains of Cappadocia. From then onwards gradually everything was sold to the pilgrims at a high price, but yet the emperor's gifts to the duke by no means grew less, for he feared him intensely. In fact when the duke observed the lack of necessities for sale, and heard with annoyance the people's protests, he would frequently go by boat to meet the emperor and make known to him the seriousness of the supply situation. Then the emperor, as if ignorant of the facts and not wanting it to be done, would once again make everything cheaper for the pilgrims.

18. Bohemond arrived and was persuaded with difficulty to become the emperor's man

Meanwhile, while the duke was negotiating these matters with the emperor, and, as three weeks had gone by already, the holy feast of Easter had arrived,[22] Bohemond stood before the city walls of Constantinople in great strength, having ten thousand cavalry and very many troops of infantry with whom he marched down through Avlona and Dyrachium and other Bulgarian cities. At the emperor's request the duke met him with twenty nobles chosen from his army, to escort him into the emperor's presence under a sure safe-conduct before they laid down their weapons or pitched their tents. When they had greeted one another and the duke had negotiated for a long time with Bohemond himself, and had persuaded him with very many coaxing words to enter the court and hear what the emperor had to say – for in fact Bohemond refused at first, and replied that he was much too afraid of the emperor because he was regarded as a crafty and sly man, but in the end he was convinced by the duke's good promise and comforting words – at last he confidently went into the emperor's palace, where he was received with a kiss of peace and all friendship and esteem. Then, after they had held several conferences and consultations between them, Bohemond became the emperor's man, and with an oath and a pledge of trust he made an agreement with him that he would not keep for himself any part of the emperor's realm, except by his favour and consent.[23] And at once gifts were brought to Bohemond, as they had been to

---

[22] Easter Day in 1097 was 5 April.

[23] AA is unambiguous on the terms of Bohemond's oath, but may have been influenced by knowledge of later events when Bohemond appropriated Antioch. Compare *GF* whose author reports that the emperor 'told Bohemond that he would give him lands beyond Antioch, fifteen days' journey in length and eight in width, provided that he would

Godfrey, wonderful and unbelievable treasures in gold and silver, vessels also, valuable in their workmanship and adornment and far more splendid than anyone can imagine.

19. Bohemond's nephew sneaks past secretly; the duke and his men are allowed to depart honourably by the emperor; Count Robert becomes his man

Meanwhile, while this agreement and treaty was being made between the emperor and Bohemond, Tancred, who was Bohemond's sister's son, crossed the straits with all the men and equipment that belonged to himself as well as to Bohemond, keeping it a secret from the emperor, the duke and Bohemond, so that he would not also be made subject to him.[24] When the emperor heard of this act of audacity he received the news with annoyance because Tancred had avoided a conference with him. But at length he wisely concealed his feelings and sent Bohemond and the duke back across the river to the army, charged with his affection and his infinite esteem and a profusion of gifts. A short time after this Robert of Flanders arrived with vast forces of men, and, when he heard of the agreement the duke and Bohemond had made, he as well entered into a treaty with the emperor and became his man. And then he as well, just as the others had been, was rewarded with enormous gifts from the emperor's hand. Then after some days he was graciously commended by the emperor, and after crossing the straits which are mentioned above, he was united with his weapons and forces which were mingled with those of his allies and Christian princes in the region and on the plains of Cappadocia.

20. The army makes its way towards Nicaea. Concerning Count Raymond and Peter the Hermit, and about certain other princes

Not long after this it was agreed in a general council by all these very illustrious men who had been brought together that as it was already a suitable time for the expedition they were waiting for, just as they had vowed, they should now continue their journey towards the city of Nicaea, which a heathen force of Turks had wrongly seized from the emperor and subjected to their own authority.[25] And

---

swear fealty ...' (p. 12). A. C. Krey proposes that this is an interpolation in *GF*: 'A neglected passage in the *Gesta* and its bearing on the literature of the first crusade', in L. J. Paetow (ed.), *The Crusades and other Historical Essays presented to Dana C.Munro* (New York, 1928), pp. 57–78.

[24] On this AA and *GF* agree (*GF* p. 13).

[25] The Saljūq Turks had taken Nicaea (İznik) following their victory over the Byzantines at Manzikert, 1071. It had changed hands among rival Turkish factions, but since 1092 it had been ruled by Qilij Arslan as the capital of the restored Saljūq sultanate of Rūm.

in fact they struck camp that very same day and made for Rufinel.[26] There they found messengers from Raymond, count of Saint-Gilles, who reported that he also had entered Constantinople and had concluded a treaty with the emperor, and he asked and demanded that the army wait for him and the bishop of Le Puy, who was called Adhémar. The allies, however, declared that they were not prepared to wait for him at all, or to delay any longer in this region, but they would go on ahead slowly; the count could follow by a mountain path that was straight and not too precipitous after he had carefully and conscientiously settled his affairs with the emperor. Peter the Hermit, who had been waiting at the same place, Rufinel, joined the princes with the few survivors of his battered crowd of followers. When they had received the duke's reply, Count Raymond's messengers returned to Constantinople. The duke, in fact, and Bohemond and Robert of Flanders, continued their journey after the emperor had bestowed on them precious gifts and very many signs of approval. Raymond, who became favoured and esteemed by the emperor, stayed on for fifteen days in Constantinople; he gained a very large quantity of rewards and gifts from the emperor, and became his man on his honour and solemn oath.[27]

21. About the siege of the city of Nicaea

At this same time Robert, count of Normandy, Stephen of Blois, and Eustace, Duke Godfrey's brother, were likewise there with an enormous company of cavalry and infantry. They also entered into a treaty and friendship with the emperor; they became his men in sworn allegiance and were honoured by him with very many gifts. The duke, meanwhile, and those who were with him, went down to the town of Nicaea where the duke pitched camp and was the first to decide that the blockade should be in front of the main gate of the town. There was only the shortest respite in the lands of Cappadocia for the princes who were following him across the aforementioned Straits of St George; but after a hurried journey and themselves pitching their tents they took up positions around the town of Nicaea, which seemed unassailable in its ramparts, walls, and fortifications of towers. In this ancient and strongly fortified town one of the princes of the Turks, Suleyman, a very noble man but also a heathen, was in charge of the government. When he heard of the arrival of the Christians' assault force he fortified the city with all the armament of brave men, bringing in plenty of food, of course, gathered from wherever it might be, and he barricaded the gates on all sides with very

[26] S. Runciman identifies Rufinel as Nicomedia: *A History of the Crusades* (3 vols, Cambridge, 1951–54), vol. 1, p. 178.

[27] According to RA who, as Count Raymond's chaplain, must be accounted better informed, Raymond refused to swear homage, but promised to respect the emperor's life and honour (pp. 41–2). This did not prevent Count Raymond and the emperor forming a 'special relationship' as described by both AA and AK (pp. 295–6).

strong bars. For indeed, as the aforesaid princes assembled around the city and its walls on their swiftest horses, some were charmed by the leaping and capering of their mounts, wondering at the towers and very strong defences, and at the double walls. But even when they saw these all around they were yet not able to feel any sense of horror, but rather they were inspired by every sort of heroism and warlike feeling and they rushed towards the city and attacked; others of the princes, indeed, provoked the defenders of the city to battle by an attack on foot and also with bows and arrows, but many of them were destroyed by the javelins of the counter-attackers which inflicted very severe blows from above: these who died were the ones who had heedlessly dared to attempt battles next to the walls with a blind rush and a sudden attack.

22. Also about the disposition of the blockading armies; which parts of the city were assigned to which princes[28]

The leaders of the army saw the people dying in this way to no purpose and in useless warfare and quite unable to harm those who were shut in the fortress, but they could think of no better plan than to apply force to the city and those guarding the walls by blockading on every side. So Godfrey, duke of Lotharingia, prince and lord of the castle of Bouillon, was established in the first blockade position with his whole company of Lotharingians. Bohemond, prince of Sicily and Calabria, took up the neighbouring position; he was a Norman by nationality, a man of high courage and wonderful talent and with every warlike attribute, very skilled in military matters and very rich in resources. Tancred, a distinguished young knight, was stationed with his companions next to this same Bohemond, who was his uncle. Tatikios, a man with a cut-off nose who was a servant of the emperor of Constantinople and privy to his secrets, was commander of the Christian army because he was familiar with the topography of the region; with an auxiliary band of imperial soldiers he applied pressure on the city in the position to which he was directed. Robert, count of Flanders, to whom no one there was equal in terms of weapons, wealth and men, and Count Robert, who was prince of Normandy, the son of the king of England, most warlike in military weapons and well endowed with property, were located in line next to those already mentioned in the siege of this same city. Warner of the castle of Grez, a soldier irreproachable in the art of war; Eustace the brother of the aforesaid Duke Godfrey, with Baldwin their brother, a most distinguished man and unbeaten in wars, likewise took up positions in line. Baldwin of the castle of Mons, count and prince of Hainaut and a very illustrious man in every military action; Thomas of the castle of Fère, a very keen Frankish soldier, together with Baldwin of Bourcq; Drogo of Nesle; Gerard of the castle of

[28] There is a similar list in *ChA* (pp. 133–4); for a detailed comparison see Duparc-Quioc, *Edition*, pp. 72–3. For identifications and biographical details see the Appendix1: People.

Quierzy; Anselm of Ribemont; Hugh count of Saint-Pol; Engelrand, Hugh's son and an outstanding soldier; Guy of the castle of Possesse, a young knight but very courageous in warfare; Baldwin of the castle of Lant; another Baldwin surnamed Calderun, of great renown in battle, together with William, count of the castle of Forez, excellent in every prowess and warlike power: all these very courageous men took up the positions which were allocated to them to keep watch on the city, which seemed scarcely conquerable by human powers.

23. Also about the same

The bishop of Le Puy, Adhémar by name, who was distinguished by every sort of goodness, increased the forces round the city with not a few troops and equipment. Stephen, count of Blois, the head and leader in council of the whole army, guarded the city on one side with a large army.[29] Hugh whose surname was 'the Great', the king of France's brother, a most illustrious ally, took up his place in line to keep watch on the city. Robert son of Gerard; Raymond surnamed Pilet; Don Walker of the castle of Chappes; also Milo surnamed Louez, a very famous soldier; Stephen of Aumale, son of Odo count of Champagne; Walter of Domedart and his son Bernard, very pleasing in every deed and delightful to look at; Gerard of Gournay; Rothard son of Godfrey, a very brilliant young man; Rodolph, who was very well endowed with troops; Lord Alan surnamed Fergant and also Conan, both princes of Brittany; Rainald of the city of Beauvais; Walo of Chaumont, William of Montpellier, undaunted men, set up their tents and took up their positions encircling the city with the rest who have been mentioned. Gaston of Béziers as well; Gerard whose city was Roussillon; Gilbert of Traves, one of the princes of Burgundy; Oliver of the castle of Jussey, a bold and aggressive soldier; Achard of Montmerle, white-haired; Raimbold count of the city of Orange, whom no one surpassed in vigour; Louis of Mousson, who was marvellous in military operations, the son of Thierry, count of Montbéliard; Dodo of Cons, red-haired and very skilled in warfare; Gozelo and his brother Lambert, very experienced in warfare, with their father Cono of Montaigu, a most illustrious man, situated their tents next to those of the aforesaid warriors. Peter of Astenois, Rainald of the city of Toul, Walter of Verveis, Arnulf of Tirs, John of Nijmegen, Herbrand of Bouillon: these surrounded the city tirelessly to meet all the heat of battle.

[29] AA seems here to be elaborating line 1450 in the *ChA*: 'Quens Estievenes de Blois estoit el cief premier', which, however, we have translated simply as 'Count Stephen of Blois was in the lead' (p. 141). In a letter to his wife Stephen claimed to have been appointed by the other princes 'lord and overseer and governor of all their acts up to that time', a claim supported by other sources. However, this was at Antioch, Mar. 1098 and AA's antedating the appointment to Nicaea must be a mistake. (See *Kreuzzugsbriefe*, p. 149; *GF* p. 63; RA p. 77.)

24. Concerning the priesthood and the non-combatant crowd; and about the lake by the city

You may be sure that with so many first-rate leaders there were not a few followers and lesser ranks, servants, maidservants (married and unmarried), men and women of every class. In charge of all of these were bishops, abbots, canons, monks, and priests to teach them and keep up their courage. The besieged town was completely surrounded by these forces, except for one place which needed guarding and was left empty: this they had allocated to Count Raymond. Such a numerous army prevented sustenance and everything which is necessary for survival being sent in by any of the gates. But on one side of the town walls there was a lake of extraordinary width and length, deep like the sea and suitable for rowing boats and sailing, through which an entrance and exit used frequently to be open for Suleyman's men and Suleyman himself to bring in necessities.[30] Of course Raymond, the aforementioned count of the land of Saint-Gilles, which is called Provence, had not yet brought up his troops and resources. For he, with his divisions, was staying a while with the emperor of Constantinople; he was closely allied to him because of the splendid gifts which were bestowed on him day after day from the royal household.

25. Concerning the prince of the city of Nicaea and about his spies

When Suleyman heard that so many warlike men had gathered together he came out of the fortress of Nicaea to enlist the aid of Turks and gentiles; he exerted himself for very many days until he had brought together five hundred thousand fighting men and knights in armour from the whole of Rūm. When he had recruited these men from all around and briefed them, a rumour reached his ears of the siege of Nicaea and the army of Christians, and it was reported to him that a number exceeding four hundred thousand by many thousands had encamped there. Moreover, he was so astonished by this rumour that, along with all the men he had recruited, he altered his route and went through the mountain regions towards the walls of Nicaea, to see if perhaps from the vantage point of the rocky heights he could detect with his own eyes whether as many thousands as he had heard had gathered there, and from which direction he could safely attack them. At last, on the advice of his men, on the fourth day of the siege Suleyman told two of them to investigate the strength and movements of the Christian army, under the false pretence of being Christians like the pilgrims, and they were to submit reports to the guards of the citadel and the defenders of the city of Nicaea in this way: 'You may be sure that Suleyman, the prince and lord of our city, sent us to you, so that you would retain constant hope of his assistance and not be inspired with terror by these troops besieging the

---

[30] This was the Ascanian Lake (İznik Gölü) on the western side of Nicaea, and its blockade by Byzantine ships was to be crucial to the eventual success of the siege.

town, who are exhausted by their long journey and have come into exile here, and will be reckoned as fools, whom Suleyman will carry off to the same punishment and martyrdom as he did previously the armies of Peter, and he is ready in the very near future to come to your assistance with a strong force numbering countless thousands.' The two men received Suleyman's mission and were sent off in advance, making their way through familiar and out-of-the-way places towards the lake which prevented a complete blockade of the city, to see if they could possibly sail secretly across to those defenders of the town and make known the things which Suleyman had charged them to: how Suleyman had formed his divisions and would attack the pilgrims in a short while, and that the entire force of Turks should burst out of the city gates and in this way, with their resolution added to Suleyman's, they would wipe out the people of God. But by God's will these two who were sent ahead by Suleyman were captured and held by the Christian guards, who were spread out round about to protect positions and paths so that no trickery or force of the enemy's could harm them: one of the spies was killed in the attack, the other was brought into the presence of the Christian princes.

26. Also about one of those spies and how carefully God's people waited for the approach of the infidels

Bohemond, Godfrey and the rest used threats of torture to force the man who had been caught to explain without any lies what was the reason he had come. He, moreover, terrified by the threats of so many excellent princes and realizing that his life hung in the balance, was insistently beseeching them for his life and safety with a tearful voice, a humble expression, and a continuous flood of tears, trembling in every limb, and he promised he would reveal the truth of the matter and that it would improve the safety of all their people. In fact he confessed that he had been sent by Suleyman, who was encamped on the mountain ridges with a countless tribe, and so close, he claimed, that they might expect to meet him in battle on the next day at about the third hour and (because of his report) to be able to guard against his tricks and sudden assaults. The spy even asked to be held in custody until the hour he had said, at which time the truth of the matter and Suleyman's attack would be proved. If, however, any of these things did not happen he had no wish for his life to be spared, but wanted to die by being beheaded. He even urged with intense and very humble prayers that he might receive baptism into the Christian faith and take communion with the Christians according to Christian law, but he sought this more out of fear of the death he thought awaited him than for any love of the Catholic faith. At last the hearts of the army's commanders were softened by the man's pitiable weeping and excessive pleading, and his promise of Christianity, and, taking pity on him, they granted him his life, but all the same he was sent into the custody he was asking for. From that moment on, the whole army of Christians was made aware of the need for keeping watch; night and day they were at the ready with arms and equipment, right up to that time when they had learnt from the prisoner's claim that Suleyman's irresistible forces would come seething out of the mountains. Duke Godfrey, Bohemond, Robert of Flanders, and all who were there sent a legation to travel all through that night to Count Raymond, saying that he should hasten his journey more than usual if he wanted to wage war on the Turks and come to the assistance of his allies. For they knew the emperor had only very recently let him go, and had distinguished and honoured him with many gifts. And the count, when he recognized the legation of so many princes and learnt that Suleyman's attack was so close, delayed no longer, but hastened his journey through all the hours of that night, and at the first hour of day, when the sun was already shining fully on the earth, he arrived with the bishop of Le Puy, in full force with a company of cavalry and infantry bearing standards of different colours and designs, armed with hauberks and helmets.

27. Suleyman's arrival. A speech of encouragement from the bishop of Le Puy, a battle, and a victory by the Christian people

The count's tents were only just being pitched when, at about the third hour, Suleyman came down from the heights of the mountains and all his company, who had formed battle lines, poured down along the different footpaths like the sand of the seashore,[31] all of them very strong men and very provident in war, heavily armed with hauberks and helmets and golden shields, and bearing before them in their hands very many standards of amazing beauty. About ten thousand of them, all archers, led the way in the first line down into the valley of Nicaea, carrying in their hands bows of horn and bone fully drawn for shooting, and all of them were mounted on horses which were very swift of movement and very skilled in warfare.[32] Thus Suleyman and his men descended, striving to burst in with a charge through the gate of the town, which was guarded by Count Raymond blockading it. But they were repulsed strongly and overcome by this same count and by Baldwin the duke's brother, who attacked from the front with Baldwin Calderun and a substantial band of men. In this horror of cruellest warfare the bishop was hurrying between the companies and his speech comforted the people in this way: 'Oh race which has been dedicated to God, you left everything for the love of God – riches, fields, vineyards, and castles – and now everlasting life is at hand for you: whoever dies in this conflict is to be crowned as a martyr.[33] Without

[31] Biblical simile, e.g. Gen. 32: 12.

[32] Like other chroniclers, AA was impressed by the speed and manoeuvrability of the Turkish mounted archers and the effectiveness of the Turks' composite bows (Nicolle, pp. 5, 6, 632).

[33] When AA puts words into the mouth of the bishop he gives them a markedly ecclesiastical tone. In this sentence images and phrases are taken from patristic and liturgical writings. For 'omnia pro Dei amore', cf. prayer on St Paulinus' feast day and Matt. 19: 29: P. Bruylants, *Les Oraisons du Missel Romain: Texte et Histoire* (2 vols, Louvain, 1952), vol.

hesitation attack these enemies who oppose the living God, and by God's gift you will achieve victory this day.'[34] After this urging to action Payen of Garlande, steward to the king of France; Guy of Possesse; Tancred; Roger of Barneville; Robert of Flanders and Robert prince of Normandy came to the assistance of their brothers in Christ without delay, galloping swiftly to and fro through the midst of the battle lines and inflicting deadly wounds. Duke Godfrey and Bohemond did not curb their horses but let them have their heads and flew through the midst of the enemy, piercing some with lances, unsaddling others, and all the while urging on their allies, encouraging them with manly exhortations to slaughter the enemy. There was no small clash of spears there, no small ringing of swords and helmets heard in this conflict of war, no small destruction of Turks was wrought by these outstanding young knights and their allies. Since by God's grace this victory rested with the Christian army, Suleyman and his men fled back to the mountains, no longer daring to join battle with God's people in this siege. From that day Christ's faithful showed every mercy towards Suleyman's messenger they had captured, because they had found out that he was faithful and true in his promise, and he was singled out and especially prized among the households of the highest leaders. The Christians cut off the heads of the dead and wounded and as a sign of victory they brought them back to their tents with them, tied on the girths of their saddles, and they returned with joy to their fellows, some of whom had been left in the tents around the city to stop those shut up inside from getting out.

28. Concerning the generosity of the emperor towards the princes; and about a Turk falsely calling himself a Christian

When the storm of this first battle had settled around Nicaea, they used to throw the cut-off heads of the Turks inside the city walls to frighten the chiefs of the fortress and the guards of the walls. Then a thousand Turks' heads were gathered in carts and sacks and loaded on waggons, and they took them down to the port which is called Civitot, and thus they were sent by ship to the emperor of Constantinople.[35] When the emperor saw so many heads of his enemies and of the soldiers of Suleyman, whose unjust force had caused him to lose the city of Nicaea by a trick,[36] he rejoiced very greatly in this triumph of the faithful and he

---

2, pp. 116–17, no. 417. For 'perpetua uita', *Rule of St Benedict: prologus* and works of Sts Augustine and Gregory the Great; also in prayer 'Largire sensibus nostris …' (Bruylants, vol. 2, p. 185, no. 662). For 'martyrio coronari', also St Augustine and compare usage in liturgy for 8 Nov. (Bruylants, vol. 2, p. 173, no. 626).

[34] 2 Macc. 15: 8.

[35] AK reports the heads carried on lances 'like standards', but not the emperor's reaction to the gift (p. 298).

[36] The Saljūq Turks held Nicaea when Alexios came to the Byzantine throne in 1081. He had made an alliance with Qilij Arslan after the latter took Nicaea in 1092, but this was

decreed that they should receive a great reward for their labour of war. And so he sent a considerable sum of money, purple clothing of various kinds and all sorts of supplies in mule and horse carts to reward every one of those responsible. At the same time he bestowed countless victuals, and granted a most generous facility for buying and selling everywhere in his kingdom. On imperial orders sailing merchants were striving to race across the sea with ships full of rations, corn, meat, wine and barley and oil; they dropped anchor at the port of Civitot, where crowds of the faithful procured all sorts of provisions to revive bodies formerly oppressed by enforced fasting. As they enjoyed and rejoiced in this abundance of food they agreed and confirmed that they would not depart until the city was overcome and taken and might be restored into the emperor's power. For they had promised with an oath not to keep any part of the emperor's kingdom, no fortresses, no cities, unless by his wish or gift. When he found out and discovered this, and saw the victory of the Christians and most cruel slaughter of the Turks, that prisoner of whom we told earlier, despairing of his life and intending to escape the yoke of Christianity, one day saw a very clear opportunity through the carelessness of the guard, and flew across the entrenchment of the city walls with a nimble-footed leap; he called incessantly and pleaded with the Turks, who were on the other side of the walls and at that moment enjoying a rest from warfare, to help him. At once they let down a rope from the walls into the hands of the false and fleeing pilgrim, and soon he was hanging on it and clinging with his hands and they pulled him up inside the walls, making a lot of shouting and din inside and outside. Yet not one of the Christians dared to follow or detain the fugitive, because the Turks were attacking with javelins from above.

29. Concerning the leading men who fell in that same siege

While they kept to their very firm resolution to besiege and destroy the city, seven weeks ran their course with the Christians in the same place around the walls, and while some of the princes were preparing machines for throwing and catapulting stones to reduce the walls and towers, others were constructing iron-clad battering rams, and were working on different inventions; they were making very many assaults, and Baldwin Calderun, who was constantly attacking the walls and excelling by his excessively rash and daring efforts, breathed his last when his neck was broken[37] by the blow of a hurled stone. Baldwin of Ghent, while he too was exerting himself there in an assault on the city and making a careless rush at the walls, expired, his head pierced in an arrow attack. After these things, while the

---

a holding ploy and once the empire was settled, by 1095, Alexios was determined to drive back the Turks: hence his appeal to Urban II: P. Charanis, 'The Byzantine Empire in the eleventh century', *Wisconsin History*, vol. 1, pp. 213–16. What 'trick' AA understood Qilij Arslan to be guilty of is not known.

[37] 1Kgs. (1 Sam.) 4: 18.

army was once again renewing its attack according to the decision and decree of the princes, the count of Forez and the count of the isle of Flanders, Walo by name, who were too impetuous and eager for war in the same attack, were shot with arrows and killed while they were striking the enemy. Guy of Possesse, the famous knight, was overtaken by sickness in that same place and passed from this life. The entire populace of Christians wept over these men, for they were considered strong counsellors and responsible for important affairs. The bishops and abbots buried these very great and very noble men with every honour and religious ceremony, distributing to the destitute and to beggars a considerable quantity of alms for the safety of their souls.

30. Likewise about others who died in that same place

Then one day while most of the princes' piles of wood and siege engines were placed close to the walls of Nicaea, and some were not labouring in vain but others were working to no effect, Henry of Esch and Hartmann, one of the more important counts of Swabia, constructed a 'fox' out of oak beams at their own expense;[38] around it in a circle they interwove a secure palisade so that they could endure the Turks' heaviest blows with close-combat weapons and all kinds of throwing spears and thus, staying inside it safe and sound they might penetrate the city by attacking it bravely. While at length this 'fox' apparatus was being completed to the last detail with workmanship and bindings, some twenty soldiers of the aforementioned princes, wearing armour, were stationed under that same cover of the 'fox'. But on account of the great surge of men and the strain applied next to the walls, the rampart not being level, the shelter subsided and was not checked by a push in the right place or by a level pull, and so the beams, the uprights and all the bindings came to pieces and in a matter of moments crushed the men who were hiding in it. Hartmann and Henry, grieving and uttering a great lamentation for the fate of their men, buried the dead honourably with a funeral, but they could not help being a little glad that they had not perished with their men in this sudden suffocation.

31. Concerning the assault on the walls and especially on a certain tower

On another day after this, while very many people's constant efforts were being squandered to no purpose, Count Raymond strongly attacked a certain tower which had been damaged by two of the stone-throwing catapults which are commonly called mangonels, but not even one stone from this ancient building and the very strong, almost indestructible masonry was susceptible to being weakened and

[38] The term 'fox' ('vulpes') seems to be unique to AA; WT calls the constructions 'sows' ('scrophae', p. 203).

loosened by such a daily battering, until as a last resort more stone-shattering equipment was added, in response to which the battered walls at last revealed cracks in places, and some of the stones began to weaken and fall because of the constant bombardment with masonry. When the army of the living God saw this it worked as one, and surmounted the rampart with a wickerwork 'tortoise' it had made, and attacked the walls in a bold move, and endeavoured to force a way through and penetrate the high tower on the walls using mattocks as grappling irons. The Turks had filled up the tower on the inside with a heap of stones so that it would stand firm more effectively with the thickness of stones, and if by any chance the outer wall were broken down by the Gauls in their efforts to enter, the accumulation of innumerable stones would be a hindrance to them. Indeed the people of the living God, their anger more and more inflamed, and feeling enraged by the massacre of their comrades,[39] assaulted the tower with a sharp point of iron, intending to breach the tower with such force that a hole in the excavated wall would appear through which two at once could enter in advance and penetrate and capture, and these two would reduce and demolish the heap stone by stone and open up a way clear to the enemy. But they were not able to succeed as they hoped.

32. God's people surround the aforesaid lake with a naval blockade

Now one night, when the people were distressed by this struggle and by the experience of the very great slaughter about the city and had withdrawn into the camp for a while, it was discovered that the Turks often sailed out of the city by way of the lake and secretly brought in relieving troops, weapons, and all necessary supplies, and that merchants from all parts came together there, and that every sort of merchandise was obtained by the Turks by way of that same lake. Because of this the princes finally held very many councils, discussing what they should do, or how they should continue, how the lake might be closed to the Turks and further sailing in and out be denied to the besieged, and saying that otherwise their own attacks or exertion could not succeed. At last in the course of very many discussions the following conclusion was reached: that unless the lake, which was so large, was guarded by ships, the enemy could in no way be kept in check, nor the city be made empty of food. So the people great and small were called together and it was announced by general agreement that countless numbers of common people, mounted and on foot, would be sent to the port of Civitot. There were ships there that had been requested from the lord emperor and granted as his gift, which they would be able to bring across on dry land all the way to the lake of Nicaea from the sea, using carts adapted by the skilful use of timbers and hempen ropes and straps of bull's hide, and placed on the shoulders and necks of

[39] Cf. Lucan iv. 797.

the men and horses.[40] The plan was carried out, and at dead of night[41] they dragged these ships, which were of extraordinary weight and size and which could hold a hundred men, on the seven-mile journey, and at sunrise they arrived at the lake of Nicaea and put down the ships on the shore and in the water. At once the princes of the army got up and came from all sides to the lake to see and to find out about the ships, rejoicing because their men were unharmed and had suffered no enemy attack, and the ships had arrived without damage. Now that the ships had arrived safe and sound the bravest soldiers of Gaul were stationed on them to use them against the Turks if they made any further forbidden exit, and to allow no more supplies to be brought in by ship. Moreover, in one of the ships there were archers from the emperor's Turcopoles, who were accustomed to fight afloat very ably in naval battles. When they saw the commotion of the people around the lake and the unusually early morning meetings of the princes, the Turks and all the guards of the fortress flocked to the walls by the water, marvelling greatly at the newly arrived ships, which beyond any doubt at all they would have reckoned to be their own, except that theirs were still to be seen moored on the other shore next to the walls and defences, chained with iron and bolts. Thus the lake was occupied by a naval blockade and, leaving behind on the river there a band of soldiers who wore mail and also bore spears, bows, and arrows, Count Raymond and his attendants and many troops from the army assembled once again at the tower mentioned above: they multiplied their assaults and stone-throwing, they upset the Turks more than a little, and they attacked, driving at the walls with an iron-clad battering ram and a loud shouting and charge of men.

33. The infidels defend strongly and wear down the Christians. Where the duke himself shoots with an arrow the most warlike of the Turks

Seeing that the walls were being struck and shaken repeatedly by the battering ram,[42] and that the tower was being penetrated by mattocks, the Turks mixed together grease, oil, and pitch with tow and strongly burning torches and poured the mixture from the walls,[43] and it burnt up completely the apparatus of the battering ram and the wicker frameworks.[44] Some killed very many with arrows shot from bows of horn, others crushed those who were working alongside the walls and tower with an attack of rocks. In the course of this defence and resistance by the Turks one of their soldiers, a man of most warlike spirit and heart, was exerting

---

40 The same strategy is described in *GF* (p. 16). AK represents it as entirely a Byzantine initiative (p. 300).

41 A common classical phrase, e.g. Caesar, *De bello Gallico* vii. 36; Livy v. 32.

42 Vergil, *Aen.* ii. 492–3.

43 This is AA's first mention of the fabled 'Greek fire': see J. R. Partington, *A History of Greek Fire and Gunpowder* (Cambridge, 1960), pp. 21–7.

44 Cf. Vergil, *Geo.* i. 95.

himself not a little with crossbow and bolts and – this is an extraordinary story – having sustained a wound, he despaired of his life and he threw his shield far away from him and clearly exposed his breast to everyone's weapons, and he hurled rocks from the cliffs with both hands into the middle of the crowd. And, as those who were there assure us is true, even though he was weighed down by twenty arrows which even yet were sticking in his chest, he did not restrain his hands from throwing stones and striking the Gauls, but wrought destruction on the people more powerfully and more fiercely. Now Duke Godfrey, seeing that this most warlike and cruel man was raging and did not falter with so many arrows sticking in him, but that more of the faithful were dying from his missiles, seized his crossbow, and, standing behind the shields of two of his comrades, he struck that Turk through the vitals of his heart. And so the man was dead and he prevented him from any further fearful slaughter. At last the crowd of Christians was weary, and the sun went down, and the attack which had been so terrible grew quiet and then the Turks, distressed by the breaching of the tower, once again collected heaps of rocks inside at dead of night, so that no easy access would be found the next day.

34. Concerning the killing of a Christian warrior who is hanged on the walls to mock the faithful

The next day when the sun returned, God's people were encouraged and armed for renewing the attack and enlarging the breach in the tower. But when they saw and recognized the pile of stones set once again in front of them in the fresh opening, the memory was still with them of the previous day's danger and anxiety, and their spirit began to weaken, and everyone told someone else to lead the way. At last one distinguished soldier sprang up from the tents of the aforesaid Robert, count of Normandy, and, concealed by a helmet and protected by hauberk and shield, he attacked undaunted across the rampart and walls, hastened to the tower, and strove to tear away the heaps of stone from the opening and to empty the entrance of the rocks which filled it up, but he gave up the attempt in a hail of rocks and a continual deluge of missiles. Moreover, when that soldier saw that he had been abandoned without any assistance, and that he could not succeed because of the crushing weight of the vast stones, he drew close to the nearby wall to avoid the Turks' javelins, which tormented the hero without ceasing. But no way or means was thus shown to him of escaping their hand. At length, after his shield had deflected from his head and shoulders so many thousands of stones, he was overwhelmed right by the walls with his neck broken, and he died wearing that same hauberk and helmet in the sight of all the faithful, who still did not come to his assistance in any way. Then the Turks, seeing that the man was still and had died now, threw down from that abominable tower a chain which had on it very sharp and grasping iron claws of ingenious artifice and workmanship, like hooks, which caught fast in the rings of the dead soldier's hauberk and held, and it was pulled up over the walls with the dead body. Then, when they had got hold of the soldier's body, although it was dead they hanged it in a noose of rope against the walls, so that they would offend the Christians further by this inhuman conduct. Offended indeed and sad, all of them wept that their comrade had perished by such a cruel death and abominable treatment. When, after this long display, he was thrown down naked from the walls they took him up with honour, along with the rest we have mentioned, and buried him in the same place as the slaughtered faithful, with the handing out of alms and a commendation from priests.

35. How a certain Lombard worked on a new kind of siege engine

Duke Godfrey and Bohemond and the other princes were troubled by this destruction of brave men, and by the harm that came to so many Christians who suffered day after day in the attack on the city, and because they were unable to make any breach in the walls by the efforts of siege engines or catapults or by assaults, and all their exertion and courage was squandered to no purpose. Then a certain man, a Lombard, master and inventor of great defences[45] and siege works, who saw the miseries and massacres of the Christians, presented himself unasked to the aforesaid nobles and raised their spirits with this sort of comfort and promise, saying: 'I see that all the siege work of your engines is labouring in vain, your men are reduced in numbers by frequent deaths around the walls, and the lives of those remaining are still threatened by great dangers. For the Turks within fight back fearlessly and in safety from the towers and walls, they overwhelm heedless and defenceless men with arrows and rocks, and indeed the wall which was built with the cunning of the ancients is not to be broken down by iron or any other show of strength. So, because I observed that all your efforts were thus frustrated, I set out to approach your highnesses and persuade you that if you agree to my plans and I get some reward from you for my work, with God's aid I shall make this tower, which seems strong and invincible, fall to the ground, without harming and endangering your fellow soldiers, and through this a way in will be opened up to get at your enemies and opponents, as long as the essentials for my craft are supplied from the common expense and assistance fund.' When they heard this man's promise they agreed with complete good will to give him fifteen pounds of the coinage of Chartres[46] as reward for his work, and to supply without fail whatever essentials he might need for the task, rejoicing and putting their trust in the hope of the promised workmanship. So, after the aforesaid

---

45 Translating 'arcium': the manuscripts all have 'artium'.

46 RA explains that the crusaders used 'moneta pictavine, cartenses, manses, luccenses, valanzani, melgorienses, et … pogesi' ('coins from Poitou, Chartres, Le Mans, Lucca, Valence, Melgueil and Le Puy', pp. 111–12). The coins from Le Puy were worth half as much as the others, of which eight or nine could be exchanged for a golden dinar. See D. M. Metcalf, *Coinage of the Crusades and the Latin East* (London, 1995), pp. 12–21.

agreement, the master craftsman prepared his inventions, joined the sloping sides together and attached hurdles of brushwood to the marvellous apparatus, so that under its protection he and those who toiled with him would keep their heads safe from the javelins of the Turks who were opposing them from above.

36. Concerning the monstrous overturning of the siege tower; and how the mistress of the city was captured

When the apparatus for their protection was perfectly finished, men from the Christian ranks, wearing hauberks and armed with shields, gathered around the engine. They used their strength to move it across the rampart, dragging it, and positioned it next to the walls, practically touching them, while all the Turks were resisting and hindering them from above. The master craftsman was left safely inside it with his other workmen after the troops of the faithful had retreated without great injury. The Turks, realizing that the apparatus of this machine could be decisive in the defeat of the city, were throwing torches burning with pitch and fat onto the siege engine, and they rolled up a mass of rocks from the walls to see if thus by any artifice the artefact brought to the wall might be destroyed and those shut in it be frightened off. But everything they threw onto the machine or tried was in vain because its sloping walls retained neither firebrands nor stones that were thrown against them. The master craftsman, who was hiding confidently within the machine with the associates whom he had kept back with him, did not leave off hollowing out the earth under the foundation of the tower with mattocks and sharpest iron, until he could set up beams, posts and other enormous oak timbers in that same excavation under the foundation, on which the walls would be supported after the earth had been taken away so that they would not suddenly fall down on top of those still digging. Once a very great excavation had been made, both wide and long, on the instruction of the master craftsman, everyone in the army, small and great, gathered twigs, stalks, sticks[47] and dry reeds, pieces of tow and all sorts of kindling and heaped it between the posts and beams and the splendid timbers, everywhere where the excavation was occupied by these pieces of wood. After this, fire was put in by the master of the siege work; it was encouraged by a great breath until, roaring and racing in different directions, the unconquerable flame grew stronger and stronger and it reduced to ashes the posts, the beams and all the wood that had been put underneath. When these things had thus been reduced to embers and there was no prop for the foundations either of earth or of wood, the building of the very ancient tower fell flat in an instant in the middle of the night, and it made such a noise that it was taken for the crash of thunder by all the people who were woken from their sleep. Although the weight, so unbearable, of the fallen tower was brought down by the sudden collapse, it

[47] Translating 'regulas': all the manuscripts have 'tegulas' and wooden shingles are possible, though improbable.

was not broken up by the shock into many pieces of masonry or stones, but the walls of the fortress were lying shattered and ruined in many places; they stood open, damaged by cracks, and offered a way in, though still difficult. Because of this collapse and devastation of the tower Suleyman's noble wife was greatly frightened, and she no longer trusted in the protection of the city, so she was sent by his men at dead of night onto the current of the lake, so that she would thus escape the Christians by boat. But her departure was spotted by the soldiers who were guarding the lake, and she was caught by their rowing up the newly brought up ships, and was placed in the care of the princes along with her two young sons.

37. The surrender of the city of Nicaea; and about a certain captive nun

The Turks defending the fortress were terrified when the tower was broken down to the ground,[48] and they were likewise stunned by the capture of this lady, and from then on they despaired of escape by sailing clear on the lake; they were devastated by the serious weakening of their men who had been killed within; they were exhausted by the long siege, and, as they saw that they could not escape, they had a discussion among themselves and they made entreaties concerning the safety of life and limb, asking that they be spared by the Christian army, having promised to hand over the keys of the city into the hands of the emperor of Constantinople, to whom originally the city was subject by hereditary law, until Suleyman invaded and brought them under his power by unlawful use of force.[49] Tatikios with the chopped-off nose, an intimate of the emperor, in answer to the entreaties of a council of the army's leaders, and after pledges had been given and received by both sides, interceded for them with the Christian chiefs, making this condition: that they should come out of the city unharmed and surrender to the emperor, along with Suleyman's noble wife who had recently been captured and was being held in the charge of the Frankish princes with her two sons who were still young.[50] When the attack had calmed down on both sides, while different discussions were going on about giving up the city, and many of the Christians' prisoners were returned, a certain nun from the convent of St Mary at the Granaries, belonging to the church at Trier,[51] was set free and returned with the rest into the hands of the Christian army. She claimed she had been captured and taken away from Peter's

[48] Cf. Vergil, *Aen*. v. 481.

[49] AA's inserting these rather legalistic clauses at this point may reflect his understanding of the leaders' undertaking to restore to the Byzantines all captured cities and territory which had formerly been theirs.

[50] AA appears not to have been informed about the role of the emperor's general Boutoumites, who negotiated the surrender of Nicaea: see AK, pp. 297–8, 300–302, 304; B. Skoulatos, *Les personnages byzantins de l'Alexiade* (Louvain, 1980), pp. 181–5.

[51] 'Sancta Maria ad Horrea' appears to be a corruption of 'S. Maria in Orreo', that is Oeren (Euren), a district of Trier west of the river Mosel: L. H. Cottineau (ed.), *Répertoire*

defeated army, and she complained that she had been taken in a vile and detestable union by a certain Turk and others with scarcely a pause. Then, while she was uttering her wretched moans about these wrongs to the audience of Christians, she recognized Henry of the castle of Esch among the nobles and soldiers of Christ. Addressing him by name in a low and tearful voice, she appealed to him to come to the aid of her purification. He recognized her at once and was affected by her misfortune, and he employed diligence and every argument of pity he could with Duke Godfrey until advice for repentance was given her by Lord Adhémar, the venerable bishop. At last, when advice about an unchaste act of this sort had been received from the priest, she was granted forgiveness for her unlawful liaison with the Turk, and her repentance was made less burdensome because she had endured this hideous defilement by wicked and villainous men under duress and unwillingly. A short time after this, only one night, she was invited again very persuasively and with many coaxing promises to the unlawful and unchaste union by a messenger from that same Turk who had violated her and taken her from the rest. For that same Turk had been inflamed by passion for the nun's inestimable beauty, and so he was excessively annoyed at her absence, to whom indeed he had promised rewards which had so possessed her imagination that she would return to her abominable husband. This Turk was even promising to become a Christian himself before long, if by chance he got out of imprisonment and the emperor's chains. At length this most wretched woman, who may have been forced to do wrong before, was now deceived by flattery and vain hope, and she rushed back to her unlawful bridegroom and her false marriage; no one in the whole army knew what cunning or lewdness could have been used to take her away from them. After this it is known from those who tell the story that she went back to that same Turk in exile where he was, for no other reason than because her lust was too much to bear. Now that the storm of war had thus abated, and the Christian prisoners from the city had been restored, and the Turks had been taken and handed over to the emperor, who received their capitulation, the army of the living God spent the day in great rejoicing and exultation right there in the camp, because everything so far had gone well for them.

38. The way in which, on the advice of the princes, God's people were divided into two parts

Now, at dawn the following day, having taken the supplies they needed, all the people moved, travelling safely through the middle of Rūm and not fearing any future opposition. And so for two days they were marching as a single armed column through the heights of the mountains and the narrow passes of the way, and then they decided that the army was so big that it should be divided, so that

topo-bibliographique des abbayes et prieurés (2 vols, Macon, 1935–37), vol. 2, col. 3210, *s.vv.* Trèves: St Irminen.

the people could live more freely and spaciously in the camp, and if a division was thus made there would be a lot more food and fodder for the horses. They came together between two mountain peaks, where a certain river had had a bridge put across it, and Bohemond with the troops who followed him separated himself completely from Duke Godfrey.[52] Some of the great nobles followed him – Robert, count of the Normans, and Stephen, prince of Blois – thus always making for and following the right-hand way, so that they would not be removed more than a mile from their comrades. The duke also and his tent companions, with the bishop of Le Puy and Count Raymond, always kept to the right. Then after this division, about the ninth hour, Bohemond went down with all his company into the valley *Degorganhi*,[53] which is nowadays called *Orellis*, in the hope of finding quarters where he might pitch camp, and his companions, who spread out all around on the grass, might attend to the needs of their bodies with food and other supplies in suitable streams and meadows.[54]

39. Concerning the immense slaughter of the Christian people through the ambushes of the prince of Nicaea

But scarcely had Bohemond and the other brave heroes got down from their horses when Suleyman appeared. Since the time he was put to flight from the city of Nicaea he had brought together assistance and forces from Antioch, Tarsus, Aleppo and the other cities of Rūm which were occupied here and there by Turks, and now he appeared, charging violently and with a large attacking force. There was no pause, no respite[55] from slaughtering and subduing the army, and as they ran through the camp some were pierced by arrows, others beheaded by the sword, several taken prisoner by the excessively cruel enemy. At these things a great shouting and shaking arose among the people, women both married and unmarried were beheaded, along with men and little children. And Robert of Paris, wishing to come to the aid of the wretched victims, was shot by a flying arrow and killed.

---

52 AK names the meeting place as Leukai (Lefke). According to her version, Bohemond had taken charge of the vanguard, while the rest moved more slowly (p. 305). AA's mountain peaks are a topographical improbability and may be the result of misunderstanding the *ChA*'s 'aigue', meaning water, as 'aigu', meaning needle or peak (Duparc-Quioc, *Edition*, p. 114: 'A un pont a arvolt, u une aigue desserre', translated: 'they reached an arched bridge which marked the point where a river spread out [*ChA*, p. 155]). See A. Hatem, *Les Poèmes épiques des croisades: genèse – historicité – localisation* (Paris, 1932), p. 172.

53 Val de Gurhenie in the *ChA* (p. 148).

54 According to FC and Ralph of Caen [RC] the battle took place in the morning, not the evening. AA presumably tried to make sense of an account which said the Turks attacked after the crusaders made camp, not realizing they were forced to do so early in the day (cf. FC pp. 189–97; RC p. 45).

55 Vergil, *Aen*. xii. 553 etc.

Bohemond, who was thunderstruck by this awful massacre, and the other nobles recovered their horses, they hastened to put on hauberks and weapons and massed together, and, having to defend themselves most unexpectedly, they joined battle with the enemy for a long time. William, a very daring youth and a very handsome young knight, Tancred's brother, was struck by an arrow and collapsed in the sight of Bohemond himself while he was fighting back fiercely and often piercing Turks with his spear. Tancred, defending manfully with his sword, only just escaped with his life, but he left the ornamental banner which he displayed on his spear in that place with his brother. The Turks, with their prince Suleyman, were growing stronger and stronger, they burst into the camp in strength, striking with arrows from their horn bows, killing pilgrim foot soldiers, girls, women, infants and old people, sparing no one on grounds of age. Stunned and terrified by the cruelty of this most hideous killing, girls who were delicate and very nobly born were hastening to get themselves dressed up, they were offering themselves to the Turks so that at least, roused and appeased by love of their beautiful appearance, the Turks might learn to pity their prisoners.

40. Concerning the messenger sent by Christ's faithful to the duke

While flocks of the faithful were being thus afflicted, and Bohemond's strength to hold out was already weakening – because the Turks had attacked them unexpectedly when their weapons were laid aside and already some four thousand of the Christian army had been killed in close combat – a messenger sped on horseback through the steep mountain slopes without pause, until he arrived at the duke's camp sad and dispirited. When Duke Godfrey, who had come forward some distance from the entrance of the tent in order to inspect the allies, spotted him in the distance approaching at a gallop and looking pale with a gloomy expression, he asked why he hurried his journey, so that the messenger would report and explain to him and the other barons. The messenger reported bitter and painful news, saying: 'Our princes, with Bohemond himself, are enduring the most violent battle of the war, and a mass of followers has already suffered the death sentence, by which our lord princes will also be killed at any moment unless your band reinforces them hastily. Some Turks burst into our camp, and as they went down through the valley called *Orellis*, or 'horrible', to the valley *Degorganhi*, they slaughtered the pilgrims without ceasing. They have already destroyed Robert of Paris by cutting off his head. They have struck down the illustrious youth William, Bohemond's sister's son, greatly to be lamented. And for this reason the whole company summons you to bring reinforcements, and let no delay or deferment hinder you or hold you back.'

41. Where the duke and those with him come to the aid of those who are dying

When he heard of this misery and the Turks' audacity, the duke ordered horns to sound loudly through all the ranks, to call all the companions to take up arms, to raise standards, to aid their allies without any delay or rest. Just as if they had been called to a party offering every sort of pleasure, they hurried to take up arms, to put on hauberks, to buckle on their swords again, to bridle their horses and to put saddles on their backs again, to take up their shields once more, and some sixty thousand cavalry rode out of the camp along with the rest of the army on foot. Already a very clear day had dawned, the sun was shining with brightest rays, and its splendour glittered on the golden shields and the iron mail; the standards and flags, bright with jewels and purple, raised high and fixed on spears, were fluttering. The swift horses were urged on with spurs, they pressed on their way, nobody waiting for companion or friend, but each going as fast as he could to the assistance and revenge of the Christians. Then, when the Turks clearly saw them arriving unexpectedly, having mobilized with all speed and readiness for battle to reinforce their companions, and being present in such a strong company, armed and armoured, with shining standards raised for battle, they took flight, and shaken by fear they turned aside from a fearful massacre, making their escape, some by out-of-the-way tracks, others by familiar paths. But Suleyman, with quite a large company and quite close formations of troops, escaped and took up a position on the mountain top to attack the Christians when they pursued him and to oppose them in that place.

42. Where the duke and certain others of the nobility are remembered by name, who performed brave deeds there for God

Duke Godfrey, on the other hand, who had ridden ahead on a swift horse with only fifty companions, after a short time joined forces with the people following and unhesitatingly climbed up to the steep slope of the mountain, to come to blows with the Turks and to engage with weapons those whom he could see gathered on the mountain top and motionless in opposition. Moreover the duke, as his men were everywhere welcomed and accepted, attacked the motionless enemies, aimed spears at them, and encouraged his allies in a loud voice to approach them steadily. When the Turks and their leader Suleyman saw the steadiness of Duke Godfrey and his men, and that at the moment they had not lost heart for war, they got ready to give their horses their heads and to flee at speed from the mountain top. The duke pursued them for six miles, striking down some with the sword, taking several as prisoners with his men, capturing not a little of their plunder and spoils, and they seized from their enemies the girls and young men and all the things they were hoping to carry off or take away. Gerard of Quierzy, riding his excellent horse and protected by his shield, saw during this same pursuit of the enemy a Turk behind him who as yet stayed on the ridge of the mountain and who was very bold and strong, so he attacked him bravely with his spear. An arrow shot by the Turk glanced off his shield then Gerard pierced him through liver and lung, and, as the Turk slipped from it and died, Gerard made off with his horse. Baldwin, count of Hainaut, a brave man and liberal dispenser of great alms, along with Robert of Flanders, scattered the fleeing Turks, urging the comrades charging all around him to kill and slaughter and never to be seen to delay in their pursuit of the enemy nor to hold back their hands. Baldwin of Bourcq, Thomas of the castle of Fère, Rainald of Beauvais, Walo of Chaumont, Rothard son of Godfrey, Gaston of Béziers, Rodolph, all of these of one accord were exerting themselves in the struggle of battle, pursuing the Turkish troops and tearing them apart with warlike valour. Heavy panting battered the flanks of the horses,[56] while steam from that same panting was thickening into a cloud all over the middle of the battlefield. The Turks, meanwhile, having recovered their strength, were fighting back courageously, relying on the force of their own great numbers, in a thick hail of arrows flying and falling. But this hailstorm passed quickly, and the troops of the faithful, keeping their weapons in their hands, were diminishing and destroying masses of them, and at last they forced the defeated army to scatter through unfrequented places and the steep slopes of the mountains where they knew the paths.

43. After the victory, what was agreed among God's faithful; and how the priesthood took care of the bodies of the fallen

Therefore the Christian victors kept all that the Turks had assembled as wages for the expedition: corn and no small quantity of wine, buffaloes, cattle and rams, camels, donkeys, horses, and mules, moreover precious gold and endless quantities of silver, tents of wonderful ornament and workmanship. At the successful outcome of this victory, everyone of one accord – Bohemond, of course, and the other princes mentioned before who were the leaders and the pillars of the army – returned to agreement and consultation, and they decided that from that day rations and all necessary supplies should be pooled, and everything should be held in common. This was done. In this battle and flight of the Turks several of the Christian soldiers were wounded by arrows and perished; moreover three thousand Turks are reported to have died. When this very cruel conflict was over the Christian soldiers rested for a period of three days around a certain river[57] and its sedge-covered banks, caring for their exhausted bodies with the plentiful food left behind by the Turks who had been killed or put to flight. Bishops, priests, and monks who were there committed the bodies of the dead to the earth, commending

---

56 Cf. Vergil, *Aen.* ix. 415.

57 This river is identified in *RHC Occ* iv. 332, note (b), as 'Thymbrim seu Tembrogium', a tributary of the river Sakarya.

their faithful souls into the hands of Jesus Christ with prayers and psalms. Suleyman, defeated now once more, only just escaped capture and climbed the mountains of Rūm, no longer having any hope for the city of Nicaea, his wife and his sons, and feeling very great grief for his men, those whom he had lost before this time, destroyed by the Gauls on the plain of Nicaea, and now those whom he had left as prisoners or dead in the valley of *Gorgania*.

Book 3

1. Where Christ's faithful pitched camp after their victory; and how many died, wretchedly tortured by thirst

After the enemy attack abated, as dusk of the fourth day[1] was drawing on, the Franks, Lotharingians, Swabians, Bavarians, men of Flanders and the whole race of Germans[2] struck camp with all the things necessary to them and the Turks' booty, and when they had pitched camp on the top of the Black Mountains[3] they passed the night in entertainment. However, when morning came the Normans, Burgundians, Bretons, Swabians, Bavarians, Germans, in fact all the army, marched down from here into the valleys called the *Malabrunias* where, because of difficulties of the terrain and of narrow passes between the rocks, they shortened their journey during the day for the sake of the countless multitude and because of the excessive heat of the month of August.[4] Then the day came, a certain Saturday of the same month, when the great shortage of water worsened among the people. And therefore, overwhelmed by the anguish of thirst, as many as five hundred people of both sexes gave up the ghost on that same day – so they say who were there. In addition horses, donkeys, camels, mules, oxen, and many animals suffered the same death from extreme thirst.[5]

2. More of the same

We actually found all this out not merely from hearsay, but from the truthful account given by those who also shared in that same trouble: that in that same trial of thirst men and women endured wretched tortures, such that the human mind dreads to contemplate and trembles to hear of such a pitiable affliction of thirst. For indeed, very many pregnant women, their throats dried up, their wombs

---

1 3 July 1097 according to RM (p. 113).

2 Unlike contemporary writers such as RM, GN and Baudri of Dol [BD], AA does not use 'Franks' to describe the whole pilgrim army, but differentiates between groupings.

3 This term was used by other writers to denote the Amanus range (Gävur Dağlari, Tu.), which suggests some topographical confusion on AA's part.

4 The battle of Dorylaeum took place on 1 July 1097, so there appears to be some chronological confusion in this section.

5 The same experience is described in *ChA* (pp. 159–60). Though the *Chanson*'s account is much less graphic, shared details like the day of the week ('semedi') suggest a relationship.

withered, and all the veins of the body drained by the indescribable heat of the sun and that parched region, gave birth and abandoned their own young in the middle of the highway in the view of everyone. Other wretched women rolled about next to their young on the common way, having forgotten all shame and modesty because of their extreme suffering in that drought. They were driven to give birth not by the due order of months or because their time had come, but were forced by the raging of the sun, the fatigue of their travels, the swelling of their thirst, their long distance from water. Their infants were discovered in the middle of the plain, some dead, some half alive. Moreover, many men, growing weak from the exertion and the heat, gaping with open mouths and throats, were trying to catch the thinnest mist to cure their thirst. It was no use at all. For a very great part, as we have said, is claimed to have died there on that day. Even the hawks, no less, tamed birds and favourites of high-born nobles, were dying of that heat and thirst in the hands of their owners who were carrying them. Dogs as well, who were excellent in the hunter's art, panting with the same torment of thirst, perished in the hands of their masters.[6] Now, while everyone was thus suffering with this plague, the river they had longed for and searched for was revealed.[7] As they hurried towards it each was keen and longed excessively to get before the rest in the great throng. They set no limit to their drinking, until very many who had been weakened, men as well as beasts of burden, died from drinking too much.

3. They advance further; the army is divided into two parts; the leaders take time off to go hunting

After this, when they had come out from the narrow chasms, it was decided with universal goodwill that because of the very great number of people the army was to be divided into two parts. Leaving the rest, Tancred and Baldwin, Duke Godfrey's brother, departed with their men and passed through the middle of the valleys of Orellis.[8] But Tancred went first with his men and went down to the cities of Philomelium, Heraclea, and Iconium,[9] in which Christian citizens were living under the yoke of the Turks, Suleyman's men. Baldwin and his men had

[6] Cf. Vergil, *Geo.* iii. 44: a description of good hunting and of Spartan hounds. Hunting was, of course, an accepted way of augmenting the diet, but it also gave rise to accusations of frivolity, for example in Eugenius III's crusading bull of 1147, *Quantum predecessores*, where hounds and hawks were condemned as 'signs of wantonness' along with elegant clothes: P. Rassow, 'Der Text der Kreuzzugsbulle Eugens III', *Neues Archiv*, xlv (1924), 302–5; trans. L. and J. Riley-Smith, *The Crusades: Idea and Reality, 1095–1274* (London, 1981), pp. 57–9.

[7] Probably the river Sakarya.

[8] This was the name given in AA 2. 38, 40, to the valley 'de Gorghani'. Once again AA's topography is confused.

[9] The sequence of towns given here is wrong: the crusaders would have reached Iconium before Heraclea.

come up against confused mountain footpaths; he with all his band was further troubled by a serious shortage of food supplies, indeed the horses, lacking fodder, were scarcely able to follow, still less to carry men. Duke Godfrey, Bohemond, Robert, and Raymond followed from far off on the royal way and, drawing near to Antioch the Less, which is situated to the side of Heraclea, they ordered a halt for refreshment at the ninth hour of the day. When evening came Duke Godfrey and the rest of the nobles pitched their tents all over delightful meadowlands, considering the district fitting and agreeable and most fruitful for the hunts in which the nobility enjoyed amusing themselves and taking exercise. As they lay near there, with weapons and all their armour laid aside, they found a wood most suitable for hunting and took up bow and quiver, girded on their swords, and went into the forests near the mountains to see if anything would appear which they would be able to shoot and chase with their cunning young hounds.

4. The duke is seriously wounded fighting a bear, but with the help of another knight the beast is killed and he is rescued alive

When at length they had spread out through the shady parts of the wood, each on his own path to ambush the wild beasts, Duke Godfrey saw that a bear of most enormous and frightful appearance had seized a helpless pilgrim out gathering twigs, and was pursuing him as he fled round a tree to devour him, just as it was accustomed to devour shepherds of the district, or at least those who went into the forest, according to their account. The duke, then, as he was accustomed and ready to help his Christian comrades at all times of misfortune, hastily drew his sword, vigorously spurred his horse and swooped down upon the wretched man; he hastened to snatch the distressed pilgrim from the butcher's teeth and claws, and racing through the middle of the thicket with a loud shout he was exposed in the way of the cruel beast. When the bear saw the horse and its rider bearing down on it at a gallop, trusting its own fierceness and the rapacity of its claws, it met the duke face to face at no less speed, opened its jaws to tear his throat, raised up its whole body to resist – or rather to attack, unsheathed its sharp claws to rip him to pieces; it drew back its head and fore-paws, carefully guarding against a blow from the sword, and, wishing repeatedly to strike, it feinted. Indeed it roused all the forest and mountains with its dreadful roaring, so that all who were able to hear it wondered at it. The duke, reflecting that the cunning and evil animal would oppose him with bold savagery, was keenly provoked and violently angry, and with the point of his sword turned towards it he approached the brute in a rash and blind attack, to pierce its liver. But by an unlucky chance, as the beast was escaping the blow of the sword it suddenly drove its curved claws into the duke's tunic, the duke fell from his horse, brought down to the ground embraced in its forepaws, and it wasted no time before tearing his throat with its teeth. The duke therefore, in great distress, remembering his many distinguished exploits and lamenting that he who had up to now escaped splendidly from all danger was now to be choked by this bloodthirsty beast in an ignoble death, recovered his strength; he revived in an instant and was on his feet, and, seizing the sword, which had got entangled with his own legs in the sudden fall from his horse and the struggle with the frenzied wild beast, he held it by the hilt and aimed swiftly at the beast's throat, but mutilated the calf and sinews of his own leg with a serious cut. But nevertheless, although an unstaunchable stream of blood poured forth and was lessening the duke's strength, he did not yield to the hostile brute but persisted most fiercely in defending himself until a man called Husechin, who had heard the great shout of the poor peasant delivered from the bear, and the butcher's violent roaring, rode at speed from the comrades scattered through the forest to the assistance of the duke. He attacked the terrifying wild beast with drawn sword, and together with the duke he pierced its liver and ribs with his blade. So, with the ferocious beast killed at last, the duke for the first time began to lose heart because of the pain of his wound, the excessive loss of blood; his face turned pale, and the whole army was thrown into confusion by the wicked news. Everyone rushed together to the place where the brave champion and man of wisdom,[10] head of the pilgrims, was brought wounded. Laying him on a litter, the chiefs of the army brought him down into the camp with great lamentation and grief of the men and wailing of the women, summoning the most skilled doctors to heal him. The wild beast they divided among them, saying that they had never seen anything like it in size.[11]

5. Tancred, having pitched his tents close to the city of Tarsus, presses for the city's surrender among the citizens, now using threats and now persuasion

So, the duke being held up by this serious wound, and his army following closely at a slower rate, Tancred, who had led the way and kept to the royal road[12] towards the coastal area, after passing over the cliffs went down before Baldwin the duke's brother through the valleys of Butentrot, through the gate which is called Judas[13] to

[10] Cf. Ecclus. 32: 22; 1 Macc. 2: 65.

[11] This heroic episode was elaborated by WT and later writers – for example they omitted that Godfrey's wound was the result of his own clumsiness – until the point where it inspired the Jesuit writer Guillaume Waha to entitle his biography of Godfrey *Labores Herculis christiani* (2nd edn, Luxembourg, 1690). Cf. WT pp. 219–20; GN pp. 285–6.

[12] Cf. Num. 21: 22.

[13] The Cilician Gates. AA's toponymical confusion and the association with Judas is interesting here, for Butentrot was the provenance of the first rank of Baligant's army in the *Chanson de Roland*: see G. J. Brault, *Chanson de Roland* (2 vols, London, 1978), vol. 2, p. 196, line 3220. The *Roland* author probably meant Butintro, Epirus, where according to legend Judas was brought up, rather than Butentrot in Cappadocia: R. Fawtier, *La Chanson de Roland* (Paris, 1933), p. 86. This passage reinforces the probability that AA was influenced by the *Chanson*: cf. C. Minis, 'Stilelemente in der Kreuzzugschronik des Albert

the town named Tarsus, or commonly Tursolt, which the Turks, Suleyman's chiefs, also held subdued with its towers.[14] There a certain Armenian, who had spent some time with Tancred and had become acquainted with him, promised to suggest to the townspeople, who were weighed down by the heavy yoke of the Turks, that they should give up the town into Tancred's own hands secretly and without the Turks' knowledge, if it so happened that they found the right time and place.[15] But, as the townspeople were cowardly and would not accept their Armenian brother's advice because of the Turks' presence and watchfulness, Tancred, who had gone on ahead, plundered the regions neighbouring the aforesaid city and, having assembled boundless supplies of booty for use in the siege, he spread out his tents all the way round the walls. When the tents were pitched, Tancred made many threats to the Turks who were stationed all over the ramparts and towers, concerning Bohemond's arrival and the strength of the army which followed, and he declared that unless they came out and opened the gates of the city, the approaching army would not withdraw from the siege of this city before it was taken like Nicaea, conquered with all its inhabitants. But if they gave in to his will and opened up the city, they would not only find favour and life in Bohemond's eyes,[16] but, receiving many rewards, they would also obtain charge of their town and of other fortresses.

von Aachen und in der volksprachigen Epik, besonders in der "Chanson de Roland"', in A. Önnersfors, J. Rathofer and F. Wagner (eds), *Literatur und Sprache im europäischen Mittelalter: Festschrift für Karl Langosch* (Darmstadt, 1973), pp. 356–63.

[14] The detachment of Tancred and Baldwin from the main army was referred to in 3. 3 above. According to *GF* the two travelled together through the Butentrot valley, but AA makes it clear that Tancred went ahead through the pass while Baldwin branched off over the mountains (p. 24). Nicholson, who discusses the question exhaustively, suggests that Baldwin hoped to benefit by the advice of his Armenian guide to arrive at Tarsus first (R. L. Nicholson, *Tancred: Crusading Leader and Lord of Galilee and Antioch* [Chicago, IL, 1940], pp. 43–4). The purpose of the detachment is an altogether bigger question. It has commonly been treated as a high-spirited adventure on the part of the two young knights, but France sees it as a serious strategic move, aimed at restoring Byzantine power in Armenia (J. France, *Victory in the East: A Military History of the First Crusade* [Cambridge, 1994], pp.190, 193, 195–6).

[15] There was a complicated political situation in Cilicia, from which the crusaders benefited. Until the invasions of the Saljūq Turks, Cilicia had been part of the Byzantine empire. In 1097 the Turks occupied the plain while Armenian princes occupied the Taurus mountains. Some, like Thoros of Edessa, were Orthodox in religion; others, such as Constantine son of Reuben, belonged to the Separated Armenian Church; all hoped to maintain their positions by playing off the other powers in the region: the Byzantines, the Turks, and now the crusaders.

[16] Gen. 18: 3; 33: 10; Num. 11: 15.

6. The citizens promise surrender; of the men of God's army, who have been separated and are far away from each other, each group suspects the other to be the enemy

The Turks were softened by these coaxings and promises, and sometimes by the impressive threats, and they promised to surrender the city to Tancred on this condition: that no further danger or trouble should be caused to them by any following band, so long as they and the city garrison were subject to Bohemond's power. Tancred, not at all reluctant, arranged for a treaty to be secured with them on these terms: Tancred's own flag was to be raised on top of the chief citadel as a sign that Tancred, in advance of Bohemond, had laid claim to this town, and so in turn it would be kept intact from any hostile attack.[17] Baldwin, Duke Godfrey's brother; Peter count of Astenois; Rainald count of the town of Toul, a man of great diligence; and Baldwin of Bourcq, a splendid young warrior, who were united in friendship, had been separated on another route and were wandering for three days away from the army through deserted and unknown places in the mountains.[18] They were afflicted by severe hunger and want of supplies, but at last, after a maze of intricate roads, they happened to be standing together on top of a certain mountain. Observing Tancred's tents from there, pitched all over the level ground of the plains to besiege Tarsus, they were afraid with a great fear,[19] reckoning this to be Turkish equipment. And in fact Tancred, seeing the men on the mountain top from afar, was no less terrified, judging them to be Turks who had hurried to the relief of their allies blockaded in the city. When at last Baldwin's men were descending, despairing of life, half-dead from hunger, Tancred, as a keen soldier, warned his comrades that they should fight for their lives.

7. The besieged citizens break the treaty; Tancred and Baldwin join forces and renew the siege; and concerning the situation of the city

Moreover, about five hundred of the Turks had assembled on the turreted walls for the spectacle and for defence, and they too, similarly thinking that Baldwin and his retinue were battle lines of Turks, were taunting Tancred and threatening him in this way: 'Look at the company of men hurrying to reinforce us. We are not in your hands as you reckoned, but you and your men are today in our hands

---

[17] AA's account of the seizure of Tarsus is much longer and more circumstantial than that in *GF*, where Tancred does not capture the town before Baldwin's arrival (p. 24). However, they are agreed on the general tenor of the three-way conflict and are in broad terms reconcilable: F. Kuhn, 'Zur Kritik Alberts von Aachen', *Neues Archiv der Gesellschaft für ältere deutsche Geschichtskunde*, 12 (1887), pp. 545–58, at 546–7. Cf. FC (p. 206) and RC (pp. 57–63).

[18] Cf. Ps. 62 (63): 3; 74 (75): 7; Mark 1: 45.

[19] Mark 4: 40.

and in our power to be destroyed. And so now you may be sure that you have been deceived in this treaty which we made to thwart you. And we have not made you stay in your camp for any other reason, except that we were expecting the hope of reinforcement from these armies which you see coming to destroy you and your men.' Tancred, undaunted warrior, paid little attention to the Turks' threats; he reacted to the taunts with a short reply: 'If you consider these to be your soldiers or chiefs, in the name of our God we think little of them; we are not afraid to approach. If with the Lord's help they are conquered by us, then your insolence and boasting will not escape punishment. But if we cannot stand firm, because our sin prevents us, yet you will never escape the hands of Bohemond and his army which is following.' This said, Tancred, with all his company who had ridden ahead with him, hastened on swift horses to meet Baldwin, bearing standards, weapons, helmets, and hauberks. The Turks thundered loudly from the walls with trumpets and dread-sounding horns to frighten Tancred. But on both sides the banners of Christianity were recognized, and friends and fellow countrymen were seen, and they dissolved into tears of joy because thus by the grace of God they were now delivered from pains and perils. And without delay the forces duly combined and by common consent they pitched their tents together before the city walls, and of the booty of cattle and herds they had collected from the mountains and from the region they killed some for food and prepared it and put it on the fire. There was absolutely no bread there for anyone, and so their long-suffered hunger forced them to devour this meat, even though it was cooked without salt. The town was walled on all sides, proper and suitable for its inhabitants with meadows and streams, lying in fertile plains. Its walls were so marvellously strong that it might be thought that it could never be conquered by human forces, unless God helped.

8. Concerning the dispute between certain princes, when even the citizens of Tarsus want Tancred to govern them

At dawn the next day Baldwin got up, and his followers, and they made for the city walls where they observed Tancred's standard, which was very well known, placed on the highest turret of the citadel in accordance with the agreement and pact made with the Turks. When they saw this they were inflamed with great indignation and anger, and burst out in bitter and mutinous words against Tancred and his men, caring not a straw for the ostentation and high rank of Tancred and Bohemond, likening them to dirt and dregs. With such bitter words the affair nearly came to blows, but peaceful and wiser men intervened with this advice: that by way of a legation of both parties they should find out from the Armenian townspeople themselves under whose ownership and authority they preferred the city to be, and whose side they favoured as the better by choice. Immediately the reply from everyone was that they would rather submit and yield to Tancred than to the authority of another prince. In fact they said this not out of heartfelt devotion, but out of mistrust, which they always felt, of an attack by Bohemond.

And that is not to be wondered at, for long before this expedition, in the lands of Greece, Rūm and Syria Bohemond's reputation was well known, and his warfare made them shudder.[20] Now Duke Godfrey's name glittered for the first time.[21]

9. About the same thing

When he heard these offensive words Baldwin, with great fury in his heart, was roused to anger against Tancred and in his presence he addressed the townspeople as well as the Turks through the words of an interpreter, thus: 'You should not believe that Bohemond and this Tancred whom you so respect and fear are in any way the greatest and most powerful chiefs of the Christian army, nor that they bear comparison with my brother Godfrey, duke and leader of the soldiers from all Gaul, or any of his kin. For this same prince, my brother Godfrey, is duke of a realm of the great and earliest Roman emperor Augustus by hereditary right of his noble ancestors; he is esteemed by the whole army, and great and small do not fail to comply with his words and advice on all matters because he has been elected and appointed chief and lord by everyone.[22] Know in fact that you and all your things, the city also, are to be consumed and destroyed by the sword and fire of this same duke, and neither Bohemond nor this Tancred will stand as your champions and defenders. But this man Tancred whom you support will not escape our hands today unless you throw down from the top of the tower the standard which he put up to insult us and to glorify himself, and you open the gates to us. If indeed you obey our will in the matter of throwing down this standard and surrendering the city we shall raise you up above all who live within these boundaries, and you will always be highly regarded[23] by our lord and brother the duke, and honoured by worthy gifts.' The townspeople and Turks were seduced by this expectation of a good and flattering promise and, with Tancred utterly unaware of what was going on, they made a treaty and pact of friendship with Baldwin, and without delay Tancred's standard was removed from the top of the tower and meanly thrown out

---

[20] Bohemond had been with his father Robert Guiscard at the siege of Dyrachium, on the Dalmatian coast, in 1081. They had not attacked Asia Minor or Syria and whether their notoriety was recognized there is questionable.

[21] AA interprets the dispute as a conflict between two factions, Bohemond's and Godfrey's, rather than a personal struggle between Tancred and Baldwin: whether this perception was correct cannot be known. See J. C. Andressohn, *The Ancestry and Life of Godfrey of Bouillon* (Bloomington, IN, 1947), p. 72.

[22] This claim is found nowhere else. Baldwin may have invented it to overawe the Turks, or AA may have done so. Andressohn suggests the statement rests on fact: that the other leaders may have chosen Godfrey to thwart Bohemond's ambitions, already clear, and that he was the obvious candidate since he held the highest rank among the crusading leaders (p. 72).

[23] Ps. 115 (116): 15.

far from the walls in a marshy place. Then Baldwin's standard was put in its place on the top of the same tower.

10. Concerning the same, and the way in which Tancred entered the city of Adana

Although Tancred was sad when he saw Baldwin's standard put up and his own taken away and thrown down, he bore it patiently. He realized dissension was mounting between his and Baldwin's followers because of this exchange of flags, and because his own side was weaker in numbers and in weapons he did not want to waste any more time in this disagreement, but went across to a neighbouring town, called Adana, which was fortified and prosperous. He found its gates closed and was not allowed to enter. For a certain man called Welf held this town, an outstanding soldier who came from the realm of Burgundy. He had thrown out and subdued the Turks and occupied the city, finding there gold and silver, precious cloaks, rations, sheep, cattle, wine, oil, corn and barley, and all necessities. For this Welf had gone ahead with the others who were separated from the army. Tancred, finding the gates closed and knowing that a Christian leader occupied the city, sent messengers under safe conduct and begged to be admitted for the sake of hospitality, and for food to be shared with him by fair buying and selling. Welf listened to his pleas and ordered the city to be opened, Tancred to be brought in with his men, and all the necessities of life to be served to them.

11. Where Baldwin is made prince of the city and will not allow in fellow Christians from Tancred's side

After this departure of Tancred, Baldwin once again warned the Turks; he urged and promised that rewards and huge prizes from the duke would follow, and not only that, but also they would be preferred to other towns if they would open the city, if they would let him and his men in with a pledge of faith made by clasping right hands. The Turks and the Armenians saw Tancred's flight and disappearance, and that Baldwin's power was stronger, and after a pledge was received and confirmed on both sides they opened the city gates, let in Baldwin and his men, but decreed they should stay on in all the turreted fortifications until Duke Godfrey and the supporting army approached, and then the matter of the town would be managed by gift and favour of the duke himself, and the other things according to Baldwin's promise to them, whether they had chosen the Christian faith or chosen to persist in the rites of gentiles. They assigned only two principal towers to Baldwin, in which he would be able to stay and rest safely and securely. The rest of the body of the army was scattered here and there throughout the houses and districts of the town. By the time these men had been let in with their leader Baldwin, and were refreshed by taking rest in quarters, the evening of the next day was already upon them, and three hundred of Bohemond's company and people who had been separated from the pilgrim army and had followed in Tancred's footsteps stood before the city walls bearing weapons and shields. On Baldwin's orders and the leaders' advice the city and its entrance were forbidden to them. These men were worn out by their long journey, they were lacking the necessities of life and exhausted, so they pleaded insistently for the hospitality of the city and the chance to buy necessities. All the common people from Baldwin's company pleaded too, because these were brothers and of the Christian faith. But Baldwin did not listen to their pleas at all, for this reason, namely, that they had come down to help Tancred, and also on account of the promise he had made to the Turks and Armenians not to receive or admit anyone except his own men into the city before the arrival of Duke Godfrey.

12. Those Christians who stay outside the gate are killed at night by the infidels

However, their brothers and pilgrims of Baldwin's company, seeing that those shut out thus could not in any way obtain admission, took pity on them because they saw they were in danger of starving. They decided to offer bread in baskets to them, and let down sheep on ropes for them to eat. Then, when they had thus been refreshed and were overtaken by a deep sleep at dead of night because of their weariness after the journey, the Turks who were in the garrisons of the towers under the protection of the promise, absolutely desperate and not fully trusting Baldwin and his fellow Christians, secretly took counsel among themselves and three hundred, carrying with them all their treasures and other things, secretly left the city while Baldwin and all his men were given up to sleep, by fording a certain river not unknown to them which flowed through the middle of the city,[24] leaving only two hundred of their lowly dependants and households in the garrisons lest there should be any suspicion of their flight among the Christians. After they left the city, however, they made a surprise attack on the Christian men who had surrendered their tired limbs to sleep throughout the meadows in front of the city, beheading some, slaughtering others, piercing others through with arrows, leaving alive no one – or few – out of all of them.

13. God's people accuse Baldwin of being responsible for this slaughter and rush to take up arms, but he satisfies the army as to his innocence and launches a violent attack on the rest of God's enemies

When morning came and the Christians who were inside the city got up and went to the walls to find out and see if their Christian brothers were still staying

[24] The river Sarus (classical) or Seyhan (Turkish).

in the meadows, they saw them all beheaded by the weapons of the Turks, and the meadows made hideous and overflowing with their blood. And in this way the treachery and injustice of the Turks was made clear. At once an uproar arose through the whole town among the Catholic people, they all seized their weapons, and, in revenge for the blood of their brothers who had been dishonourably killed, they made haste to break down the towers, to put to death the Turks they found there, stirring up a considerable riot with trumpets and loud shouting. Baldwin was astonished by such a violent din and by the excited gathering of the people. He rode swiftly from the garrison in the tower through the middle of the city, urging the troops of armed men to stop fighting and to return to their quarters, lest the treaty exchanged should be breached so soon, until the slaughter of the Christians was made more fully known to him. But the uproar was becoming more and more violent, and the people were very angry at the murder of Christians and were shouting that Baldwin was guilty of this massacre through his fatal advice. The tumult and discharge of arrows became so fierce and so great against him, that he was forced to enter the tower for refuge, driven by the necessity of saving his life. There, when he had returned to himself, after the fierceness of his feelings had died down, to placate the people he defended himself on all charges, and claimed that he was ignorant of the cruelty of the Turks and he had not shut out the people of the living God for any other reason than the vow he had sworn to the Turks and Armenians that no one would be admitted except his own men before the duke's arrival. After Baldwin had thus exonerated himself and was reconciled with his people, he attacked and overcame tower by tower the Turks who had stayed behind because they were of lowly family and household. His men attacked them too, until they had beheaded nearly two hundred in revenge for their colleagues. In fact very many distinguished women of the town were accusing those same Turks, showing the Christians ears and noses which the Turks had cut off them because they did not find them willing to be defiled. The people of Jesus Christ were more greatly inflamed to hatred of the Turks by this scandal and horrendous accusation and they further increased their slaughter of them.

14. Where Baldwin's men make a treaty with some Christian pirates, and they make for Tarsus too

When a few days had passed after this, Baldwin's men, who were scattered along the walls, observed from afar in the middle of the sea, three miles from the city, a great number of ships of different kinds and workmanship. Their masts were of a wonderful height and covered in purest gold so they shone in the rays of the sun. And they saw men disembarking from those same ships onto the seashore and dividing among themselves a great deal of booty, which they had brought together over a long period of time, nearly eight years. When they saw these men they thought they were hostile forces summoned by those who had fled from the nocturnal slaughter of the Christians. So they armed themselves eagerly and rushed together to that same shore, some on horseback, some on foot, enquiring fearlessly why they had come and what nation they had come from. The men replied that they were soldiers of the Christian faith, acknowledging that they had come from Flanders and from Antwerp and Frisia and the other parts of Gaul, and that they had been pirates for eight years until this day.[25] The men who had sailed in were also asking why they too had come down from the lands of the Romans and Germans and come into such a remote exile among so many barbarous nations. They testified that they had come for the sake of pilgrimage and to worship in Jerusalem. And so each side recognized the speech and language of the other, and they made a treaty, giving their right hands, all to go to Jerusalem. In this naval association there was a certain man called Winemer, the chief and master of all the sworn brothers, from the land of Boulogne and a member of the household of Count Eustace, the splendid prince of that same land. Once they were strengthened by an exchange of promises on this side and that, they left their ships and entered the city of Tarsus with Baldwin, taking the booty and all their baggage, and they rejoiced and feasted for some days on all the good things of the land there. Then, when they had consulted among themselves, three hundred were chosen from the naval force to guard and defend the city. Two hundred more were appointed from Baldwin's troops. Having arranged and organized this, they set out with their combined weapons and forces and they marched up the royal road to the sound of trumpets and horns in a great display of power.

15. Tancred captures the city of Mamistra by force of arms, and at the instigation of a certain Richard he makes a hostile attack on Baldwin's camp

Meanwhile Tancred left the town of Adana and its chief, Welf, and came down to the town of Mamistra,[26] which was occupied and fortified by the Turks. When the town resisted and opposed him he attacked it vigorously with his armoured band. He quickly threw its walls down to the ground, demolished its gates and iron doors, and wore down by cruel slaughter the arrogance of the Turks which had ruled supreme. When the enemy had been destroyed and driven out, Tancred

[25] OV, discussing events at Latakia, also refers to a large number of pilgrims arriving by ship: 'About twenty thousand pilgrims, journeying from England and the other islands of the Ocean to the Lord's sepulchre' (v. 271). This was probably the same group: P. Riant, *Expéditions et pèlerinages des Scandinaves en Terre Sainte* (Paris, 1865), p. 134, n. 3. Note AA's ready identification of merchants with pirates and with pilgrims (cf. the sea-captain Godric, 9. 9).

[26] Nicholson points out that RC has a different account of events at Mamistra and suggests that AA was mistaken, as Tancred would scarcely have omitted to relate to his panegyrist such a victory (p. 50 n. 1; RC pp. 66–7). Equally, it is possible that the aftermath of the capture of Mamistra, when crusader was fighting crusader for the first time, persuaded Tancred to suppress the details.

garrisoned the towers with a guard of his own men; he distributed among the Christian confederates food, clothing, gold, and silver which he found there in great quantity and stayed in the place for some days. And while he was stopping there in safety, concerning himself with the care of the city, Baldwin the duke's brother, marching with weapons and companions on the royal road, descended into the territory of that same town, and he and his supporters and fellow nobles pitched their tents in a row in a certain large garden planted with trees which was next to the city. A certain Richard, prince of Salerno, a town in Italy, a Norman by descent and close kin to Tancred, considered these things and took them ill, and he reproached Tancred with very bitter words on the subject, saying: 'Ah, Tancred, today you have been made the most worthless man of all. You see Baldwin in command, by whose injustice and envy you lost Tarsus. Ah, if you have got any manhood in you now, remind your men directly and return the injury against you on his head.' When he heard this Tancred groaned in spirit[27] and, calling for weapons and soldiers on the spot, he sent his archers ahead in great strength to challenge the enemy in their tents and to wound the horses which were wandering all over the pastures and meadows. He himself suddenly charged on horseback with five hundred armoured cavalry into the camp and against the followers of that same Baldwin, so he could take a worthy revenge for all the wrongs he had done to him.

16. Baldwin and Tancred join battle, in which Tancred comes off worse

When Baldwin and his namesake Baldwin of Bourcq and Giselbert of Clermont and all his company recognized Tancred's sudden attack and charge, they took up their swords at once and raised their banners. And, having warned their comrades with loud shouts, they hastily rode to meet Tancred with much sounding of trumpets and horns, engaging heavily in conflicts on both sides and falling with serious wounds. But Tancred's army, unequal in number and strength, turned tail, unable to bear the intensity of the battle, and with Tancred himself they took flight into the protection of the city, only just managing to slip across the narrow river bridge away from the storm of battle. On this narrow bridge Richard prince of Salerno, Tancred's nearest kin, and Robert of the town of Anzi, very brave soldiers, lingered too long, and they were captured and held back; very many cavalry and infantry of Tancred's company died, some killed at once, others dying later from their wounds. Only Giselbert of Clermont pursued too hotly and was caught up in the middle of the enemy, captured on that same narrow bridge and taken away. Baldwin and his men, thinking he had been killed, wept for him with great lamentation.[28]

---

[27] John 11: 33.
[28] Biblical, e.g. Gen. 50: 11; Zech. 12: 11; 1 Macc. 1: 26.

17. Tancred and Baldwin make peace between them again. Concerning Baldwin's success in attacking fortifications, and about the treachery of a certain Armenian

When the sun rose the next day they were grieving on both sides for the absence of the noble men who had been captured and they recalled that both sides had done wrong in the Lord's sight, and their devotion to the most sacred way of Jerusalem had been violated, so on the advice of the leaders of their army they made a lasting peace agreement, with an exchange of prisoners. When this peace was made and all the booty and prisoners returned, Baldwin, keeping apart with his seven hundred cavalry, entered the land of Armenia on the advice of a certain Armenian soldier called Pakrad and besieged a fortress of wonderful workmanship and strength called Turbessel.[29] The Armenian townspeople, men of the Christian faith, saw this and, when they had secretly taken counsel with Prince Baldwin himself, they handed it over into his possession, the Turks having been driven out who were in command of the citadel, because the Armenians wished rather to serve under a Christian duke than under gentile power. And so when this town with its fortress citadel had been subjugated and his men placed in it, he laid siege to and captured in the same way Ravendel, a fortress impregnable by human forces. The Turks, frightened by the capture of Turbessel, are reported to have fled and gone away from there. He also took many cities with their surrounding fortifications, as they were frightened by the look of the army making for Antioch.[30] The Turks were also guarding these, long subjugated, but now they were struck with terror and took flight by night, abandoning them. When Ravendel had thus been taken Baldwin entrusted it to Pakrad, the aforesaid Armenian, an untrustworthy man and one of great treachery, whom he detained at Nicaea after he had escaped from the chains of the emperor of Greece: he did this because he had heard that Pakrad was a warlike man and one whose talents took a thousand forms, and because all Armenia, Syria, and Greece were familiar to him. Pakrad, being both treacherous and cunning, was especially well known to the Turks; he thought he could hold by force the land of this fortress of Ravendel which had been entrusted to him,

[29] For Baldwin's successful campaign in Armenia AA's is the most detailed account. It was analysed exhaustively by A. A. Beaumont and compared with those of FC, who accompanied Baldwin yet wrote quite briefly, the Armenian historian ME, and an anonymous Syriac chronicle. Beaumont concluded that AA's narrative was of great value and used eye-witness evidence: 'Albert of Aachen and the County of Edessa', in L. J. Paetow (ed.), *The Crusades and Other Historical Essays*, (New York, 1928), pp.101–38; FC, pp. 203–15; ME, pp. 168–70; J. Chabot, 'Edesse pendant la première croisade', *Comptes rendues de l'Académie des inscriptions et belles lettres* (Paris, 1918), pp. 431–42, at 436.

[30] The capture of this great city was an important interim objective of the expedition, since it was the key to northern Syria. It had been an important Byzantine trading centre and frontier town before its capture by the Turks in 1085 and its repossession was therefore of prime importance to Alexios Komnenos, while the crusaders knew they could not afford to leave it behind them in enemy hands as they marched on to Jerusalem.

letting in none of Baldwin's company, and he stationed his son, a distinguished youth, in it, and yet he did this deceitfully and, staying and walking with Baldwin, he concealed it.

18. How unwillingly that same Armenian surrendered the fortress that had been entrusted to him

There were certain princes who had heard of Baldwin's hard work and noble birth, and so had made a treaty with him. They were Armenian men; one of them was Fer, commander of Turbessel, and the other, called by the name of Nicusus, had fortresses and ample estates near Turbessel. At length, having found out the treachery which Pakrad had devised with the Turks, and knowing that he was an odious and resourceful man, they reported it to Baldwin, declaring that if he entrusted the fortress of Ravendel any longer to such a man, and one who had broken his oath to the emperor so criminally, he could soon lose the land he had subdued. Baldwin, when he heard this from these trusting and faithful men and because he knew Pakrad's tricks from his own frequent experience, asked for the fortress he had entrusted to him. Pakrad stubbornly refused to return it into the hands or care of the Gauls. Finally Baldwin, after making a very pressing demand for the fortress, was angry, and on a certain day he ordered the man who was resisting and defying him to be taken, to be bound with chains, and tortured until he was forced to give up the fortress. But he was still not driven to give it up by undergoing any method of torture or out of fear for his life. Baldwin, overcome by loathing of the man's tortures, finally ordered that he should be torn limb from limb while yet alive unless he gave satisfaction to him concerning the fortress's return. He, fearing the hideous rending of his limbs and sinews, sent letters to his son by Fer's hand, telling him to surrender the fortress hastily for the deliverance of his life and his limbs. This was done and Pakrad was freed from his chains and then cut off from Baldwin's fellowship. Baldwin transferred the surrendered castle to the guard and trust of his Gauls and withdrew from Turbessel, which is called Bersabee, reducing the land and region on all sides and subjecting it to his power.

19. The duke of the city of Edessa has made a direct appeal to Baldwin to go to his assistance; Baldwin is barred by the Turks but he hastens to go again

Some days passed after this, and Baldwin's reputation was increasing far and wide, and the heroism of his battles over all his enemies was becoming known. The duke of the town of Rohas, which is called Edessa, situated in the region of Mesopotamia, sent the bishop of that city to Baldwin himself, along with twelve of the greater governors of the town, whose advice was trusted by all ranks of the town and region, to ask Baldwin to come down to the city with his Gaulish soldiers, defend the land against the Turks' attacks, and take possession with the duke, in shared power and absolute authority, of all the revenues and taxes. He at length agreed, after he had taken counsel, and went down with only two hundred cavalry; the rest of the army was divided and left at Turbessel, Ravendel, and in many places which, now that the Turks were driven out, submitted to his power. However, when he had travelled swiftly as far as the great river Euphrates and he had set about crossing it, Turks and other hostile armies had marched out and gathered on all sides on the advice and prompting of Pakrad, whom he had released from chains; as many as twenty thousand were there, obstructing his way as he wanted to cross. But when he found out their strength and their cavalry, and as he was not strong enough now to meet and overcome so many thousands, he returned to Turbessel by the road along which he had come. Then when the Turks had scattered and gone back to their strongholds, Baldwin once again took his two hundred cavalry and set out for Edessa with his escort of faithful men. His journey was completed without hindrance and hostile attack, and the river Euphrates was negotiated with complete success.

20. The manner in which Baldwin was received in Edessa, and how magnificently he rejected the gifts of that duke; and about the petition from the senators

As the news of the arrival of such an outstanding and very celebrated prince reached the ears of the city's senators,[31] it caused joy and delight in all who heard it, and with trumpets and all kinds of music they assembled to meet him, great people and lesser ones alike, escorting him into the city with all honour and joy as befitted so great a man. When Baldwin had been escorted with such honour and glory through the town gates, and when he had arranged lodgings suitably with his men, the duke,[32] who had summoned him to a council of the twelve senators to oppose the town's enemies, was angered over the praises and honours which the people and senate had shown to Baldwin, and began deep down in his heart to envy him vehemently, but he also forbade him utterly to take command of the town and region, and said he would not be his own equal so far as any revenues or taxes were concerned. He said that he would give him a very great deal of gold, silver, and purple, plenty of mules and horses and weapons, if he would agree to be a champion and supporter for him and the citizens and the region against the ambushes and attacks of the Turks, in places appointed for him. Baldwin refused absolutely these gifts from the duke which were to be accepted under such a mean

[31] AA uses the classical 'senatores' for the prince's counsellors, or elders of the city.

[32] Named elsewhere as Thoros (or T'oros), the duke was entitled to feel vulnerable since he claimed authority as a Byzantine appointee and also recognized the suzerainty of the neighbouring Turks. Furthermore he was an Orthodox Christian rather than a member of the Separated Armenian Church as were most of his subjects: J. Laurent, 'Des Grecs aux croisés: Étude sur l'histoire d'Edesse', *Byzantion*, 1 (1924), pp. 404–34.

agreement, asking only for the assurance of a safe conduct, so that he could return safe and sound to Duke Godfrey his own brother, without danger and unfair tricks. When the twelve leading senators and the most eminent men in the town and the rest of the crowd heard that Baldwin could not be restrained by gold or silver or any precious gifts, they went to the duke, urging him in all ways and with every entreaty not to allow such a noble man and so very strong a champion to depart, nor to estrange him from himself, but to make him his ally in matters of the kingdom and town, for with his protection and military strength the town and the land could always be defended, and he should never bother the man about what he had promised.

21. Baldwin is adopted as son by the duke of Edessa; at the duke's request he attacks the city of Samosata, but after a fruitless siege he returns empty handed

In view of the twelve governors' and all their fellow-citizens' steadfastness and goodwill towards Baldwin, the duke had to grant their request whether he liked it or not, and he made Baldwin his own adopted son according to the custom of that region and people, binding him to his naked chest and clothing him once for all under the garment closest to his own flesh, with pledges given and received by both parties.[33] With the father-and-son relationship thus confirmed on both sides, the duke one day suggested to Baldwin, in his position as son, that he call his men together, all the army and those serving for pay, taking the citizens of Edessa likewise, and set out for the fortification at Samosata,[34] which was next to the Euphrates, and conquer Balduk, prince of the Turks, who had unjustly seized that same citadel, which belonged to Edessa, and was holding it. That same Balduk had inflicted unbearable harm on the citizens. For he had used threats to force them to give him several of the leading citizens' sons as hostages, for the annual revenues and tributes of bezants which they had been accustomed to give him to redeem their vines and crops. Baldwin did not refuse this first request of the duke and the leading citizens; he took with him two hundred comrades and the town's entire company of cavalry and infantry and attacked the fort at Samosata, directing a great force against the enemy in the strength of his men. But the attack was strongly resisted by Balduk and his men, who met them with a hail of arrows and a blast of trumpets. For an innumerable band of the effeminate Armenian townsmen, who were fighting carelessly and slowly, fell in that place and as many as six of

[33] The adoption is described by AA and, following him, mentioned by WT; it is also found in BD and GN (who associates Thoros's wife in the ceremony), but not in the two eye-witness sources, FC and ME (WT pp. 236–7; BD p. 81 [intercalation from ms G]; GN pp. 163–4). These sources say Thoros was childless, but according to *ChA* Baldwin was married to the prince's daughter in a bizarre ceremony (p. 166).

[34] The expedition to Samosata is confirmed by ME, pp. 168–9.

Baldwin's excellent and vigorous soldiers were shot with arrows and died. In their funeral rites, carried out according to the Christian custom, there was lamentation and great grief throughout the whole city. Baldwin realized that the citadel of the fortress at Samosata was unconquerable, and that the Turks in it were very resolute and tireless in war, so he left his men, armed with hauberks and helmets and horses, at St John, in a fortress which was not very far from the citadel, so that they would always ride out to oppose the Turks and trouble them with constant warfare, while he returned to Edessa with only twelve Gauls.

22. Baldwin wants to quash a conspiracy by the people against their duke, but he gets nowhere

A few days passed after this, then the senate and all the citizens assembled and considered Baldwin's wisdom and steadfastness against the ambushes of the Turks, and decided that the state could most likely be saved and defended under his power and his protection. Constantine,[35] a very powerful man, had been summoned from the mountains to the general council and he proposed that they should kill their duke and raise Baldwin to be duke and lord in his place. For the duke was very strongly opposed to them; he had often treated them dishonestly and had taken huge amounts of gold and silver from everyone. If anyone opposed him, he would encourage the enmity and hatred of the Turks not only to imperil his opponent's life, but also to mow down his vines and crops and plunder his herds. After this council had been held, one day everyone in the city, small and great, flocked to arms, and, fully armed and armoured, they spoke to Baldwin, demanding that he hurry with them to destroy their duke, claiming that by common consent they had decided that he should become lord and duke in his place. Baldwin refused with every objection to undertake such a crime, because he had been appointed the duke's adopted son and had not yet discovered any sort of cause or evil in him which would make Baldwin agree with and take part in his destruction. He said: 'It would be a sin beyond estimation in the sight of God for me to raise my hand without cause against this man whom I have taken to myself as father, and to whom I have also given my pledge. But I beg of you not to let me be dishonoured by his bloodshed or death,[36] and not to make my name become worthless among the leaders of the Christian army. I also ask you to let me talk to him face to face in the upper room of the tower, where he has been used to remain up to now, raised up by your gift.' They immediately agreed to this. And so he climbed the tower and talked to him thus: 'All the citizens and senators of this state have conspired for your death and they are hurrying to this tower carrying all sorts of weapons, full of rage and passion: I am sorry I bring you this bad news. But I did not neglect

---

[35] ME's account of the plot is similar in outline, but according to him Baldwin was deeply implicated (pp. 168–70).

[36] Cf. Isa. 59: 3.

to come ahead of them so that you could be delivered by some method, or by the granting away of your possessions.' Hardly had the duke heard his speech when a crowd of citizens flocked around the tower to besiege and attack, shaking the walls and the doors of the tower with an unceasing bombardment of mangonels and arrows.

23. How wretchedly that same duke was slain

As the duke saw that his life was in danger, he revealed to Baldwin his matchless treasures – in purple, in vessels of gold and silver, in plentiful bezants – asking him to take them and to intercede with the citizens for the duke's life and safety, so that they would allow him to leave and go away from the tower, naked and empty-handed. Baldwin listened to the man's entreaties[37] and was moved to pity by his despair; he urged the people's leaders and he insisted resolutely and persuasively that if they should spare their duke and not kill him, then they would be able to divide among themselves the countless treasures which he had seen. The senate and all the citizens paid little attention to Baldwin's words and the promise of treasures; they were shouting out as one voice that the duke was not going to escape alive and well in return for any exchange or gift of things; they were reproaching him with the insults and injustices they had often suffered under him and from the Turks at his instigation. Therefore the duke, despairing of his life and seeing that neither his entreaties nor any precious gifts would be of any use to him, sent Baldwin from the tower and left it, letting himself down on a rope from the upper room through the window. His destroyers brought him down in the middle of the street, shot with a thousand arrows in a moment. They cut off his head and carried it fixed on a lance through all the quarters of the city for everyone to mock.

24. Baldwin takes the place of the slain duke; he disdained at first to buy the citadel of Samosata which was put up for sale, but soon afterwards, on the advice of his men, he bought it with precious things

On the following day they appointed Baldwin duke and prince of the city, although he was very reluctant and made very many objections. They bestowed on him the unassailable tower with all the dead duke's treasures found in it, and bound themselves by oath to be his subjects and faithful to him. When Balduk heard about Baldwin's new advancement he was struck by a great fear that he might lose Samosata if it was besieged by the strength of the Gauls, those warlike men.

---

[37] The phrase 'preces … exaudire' occurs in the Bible (e.g. Gen. 30: 17; 3 Kgs. (1 Kgs.) 8: 45, 49) and also in the liturgy, notably in votive masses, including the mass 'Pro peregrinantibus et iter agentibus' (Bruylants, vol. 2, p. 143, no 528; vol. 1, pp. 185–6, no 560).

So a deputation was sent to Baldwin; Balduk offered the citadel for sale for the sum of ten thousand bezants and said that for an agreed sum of money he would serve him faithfully as soldier from then on. Baldwin took no notice of his words, because Balduk had taken this citadel from the Christians unjustly, which formerly, not long before this time, belonged to the state of Edessa. Balduk, seeing Duke Baldwin's fierceness and stubbornness, said that he would burn down the citadel, behead the many hostages of the citizens and senate whom he held, and always set ambushes for Baldwin, night and day. At length, when some considerable time had passed, Baldwin took his men's advice and gave Balduk a large sum in gold and silver and precious clothes in royal purple, horses and mules worth no small price, and thus he bought back the fortress of Samosata from enemy hands and power. From that day on Balduk became subject to Baldwin and he was established as a member of his household and a familiar acquaintance among the Gauls. Baldwin garrisoned the fortress he received with a faithful guard of his own men; he restored the hostages he found there to the appropriate senators and citizens. After this, because it was not equally fair to both the gentiles and the Christians, and as they were always suspicious of one another, Baldwin asked Balduk for his wife and sons to ensure that he would keep faith. He willingly agreed but from day to day he found pretexts to put off giving these hostages.

25. The fortress of Sororgia is handed over to Baldwin, though not without exertion on his part; and Balduk is found to be deceitful

After Baldwin had thus been raised up as duke and his military reputation was widely known, Balak, who was himself also a prince, and usurper of the fortress of the town of Sororgia, sent a delegation to Duke Baldwin asking that he should come down with a joint army to a town which was at a distance from the fortress and the mountains and was still holding out for the rebels, and that when the city and citizens were overcome he should restore the fortress to Balak's hands without any delay. For the citizens were Saracens who were holding out against him, and they scorned to pay tribute.[38] Baldwin believed his promises, and after a treaty was agreed on both sides he arranged to besiege and attack the city with all his equipment, until the defeated citizens yielded and then became tributaries. When the citizens found out about Baldwin's approach and his anger, at Balak's instigation they summoned Balduk with an agreed sum of money and the other Turkish soldiers with many prizes, hoping they would be able to hold and defend the city walls under their protection. Balduk, a soldier and one of the princes of

---

[38] AA distinguishes between Turks and Saracens throughout his narrative, in contrast with other and later western writers who use 'Saraceni' indiscriminately to refer to Muslims: see H. Szklenar, *Studien zum Bild des Orients in vorhöfischen deutschen Epen* (Göttingen, 1966), pp. 193–6. By Saracens, AA probably meant the settled, Arabic-speaking peoples, as opposed to the nomadic Turks.

the Turks, who was already corrupted by greed for bezants, came down with his men to the city, hoping he might yet become the chief and master of that same city. Duke Baldwin, knowing this, arranged to set out on the appointed day with a strong force to besiege the city of Sororgia, equipped with mangonels and all sorts of weapons with which the city could be torn apart and overcome. When the Saracen citizens learnt of Baldwin's forces and irresistible weapons they were horror-struck and sent messages to him to come down to them peacefully and to take the city without opposition; then they would not refuse the revenues each year to his authority. Baldwin yielded to their entreaties and he fixed a day for all these things to be settled with a sure and trusting peace and pledge. Balduk, seeing that the citizens had abandoned the defence and that they were terrified and they could not resist so great a prince, left the city with his men and, pretending he could be trusted, came down to Edessa to Baldwin himself, with these words: 'You should in no way believe or suppose that I entered the city of Sororgia in order to bring support to the citizens against you, but I came to dissuade them from starting their rebellion by whatever advice I could, and to make them subjects and tributaries to you.' Baldwin accepted this patiently and allowed Balduk on this excuse to stay with him from that day, but nevertheless he put little faith in his honesty. Soon afterwards the city was delivered into his hands, the citizens were made tributaries, and Balak put the fortress which stood out in the mountains into his hands and the guard of his men. When he had received the town with the fortress Baldwin left Fulcher of Chartres,[39] a warlike man and very skilled in battle, to manage and guard their defences while he himself returned to Edessa in great glory.

26. Tancred destroys fortresses that are harming the Christians, and prudently puts away gifts offered to him by the enemy

Tancred, who had been separated from Baldwin at Mamistra and had stayed on the coast, used his forces, enlarged by the navy which Baldwin had brought, to besiege and conquer the Castle of the Maidens, which is commonly called Debaiesses, and in the same way he conquered and demolished the Castle of the Shepherds; with his band of strong soldiers he also cast down and destroyed the Castle of the Young Men, which is called Debakelers, all of which were fortresses in the Turkish mountains. He gained Alexandria the Lesser, having overcome it and demolished its gates and walls. He put the Turks he found in these places to the sword's edge. Moreover, he either captured or burnt down all the castles and fortresses which had till then been harming the pilgrims, and of the enemy gentiles he found in them,

[39] Fulcher was evidently a common name in Chartres and this Fulcher must be distinguished from the historian, who had also accompanied Baldwin to Edessa (FC pp. 163–4, 206–8) and the Folcher who had been killed in Asia Minor (1. 21 above). The death of Fulcher, count of Sororgia, 'a brave and mighty man and a person of saintly and pure conduct,' was recorded by ME in 1100–01 (pp. 177–8).

some he killed, others he held captive. Now that the enemy, who had scattered through the mountain regions after overcoming the Christians and had occupied the Christians' fortresses and places unjustly, heard of his warlike strength, some took flight, others sent mules and horses and precious gifts of gold and silver and were joined in friendship with him, so that they might find him peaceable in all the lands they possessed. Tancred refused none of all these things which they were offering, but like a cautious and provident man he accepted everything and stored it away, remembering the difficulties of the past and believing greater ones were yet to come.

27. Concerning the city of Marash where, too, Baldwin's wife died

Meanwhile the great army was hastening with its entire equipment and strength on a direct route through the middle of Rūm, marching through steep mountains and sloping valleys. It was governed by Duke Godfrey, Bohemond, Count Raymond, Robert of Flanders, Adhémar bishop of Le Puy, Robert of Normandy, who took counsel together[40] and led as equals. These men, coming down in a strong company to the town which is called Marash, were quartered for the night there, spreading out their tents in the green places in front of the city walls, and not using any force on the Christian citizens there, but receiving peacefully from the city necessary supplies for sale. The Turks, who had learnt of the arrival of such great princes in such great numbers, fled from their occupation of the city which they had suppressed by undue force and unfair tributes for many years past. Baldwin had brought his noble wife from her English homeland, and in this region of Marash her bodily ills daily grew worse. She was entrusted to Duke Godfrey, but she breathed her last and was buried with Christian rites: her name was Godevere. Udelard of Wissant died there in the same way, carried off by sickness, and was buried with honour in a grave in that place. He was an irreproachable knight, useful in every council of war and in action, a member of Duke Godfrey's household and always privy to his secrets before anyone else.

28. Concerning the city of Artah, where Armenian Christians cut off the heads of the Turks who live alongside them, and receive their brothers in friendly fashion

When they left the mountains and region of Marash, with all their troops following, the aforesaid leaders learnt from some Christians of Syria who met them that the town of Artah was not far away, rich in the necessities of life but occupied by Turks. When he learnt this, Robert of Flanders rose from the army, taking with him some men who were very careful in warfare – Roger of Rozoy, Gozelo son

[40] 2 Macc. 15: 36.

of Count Cono of Montaigu – and a thousand armoured men, and they went down to the town of Artah which was very well fortified with a wall and ramparts and a turreted fortress and where the Turks had brought the remaining Armenian Christians under the yoke of slavery. And so, as they approached the city and its ramparts, holding high beautiful banners of every colour, their bronze helmets shining as brightly as gold, the news of their arrival alarmed the whole region. The Turks who were on the ramparts of Artah and in the fortress intending to defend and resist stood stock still, terrified at this sudden attack by the Gauls, and they secured the town gates with a bar and bolts. The Armenian citizens, whom those same Turks had long oppressed with slavery and who were now with them within those same defences, called to mind the injustices which they had borne from those same Turks for a long time – the rape of their wives and daughters; the other crimes they committed; the levying of unjust tributes – and now, relying on the arrival and support of the Christians, they attacked the Turks and killed them with the sword's edge, they cut off their heads and threw them from the windows and walls, and, opening the city gates to their Christian brothers, they delivered up a safe entrance by their massacre of the gentiles, by their throwing out of dead bodies. They led in their faithful brothers courteously and received them with every proper ceremony, relieving them of their weapons and packs in a friendly way, and refreshing them with different foods and pleasing drinks, and detaining them with agreeable hospitality and they provided their horses and mules adequately with fodder.

29. God's people are surrounded by an infidel horde; they open up a way for themselves with the sword and only just escape; those under siege fight loyally

The distance from where this city stands to Antioch is reckoned to be ten miles: the news of this latest slaughter of Turks sped the distance on winged feet[41] and summoned Turks from Antioch and from all their territories – some twenty thousand of them gathered – to the aforesaid fortification of Artah. Thirty of the more cunning and nimble out of these thousands of Turks, riding horses which galloped like the wind, went ahead as a trick, leaving behind them in ambush the entire legion, so as to be able to provoke and draw out the Gauls from the fortress using the bow of horn and bone. The Gauls, of course, knowing nothing of the tricks and hidden ambush, went out on foot and on horseback, armed and armoured, and met them in the middle of the plain to do battle with their enemies. But no successful outcome was possible for them in any conflict. For the Turks, who lay in ambush across their route, took the road before them in a great horde, so that the Gauls, who had come out and had no way of returning or taking refuge in the city, would be killed instantly. When they saw this sudden and unexpected

[41] Cf. Ps. 13 (14): 3; Prov. 6: 18; Rom. 3: 15.

attack Robert of Flanders and Roger and the other army chiefs, after warning their comrades forcefully and gathering as one, sped on a tight rein from the level plain through the middle of the dense Turkish battle-lines and charged the enemy with lances held rigid. The whole company also charged with such manly boldness that they escaped from the enemy's hands unharmed inside the gates and ramparts. The Turks pursued the men who had escaped inside the gates with a hail of a thousand arrows, trying to enter the gates with them. But they were pushed back from the threshold by a strong, though small, band, and they were in no way allowed to enter the gates with the Gauls. Many armed men, both cavalry and infantry, were wounded on this side and that in the sudden bombardment of arrows, also mules and horses. The Turks, therefore, seeing that they had not succeeded, and still trusting in their numbers, decided on a siege around the aforesaid city. But the faithful people shut inside remained safe and calm because they had a sufficient supply of food, discovered in the fortress, and the strength of the walls was sure and unassailable. There in the fortress of Artah Gozelo, son of Count Cono, was overtaken by a very great lassitude and after some days he departed from life, and from his Christian comrades he received the honourable and Catholic burial which was due to him.[42]

30. The infidels besieging Artah, informed by spies of the approach of the Christian army, nevertheless do not lift the blockade until after nightfall

Meanwhile it was not long before the great army of Christians hastened on their journey. Spies were lurking among them who saw their chance and withdrew themselves secretly from the army. They reported to the Turks what they had heard and found out about the approach and the plans of the Christian army. These informers, hearing that news from Artah of their comrades' siege had reached the ears of the princes Godfrey, Bohemond and the rest, and that they had made a plan to rescue them, returned in haste to the Turkish camp, announcing that the Romans, Franks, and Germans were already close and were coming nearer, and the Turks could neither withstand their forces nor be rescued from their hands unless they left the town and returned quickly to their own defences. Yet the Turks were not at all terrified by these dark warnings; their very many thousands made them overconfident and they attacked the city throughout every hour of one day and worked on many assaults. But they squandered the effort in vain, as the Gauls fought back resolutely from the citadel and the ramparts.

[42] According to *ChA* Gozelo ('Gosson') was killed in battle at Artah (pp. 166–7).

31. As the army of God approaches, Artah is fortified by the protection of the faithful; Baldwin, renowned for his victories, is exalted by a new marriage

Then, when night returned and darkness was falling, they held many councils among themselves and a plan was devised that as first dawn appeared they would set about returning to the bridge on the river Orontes and they would enter safely the city of Antioch, which was made secure by towers and walls and could not be overcome by human forces, and, with the bridge and river defended from the Christian army, they would not suffer the danger to their lives of being conquered. The aforesaid Turks had only just sneaked into Antioch when, at dusk on the following day, the great army of Christians pitched camp in the district of Artah, spending the night there in happiness and joy. There on the decree of the leaders one thousand five hundred armoured men were chosen and sent to Artah to the assistance of their comrades who were in the citadel, so that in this way they might retreat safe and sound to the main army with their strength and forces combined, and worry less about enemy attack on the journey together. With the town of Artah defended by the faithful protection of the Christians, they returned to the army without any trouble. Tancred also returned from lesser Alexandria and the coastal regions, and everyone returned from whatever places they had been sent and scattered in order to subdue the land and the castles and the towns, except Baldwin, Duke Godfrey's brother, who had set out for the southerly region into the land of Armenia to conquer the Turks and was engaged in bringing Turbessel and Ravendel and other fortresses under his authority. This same Baldwin – whose wars and victories were increasing so, more and more, day after day – took in a splendid and legal marriage, on the advice of the twelve senators of the state, a very noble wife from an Armenian family, daughter of a certain prince who was brother of Constantine, called Taphnuz, who occupied many fortresses and defences in the mountains, to all of which he appointed Baldwin his heir.[43] He also promised to give him sixty thousand bezants, paying an agreed sum of money out of this for his soldiers, so he would hold the land effectually against Turkish attacks. He promised, but he only gave Baldwin seven thousand, putting off from day to day paying the rest he owed. Since Baldwin's wedding had been celebrated with incalculable pomp, it was proclaimed on the advice of the more important men of the city and region that this same Taphnuz should discuss with his son-in-law the situation in the land and the circumstances of the town, because he was a

[43] WT says Baldwin married the daughter of Taftoc, who was brother to Constantine and son of Reuben (Roupen) of Armenia (p. 453). During the nineteenth century the bride was awarded the name 'Arda', but there is no contemporary authority for this: FC, pp. 241–2, n. 7.

man of advanced age and sensible advice, and so they would hold one another in mutual esteem.[44] And this was done.

32. Christ's people are united and not to be divided again; the bishop of Le Puy warns them in a fatherly way to be careful

After they had gathered in one body, from that day onwards they were not separated, because of the Turks' countless forces who, having fled from the mountains and all Rūm, had hastened for defence to the city of Antioch, which was unassailable. Without delay Bishop Adhémar of Le Puy, making a speech to the people, gave them all a fatherly warning, and told them, with encouragement of this sort, to which the present emergency and constant news from nearby Antioch were driving him: 'Oh, dearest brothers and sons, be sure that the very nearby town of Antioch, as we have on good authority, is secured with a very strong defensive wall which cannot be broken down with iron or by stone-throwing, being built in an unheard-of way, both from indestructible masonry and with a massive structure of great rocks. In it we understand without a doubt that all the enemies of the Christian name, Turks, Saracens, Arabs, have come together, fleeing before us out of the mountains of Rūm and from every direction. For this reason we must be extremely careful not to make any further division of our men, or rashly to go on ahead; but we have made a limited decision, on the wisest advice, that tomorrow we shall travel in one single-minded force as far as the bridge on the Orontes.'[45]

33. Leaving Rūm behind, and following the standard-bearers they had chosen, they arrive at the bridge on the river Orontes, where they are surprised by a Turkish attack

All the people, therefore, agreed with the honoured priest's suggestion and at sunrise the next day, with comrades they welcomed from Artah, Tancred and Welf of Boulogne, who had come back from the coastal regions with all the Gaulish comrades, with camels and donkeys and all the waggons of baggage and provisions, they set out in one convoy, confident of their armed strength, to the bridge on the river Orontes, which is called Farfar, leaving behind them the rough, high mountains and valleys of very pleasing, very rich Rūm. On this day, in fact, Robert count of Normandy was appointed to go in advance of the army with his thousands, as is the custom in every well conducted army, so that if any

[44] In her notes to *ChA*, Duparc-Quioc suggests that the *Chanson*'s 'Old Man of the Mountains' is the result of 'Graindor de Douai's eliding AA's references to Taphnuz's living in the mountains (previous paragraph) and to his advanced age ('Li Viels de la Montaigne', line 2457): *Edition*, p. 140.

[45] Cf. *ChA*, p. 168.

opposition force had hidden it would be reported to the generals and leaders of the Christian army, and they would hasten to put on weapons and armour and take up battle formations as quickly as possible. In this band, among the thousands, Roger of Barneville and Everard of Le Puiset, praiseworthy knights in every military engagement, were bearing the standards and controlling the cavalry, until they took up position without delay at the aforesaid bridge. This bridge took the form of an arch of wonderful craft and ancient workmanship, beneath which the river Farfar of Damascus,[46] commonly called Orontes, scoured the river bed with its very swift flow. On each side of the bridge two towers overhung, indestructible by iron and perfectly adapted for defence, in which there was always a garrison of Turks.[47] A company of two thousand infantry followed after these distinguished men, and they also took up position at the bridge, not being allowed to cross. For the Turks, of whom a hundred or so had been posted in the bridge towers to defend them, were fighting back vigorously with bows and a hail of arrows against those who were wanting to cross; they struck the horses with frequent wounds, they pierced with flying arrows very many of the horses' riders through the covering of their hauberks.

34. A hard fight between the faithful and the Turks for the river crossing

A serious dispute arose on this side and that, with these men wanting to cross, those on the other side fiercely forbidding the crossing and so far winning. Seven hundred Turks, who had been summoned and had come out from Antioch, seeing their men's steadfastness and defence on the bridge, galloped up on swift horses, very excited by the battle, and took possession of the fords to stop any of the Christians from being able to cross. The Christian cavalry and infantry, seeing the forces of armoured Turks spread out for defence on the river banks, themselves spread out widely on the other bank, and, as on both sides arrows were twisted and loosed in bold endeavour, the struggle would be a long one. Very many men and horses were shot on both banks and, fatally wounded, were falling and failing. At last when the Turks were emerging very much the winners, and were outdoing and outlasting in the accuracy and effectiveness of their arrows, the army of the faithful, provided with weapons and horses, came quickly from all parts to the assistance of the comrades they had sent in advance. But even then the Turks did not retreat from the bank; they preferred to die rather than to yield, resisting those who wanted to cross with an unceasing assault of arrows.

---

[46] Damascus is on the river Barada, not the Orontes.

[47] Cf. the description of the bridge in *ChA* (p. 168). It is often called the Iron Bridge, a mistranslation of 'pons ferreus' or bridge on the river Far: *GF* p. 28 n. 1. WT corrected this mistake (p. 243).

35. Encouraged by the bishop of Le Puy, they take the bridge; after joining battle Christ's warriors return victorious; they send a hard message to the prince of Antioch

The bishop of Le Puy heard of this very serious conflict, so he went before the great army. He saw that the hearts of his men were weak from fear and failed them a little because of the injuries to the horses and the wounds to their own chests, so he addressed the people and strengthened them for defence in the name of the living God, thus: 'You should not fear the enemy's attack. Stand firm, rise against these tormenting dogs. For now, today, God will fight for you.'[48] At these words and warnings of so distinguished a bishop a shield roof was made, heads were protected by helmets, breasts by hauberks, and they attacked the bridge boldly. The enemy withdrew their lances from the bridge and took flight. Some Christians, seeing that the whole army had come to their aid, put too great reliance on them and they entered the fords and swam their horses across; others, discovering the fords on foot, made haste to cross the waters because they were keen to wage war; although they sustained wounds from blows and slingshots, they attacked the Turks in a blind assault and put them to flight from their position, then they stationed themselves on dry land on the other side of the river. Walo, steward of the king of France,[49] attacked the Turks with horse and lance. Rainald of Beauvais, a very rough recruit, took very little notice of the archers' shafts, and hurried on ahead into the midst of the enemy with lance and sword, engaging in very brutal massacres. The divisions of faithful and infidels were completely mixed up in the violent attack, and they grew hot with the exertion of battle; the slaughter and massacre grew worse. Bohemond, Godfrey, Raymond, Robert, and Roger governed the battle order and the war standards which were of many colours and very beautiful, until the Turks, taking flight on swiftest horses, turned back to Antioch, speeding their way through the steep mountain slopes and places known to them. The Christian victors turned back from pursuit and very great slaughter of their adversaries, and they chased the enemy no further, because the ramparts of Antioch seemed to be much too near and the forces of all the gentiles had poured in there and they spent the night next to the river Orontes. They collected plunder and spoils from everywhere and they freed from chains very many of Peter's army, whom the Turks had kept apart all over the region of Antioch.[50] When Yaghi-Siyan,[51] prince and chief of the city, heard this bad news and the turn

---

[48] Exod. 14: 14 and *passim*.

[49] Probably Walo of Chaumont; see 2. 23 above.

[50] Cf. *ChA*, which further specifies that the freed captives were 'Alemans', i.e. Swabians (translated as Germans, p. 171).

[51] Yāghisiyān had been appointed amir or ruler of Antioch by the Saljūq sultan Malik-Shāh. In the political fragmentation following Malik-Shāh's death in 1092 he had achieved a large degree of practical autonomy: P. Holt, *The Age of the Crusades* (London, 1986), pp. 14–15.

of events against his men, his expression was downcast, his heart was worn down by fear, and he was weighed down by great sorrows, turning his mind to different solutions, what he should do so that the same thing would not happen to him as had happened to Suleyman when he lost the town of Nicaea.[52] Without delay, brooding over many different plans, he plotted ceaselessly to bring in food, to collect together weapons and troops of allies, and he went on protecting the gates and ramparts with a trusty and safe garrison.

36. The journey to Antioch is proclaimed, the bishop addresses the people, and through him it is appointed which princes should be in the vanguard, and which should watch over the rearguard

When the following day dawned Duke Godfrey, Bohemond, and all the captains of the army got up and put on their weapons and hauberks and helmets again, and told everyone to resume their interrupted journey to the city of Antioch with all the necessary equipment and all the kinds of livestock and the cartloads of food of which so great an army has need. When these men were assembled and ready for the journey the prudent bishop spoke to them in this way, saying: 'Men, most beloved brothers and sons, do not be reluctant to listen carefully and take heed of the things I am saying to you. The city of Antioch is very near and close to us. There are four miles between us and the town. This wonderful city is the incredible work of King Antiochus,[53] built with most enormous rocks and towers, reckoned to number three hundred and sixty. We know that Sansadonias, son of King Yaghi-Siyan, rules as very strong prince in this city, and we have found out that four amirs, very noble and very powerful as if they were kings, have been summoned and have come together at Yaghi-Siyan's command, and they and their men, because of their fear of our approach, have taken warning and have armed in a strong force. Their names are Adorsonius, Copatrix, Rosseleon, Cazcornuz.[54] King Yaghi-Siyan is reported to be head and lord of all of them. These four amirs, out of thirty states from far and wide around which belong to Antioch and have submitted as tributaries to King Yaghi-Siyan, hold four of the more wealthy in benefice by gift and favour of Yaghi-Siyan himself, each one with a hundred castles. Because of this they have now been summoned in considerable strength by Yaghi-Siyan himself, king of Syria and all Armenia, to defend the city, mistress of all these cities and realms, and they are said to have arrived. And

---

52 Cf. *ChA*, p. 173.

53 Antioch was founded by Seleucus I Nicator *c.*300BCE and named for his father.

54 Shams al-Dawla is thought to have been in Damascus at this time, raising reinforcements. When he set out to relieve his father he was accompanied by Duqāq and Ṭughtigin and a sizeable army. The amirs named by AA in this passage do not equate to any known historical figures, and one of them, 'Rosseleon', seems to be the fabulous 'Rouge Lion' of *ChA* (*passim* pp. 213–312).

so we must proceed in a careful and orderly fashion.[55] We joined battle, as you know, late in the day. We are tired and our horses' strength is exhausted. Duke Godfrey, Bohemond, Rainald of Toul, Peter of Astenois, Everard of Le Puiset, Tancred, Warner of Grez, and Henry of Esch are going ahead to bring together and control the army in the vanguard when the battle-order has been drawn up. Robert of Flanders and Robert count of Normandy, Stephen of Blois, Count Raymond, Tatikios, member of the emperor of Constantinople's household, Adam son of Michael, Roger of Barneville – if the plan is acceptable – will govern and protect the rearmost battle lines of cavalry and infantry.'

37. Arriving at Antioch, what the army of God did, and what its numbers were estimated to be

So, according to this plan, when everyone had been positioned by the bishop and the other shrewd men, they set out of one accord on the royal road to the very walls of dreadful Antioch, splendid with their shields of gold colour, green, red and every shade, and with their banners held high, picked out in gold and visibly ornamented with all kinds of workmanship in royal purple, on horses very suitable for war, wearing quite magnificent hauberks and helmets. They put up their tents in strength next to the place which is called Altalon. There they cut down apple trees and trees of other kinds with axe and hatchet and uprooted them,[56] taking over the ground with their swelling tents. When these were pitched they eagerly indulged in the business of nourishment, making a lot of noise with thousands of horns, everywhere pursuing plunder and horse fodder. Their din and noise, it was reported, could be heard almost as far as a mile away. No wonder, when the number of so great an army may be reckoned by all beyond doubt at three hundred thousand[57] fighting men, not counting women and children following, of whom there seemed to be very many thousand. At this approach of the Christians and fresh siege the city was quiet that day with such a great silence that neither sound nor noise could be heard from the city, and the city might be thought to be empty of defenders when in fact it was overflowing, full of very many weapons and gentile troops in all its towers and fortresses.

---

[55] Cf. 1 Macc. 6: 40.

[56] In a note to the parallel passage in WT (p. 252), Huygens points out that the cutting down of orchards during a siege, though common enough, was contrary to scripture: Deut. 20: 19–20.

[57] The early editions had six hundred thousand, a figure for which there is no authority in extant manuscripts. Since AA had written of only four hundred thousand at Nicaea (2. 25) it appears a copyist's mistake undermined his veracity.

38. A description of the way the city was besieged

It was Wednesday[58] when they entered the land of Antioch and besieged its walls. On that day Tancred first took up position beside Altalon. Next to him his ally Roger of Barneville was added. Adam son of Michael was stationed next to him with his followers, so that no supplies could be brought in by the Turks on this side. Then at the gate which looked back towards the Persian plain,[59] where the mountain ridges began to run out, Bohemond took up his place with a band of hardy men, and there, with his position established, he stayed in safety. Then Tatikios, of the emperor's household, pitched his tent a little further from the city on the plain called Combrus, all the time intending to flee.[60] In front of that same Tatikios Baldwin count of Hainaut took up position with his contingent. Next Robert count of the Normans and Robert of Flanders were appointed to lay siege to the walls with all their military company. Stephen of Blois was likewise settled in his place to surround the city next to the princes already mentioned. Hugh the Great, brother of King Philip of France, in the same way took up position with his allies at this siege.[61] This city of Antioch, so they say, is fully two miles in length, one and a half in width. The aforesaid river Farfar flows past it and embraces walls and towers, whose defence and siege work extends right to the ridge of the mountain where a more important citadel stands, established as mistress of the city and of all the towers. Around this fortress are said to be positioned the four insuperable towers, for the purpose of guarding the middle citadel in their midst, and they have given their names to the four amirs mentioned above, who were always King Yaghi-Siyan's guardians and defenders.

39. More about the same thing

The bishop himself also assisted at the besieging of that same Antioch, which you have heard is so large, at the gate which is called *Waiferii* by modern people, which is unconquerable. Count Raymond was allied with him, and with them Provençals and Gascons and all their followers took up position. In a further place, where afterwards a bridge was built by joining ships, Duke Godfrey besieged one gate of the town on the bank of the river,[62] with countless thousands of Lotharingians, Saxons, Swabians, Bavarians, murderously fierce. With this same duke were

---

[58] 21 Oct. 1097 (*GF* p. 28).

[59] WT says it is 'now' called St Paul's Gate (p. 251).

[60] Only AA and *ChA* give Tatikios' position: the *Chanson* says he 'set up camp on a sandy bit of ground' (p. 175). However, while AA refers to his future flight, in *ChA* he is still 'lion-hearted'.

[61] AA's description of the disposition of the blockading forces is largely supported by RC (pp. 74–5). For an analysis and plan, see France, *Victory*, pp. 225–6 and 221, fig. 8.

[62] Later called the 'porta ducis', WT p. 252.

Rainald of Toul and Peter of Astenois, who had been separated from Baldwin the duke's brother at Mamistra and had returned to the army and the duke. Cono of Montaigu, Henry of Esch, and his brother Godfrey, soldiers always very dangerous to the enemy, likewise took up position to forbid entry and egress to the Turks. The more frequent and greater task fell to these men.

40. Concerning the river bridge, for the destruction of which a siege machine is skilfully built

Over this river we mentioned, which reached right to the sea through a very long channel, flowing past the walls, a stone bridge stretched from the city itself, of ancient workmanship but not much turreted, and this bridge remained entirely unbesieged on this side, as the army finished before it. In fact the Turks used to come out frequently across the bridge and, with the army watching, they broke through with their men and came back, bringing in supplies, and they were often sent out by that same bridge and slaughtered the people of Jesus Christ who had scattered through the districts and the mountains to look for sustenance or fodder for the horses, because the Turks realized they were scattered in this way. In the same way, from that very *Waiferii* gate which Bishop Adhémar and Raymond were watching, another bridge was also dangerous, built by the genius of the ancients, stretching across a certain marsh, muddy enough and very deep from the rush and flooding of a spring which flowed incessantly next to the city outside the walls. Now and then the Turks would come out across this bridge, either in daylight or in the darkness of night, and would hurl arrows at the army who had forgotten their ambushes, or they would put some to the sword in a charge, and would escape by a hasty retreat across that same bridge into the protection of the city. The bishop and the entire leadership, complaining bitterly about the problem of this bridge, took counsel and plotted for its destruction, and on the appointed day they provided themselves with iron hammers, mattocks, and axes and left the camp. But their strength was in no way powerful enough for the ruin of this bridge. For it was an indestructible piece of craftsmanship, built with the masonry and skill of the ancients. When the army was thwarted here in its attempt with hammers, the princes ordered them to build a siege engine from a pile of timbers and interweave it with wickerwork. Its ties were made of iron and connected; then they covered them with the skins of horses, of bulls, of camels, so that the engine would not be set alight by the Turks throwing on fire with pitch and sulphur.[63] When they had finished this engine they brought it right down onto the middle of the bridge at the *Waiferii* gate by means of a force of armoured men, and they appointed Count Raymond guardian and master of the engine.

---

63 The engine is described in the *ChA* (p. 182).

41. A fierce battle at the bridge, where the Christians' engine is reduced to ashes and other siege weapons are set up

When they saw this structure the Turks hurried to the ramparts and struck the Gauls with arrows and by firing ballistas as they struggled on the bridge, so that they could keep the men off the bridge and the engine by thus striking them. Similarly from the other side the Christians were fighting back with arrows and crossbows, attacking the enemy on the ramparts vigorously, till they pierced the son of a certain amir with an arrow through the liver. The Turks, angry at his death and at the Christians' resistance, raged more furiously, and at last, when they had gathered their forces together, they suddenly opened the gate and sallied forth. Once out they vigorously leapt upon the siege engine and at once pursued and overcame the guards. They boldly hurled into the machine fire and torches of pitch, and warm sulphur, reducing the whole thing to ashes.[64] The guards of the machine, fearing for their lives, were forced to come out, although unwilling, and they only just managed to protect themselves and escape in headlong flight. The soldiers and princes of the pilgrims, moreover, seeing they were getting nowhere, on the next day set the equipment of three ballistas before the bridge, which would shatter and wear away the *Waiferii* gate and its tower and its ramparts with repeated bombardment and attacks with rocks, and would weaken the outer walls, which stood before the walls and which the Franks call barbicans,[65] into very many pieces. But they were not able to break down the gate in this way. Since nothing was of any use, one day they decided on a plan together and, using the strength and effort of a thousand armoured men, they rolled across the bridge to the gate some enormous oak trees, scarcely movable, and boulders of extraordinary weight and size as an obstacle to the Turks who wanted to come out and do them harm.

42. Concerning the bridge of boats built by the faithful to avoid the Turks' ambushes

Very many injuries and attacks had assailed the army of Christians from both these bridges, but now, the *Waiferii* gate and bridge being filled and blocked by the strength of timber and by enormous rocks, ambushes were set more often to destroy the faithful from that bridge which was in another part of the town across the river Farfar (we have described its position) by which there was a way out for the Turks and which remained unbesieged because of the size of the town. The Christians, therefore, decided to construct a bridge out of boats with rope ties, by means of which they would have free access to the port of St Symeon the hermit.

---

[64] The attack on the siege engine is recounted in vivid detail in *ChA*, including the use of Greek fire (p. 183). After this episode the two narratives diverge.

[65] Ducange, s.v. 'barbacana', gives 1163 as first usage; he lists AA as first to use 'barbicana'. He further suggests an Arabic origin for the word. Cf. RC, p. 72.

For previously they had crossed over from one bank to the other one by one and slowly on a sluggish boat, watching anxiously. Now, this boat bridge was built for this reason, so that when the Turks had set out across the stone bridge over the Farfar to ambush Christians, the Gauls would run hastily across this wooden bridge and help their men who were bringing food supplies from the seaport and would drive back the Turks without delay. The distance from the stone bridge over the Farfar to the bridge of boats equipped with ropes and a wicker framework was half a mile.

43. The way the Turks secretly attacked the Christians sent out to get fodder for the horses

Now, when they had finished making the bridge by bringing and joining together boats, three hundred Christians, both knights and foot soldiers, crossed the river Farfar one day to look for fodder for the horses and for vital supplies. The Turks, realizing this, and watching from the ramparts, hastily assembled allies, took weapons and quivers, and mounted their horses to sally forth likewise across the stone bridge of the city, and they appeared unexpectedly behind the Christians sent out to forage. They left very many of the Christians' bodies thrown to the ground with their heads cut off; they pursued others, who had the opportunity to flee, all the way to the new bridge. Lucky men, who were able to escape so cruel an enemy. Others, who were making for the fords because the new bridge was denied to them on account of the great number of people fleeing, were suffocated when the current swept them away to die as they fled before the Turks.

44. The faithful rise up to avenge their comrades, and after mutual slaughter some are put to the sword, some drowned in the river

When news of this great disaster reached the army chiefs nearly five thousand armed, as many put on hauberks, and they swept out of the tents on horseback to force back the audacious enemy. Henry, son of Fredelo of the castle of Esch, keen to pursue the enemy, as he was very famous in warfare and deeds, swam across the river on horseback although he was weighed down by hauberk and helmet and shield, for he could not wait to cross the ship bridge because of the long delay. The very deep waters closed over his head as he recklessly entered the waves with his horse. Nevertheless, with God protecting him, whose favour placed life before danger, he reached dry land alive and unhurt and still sitting on his horse, along with the others who swam across, and, continuing tenaciously in the pursuit of the Turks, he was undaunted as he urged his comrades, cavalry and infantry, to chase them right to that very town bridge. And so some of the Turks were held back, others escaped with difficulty, and they summoned to their aid with a loud noise of shouting their allied forces who were gathered at the Farfar bridge and on the gate. And in the rush and noise of the relieving troops they were giving their horses their heads, and they turned into a serious rout the Gauls who had up till then been pursuing them, driving them back to the very bridge they had made of ships. Very many infantry died, shot by Turkish arrows in this severe harrying and driving into the water by the Turks, and the swift flight and retreat of the Christians to the bridge. Many at the rear, seeing that death was imminent and putting their only hope of escape in the water, were carried into the waves of the deep river. Not a few of them were seen to be submerged by the water and to risk drowning and death. Others, with their very horses and shields and hauberks, were falling from the bridge because of the pressure from those fleeing, and they sank under the waters and died, and were never seen again.

45. Guardianship of the gate is assigned to Tancred for an agreed sum of money

With the Turks making these frequent sorties to harm the Christians from the gate and this bridge, and from the gate through which the city was afterwards betrayed, which was placed to provide an exit up into the mountains, the princes of the army took counsel and decided that Tancred should keep watch there in a specially positioned garrison post, and force back any Turks who dared to come out from either gate. And for this watch duty he would receive from the army every month the agreed sum of forty marks in silver. One day while he was keeping watch across the river Farfar at the post in the mountains next to the Turks' sacred sites, that is to say in the place where the river channel was almost half a mile from the city, he attacked the Turks in strength while they were crossing in their accustomed way, and joined battle with them, in which he eventually prevailed, killing four of the Turks with the sword and sending the rest fleeing back across the river to the place where their herds were grazing. When these had been put to flight across the river he carried off booty from the herds, along with one camel, and returned in triumph to the new garrison post which he had established.

46. About the clerk and the woman who were sneakily killed while playing dice

With Tancred keeping watch on these two gates, the one towards the mountains and the other towards the stone bridge, and the Christian army quiet and somewhat unconcerned with warlike things, and with some of the comrades meanwhile taking to dicing because of the leisure, it happened one day that the son of Count Conrad of Luxembourg, named Adelbero, a clerk and archdeacon of the church at Metz, a very high-born young man of royal blood and related to Henry III, emperor of the Romans, was also taking his recreation and occupied playing dice with a certain woman of great birth and beauty in a pleasure garden full of apple trees, but also as dense as a forest with an abundance of plants, which was next to the position and that same city gate which Duke Godfrey and the Germanic company were blockading. While these two, as I have said, were intent on resting and playing dice, the Turks sneaked out of the gate with the idea of ambushing and killing Christians, and, hiding themselves carefully among the tall and towering plants and the density of trees, they attacked with a sudden shout the archdeacon and the woman playing with him, catching them unaware and by surprise; they shot them with arrows and scattered and wounded the comrades who were there as judges of the game, and who now forgot about dice games in their fear. The Turks cut off the archdeacon's head, and having done this they suddenly and instantaneously retreated, taking the head with them. They seized the woman alive and unhurt by force of arms and dragged her into the city, where they tormented her all night with the unchaste intercourse of their excessive lust, showing no kindness towards her. At last they led the woman they had abused with this very abominable and most wicked coition to the ramparts and they put her to death. Then they put her head in their mangonels together with the archdeacon's and they hurled them far from the walls into the middle of the plains. And so the heads of both were found and taken to Duke Godfrey and shown to him. He recognized the archdeacon's and ordered the grave to be opened where his body had already been buried, and the head to be restored to its proper place, so that the parts of such a noble man should not remain unburied.

47. About the knight brought down by his own carelessness; and about the orchard cut down because it is injurious to the faithful

Then another day the Turks, pleased with the success of their deception and thinking to carry out a similar one against the Christians, came out of the gate and secretly approached among the thickness of the rushes and the slender reeds of the marsh. They rose up against some pilgrims in the aforementioned orchard with their usual fierceness and noise. But soldiers came from all sides to aid the pilgrims and the Turks were forced back and put to flight. No one was hit by them then, or wounded, except Arnulf of castle Tirs, who was a knight always spoiling for a fight and usually careful, though now he was careless and rushed into the orchard when he heard the pilgrims' shouting without the protection of his shield or putting on his sword. There he was mortally wounded by the blind and randomly shot arrow of some Turk, and he died. The duke, therefore, and his tent mates took it ill that the Turks were setting ambushes for Christians from this orchard and that such eminent men had died there by trickery, and they ordered that Christians should come from the army with axes and hatchets and root it out, cut down plants, rushes, and reeds so that no deceitful band would any longer be able to hide there or do harm. Some Turks, seeing that Jesus Christ's people were taking precautions against their tricks in this part and from this gate, came out again across the Farfar bridge intent upon the destruction of the pilgrims crossing on the ship bridge, who were collecting brushwood and searching out plants and fodder for the horses, and they pursued instantly and killed with swords and arrows anyone they spotted from the mountain lookout who was wandering here and there for necessary supplies.

48. About Count Hugh who, lamenting the slaughter of the faithful, valiantly deals with the trickery of the Turks

So, while these massacres, ambushes, and attacks took place morning, noon, and night and on every single day, and a daily lament over those killed might be heard in the camp, and Tancred was unable to attack the enemy so often because of different ideas about enemy trickery and because they would often sally forth across the bridge when he was unaware, Hugh of Saint-Pol in the kingdom of France was moved to pity by this daily slaughter of the faithful who were serving him and the other nobles and bringing in necessary supplies. For this reason he made the fatherly suggestion to his son Engelrand,[66] a recruit who was swift to arms, and to the rest of his household, that, fired with him to a single purpose, they would deliver and revenge their poor and brother Christians from so many Turkish massacres and attacks, and frighten away the enemies who were so often pursuing them. When these things had been done and volunteers had been found, the aged father himself was the first to call for weapons and horse and to mount, and, crossing over the ship bridge in the darkness of night, he concealed himself in a hiding place in a valley next to the mountains with his beloved son and the companions he had taken with him. When morning came he left a Christian foot soldier on the level plain where he would be clearly visible to the Turks. The Turks, therefore, with their own cruelty and Christian slaughter in mind, set out again from the city across the bridge over the river Orontes or Farfar and halted on the mountain top, as was their custom, from where there was a long lookout for almost two miles from one mountain range to another across the level plains. There they observed the lone pilgrim going to and fro collecting brushwood and they charged their horses at speed to kill him, they frightened him with a sudden shout, then in the course of chasing the fugitive all the way to the mountains and scrubland they passed close by the ambush of the hiding Christians. The pilgrim had already taken cover in the mountains, so these four Turks took the road back near the Christians' ambush, hoping confidently to return. But immediately the count and his men rose out of the valley and rode at them at speed, leaving two destroyed in a single moment, whose horses and armour they took away, and taking the other two alive, whom they brought back in fetters to the army. The pilgrims ran from all sides, nobles and lesser men, to see the Turkish prisoners, giving glory to God for this favourable outcome. And they heaped praises on Count Hugh and his son Engelrand, by whose wisdom and manly courage such criminal opponents had been captured and destroyed.

---

[66] Engelrand's role at Antioch is greatly enhanced in *ChA* (p. 169 and *passim*).

49. Where the son of that same count puts an end to the fiercest of the Turks and, after considerable risk to his life, returns victor

The Turkish leaders and all their horde heard about the destruction of their men and their anger was sharpened by grief. They took counsel as to who would shortly avenge their fellows and pay the Christians back with crueller losses. So one day twenty who were more bold and fierce in spirit were chosen out of their thousands to challenge the Christians, and they were sent ahead to the ship bridge on horses whose speed was like the wind. They rehearsed with many runs to and fro on the shore next to the bridge, and shot arrows, then they tried to mobilize the whole army in pursuit so that the forces of their Turkish allies, rushing out suddenly from the city, could inflict martyrdom on some of them as they were accustomed to do. But Christ's faithful had sufficient and frequent enough experience of their stratagems and they restrained the people from rash pursuit. But so that none could claim the Christians were beaten by war-weariness, they sent out Engelrand, son of the aforesaid Hugh, to meet the Turks with some comrades. They also in their own style would turn their horses to and fro, trying to trick the cunning enemy into a pitched battle. At once they crossed the bridge and spurred their horses to races to and fro among themselves, and some took turns to aim lances to strike, some shot arrows to pierce. At the very last, after much strife and charging to and fro, with God's help the honour and praise of victory were bestowed upon Engelrand. For he overcame a Turk who was more remarkable and fiercer in the charge than the rest; he cast him down from his horse and pierced him with his lance, all in full view of his father and of all who had gathered to see the outcome of the affair and were standing on the other bank. Then with his Christian comrades he eagerly pursued the rest, who were stunned by their companion's fate and misfortune and were soon put to flight, but the Christians did not go far from the bridge on account of the raids which frequently took place from the city and deterred pursuers. When the son came back safe from this, and his other comrades, the heart of his aged father was raised to very great happiness, and the glorious youth was lifted on high by the favour and acclamation of all, great and small, along with his assistants and co-victors.

50. Since victuals are lacking, princes chosen for this purpose are bringing back countless quantities of plunder from the lands all around

A period of some time was spent in these sports of ever-present Mars and in very frequent attacks, then the people of God began to run short of supplies and rations because of a shortage in the cities and regions which such a great army had exhausted all around. So, with hunger growing daily more severe, and the army dying from want, and especially the humble people, wretched groans and laments assailed the most pious bishop and all the princes of the great army, and they were distressed, so they conferred about these problems and how the people could be nourished. Yet no way was found by which the people could be helped, and it seemed to all that they should send Bohemond, Tancred,[67] and Robert of Flanders with a company of cavalry and infantry into the very wealthy land of the Saracens, which was as yet untouched by looting, to seize plunder and supplies by which hunger could be assuaged and the people relieved from want. Tancred had then already returned to the army from carrying out guard duty in the mountains. Bohemond and Robert, and that same Tancred, in accordance with a decree made at the beginning of the expedition, that no one great or small was to oppose whatever the army commanded, took fifteen thousand infantry and two thousand selected armed cavalry and entered the gentiles' lands for a period of three days. They seized incredible quantities of plunder, of herds and every sort of livestock, which they carried off without hindrance over two days. But when the evening of the third day arrived they were tired by the travelling and weighed down by the burden of booty and the whole fellowship decided to rest on the level plain next to the mountains.

51. Where the plunder is seized by the infidels

Meanwhile the rumour and noise from all the regions round about wasted no time in reaching the gentile chiefs' ears and it brought out so many thousands from different parts and mountain posts to pursue Bohemond, Robert, and their people and to take away the plunder that it is amazing to say and hear. Since Bohemond knew nothing of this and foresaw no difficulty, but was sleeping soundly, as was Robert, when at first light on this day the thousands of enemy were at hand and they saw that they and their men were surrounded by them, they were amazed that they had increased on all sides like a very thick forest. When they saw them the Christian leaders were stupefied and despaired of their lives, so they assembled the cavalry at their side, declaring openly that they could not join battle and withstand the strength of so many thousands. Accordingly, they made a shield roof and a massed front rank of knights and they reconnoitred possibilities of access and flight, but these made their assembly seem even thinner and weaker. Soon they drew their swords, gave their horses their heads and charged together, they penetrated the opposing battle line and, intent only on flight, they made swiftly for the mountains, leaving the infantry deserted with all the plunder and spoils they had collected. Once these soldiers had taken themselves off through the steep mountain slopes and out-of-the-way places, yet leaving very many of their followers captured and destroyed, the gentile battle lines swept down on the wretched and fleeing infantry and did not hesitate to cut them down with swords and arrows. Some, however,

[67] According to *GF* Bohemond and Robert were the two leaders of this expedition – not Tancred – and they set out on 28 Dec. 1097 with a force of over 20,000 cavalry and infantry (p. 30). Although AA appears make a point of Tancred's participation, his role in events is not described.

they captured; they robbed them of their weapons and took back the plunder and everything which had been stolen from them and their people.

52. About Count Robert's plunder, and, as the famine grew, what the lesser people did or what they suffered

Bohemond was troubled by this wretched loss, and he returned to the army and his brother soldiers humbly, his face tear-stained. The people lamented violently: women, youths, boys, fathers, mothers, brothers, and sisters, who had lost their very beloved friends, sons, and relatives. Robert of Flanders had also gone down into Saracen territory with that same Bohemond to plunder, and now that Bohemond had been defeated with his forces and put to flight, and he had been separated from him and had returned, albeit unwillingly, he reassembled two hundred cavalry on the following day and rode against the Turks and Saracens who were scattered and marching carelessly. He fought with them vigorously, put them to flight, and won a glorious victory, and he returned to the camp at Antioch with enormous supplies of plunder which the fleeing Turks had left behind there, bringing much comfort to the people, whom Bohemond's disaster had made desperate. A short time after this, since Robert's loot had been consumed in a few days, and no one dared any longer to seek plunder far from the army because of the cruel slaying of Bohemond's companions, the famine among the people began to grow more widespread and severe, and a very great mortality happened to the humble people, and the army began to be weakened. No wonder. For a single little loaf which previously could be purchased for a penny of Luccan money was now sold to the poor for two shillings. An ox was sold for two marks, which a short time before could be obtained for ten shillings; a little lamb cost five shillings.[68] So, with this very serious scarcity afflicting the people of the living God, many wandered to and fro, taking themselves away into all the region of Antioch to look for food, three hundred or two hundred acting together for defence against Turkish attacks, and for the fair division of all the things they managed to find or to capture. When the Turks heard and understood the people's anguish and the misery caused by famine, and Bohemond's recent disastrous defeat, and the army's energetic pillaging, they sallied forth from the gate into the surrounding countryside from that part of the city which jutted out into the mountains and was not besieged, a very great distance from the gate which Bohemond was watching, and they went down through the sheer rocks, pursuing Christ's faithful who were scattered all around and destroying them with a horrific slaughter.

---

[68] The anonymous author of *GF* also refers to the terrible famine and high prices. He describes native Christians profiteering by selling an ass's load of provisions for 120 shillings (p. 33).

53. The hideous death of a certain archdeacon and his companions

One day, as the famine grew and became more pressing on many, both noble and lesser men, a certain archdeacon of the church at Toul, called Louis, was forced by the disappearance of his pay and brought low by the sword of hunger, along with three hundred other clerics and laypeople also compelled by want, to leave the army for a region which was rumoured to be rich in food supplies, situated next to the mountains of Antioch at a distance of three miles, where they believed they would be safe to plunder and stay. However, the Turks discovered their departure through spies who lived constantly among the army in false friendship, and some six hundred cavalry set out secretly in pursuit of the armed pilgrims from that same part of the city mentioned above, along paths known to them, to the place to which they had decided to go in the hope of replenishing their food supplies. They fell upon them with fierce cries, shooting arrows through head and side and bowels, tearing all of them to pieces as wolves do sheep, and scattering them in flight. The archdeacon tried in vain to escape to the mountains, but a Turk rode quickly after him and pierced him with a swift arrow. And he took out his sword and from both sides of his neck he cut his shoulderblades, wounding him very severely, and so, with a stream of blood spilling onto the ground, he gave up the ghost. When the army leaders heard this cruel news they were overcome by a feeling of grief, angry that the Turks had inflicted so many massacres day after day by way of the gate which was not blockaded, and now mourning the more because of the killing of so eminent an archdeacon and because repeated lamentations were to be heard for the loss of their friends.

54. Concerning the death of the Danish king's son and of Florina, a certain woman; and of those who were killed while bathing

While these many disasters were still fresh, a wicked rumour reached the ears of all the sacred army that after the conquest and capture of Nicaea the son of the king of Denmark, called Svend, high-born and very handsome, had been detained for some days and graciously received and honoured by the emperor of Constantinople, after which he continued his journey through the middle of Rūm confidently, having heard of the Christians' victory, bringing with him fifteen hundred warlike comrades to assist at the siege of Antioch. But Suleyman had given the Gauls the slip after his defeat and taken refuge in the mountains between Philomelium and Ferna, cities of Rūm, and as the prince was lying down in the middle of a very dense thicket of rushes and reeds he was killed by a hail of arrows, and all his company was destroyed by the wicked killers in that same martyrdom. It is no wonder that they were all overcome by the Turkish forces and died. For their presence was betrayed by certain wicked Christians, that is to say Greeks, and they were surrounded unawares by Suleyman's band, which had come together from the mountains. Nevertheless, the king's son Svend resisted with great strength of arms, scattering many of the Turks with his sword, and his men did so too. But in the end they were weary and stripped of their weapons, and they could not withstand the unspeakable multitude of enemies, and all alike were shot with arrows and killed. In that same place a certain woman called Florina, daughter of the duke of Burgundy, who used to be married to a prince of Philippi but was now unfortunately widowed, was in that same company of Danes, hoping she would be joined in marriage to that same great nobleman after the triumph of the faithful. But the savagery of the Turks cut off this hope. For they shot her with six arrows as she rode on her mule, fleeing towards the mountains. Although she was hit she did not fall off her mule; she still thought she could escape death until at last she was overtaken in her flight and put to death with the king's son. The Turks, therefore, Suleyman's soldiers, rejoicing at their victorious outcome and the immense slaughter of Christians, rode swiftly to a lake of warm springs which steamed there next to Philomelium. They found needy and fever-stricken pilgrims bathing in the waters to cure their weak bodies, and they pierced them through with arrows, turning all the water bloody. And they forced others, who hid their heads beneath the water to avoid the blows they struck, to suffocate in cruel death by drowning.

55. While the gate is bringing death to Christians, Count Raymond somewhat restrains the infidels from attacking the faithful

The army leaders were troubled by these frequent Turkish raids and the constant sorties from the unguarded gate and the wretched fates which befell their fellows, and their anger grew sharper, and they resolved to block the aforementioned gate, which they had not been able to besiege because of the difficulty of the mountains and the unevenness of the rocks, with this obstacle, that is to say, they would position a fortification on the ridge of a certain standing rock at the foot of the mountains, well fortified with a rampart and pile of stones. For there was a shortage of timber there. In this fortification, accordingly, each of the leaders kept watch for an agreed time, and the Turks' going out from the gate through the mountains and known paths of the valleys was observed from the lookout on the rock and from the fortification, and as they were going down across the plains of the region they could be suddenly pursued and prevented from slaughtering Christians. Then, when this same fortification had been made and it was Count Raymond's turn to stand guard in it, one day, after secretly setting ambushes of their soldiers, about two hundred armed and armoured Turkish cavalry sallied forth at first light of dawn; leaving from their usual gate and riding down the mountain sides they made purposefully for the fortification in a sudden assault, attacking the garrison within, and they endeavoured to pull down the piled up stones of the walls, because they had opposed their sorties and raids. At length, as they laboured in vain around the new fortification, Count Raymond's raiding party charged on swift horses, hurrying to the relief of their comrades who were in the garrison. And they overpowered with a violent attack the Turks who were already anxious about the full daylight and making haste to ride back up to the gate. They captured only one young man, born of noble family; the rest escaped. And with this one young man captive, and the rest fled, Count Raymond's soldiers returned to the army in the camp in happiness and victory. The Turks went back to their fellows in sadness, and for a few days they were quiet, from that day on, not daring rashly to pursue Christians as they roamed around.

56. To ransom a certain captured youth, his parents wanted to hand over their tower to the Christians, but they were expelled and their son was killed by the Christians

On the following day the Christian princes, realizing this same young man was born of the Turkish nobility and he might affect the hearts of his people with very great grief, presented him to his blood relations who had been stationed in one of the high towers by King Yaghi-Siyan for defence, to see if they would be moved by pity and would surrender the citadel they commanded to ransom him, and would secretly let the Christians in. His kinsmen entirely refused to hand over the tower, but offered a great deal of money for the youth's ransom and life; however, the Christians refused to consider anything except the city and the citadel, because they knew he was of high parentage. The hearts of his relatives began to soften, and secret talks were held between them and the Christians, until the affair became common knowledge and reached the ears of Sansadonias, King Yaghi-Siyan's son, that peace might be made between his relations and the Christians for the ransoming of the captured youth, through which, unless they were careful, the city could be betrayed and soon lost. Therefore King Yaghi-Siyan and his son Sansadonias, when they perceived plainly at last what was going on, took counsel with their chiefs and ordered all the relatives of the captured youth, and his brothers, and all his household to be expelled from that same tower which they commanded, so that the city would not be betrayed by admitting Christians through that tower as ransom for their kin. Once these people had been expelled and their plans revealed, the Christians had no longer any hope of the tower's being surrendered, because everything had been done too openly, so they put the youth to death by beheading, dragging him before the city walls in full view of all the Turks: by this time he was wretched and scarcely breathing on account of torture, since for not much less than a month constant baiting and different torments had been inflicted on him. In particular he was executed following the accusation of Greek Christians, who reported that this man had killed over a thousand Christians with his own hands.

57. The decision of God's people and the public shaming of two who were taken in adultery

When these things were done, and the persecution of the Christians arising from the new fortification and the youth's execution had been somewhat curbed, the Christian princes gave consideration to the sufferings of their men and of Bohemond and the weakened fellowship, and reflected upon the affliction of famine and the devastating mortality among the people, and they claimed these things arose from the great number of sins. For this reason a conference was held with the bishops and all the clergy who were there, and they declared that all injustice and wickedness was to be cut out from the army, meaning that no one was to cheat a Christian brother in weight or measure, nor in changing gold or silver, nor in purchase of anything, nor in business; no one was to commit theft; no one was to take part in fornication or adultery. Anyone who disobeyed this order would be subject to the most severe penalties if caught, and thus God's people would be sanctified from filth and impurity. When, indeed, many of the pilgrims disobeyed the decree they were severely sentenced by the appointed judges: some were put in chains, others flogged, others shaved and branded for the correction and improvement of the whole army. In that place a man and woman were caught in the act of adultery and they were stripped in the presence of all, and their hands were tied behind their backs and they were severely whipped with rods by floggers, and were forced to go around the whole army so that their savage wounds would be seen and would deter the rest from so very wicked a crime.

58. Duke Godfrey, now recovered in health, and Count Raymond are allocated different regions and sent out to take quantities of plunder

This justice among God's people was enforced by the will of the leaders, so that God's anger might be assuaged. Duke Godfrey was now recovered from the illness caused by his wound and the army sent him into Saracen and Turkish territory to seek out again the plunder and spoils which Bohemond had abandoned when he was defeated and fled, so that he might carry back to the famished and weakened people joy from ill fortune. With God's approval this was done. But he did not bring back much plunder. For since that time when Bohemond had entered their land and carried off booty, the Saracens and gentiles had prudently hidden their herds with all their possessions and money throughout the mountains and inaccessible places. In the same way Raymond and the other princes were sent out on the army's orders. But they collected few spoils because the Saracens had dispersed with their possessions, herds, and flocks throughout the mountains and distant region.

59. The embassy of the Egyptian king to God's people; and how Winemer both captured Latakia by his energy and lost it by his stupidity

When this long siege had gone on for some time, and the people had undergone very heavy punishment in terms of the burden of keeping watch, of famine and disease and frequent Turkish attacks, the king amir of Egypt,[69] because there had been very severe discord and hatred between him and the Turks long before this expedition of the Christians, and knowing the Christians' intentions by means of a certain abbot sent as emissary, sent fifteen envoys who were skilled in different languages to the army of the living God, about a mutual alliance for peace and his kingdom, bearing this message: 'The marvellous king of Egypt, who rejoiced at your arrival and that you have done well so far, sends greetings to the great and small princes of the Christians. The Turks are a race foreign to me and dangerous to my kingdom; they have frequently invaded our lands and held on to Jerusalem, a city which is subject to us. But now with our forces we have recovered this city before your arrival, we have thrown out the Turks, we have struck a treaty and a friendship with you, we shall restore the holy city and the Tower of David and Mount Sion to the Christian people, and we shall have discussions about acknowledging the Christian faith. If, when we have discussed it, it pleases us, then we are prepared to embrace it. If, however, we should persist in the law and the ritual of the gentile faith, yet the treaty which we have between us shall not be broken. We entreat and we warn you not to withdraw from this city of Antioch until that which was unjustly stolen is restored to the emperor of the Greeks and to the Christians.'[70] Winemer, who had withdrawn to the coast from Baldwin and Tancred at Mamistra, sailed again for Latakia with all the military equipment of the navy. He laid siege to the walled town by sea and overcame it by his forces and captured it, not offering or granting any help or consideration to his Christian brothers who were besieging Antioch from all the things he had gained. Then, while he possessed captured Latakia in safety, and his fellow soldiers and co-pirates enjoyed some leisure, and they delighted in the benefits of the territory and town, they were intentionally struck down and overwhelmed by the Turcopoles and soldiers of the Greek king; the town's citadel was recaptured, Winemer himself

[69] AA always uses 'Babylonia' to refer to the Fāṭimid dynasty ruling in Cairo. The effective ruler was al-Afḍal, vizier 1094–1121.

[70] There is no doubt that the Egyptians, who maintained good relations with the Byzantines and were implacably opposed to the Turks, suggested an alliance to the Franks, but AA's report of the message is invented. In particular, the Egyptians had not yet recaptured Jerusalem from the Turks: this is clear from the other Latin sources and also from Ibn al-Athir [IA]: *al-Kāmil fī'l-ta'rīkh*, trans. D. S. Richards, vol. 1: 1097–1146 (Aldershot: Ashgate, 2006), p. 21. AA's invented speech may be compared with RM's (equally fictitious) one (pp. 136–7).

was taken and put under guard in prison, while Godfrey and the other princes at Antioch as yet knew nothing about it.[71]

60. A plan for besieged Antioch is put to the Christians. The bishop of Le Puy and Duke Godfrey encourage God's people with comforting words

Meanwhile the Turks who were besieged in the city of Antioch were not slow to seek assistance and to warn their friends, and they brought together from the mountains and adjoining regions great and numerous forces of Turks, of whom in a little while thirty thousand were gathered together. For the besieged had arranged in their intention and resolution that at first light an attack on the holy army of God would be made by these external forces, then those within the city would set on to strengthen and increase the attack, to harass the Christians with weapons and a hail of arrows, until they were all fatally wounded and put to the sword's edge. Information about the wicked plans and criminal conspiracy arrived in the camp of those Catholic men, Duke Godfrey and the bishop of Le Puy and the other leaders, among whom there were no more than a thousand fit horses, on account of the shortage of corn and the long-term weariness and other harm. Now the bishop put forward his ideas for this anxiety and distress, in this manner: 'Most Christian men, and you who are the chosen flower of Gaul, I do not know what it may be useful to suggest as a plan now, except that you have hope in Jesus' name and attack the enemy unexpectedly. Ever so many gentiles have come together from all sides in so many thousands and are close by, as you have heard. They are not weighed down by labours, nor have they left on a long journey from their own land and become tired; they have set out for the town of Harim, yet it is not difficult for so many thousands to be confined in God's hand and destroyed by your few forces.' To these words of the bishop Duke Godfrey, always unflagging in the service of war, replied thus in the hearing and presence of the army which had secretly been called together: 'We are followers of the living God and Lord Jesus Christ, for whose name we serve as soldiers. These men are gathered in their own strength: we are gathered in the name of God.[72] Let us trust in his favour and not hesitate to attack the wicked and unbelieving foe, because whether we live or die

[71] Latakia's history during this time remains obscure. David set out as clearly as possible the contradictions within and between the sources (C. W. David, *Robert Curthose, Duke of Normandy* (Cambridge, MA, 1920), pp. 230–44). RA was in a position to be well informed, and according to his account an English force held Latakia throughout the siege of Antioch and did send help to the crusaders (p. 108). This agrees more closely with AA's second version of events (see below, 5. 24, 6. 55), and to some extent with AK who reports that Alexios instructed Raymond of Toulouse to hand over Latakia in 1101 or 1102 (p. 317). See also R.-J. Lilie, *Byzantium and the Crusader States, 1096–1204* (Oxford, 1993) Appendix 1, pp. 259–76.

[72] Cf. Ps. 19 (20): 8.

we are the Lord's.[73] For as we love safety and life, so this word of yours should not be proclaimed, lest the enemy, being careful and forewarned about our approach and attack, will be less frightened and not greatly afraid to join battle with us.'

61. Knights are chosen to attack the enemy camp, and they are not afraid of the great host that is on its way

With the duke warning and encouraging in this way, seven hundred cavalry, good fighting men, were chosen, from whom, however, the affair was utterly hidden other than some leaders of the army. Very many of them lacked horses, on account of different misfortunes as we have said, and very few horses were fit. So some were riding packhorses, others mules or donkeys, just as necessity drove, when they moved off in the silence of the dead of night, crossing over the ship bridge, with the Turks who stayed in the fortress of Antioch to defend it unaware of these developments. Bohemond, Tancred, Robert of Flanders, Robert of Normandy, together with Duke Godfrey, all met in the appointed place. Roger of Barneville had also been called up and was there: he was very active against Turkish raids and frequently brought about defeats, and he had gained such renown among those same Turks as a remarkable and famous soldier that he was frequently employed between the Christians and them as mediator in any settlement of prisoners on both sides, or negotiation of any matter. Likewise the bishop himself followed as their comrade and as a reminder of all holy things to strengthen the men. These men completed the journey during the night and were approaching the Turkish camp. A certain Bohemond – a Turk who had perceived the truth which is Christ[74] and received the grace of baptism, and, since he had recently been raised from the holy spring by Bohemond the prince, was called by his name – and Walter of Domedart were sent ahead, creeping up very cautiously, so that in the very first light of day they observed the infinite army coming to relieve the Antiochenes, and how they hastened their journey from the woods and scrubland on all sides. Once these two had looked at the enemy from a distance they prepared their return and rode back to their seven hundred comrades at a gallop, reporting exactly how things stood but taking away all fear with good consolation.

62. The pilgrims, fortified by a sermon from the bishop, are clearly victorious over seven hundred of the enemy and they disgrace them by cutting off their heads

When the eminent bishop heard what Walter and Bohemond had to say he told his comrades, who were wavering a little from fear and anxiety, that they should not

[73] Rom. 14: 8.
[74] 1 John 5: 6.

hesitate to die for love of Him whose footsteps they had followed with the sign of the holy cross, and for whose favour they had left their homeland, kindred, and everything, certain that he who happened to die here today would possess the heavens with Lord God of Hosts. Strengthened now by this blessed advice they declared as one that they would rather die than despicably turn their backs on the enemy. At these words Count Raymond cheerfully brandished his lance and brought his shield up to cover his chest, Duke Godfrey was burning no less with the desire to join battle, and the other seven hundred warlike men galloped unexpectedly through the midst of the enemy and broke their lines, throwing their great multitude into confusion, and by God's gift they received the palm as victors, while the Turks were destroyed and put to flight. By God's help and mercy also, the strings of their bows were unusable because they were wet and weak from the rain, which was a great problem to the Turks and an increase in triumph to the faithful. Therefore, when the Christians saw they had prevailed as victors and few of their number had fallen, they dismounted and cut off the heads of those killed, tied them to their saddles and carried them back in great happiness to their many comrades who were awaiting the outcome in the camp around Antioch, along with a thousand fit horses and many spoils they took from the defeated enemy. The king of Egypt's envoys were in that same battle and they also took back to the army on their saddles the cut-off heads of Turks. This victory happened to the Christians in a band of few on the day before Ash Wednesday.[75] While these faithful were returning in great glory to their people and to the tents they had left on the plains of Antioch, the Turks who were besieged and were waiting for assistance from the destroyed army were standing on the ramparts, and they saw from a distance the victory banners of the faithful, which they believed to be those of the expected army, so they quickly hastened to arms with the sound of shouting and the blast of trumpets and spilled out of the gates in strength, thinking that the entire holy army would be destroyed instantly from inside and outside. But as the Christians drew near and they saw the heads of the Turks, and recognized also their equipment and ponies, they suppressed the noise and sounding of trumpets, stopped rejoicing, and fled back swiftly into the defences. Then to increase the Turks' grief the Christians hurled some Turkish heads over the walls and ramparts; about two hundred others they fixed on lances and stakes and carried them up to the walls in view of all who were standing on them.

63. While Bohemond and his companions are striving to make the bridge impassable for the enemy, some are killed and some are injured, and this is announced to Duke Godfrey with weeping

When the next day came the princes of the faithful, happy from the recent victory, made careful plans to position the defence of a siege engine next to the

[75] The Lake Battle took place on 9 Feb. 1098.

aforementioned town bridge which stretched across the river Farfar, so that when the engine was in place they could take away the way into and out of the city from those going to and fro and bringing in supplies, and setting up raids on the Christians across that same bridge. At length the plan was made and they sent Bohemond prince of Sicily and Everard of Le Puiset, Raymond count of Provence and Warner of Grez, with many infantry, to the seaport which is called Symeon the Hermit's, to buy food and to call on those comrades who were hanging about on the seashore because of the ships which used to bring supplies, for aid in building the siege engine. In that same company they brought down the king of Egypt's envoys, who had been honoured with magnificent gifts, and sent them back safely by ship in good faith. The plan and decampment of so many eminent men was discovered and made plain to the Turks by spies and they rejoiced with great joy.[76] They assembled four thousand picked soldiers and set out from the city across the aforesaid bridge to pursue those army leaders along paths known to them, the army being totally unaware of this, and they set up an ambush in the mountains among the thornbushes and scrub at the point where the princes sent to the seaport would return. As the comrades were returning on horseback and on foot – at Bohemond's urging and that of the other leaders four thousand of them had now gathered – the Turks leapt out suddenly from the ambush and attacked them, unprepared as they were and laden with supplies, piercing them with arrows through chest and stomach, and slaughtering others with the sword. And because victory was properly theirs, they did not hold back their hands from martyring the faithful until they had killed five hundred by cutting off their heads in the woods and on the plains. There were countless wounded and captured. Therefore Bohemond, who was keeping guard at the rear with other splendid men, when he knew about this very cruel slaughter, and since he saw his men half-dead on the mountain-slopes, hiding in dark places, fleeing swiftly here and there, and since he saw he could not be any use at all to the fleeing and the conquered, but was himself about to die, he reined back with his mounted comrades and withdrew, and he made for the maritime road again and retraced his journey with a few men. Soon one of the knights, who had only just escaped by the speed of his horse down the hill slopes and had avoided the weapons, disturbed Duke Godfrey, who was coming across the ship bridge from the army and was in the middle of the plains and who on the bishop's advice had forced the Turks and their herds to return into the city, with the serious news, telling how Bohemond and the other co-leaders were in danger of death, that they were in a tight spot between enemy ambushes, and with what great cruelty the people returning from the port had been destroyed.[77]

---

[76] 1 Chr. 29: 9; Tobias 11: 21; Matt. 2: 10.

[77] This messenger also appears in *ChA* (p. 191).

64. The faithful rise up to avenge their comrades; for some time risky flight is undertaken by both sides

When he heard these things the duke sent criers through all the tents to announce the cruel news, and to prepare everyone for all the things which were now going against them. All the faithful were troubled and afraid and they rushed together from all the tents straight away; they carried their scaly iron garments on their shoulders; they fixed banners on their lances; they swiftly recovered their horses with harness and saddles. They formed their divisions, having swiftly decided to make for the approach to the bridge and city by which they hoped the enemy would return to the protection of the city. These men crossed the ship bridge without any delay and found Duke Godfrey in the middle of the plains across the river, his sad face transformed by grief at the killing of his comrades, and then another messenger arrived who was sent by Bohemond, Raymond, Warner, and the rest, who were making their escape through the mountains and warned the duke on the plain and the other leaders who were with him to return to their tents because of the ambushes and attacks of the Turks, whose strength and number they judged to be more irresistible than they had been before. The duke was unafraid and thirsting for revenge for the destroyed Christians, and he refused absolutely to move from there or to desert this place out of any fear, but he declared with an oath that either he would today ascend the mountain on which the fortress had been built, or he would lose his life with his men on that same mountain. The princes named above, Bohemond, Raymond, and Warner, arrived safely as the duke made this reply and affirmation and disposition of troops. Everyone was happy and cheered that they had arrived and were still alive, and they made for the place on the aforesaid mountain, in front of the city bridge, and sent ahead ten horsemen chosen from the great army to the summit of that mountain in order to see if the Turks had set ambushes in the other valley of the mountain next to the mountainous region. The ten knights sent ahead on horseback had only just reached the steep part of the mountain when they saw the whole army of those Turks, that is to say those who had returned from the recent slaughter of Christians secretly and in a roundabout way through the mountains and paths known to them. They spotted twenty of these riding in front towards them to cut off the ten from the peak. The ten Christians gave way because there were too many Turkish ambushes in that vicinity, and the twenty Turks reached the summit. Thirty fellow Christians came to support them and they attacked the twenty Turks valiantly and forced them to flee from the mountain peak back to the Turkish lines. As the twenty made good their escape to their company, sixty Turkish cavalry burst out from ambush, very strong men and very skilled on horseback, who soon drove away the thirty Christian horsemen with bow and arrow, and held out on the peak. Since they saw the boldness and attack of these men, sixty Christian cavalry likewise attacked the sixty Turks on the mountain; meanwhile the whole Christian army was approaching close at hand and they sent back in swift flight those who had suddenly fled from the mountain into the valley where the Turks' army and strength had been assembled next to the mountainous region. At this point the entire Turkish force rose up together from ambush and began to harry with a very threatening pursuit the sixty Gaulish horsemen who now held their prize of the mountain, and they forced them back all the way across the middle of the mountain peak to that same valley which the approaching Christian army had already occupied.

65. Where the duke divides an armoured Turk through the middle with one blow; and after a bloody battle victory attends the faithful

Some Turks, seeing that they had advanced too far and that the Christian army was holding firm and could not be turned away from their intention by fear, but were hurriedly riding against them, took flight in vain. The Gauls, notwithstanding, pursued them eagerly and were in among them in a moment because they had met one another close at hand, and they inflicted a cruel slaughter on the Turks in revenge for their colleagues killed returning from the port of St Symeon. As the Turks fled and the Christians approached, not falling back before them at all, many troops who had gathered at the gate from the ramparts all around were concerned with the return of the outside Turks, but now they saw their luck changed for the worse, and their wretched overthrow, so they opened the gate and went out armed onto the open plain to increase the strength of their forces and give courage for entering the city. From all sides the cavalry and infantry of the faithful and the infidels were mingled together. Duke Godfrey, whose hand was very schooled in war, is reported to have cut off many heads there even though they were helmeted: this is said by those who were present and saw it with their own eyes. While he was thus exerting himself in the great labour of war and inflicting a great massacre in the midst of the enemy, amazingly he cut an armoured Turk who was threatening him with his bow into two parts with his very sharp sword. The half of the body from the chest upwards fell to the sand, the other half still grasped the horse with its legs and was carried onto the middle of the bridge in front of the city ramparts where it slid off and remained.[78] Rejoicing at this happy outcome, Robert of Flanders, with Robert count of Normandy, Cono of Montaigu and Count

[78] This exploit is to be found in *ChA* (pp. 192–3). F. Reiffenberg (*Le Chevalier au Cygne et Godefroid de Bouillon* [3 vols, Brussels, 1846–54], vol. 3, pp. lxix–lxx) draws attention to a parallel in *Pseudo-Turpin*, referring to Charlemagne: *Historia Karoli Magni et Rotholandi ou Chronique du Pseudo-Turpin*, (ed.) C. Meredith-Jones (Paris, 1936), p. 177; *An Anonymous Old French Translation of the Pseudo-Turpin Chronicle*, (ed.) R. N. Walpole (Cambridge, MA, 1979), p. 71. Roland sliced at least four of the enemy from scalp to saddle, and his feat was emulated by Oliver: *Chanson de Roland*, (ed.) Brault, vol. 2, pp. 82–4 (lines 1326–34), 86 (1371–5), 96 (1543–5), 98–100 (1601–6), 116 (1871). However, it should be noted that Godfrey's cut was lateral, not vertical; also that it is reported in several contemporary histories, so may be more than a poetic conceit: RM p. 133; OV, v. 84; RC p. 79. On the other hand, none of the eyewitnesses recounts it, and RA writes of this skirmish that Godfrey 'hostes … per medium dividebat' (divided the enemy through the middle), a phrase

Raymond, and all the nobility of Gaul which was there, broke through the enemy with a cavalry charge and pierced through many with lance and sword, forcing the dying to fight on the bridge where, because the pressure was more than the bridge could sustain and because its width was not sufficient for so many fleeing people, very many fell from the bridge and were covered by the waters of the Orontes. Bohemond, who had escaped across a ridge of rocks accessible only to mountain goats, by the grace of God had returned safely with his comrades to the army and was exerting himself fiercely in that same bloody work; he advised and strengthened his comrades, he slaughtered with his sword enemies who had been pierced by lance wounds and were slipping off the bridge. Then the infantry, who were rejoicing at this triumph, attacked the Turks with lances as they tumbled down and were pressed together on the edge of the bridge and the banks of the river bed, not holding back from killing until the whole river was changed by the blood of the killed. When these things had turned out well, therefore, and the Christians were reunited and were still pursuing the Turks on the bridge and trying to enter the gate with them, the gate was barricaded quickly by those inside, and they left their wretchedly excluded comrades in the hands of the killers. These struggles and the fresh revenge of the Christians were carried out on one day in March, and the Turkish dead were estimated to be fifteen hundred, counting those who fell in battle and those who perished in the waters.

66. Certain of those besieged in Antioch take refuge secretly with the Christians; and a fortress built next to the bridge is assigned to Raymond

After these savage Turkish forces had been conquered in the name and strength of Lord Jesus Christ, and they had been forced into the city gate by cruel slaughter and flight, and the Christians had gone back into their tents with great glory of victory, from that day onwards the minds of the gentiles began to soften and their attacks which were previously very frequent ceased from then on, their ambushes stopped, their strength decreased, fear beset many of them to such a degree that some of them left the town and their comrades by night and, claiming that they wished to become Christians, they commended themselves to the leaders of the Christians. Once commended and allied to the Christian troops, they reported how many injuries they had endured of their own people, and how many lamentations for their fate had risen up throughout the whole city. Also they claimed that twelve of King Yaghi-Siyan's most powerful amirs had fallen on that evening in the same battle, and that all of Antioch was troubled by mourning and grief for their death. Moreover, when the fourth day after this dawned, the duke and all the princes of God's army sallied forth in great strength from the tents and with a very secure rampart they reinforced the fortification which they had set up on the top of the

which may have been the origin of the tale (*RHC Occ* iii. 249; the Hills' edition erroneously has 'dividebant' [p. 61]).

aforesaid mountain in front of the bridge and gate of the city, building it with a pile of stones and a mortar of weak lime, and placing Count Raymond's garrison in it with five hundred men of military dedication and courage.

Book 4

1. When the prince of Antioch hears of the Christians' victory, he consults his loyal men as to what needs to be done

In this way the enemies of the Christian people were conquered and overwhelmed in the river waters, and the fortification was established in the absence of further resistance. A messenger hurrying from the Turks sped across to the tower and palace of Yaghi-Siyhan, the ruler of Antioch, which is in the mountains;[1] he revealed to him the extent of their losses and suggested that unless Yaghi-Siyhan took diligent and careful precautions he would soon lose Antioch and all its adjoining territories. King Yaghi-Siyhan, an aged man, heard of this fortification being established and of the irreversible destruction of his men: up till that point he had slept soundly in his upper room through all the fighting and outcome of different affairs; now for the first time he was distressed, and with a deep sigh he summoned his son Sansadonias, and all the men of first rank who were his subjects, to his council.

2. A record of Yaghi-Siyhan's messages and who they are whom he is calling upon for assistance

Among those in the presence of this same ruler was Suleyman who had been driven out of Nicaea and the lands of Rūm, and the aforesaid Yaghi-Siyhan addressed him, asking him in all earnestness to become the bearer of his message, knowing him to be a man of eloquence and very renowned in all the kingdoms of the gentiles, saying to him: 'Neighbour of my people, you shall set out for Khurasan in the land and kingdom of our birth with twelve legates from me and my son Sansadonias. Copatrix and Adorsonius, two of the most faithful of my princes, shall go with you on this legation, to make complaint of our injuries. As you travel through, summon Ridwan of the city of Aleppo, our brother and friend, to our assistance.[2] In the same way call on Pulagit, whose soldiers and weapons are plentiful, to bring us aid, because he is allied to us by a permanent treaty.

[1] The city of Antioch enclosed the north-western slopes of Mount Silpius (Habib Neccar). Its walls climbed from the Orontes valley up the slopes and along the ridge. Near the highest point was sited the citadel, from where Yaghi-Siyan overlooked the city. The ground fell away steeply both before and behind the citadel: see below, 4. 24.

[2] Although AA associates Riḍwān with the siege of Antioch, he did not, in fact, come to Yaghi-Siyan's aid.

Moreover, expound our misfortunes and injuries to the royal sultan of Khurasan,[3] who is the chief and prince of the Turks, and suggest that Karbugha[4] the sultan's friend should produce for me auxiliary resources and troops. Let my scribe and secretary be called so that you may carry with you letters and my seal so that they will believe our difficulties more confidently. For very many days have passed since at the beginning of this siege of this city, my son Buldagis[5] preceded you to Khurasan to inform our brothers and princes of the arrival of the Christian people and to warn everyone against them so they would come to our assistance.'

3. The case put forward at the court of the king of Khurasan

When they had heard the king's wish and command and received letters with his seal, they set out from the city and the royal palace and went into the land of Khurasan. So they came to a certain town called Samarthan, which belonged to the kingdom of Khurasan, in very great splendour and extravagance and in great magnificence. There they found in great glory the great prince and sultan himself, ruling over all kings and princes in the eastern region, and Prince Karbugha the king's second-in-command. Suleyman greeted him because he was his elder and greatly renowned for his diligence and eloquence. However, having greeted the king, before he revealed the purpose of the legation, the envoys followed the custom of the Turks when they are lamenting misfortune and injuries, and in full view of that same great and all-powerful king and in the presence of his men they took off their hats and threw them to the ground, they savagely plucked out their beards with their nails, they pulled at their hair and tore it out by the roots with their fingers, and they heaved sighs of great lamentations. When he saw the Turks tearing themselves to pieces in this way the king of Khurasan replied thus, very haughtily: 'Suleyman, our friend and brother, explain what has happened to you and reveal the injuries against you. We shall not countenance the continued existence of anyone who has the temerity to trouble you.' Suleyman rejoiced and trusted in the replies of this very powerful king and in his strength, and he told of the bitterness which lay heavily on his heart, and reported the whole affair in order, and what he could not deliver in his own words he was reminded of by the prompting of the letters: 'We acquired,' he said, 'Nicaea, that city which you know is very famous, and the land which they call Rūm, from the kingdom of the Greeks, and it was granted to us by your assistance and forces and from your gift and favour. Now a people has arrived whom they call Christians from the realm of Francia and they have stolen Nicaea from us with a strong force and a powerful army and have handed it over with my wife and two sons to the emperor

[3] Barkyārūq, Saljūq sultan 1094–1105.

[4] Karbugha was atabeg of Mosul (equates roughly to commander-in-chief).

[5] According to Kemal al-Din,Yaghi-Siyan's second son was called Muḥammad: *RHC Or* iii. 578.

of Constantinople. Moreover, after they had defeated me and put me to flight, they pursued me in strength to the city of Antioch, in which I hoped to stay. There they have laid siege with an armed force not only to me and mine, but also to King Yaghi-Siyhan, most noble man of our people, who is your subject and friend and holds the city and lands by your gift. This same prince and subject of yours, Yaghi-Siyhan, our superior and kin, has sent us to you that you may deign to assist him in what great strength you can. For our need is very pressing and greater than we thought. Our people and army are destroyed; our land and region are overthrown. Our lives and all our possessions are now in your hands, for we have faith in no one else as we do in you.'

4. The manner in which the king himself received the words of the messengers

The king of Khurasan heard the man's words and complaints with laughter and mirth; he listened frivolously, for he confessed that he did not in the least believe that these injuries could have been inflicted on the Turks by people from any region of the world, and in the hearing of his assembly he said he did not think much of Suleyman's strength – hitherto so renowned – and the boldness of his military forces. Suleyman, as someone who had recently experienced the strength of the Christians, did not hear the king's opinion lightheartedly. And so, because he had been unable to make everything clear in his own words, he opened the letters with Yaghi-Siyhan's seal, in which were listed the names of the kingdoms and the names of the princes of all the Christians who were fighting the Turks, and the size of their armies and their strength. The minds of the king of Khurasan and all the other gentile nobility who were with him were overwhelmed when they knew the content of the letters and the possessions and forces of the Gauls; they cast down their gaze to the floor and no longer wondered vainly about Suleyman's complaints. Now the king sent royal messages in a constant stream throughout all the lands of his kingdom, ordering all his nobility and amirs to assemble on a given day which then seemed suitable.[6]

[6] Cf. *ChA* (pp. 220–21). At this point, according to Duparc-Quioc, the lines are by Graindor de Douai, hence AA could not have known them (*Edition*, pp. 254–5, note to lines 4945–75). For the whole vexed question of the relationship between AA's *Historia* and the *Chanson*, see R. F. Cook, *'Chanson d'Antioche', Chanson de Geste: Le Cycle de la Croisade est-il épique?* (Amsterdam, 1980); S. B. Edgington, 'Albert of Aachen and the *chansons de geste*', in J. France and W. G. Zajac (eds), *The Crusades and their Sources: Essays presented to Bernard Hamilton* (Aldershot, 1998), pp. 23–38.

5. Karbugha's insulting speech against the people of God in the presence of those the king has called

When the day arrived they all met according to the king's decision and command, and the king shared with them Suleyman's words and complaints and the injuries inflicted by the Christians, saying: 'All of you who have assembled, think – and you must think of this – unless the Christians who have arrived are checked they will do to us as they have done to the other states and our allies and brothers.' Karbugha, a friend and favourite at the royal court and second to the king in the kingdom of Khurasan, a stubborn man and full of fierce arrogance, did not think much of the Christians' strength and burst out with these words in a spirit of arrogance: 'I wonder at the words and complaints of Suleyman and of Sansadonias and Buldagis, the sons of King Yaghi-Siyhan, over the attack of the Christians by whose siege Suleyman lost his lands and cities, and from whom they could no more easily be defended than if they had been besieged by so many wretched and irrational animals. Once I laid waste a hundred thousand Christians and cut off their heads next to Civitot, where the mountain regions end, after I was summoned to Suleyman's assistance against the emperor of the Greeks and we had scattered and put to flight their army from the siege of the city of Nicaea. After this my satellites who were sent to aid Suleyman destroyed the countless troops of Peter the Hermit, and their corpses and bones could never be cleared from the region's plain.'[7]

6. The prince of conquered Nicaea asserts the courage of the Christian army

Suleyman, who was a man of great and wonderful diligence, listened to his arrogance and boastful words and gave him this reply in an even-tempered way: 'O Karbugha, our brother and friend, why do you thus think so little of us and add that we show too little daring, and that our men conquered and destroyed the emperor of Constantinople and Peter the Hermit's infinite thousands only with your help? The imperial army is made up of soft and effeminate Greeks, who have rarely been troubled by the exercise of wars and could easily be overcome by the strength of hard men and, once overcome, decapitated. Similarly, I have established that Peter the Hermit's troops were in reality a weak and beggarly band, footsoldiers and a useless mob of women all exhausted from the long journey, only five hundred cavalry, whom it was not very difficult for us to destroy with a trifling charge and slaughter. But these men whose names, strength, and warfare, and talents you have learnt from the letters, and against whom it is difficult to wage war – know that they are very courageous men, knowledgeable about the wonderful ways of

[7] In Book 1 AA made Qilij Arslan solely responsible for the attack on Peter's followers. He contradicts himself here, perhaps because of a confused recollection of *ChA* (pp. 112–14): see P. Paris, *Nouvelle étude sur la Chanson d'Antioche* (Paris, 1878), p. 32.

horses,[8] and they cannot be frightened away by fear of death in battle or by any sort of weapons. Their iron garments, their shields studded with gold and jewels and painted with different-coloured flowers, their helmets shining on their heads glitter more than the brilliance of the sun, the ashen spears in their hands are tipped with sharpest iron, like long staffs. Their horses are very experienced in running and warfare, the standards on their spears with their golden knots and silver threads make the mountains round about glitter with their great embellishment of light. Know that their boldness is so great that if a thousand of their knights go into battle they do not hesitate to take on twenty thousand of ours, like lions and wild boars, hurling thunderbolts with the death-dealing blows of their weapons.[9] Moreover, I myself thought very little of their forces and I imagined they would not stand up to me; I assembled my men in strength, but I hoped to wear down the strength of their men in the same way I had destroyed Peter the Hermit's army a short while before. I also hoped to be able to frighten them away from the city of Nicaea by the strength of my forces and set free my wife and my sons, my soldiers and princes, who were within the city walls. Once more I waged war with them, but my labours were in vain and I only just escaped their hands over the mountain ridge, leaving not a few of my men dead. They were not greatly troubled by the slaughter of their comrades and, having destroyed my men, they returned to Nicaea where they reimposed the blockade more strongly and securely than before, until they made my defeated men capitulate, with my wife and my sons, and handed over the city with its keys to the emperor of Constantinople. Besides conquering and subduing towns and castles in Rūm which were subject to my jurisdiction and restoring them to the same emperor, they invaded very many of our castles. None of all the lands and towns and castles which I used to hold is left to me beyond Foloroca, the citadel which is next to the sea and the borders of the kingdom of Russia. Then these Christian soldiers, whom you believe to be weak, conquered and occupied Tarsus, Adana, and Mamistra, towns in Rūm with very many fortifications. The towns and castles of Armenia, Dandronuch, and Haruni and Turbessel, and the mountain stronghold of the Armenian prince Constantine and the region belonging to Pakrad and the land of Duke Kogh Vasil were forced by iron and armed strength to submit. They occupied the state of Edessa, which is very strongly fortified with ramparts and built walls and very famous indeed for its fertility, and one of their princes, Baldwin, the chief and leader of this Christian people, even took a daughter of the prince of the land as his wife and was put forward in the place of the dead duke by the citizens, and he made the whole land and region tributary to him, and thus these same Christians have invaded all places and kingdoms as far as Melitene. Now, having subdued these places to right and left, they are besieging Antioch. These are peoples of amazing industry and experience, they do not look after their bodies[10] with any stopovers or rest, but day after day they seek out their

[8] Cf. Vergil, *Geo.* iii. 192.

[9] Lucr., iii. 486 *et passim* (*HL* vol. 2, p. 372).

[10] Vergil, *Aen.* viii. 607; *Geo.* iv. 187.

enemies and those who oppose them, and when they find them and defeat them they send them to damnation.'

7. Karbugha boasts that he will shortly put the Christian soldiers' bravery to the test

Arrogant Karbugha heard Suleyman's tale, then opened his lips further to pride and boasting, thus: 'If I am lucky enough to live, before six months shall pass I shall put these Christians to the test and find out whether they are as strong as you claim, and I swear by my god that I shall destroy them in such a way that all their posterity shall grieve.'[11]

8. The king of Khurasan consults magicians concerning the outcome of the war; and the princes of the Turks are called by name

However, while these two, Karbugha and Suleyman, were striving against one another in verbal dispute, the king of Khurasan summoned magicians, prophets, and soothsayers[12] of their gods and asked about future victory. They foretold that all things would succeed as the king wished, that he would triumph over the Christians and easily conquer them in war. When Karbugha heard this reply of their priests, which confirmed the purpose of the king's heart and resolution, he sent out a great number of envoys through the whole kingdom of Khurasan and summoned, on the august order of the king, all the high-ranking and noble men hurriedly to prepare weapons and arrows and waggons of supplies for the expedition. He directed smiths who lived all over the region to manufacture fetters and chains, in which the conquered and captured pilgrims would be led off into exile in barbarous lands. The king of Khurasan's legation summoned to the common cause Pulagit, who was one of the most powerful of the Turks and who lived next to the river Euphrates, and Ridwan of Aleppo – a splendid state – who himself also had plenty of protection, to revenge the Turks and the injuries which had been inflicted by the Christians on Suleyman and on Yaghi-Siyhan king of Antioch, friends and kinsmen of the Turks; it explained the matter and announced officially the present exigencies.[13] The same news and legation also

---

[11] Needless to say, this is a fantasy scene. There is a parallel in *ChA* (pp. 223–5), while *GF* has Yaghi-Siyan send an envoy to Karbugha in Khurasan and has an elaborate description of dialogue among the enemy, including advice from Karbugha's mother (*GF* pp. 49–56).

[12] Deut. 2: 27.

[13] The list of oriental chieftains which follows is fabulous, according to C. Cahen, *La Syrie du nord à l'époque des croisades et la principauté Franque d'Antioche* (Paris, 1940), p. 215 n. 35. FC likewise assembled all the names of Turkish leaders he knew (pp. 249–50

alerted and warned the prince of Damascus.[14] He himself had subdued the land of Syria to a large degree, and the fertility of his land and the strength of his cavalry had made him powerful. The king's legation likewise also stirred up Amasa from the region of Niz, situated on one side of Khurasan, the fame of whose bravery and boldness was very widespread, because this man was always standard-bearer in the vanguard in any danger. The spear and arrow of this same Amasa was unequalled by the arrows of any other Turk, and he led them all in shooting with the bow. In any expedition he was equipped with no less than a hundred horses of the fastest pace, so that if one was struck by an arrow, or another died in an unlucky fall, the rest were enough to ensure his constant presence in battle, and he would always be speeding ahead and harrying the enemy. Boesas, from the same group of Turks and not unlike in equipment and weapons, was summoned. Another Amasa, of Curzh, a very large and wealthy land, having many bowmen, was similarly called to attend on the king's orders. Balas of the fortress at Amacha and the town of Sororgia and Balduk of Samosart, cunning Turks and knights well known in weapons and warfare, and Karageth of the town of Karan, very well fortified with walls and ramparts, were called to be present on the same day of the expedition. These men, those who were in the kingdom of Khurasan on the royal summons and those who were scattered in charge of other kingdoms, were called up for this expedition, and from the start of the siege of Antioch and from the day on which the second legation from King Yaghi-Siyhan was made through Suleyman they gave attention to necessary supplies for Khurasan, they armed their soldiers, they came forth eagerly in great numbers and without ceasing, with all the equipment of war.

9. About Baldwin's generosity towards the princes and about the tent he sent to the duke

The army of Christians and all the princes who were involved in the siege and hardship around Antioch knew absolutely nothing about this expedition, but day after day they were hard pressed by the lack not only of food but also of horses and weapons, and this severe poverty caused them more anxiety than all other concerns. While this long-term need grew greater and greater and very many were in despair because of the diminution of necessary supplies, Baldwin, who had subdued the state of Edessa, or Rohas, and had been made duke, sent very many talents of gold and silver to his brother Duke Godfrey, Robert of Flanders,

---

and nn.). According to Hill and Hill, this passage demonstrates that AA had access to a source also used by PT, *GF* and RA, 'a common list of kings and leaders', but this would require AA to have been uncharacteristically selective in his use of the list: Peter Tudebode, *Historia de Hierosolymitano itinere*, trans. J. H. and L. L. Hill (Philadelphia, PA, 1974), pp. 10–11.

[14] Duqāq ibn Tutush was ruler of Damascus.

Robert count of Normandy, Raymond, and the other chief leaders by way of his great favourite Gerard, to make good the lack which he realised the great and noble princes were enduring. He also sent to this same brother and the rest of the princes horses which were remarkable runners and of excellent build, with valuable decoration on saddles and reins. He also sent weapons of wonderful value and ornament. Then after some days Nicusus, the Armenian prince from the region Turbessel, sent a pavilion of wonderful handwork and ornament to Duke Godfrey, in order to acquire favour and friendship. But Pakrad set an ambush, and the pavilion was stolen from Nicusus' young men and sent as Pakrad's gift to Bohemond. When Duke Godfrey and Robert of Flanders, who were allied one to the other as beloved friends and comrades, found out from Nicusus' young men's words that the pavilion had been taken to Bohemond, they suggested in a peaceful way that he should hand over what he had unfairly received. But he flatly refused their suggestion and request. The angry princes, on the advice of their nobles, once again asked for the stolen pavilion. Bohemond declared that he would never give it up, but by this provocative reply he stirred up anger against him in the minds of the aforesaid princes. And, being thus roused, they announced that they would call on Bohemond in his own camp with a chosen band of their men, unless he sent back at once the pavilion he had unfairly received. At last Bohemond, on the advice of his fellow leaders in the army, restored the pavilion to the duke to avoid a dispute among the people, and peace was made and once again they became friends with each other.[15] Then, as the famine grew, and supplies of food around the region of Antioch dwindled, Baldwin settled all the revenues of Turbessel on Duke Godfrey, his brother by birth, in corn, barley, wine, and oil; in gold alone they amounted to fifty thousand bezants a year.

10. Concerning the congress of the nations hastening to the Christians' siege and about the accusation against Baldwin

Now the appointed day approached for the king of Khurasan's expedition which had been announced and in preparation for a long time. And there, indeed, were all the nations of his kingdom and the princes named above who came from throughout the regions of Armenia, Syria, and Rūm, assembling at the castle of Sooch with weapons and plentiful equipment: two hundred thousand warlike cavalry, not counting poor people and women, nor counting packhorses and camels and other animals whose number could not be calculated by anyone. Karbugha the prince and army general was there too, and he was better off than all the rest in supply

[15] The incident of the pavilion reveals tensions within the expeditionary force, which are explored by Beaumont (pp. 114–15). Although Godfrey and Robert had been enemies in Europe, he suggests that they drew together as a neutral party between the antagonistic Normans and Provençals, and as Godfrey and Robert thus held the balance of power Bohemond was willing to give in over the pavilion to buy their support.

waggons, in forces and weapons for the soldiers, in tents and great quantity of equipment. All the princes and peoples who had assembled honoured him as if he was a god, and they listened to him as master and teacher in all things. Here, once his army was gathered into one, he slowed down the journey for many days because of the loads on his vehicles and the burdens on the pack animals and camels, until he entered the land and region of the state of Edessa, where he delayed and spent some days. As he went down through this region, shortening each daily journey on account of the very great press of people and pack animals, many people met him from different places and reported many things about the army and the siege of Antioch; among these various things Baldwin stood accused, because he had not only destroyed and driven the Turks out of the town of Edessa, but had also brought under his rule all the fortresses round about.

11. Baldwin meets the infidels preparing to besiege Edessa, fights them, and is victorious

When they heard this Karbugha and the officers of his army consulted among themselves and agreed that they would besiege and subdue the city of Edessa and would capture and punish Baldwin and his fellow Christians, restoring the state and region to Turkish rule. But when Baldwin, whom threats and other fears had failed to move, realized that Karbugha was approaching and that his purpose was inimical to Baldwin and the state of Edessa, he called to arms all his troops on their powerful chargers and rode out to meet Karbugha's soldiers who had been sent ahead to lay siege to Edessa. He attacked the Turks bravely and fought them with the bows of the Armenians and the lances of the Gauls, until he put Karbugha to flight back to his camp, carrying off spoils into Edessa: camels and mules sent ahead with provisions. Karbugha wondered greatly that Baldwin would dare to take this action against him when he was present, much less when he was absent. He was indignant at his audacity and vowed by his god that he would never leave off the siege around Edessa, but would summon his army and invade at once and take Baldwin prisoner.

12. Karbugha blockades Edessa for three days in vain; Baldwin pursues him aggressively when he retreats

Karbugha, the prince and a man to be feared, had no sooner summoned his allies than they all charged and besieged the city of Edessa in the blare and din of trumpets and bugles, applying great force and attack for three days around the ramparts and gates of the city.[16] But they realised that they were being strongly

[16] FC records the siege as lasting three weeks (p. 242), while ME has forty days (p. 170). It is possible they are referring to the whole period of time Karbugha was in Edessan

repulsed by the defenders and guards of the city, and that they could not make progress at once or in a short space of time because the city was unassailable with its walls and towers, and so they advised Karbugha that he should now move the camp away from the siege, make haste on the road he had decided to Antioch, and when Antioch was conquered he could return and repeat the siege around Edessa, until he slaughtered Baldwin and his men like so many sheep in the sheepfold. Karbugha agreed with those who gave this advice and continued his journey towards Antioch. Because of the difficulties of the mountains, and because it took a long time for so many thousands to cross the great river Euphrates by boat, he divided the infinite thousands of his army into parts. The faces of Baldwin and those who were with him in the city did not change when presented with the problem of such a great multitude, but they mounted their horses, and as Karbugha withdrew from his position by the city they pursued the rearguard of the army in the hope that some part would linger and could be opposed. But when they were unsuccessful, on account of the Turks' wariness and watchfulness, they returned to Edessa, imploring God in heaven to have mercy on Duke Godfrey, Robert, Bohemond, Raymond, and all the Christians, and to defend them from the host of enemies approaching in such strength and to protect them with his favour. At once the rumour of the approach of Karbugha and his thousands began to be spread abroad by Syrian and Armenian spies and to reach the ears of the Christian army. But some refused to believe it; others believed and pestered the duke to take care of the matter.

13. Certain men of the Christian army withdraw secretly from the camp, and diligent men set out to investigate the movements of the infidels

Among all these different rumours, Stephen of Blois for some reason declared that he was very unwell and could no longer stay in the siege. He wished his brothers well and left them on this pretext of illness, and set out towards the coast for lesser Alexandria. When he left, four thousand men of war followed him, who had been of his company.[17] Duke Godfrey, Bohemond, Robert, Raymond, the army captains, were increasingly astonished by the rumour of the approaching gentiles, so they decided unanimously to select diligent men from the army and send them

territory, while AA refers only to the assault on the city. The *ChA* agrees with ME in giving famine as the reason for the Turks' withdrawal (p. 232).

[17] Stephen's desertion is reported in much less derogatory terms than in *GF* (p. 63), perhaps because AA knew Stephen was to redeem his reputation by a martyr's death in 1102. It has been suggested that Stephen had been planning to leave since late March when he wrote to his wife (*Kreuzzugsbriefe*, p. 152) and he had waited only to see Antioch in Christian hands. However, in view of the fact that Karbugha was known to be approaching, this does not make his action any less indefensible. See J. A. Brundage, 'An errant crusader: Stephen of Blois', *Traditio*, 16 (1960), pp. 380–95.

out through the mountains and inaccessible places from where they could quite safely keep watch and find out the truth of the matter. Those sent out were Drogo of Nesle, Clarembald of Vendeuil, Ivo of the kingdom of France[18] and Rainald of Toul, very eminent and careful men, who were to report to the army without delay if anything which they knew was true concerning the gentiles' arrival came to their ears or caught their eyes, so that the princes would be forewarned and would be less fearful of the attackers' javelins. The knights who were sent out to reconnoitre spread out and some went to Artah, some towards Rossa, some towards the road from Rūm to observe the truth of the matter, and they saw the army swarming from all sides, from the mountains and different roads like the sands of the sea; they marvelled at their infinite thousands and were totally unable to count them.

14. When the tribes had been observed, what plan the princes made

Moreover, when they saw so many thousands and Karbugha's incomparable weaponry and the splendour of his possessions, they returned to Antioch with all speed, seven days before Karbugha and his troops would reach the boundaries and the plains of the region of Antioch. On their return the men reported to the duke and other princes, just as they had learnt and seen it with their own eyes, the approach and all the equipment and all the soldiery which Karbugha had led out. They did this privately lest the terrified people should despair, because they had been afflicted by the long siege and serious famine, and lest they should put up less resistance and prepare for flight in the gathering darkness. Duke Godfrey, Robert and Robert of Normandy, Raymond, Bohemond, Eustace, Tancred,[19] and all the leadership called a meeting together on the day following the return of the knights who had been sent out to reconnoitre Karbugha's army, and they discussed what they should do for the best, what was the most sensible plan if they were not to be suddenly seized by the invading thousands of enemies and destroyed by sword and bow. Duke Godfrey, Robert, and many others were struggling to rise up and meet Karbugha as he approached with his thousands, putting on hauberks, helmets and shields, taking upright standards and forming orderly ranks. They put all their hope in Lord Jesus that they might join battles with the Turks and in God's name might end their lives in that place in martyrdom. Some were advising that a part should continue to besiege Antioch, in case the Turks burst out of the city to assist Karbugha, while the stronger part, in accordance with the plan of the duke and Robert of Flanders, would go to meet the enemy no more than two miles away.

---

[18] Ivo of Grandmesnil.

[19] Here and later (4. 22) AA says Tancred was present at meetings of the leaders, and further that he took part in the storming of the city, but this is disproved by the eye-witness accounts and above all by RC: see Nicholson, p. 65, n. 2.

15. Bohemond's mysterious secret plan for the betrayal of Antioch

While people were offering their opinions in these meetings Bohemond, a man exceedingly wise and shrewd, took Godfrey, Robert of Flanders, and Raymond apart from the conference of allies, and in a secret place he told them everything he had in his heart in this way, saying: 'Lords and my most beloved brothers, I have a secret which I am now going to entrust to you, and with God's agreement and assistance it will enable all the army and our princes to be delivered and saved. I was promised as much of the state of Antioch as might be handed over to me, and now seven months have passed and this pact has been made between me and a traitor who is bound by his promise, which cannot in any way be dissolved or changed, that, at whatever time I shall advise, one of the towers which allows entry into the city, and in which that same traitor lives, shall be handed over to me. I have exerted myself a great deal for this thing, observing that the city is unconquerable by human forces. I have agreed to give him a great and infinite sum of money, and I have bound myself by a solemn oath to raise him up and enrich him among my people no less than Tancred, the son of my sister. Bohemond my namesake, a man of Turkish race, was the author of this secret agreement and betrayal from the beginning of his becoming a Christian.[20] And now his account is due to him, so that he will not disappoint with respect to any of the things he has promised as traitor, and he will find me prepared to grant him the great reward I vowed. Hence, because I am obliged to pay a considerable sum to him, and I am sustaining the entire weight of this matter, I am revealing it in secret to all of you who are the pillars and captains of the army, namely to see if it is your will, and that of the others, that if the city is captured it is handed over to me. I shall close this agreement and plan, and from my own means I am prepared to grant what I agreed to the traitor at once.'[21] When they heard this the princes rejoiced with great joy, and with complete goodwill they promised the city to Bohemond, and they associated the other nobles likewise as voluntary participants in Bohemond's gift and grant.

16. How cautiously that same plan was discussed among the leaders, while the rest remained in ignorance

After the captains were all made willing participants strictly on their honour, pledging with right hands all round, it was announced that no word was to become public, but the matter suppressed in silence and revealed to no one. Some people also said that in the attack and struggle of people fighting to and fro the young son

[20] See 3. 61, above.

[21] The story of the traitor Firuz from the Arabic side may be read in IA (pp. 14–15).

of that same Turk was captured and by chance came into Bohemond's hands.[22] For the sake of his ransom the boy's father began to be a confidant of Bohemond, and, at the last resort preferring the life of his son to the safety of all the inhabitants, he decided on treachery against King Yaghi-Siyhan and entered into an agreement with Bohemond for the restitution of his son, and thus he admitted the faithful soldiers of Christ into the city. The city was granted to Bohemond if he could take it. So, as evening was already covering the earth, it was decided on Bohemond's advice that Duke Godfrey and Robert of Flanders should take seven hundred eminent knights from the army and, while the Turks were scattered throughout the ramparts intent on household cares, they should make for the mountains in the darkness of night, as if they were setting out to ambush some of Karbugha's army as they led the way to the city. As these seven hundred were making their way under cover of darkness towards the mountains through out-of-the-way and scarcely penetrable places, led by Bohemond's recent Christian convert along the narrow defiles, Duke Godfrey enjoined these things confidently, saying: 'Men, brothers, and pilgrims devoted to God, we have decided to go to meet the Turks and their hostile divisions who are encamped close to us, to fight with them to see if by any chance a victorious outcome will be granted to us. We forbid any noise and din to be made among us on pain of death.' But he had something else in mind than that of which he spoke to the people. For with those comrades who alone knew the plan, he was striving to reach the mountains, that is to say that part where Yaghi-Siyhan's city and fortress was sited on the highest peak, and he passed over the valleys and mountain-slopes and, taking up position in a retreat far from the city and hidden in a valley, he organized with Robert of Flanders everything which was sensibly to be done about the betrayal of the city.

17. How carefully the interpreter of the faithful and the betrayer of the city met together

Therefore, after everything had been organized according to the careful plan, they sent ahead a certain interpreter of languages, a Lombard by race and a member of Bohemond's household, to the tower which the traitor was guarding, to remind him of the agreement on Bohemond's part about letting in the Christians, to listen to his reply on this matter and to bring it back to the princes.[23] The interpreter reached the walls and called in Greek to the traitor who was stationed in the window of the tower that same night, waiting ever-watchful for the Gauls. He asked if the

---

[22] AA gives two accounts of the city's betrayer. This one would appear to be oral testimony and is related to the story in *ChA* (pp. 234–44).

[23] Bohemond's interpreter, whom AA calls a Lombard, probably came from southern Italy where Greek was still widely spoken. Greek was also in daily use in Antioch. According to *GF*, the traitor Firuz addressed the Franks in Greek (p. 46). The presence of Greek- (and possibly Arabic-) speakers in Bohemond's contingent was clearly advantageous to him.

traitor was alone, so that he might discuss Bohemond's message with him more confidentially. When the man had recognized his words and Bohemond's very sure token, that is by means of a ring which Bohemond had received from him and now had sent back to him as a token, from then on he did not refuse to believe the interpreter's words, but questioned him closely as to whether Bohemond or his men were at hand. The interpreter perceived that the traitor was not talking to him in an attempt to deceive, and he acknowledged that Bohemond's soldiers were not far away and that they were ready to do everything they should according to his advice. He advised them to approach without hesitation and fear, to climb the walls in safety, and not to put it off at all, because of the short period of darkness and dawn drawing near. He also begged them earnestly on this account, that the guard on the walls, who carried a small torch in his hand when it was his turn for the watch and he went on his rounds of the ramparts, walls and towers to check all was well, should not reveal that people were climbing and so put them in danger of their lives by awakening the enemy.

18. Godfrey and Robert encourage the warriors chosen for this task, lest they dread the first ascent of the walls

When the interpreter had heard the traitor's advice he ran back to the princes he had left in the mountains and told them everything he had heard, and pleaded strongly with them to select those they considered bold enough, who would climb the walls without ceasing and would be admitted to the city. The men were chosen straight away for the ascent of the walls. But their hearts were struck with fear and very great doubt, and each of them was reluctant and very much against being first in and climbing the walls.[24] Godfrey and Robert saw that the men were becoming alarmed in this way and they could not establish which would go first, because the men did not trust the Turk's promise and thought these were stratagems of deceit, and so they spoke angrily, putting new heart into them in this way: 'Remember in whose name you left your country and your kindred,[25] and how you renounced earthly life, not fearing to undergo any danger of death for Christ. Not that you should believe that you will die, but that you will live in happiness with Christ,[26] and hence by His grace and love you should accept in a calm and willing spirit whatever may happen to you on this journey. Alas! Most faithful soldiers of Christ, you do not run this risk for earthly recompense, but in expectation of His reward, who is able to grant to His own the prizes of eternal life after present death. For we all have to die somehow. Already some light of day is revealing our plan, already if the citizens and Turks spot us then not a single one of us will escape alive. Go,

24 Cf. *ChA* (pp. 245–8).

25 Cf. Acts 7: 3.

26 Cf. Rom. 6: 8.

and as you climb offer up your life to God, knowing that it is the charity of God to lay down one's life for one's friends.'[27]

19. The way that wise men were admitted into the city by way of a ladder made of hide

The doubt in very many minds was allayed by these words of comfort from such high-minded princes. And they took up the ladder, which was made of bull's hide and very suitable for this business,[28] and crept up to the wall with their interpreter, to where the traitor was waiting on the ramparts for the approaching men. As some of those sent forward arrived – some from the duke's household, others from Robert's company, and certain from Bohemond's group – the interpreter told the Turk who was waiting for them on the ramparts to throw down a rope from the ramparts by which means the knotted ladder could be drawn up onto the ramparts so that soldiers could climb it and be let in. Just as he had promised, the Turk drew up the ladder on the rope, tied it firmly around the ramparts and, encouraging the men in a low voice, he assured them they could climb without hesitation. At once the bold men climbed the ladder, wearing hauberks and helmets, their swords buckled on, leaning on their spears and dragging them in their hands. Others followed them, in uncertain hope of survival, until some twenty-five had entered. As these who entered first were keeping still and completely silent their comrades stationed next to the walls and waiting for the outcome of the affair, hearing no one, thought the men sent in had had their throats cut and had been suddenly strangled in bad faith, and so they hung back from climbing and following.

20. Some die when the ladder breaks, but once it is mended again they mount it loyally

The soldiers inside, realizing that this great fear had affected their fellow Christians to such an extent that they had moved stealthily away from the ladder, leaned over the ramparts from the wall and in a low voice they encouraged their comrades to climb, telling them nothing dangerous would happen to them there. These heard from the sound of their brothers that they were still alive and they strove with fierce intent to climb the ladder and to enter the city, until the ancient and aged ramparts were riven and ruined and the rocks and masonry crumbled

---

27 Cf. John 15: 13.

28 AA's description of a rope-type ladder is confirmed by FC and by the *ChA*, where it is said that 'at least 1000 deer hides' were used (FC p. 232; *ChA* p. 240). However, Raymond and the *GF* author, both present during the siege, refer to a rigid ladder (RA p. 64; *GF* p. 46). It is interesting that AA specifies that the group was not just Bohemond's men: possibly the other leaders had imposed a condition on him.

from the great pressure and weight of the people climbing, and so the ladder had no hold and fell right down to the ground with the men who were still standing on it. Moreover, there were shafts of lances positioned upright next to the walls, onto which those who had fallen were driven; others who fell from the stones of the wall were crushed and half-killed, some dead. The people of God shook with horror at this, thinking all these things had happened by Turkish trickery, and that now all those sent in had undoubtedly perished by a hostile death. No sound, no outburst was heard in the city nor on the ramparts, even though those who fell and were pierced made a great noise. Lord God raised a strongly blowing wind that night. The Turk, obedient to the vow he had made to Bohemond concerning the betrayal of the city, once again let down the rope to draw up the ladder. Once it was more strongly wrapped around the ramparts in the same place a second time, he called to the forsaken and terrified men again, through the interpreter, urging them all faithfully to repeat the climb. The men hesitated no longer but, strengthened by the interpreter's words and the knowledge that their brothers were safe, they climbed the ladder a second time and were brought inside the ramparts, until some sixty had been brought in over the walls and were in position.

21. Those admitted carry out the slaughter of the guards; other infidels are awoken from sleep and attack the Christians

Meanwhile the guard on the walls who patrolled the ramparts in a circuit of the town to call on the watchmen of the towers and warn them, carrying a small torch in his hand, met the men sent inside. But they cut off his head instantly with a blow of the sword, crossed over and entered the neighbouring tower. Once inside, they put to the sword everyone they found in the tower while still heavy with sleep, and as part of the same attack they rushed into other towers and inflicted a very great slaughter, until they killed some ten guards of the towers in this part of the city while they were still fast asleep and without any outcry. When these were thus laid low by the sword, a large party formed from the seven hundred suddenly broke the bars and entered through a certain postern gate which was in the mountainous region next to that same place where they had climbed in. And, making a loud noise with bugles, they summoned Godfrey, Robert, and the other nobles to penetrate the city as hastily as they could to reinforce those sent in already. When these nobles heard the bugles and recognized them as the agreed signal, because they were privy to all the secrets, they sped in a strong company to the gate which jutted out upwards in the mountains, and they strove to enter. From Yaghi-Siyhan's chief citadel, which was very close to this gate, the Turks heard the din and leapt up, they drove away the Gauls by throwing stones, and did not allow their comrades who had been sent in first to reach the gate and open it. So as they returned to the postern gate mentioned above, the soldiers who had entered the city by the ladder enlarged the breach in this postern by breaking down the wall, with their sharp swords ready for the stratagems of the Turks, and thus the princes and their comrades, riding and on foot, were admitted through an ample gap.

22. While there is uproar from this side and that, the princes for the first time reveal to the crowd that the city has been betrayed

The Turks were woken up by this sudden outcry and din of trumpets and blaring of bugles and they armed hurriedly, seized bows and arrows, and defended the towers, both sides joining battle one against the other with intense struggles up and down. In this noisy, to-and-fro contest Yaghi-Siyhan's soldiers, who were on the mountain top in the chief citadel, sounded their horns loudly so that the Turks, who were still snoring in the city and tower fortresses at very first light, would wake up and charge to the relief of their comrades, and thus they would be able to resist the Christian invaders. When the great army which was still stationed outside the walls in another spacious part of the city heard this, they thought those in the mountains and the citadel were raising their voices, sounding horns and rejoicing together at the approach and invasion of Karbugha, not in the least aware that the city had been betrayed into the Gauls' hands and captured. Bohemond, Raymond, and Tancred, who knew about the whole affair, and everyone who had remained in the siege, put on hauberks, buckled on weapons and raised banners, and sped to attack the city from outside, greatly strengthening those who were unaware of what had happened by explaining the whole affair to them during the attack on the city.

23. The faithful open the gates of the city; Bohemond's banner is flown on the citadel; at dawn warlike Mars prevails

Meanwhile, while the Turks inside and outside were being hard pressed in battle, the Greeks, Syrians, Armenians, citizens and men of the Christian faith, rushed joyfully to break apart the bolts and to open the gates through which Bohemond and the whole army were admitted. Indeed, at first light, in that area where the betrayal of the city took place, Bohemond's banner, which was the colour of blood, glowed redly over the walls in the mountains, to show everyone that by God's favour and assistance the city which was invincible by man had been betrayed into the hands of Bohemond and all Christ's faithful and captured. Thus, with bolts drawn back and gates standing open on all sides, everyone wondered and rejoiced, since Bohemond's plan was not common knowledge, and once awake they swiftly seized weapons, one warned the other, and everyone armed on the run and hurried to enter the city and gates. There was time for someone to run a mile before the whole number of Christians was admitted. Soon the Turks were stupefied by the violent crash and din of so many thousands going in, and the fearful sound of trumpets, and the widespread raising of banners, the loud shouting of armed men, the neighing of horses, and some who were still asleep in bed woke up unprepared and unarmed. A part of them got together at once in the hope of resisting, grabbing bows and weapons; others remained steadfastly on the towers and defences and shot with arrows many careless Christians of the non-combatant crowd, men and women. Charges and various fights took place among them and were decided by the random chance of war.[29] The Christians, whose strength and forces were great and growing stronger and stronger, were putting to the sword the Turks who were scattered and roaming through homes, through streets and quarters of the town. They spared none of the gentile kind on grounds of age or sex until the earth was covered with blood and the corpses of the slaughtered, many of them also the killed and lifeless bodies of Christians, Gauls as well as Greeks, Syrians and Armenians mixed together. No wonder, since there had still been darkness over the earth,[30] with the light scarcely discernible, and they were entirely unaware whom they should spare or whom they should strike, for very many Turks and Saracens, fearing for their lives, deceived the pilgrims with speech and tokens of the Christian faith, and so they lost their lives in the common massacre. There were ten thousand killed whose bodies lay all over the quarters and streets of the town and had been killed by the Gauls' weapons.

24. Every pagan fled as best he could; some fell from very high cliffs and were dashed to pieces and died

Many of the Turks, seeing the grave slaughter which was happening, and that all the city was overflowing with the Gauls' forces and weapons, despaired of their lives, and, fleeing from the towers, the districts, and defences of the town, they made for the mountains using their knowledge of the winding ways, and there they entered the fortress of the chief citadel and escaped the weapons of the pursuing Gauls. For this citadel and palace sited in the mountains could not be conquered by any stratagem or strength; no one could oppose or harm those who remained within. There were about a thousand others who had been summoned to assist from distant parts; they were sent in, and had been frightened by the blare of trumpets and bugles, and had lost heart because of the very great killing of their men, and they had absolutely no knowledge of the ways and the escape route. They likewise were hurrying to the mountains and Yaghi-Siyhan's fortress, which dominated them, to escape the Christians' army, but they blundered onto a narrow and unfamiliar path where there was no possible way for them to reach the hilltop, nor was there any longer a possibility of turning back, and so they fell from above with their horses and mules down the slopes and the very difficult and impassable cliffs, and everyone perished with broken necks, legs, and arms, and all their limbs in an incredible and amazing fall.

[29] Vergil, *Aen*. ii. 335; ix. 518.

[30] Exod. 10: 21; Ezek. 32: 8; Matt. 27: 45.

25. About the resources found in the city, and what day the city was captured

The people of the living God returned from the slaughter and pursuit of the gentiles who fled into the fortress and the mountains. The sun was already shining quite high in the sky and the day was very well advanced. They patrolled the city, looking for provisions, but they discovered few. They found many purple garments of different kinds and colours, also pepper and very many spices, the gentiles' clothes and tents, gaming pieces and dice, also some money but not much. No wonder, for, blockaded for nine months during the long siege, the many thousands of gentiles assembled in that place had used it all up.[31] The Thursday was a very fine day, when on 3rd June the town of Antioch was betrayed into the Christians' hands and captured, and the Turks destroyed and put to flight.

26. Concerning the flight and killing of the king of Antioch

When Yaghi-Siyhan, the king of Antioch, realized his men had fled and that the entire fortress and citadel was full of fugitives, he was afraid that the band of Gauls who had captured the city might surround and storm the citadel. So he mounted his mule and left in order to lie low in out-of-the-way places in the mountains until he might find out more fully the end and outcome of the affair, and whether the citadel could be held by his men against the Gauls. While the fleeing king was wandering alone through the out-of-the-way places in the mountains some Syrians, men of the Christian faith, who were travelling through the mountain regions for supplies, saw him from a long way off and recognized him, and they wondered a great deal why he had turned aside alone from the fortress citadel into the out-of-the-way places. And so they said to one another: 'Look, our lord and king Yaghi-Siyhan is not journeying through these mountain wildernesses for no reason: perhaps the city has been captured and his men killed; he himself is certainly intent on flight. Let us see that he, who has inflicted on us so many losses, injustices, and sharp practices does not escape our hands.' In this way the three Syrians were plotting Yaghi-Siyhan's death, but they hid all their feelings and showed him false reverence with heads bowed, greeting him deceitfully and coming close to him until they seized and drew his own sword and threw him down from his mule, cutting off his head and putting it in their bag. They soon took it into the city of Antioch, into the view of all the Christian princes. The head was of enormous size, the ears very wide and hairy, his hair was white and he had a beard which flowed from his chin to his navel.

[31] RA says they won unimaginable quantities of booty (p. 66).

27. Concerning Roger, who valiantly intercepted advance riders of the infidel army but was unexpectedly forestalled by death

Then, because they were already aware of the very near approach of Karbugha and his men, and there was little food to be found in Antioch, they hastily sent to the port of St Symeon the Hermit and purchased with money, each one according to his means, foodstuffs brought in by sea, which they took into Antioch that evening and the following morning. When this had been carried out, and with the Turks partly killed and partly put to flight to the fortress, and the Gauls spread out all around on towers, houses, palaces, and ramparts, on the following day, which was a Friday, three hundred Turkish cavalry of Karbugha's people, armed with bows, quivers, and arrows and carrying purple banners, rode out ahead of the entire gentile army to inflict sudden death on any of the faithful whom they found unsuspecting outside the walls. Of these three hundred, thirty who were men very skilled in warfare and very nimble on horseback were advancing towards the walls and gates of the town at a gallop; behind them were comrades left in a certain valley to ambush and attack the faithful if by chance they should pursue the thirty sent ahead as far as the valley and they rushed in a charge on top of the hidden forces. Therefore, as these thirty were approaching the town wall and eagerly challenging Christ's faithful, spread out along the ramparts, with their bows, Roger of Barneville, riding with fifteen most excellent comrades, wearing weapons and hauberk, hurried from the city to meet them and to do something remarkable with them.[32] But at once the Turkish advance party turned back their horses and fled, making for the ambush, luring Roger, who was urging his men on to a gallop, to the place of the ambush. When Roger saw the ambush swarming out of the valley there he drew in his reins and swiftly retraced the road to the city with his comrades. The Turks on their galloping horses drove on the fleeing knight no less hard, until he drew near the town wall and almost escaped across the shallows of the Orontes with his men. But luck was against him and in full view of all those who were standing around the ramparts the very noble champion was beaten by a Turkish soldier on a faster horse. An arrow pierced his back and penetrated his liver and lung, and so he slipped from his horse and breathed his last. Therefore, since so eminent a man was dead and destitute of help from all his men, the cruel murdering Turks dismounted from their horses and cut off his head from the neck, and they retraced their journey to Karbugha and the army bearing the head stuck on a spear as an exhibition of their recent and unprecedented victory. Exulting then in this happy outcome, the legions of the gentiles took great heart from this, because they had thus acted boldly right next to the walls, and they had seen no one from the pilgrims come out from the city to help Roger when he was killed and beheaded, or dare anything at all.

[32] Roger rode out with three companions according to *ChA* (p. 260) and RM (p. 151).

28. The reason why his brothers did not help him when he was dying before them; and concerning Roger's funeral

This should not seem surprising to anyone, and no one should think that dullness of mind or fear of the attacking multitude had stricken the Gauls and made them soft, and this is why they held back from helping and revenging their brother who had been struck down and beheaded in full view of everyone, since no region in the world excels Gaul by nourishing bolder men or more keen in battle. But in truth it may be believed beyond doubt that they were held back by lack of horses, which they had lost at various times from infectious disease or long-term hunger, or occasionally to a cunning arrow from the Turks. For hardly a hundred and fifty horses remained to the Gauls and those were enfeebled by shortage of fodder; the Turks', however, were sleek and not worn out, on which account they were able to escape by galloping swiftly and the Gauls could not pursue them at all. As many as four hundred Turkish horses were found and captured in the city of Antioch alone, which they had not yet started to tame for riding according to their custom, or learnt to turn about in pursuit of the enemy and urge on with spurs. Then, after the Turks had left, the sad and grieving pilgrims brought Roger's body into the city, lamenting with great wailing and weeping that one of the strongest of the people had fallen. He was always watchful in ambushes and in the slaughter of the gentiles and his extraordinary deeds were much greater than our pen can explain. His fame was even pre-eminent among all the Turks and they used willingly to see and hear him in any business they were doing with the Christians, or in the restitution of prisoners on both sides, or when at any time they were arranging a truce between them. This same very celebrated knight was buried in Antioch in the entrance of the basilica of blessed Peter the apostle[33] by the princes of the Christians, and by the lord bishop of Le Puy, and by all the Catholic clergy who were there, and his soul was commended with the sacrifice of prayers and the singing of psalms to Lord Christ, for whose love and honour he had become an exile and did not hesitate to die.

29. The blockade of the infidel nations around Antioch

No sooner was the famous warrior's funeral ended than, on that same Saturday morning, which was the third day after the city was captured,[34] all the barbarous nations and legions of the gentiles appeared, with a large amount of equipment, which Karbugha had drawn together from all the kingdoms, lands and places of the eastern region, and they camped on the fields and plain, laying siege around

[33] St Peter, chief of the apostles, preached in Antioch and early tradition claims he was the first bishop there: Gal. 2: 11–14; S. Eusebii Hieronymi, *Liber de viris illustribus* (*PL* xxiii. 607–8); idem, *Commentarium in Epistolam ad Galatos* (*PL* xxiii. 341).

[34] 5 June, 1098.

the walls and ramparts of the spacious city. Then, on the third day after he besieged Christ's faithful, at that point staying at a distance from the walls, Karbugha made a plan to be quartered closer to the town, he struck camp, and with his great strength in numbers he took up position on top of the cliffs in the mountains around the chief citadel and in that part where the city was taken, so that he could encourage Sansadonias and Buldagis, Yaghi-Siyhan's sons, and the others who remained in the fortress, and so that he might see the spot where the city was betrayed and through which Christians had been let in. Similarly, in a show of strength others of Karbugha's people pitched their tents in those mountains, on the slopes on the right-hand side of the fortress, where Duke Godfrey was protecting the tower and this gate from within, which Bohemond previously had besieged from outside before the capture of the city, so that the Christians would be allowed no freedom or opportunity to leave on any side.

30. Duke Godfrey goes into battle but is put to flight, and very many of his companions are brought down by different deaths

Duke Godfrey saw how greatly their strength and steadfastness against him had grown, so at once he sallied forth through the gate against the enemy with an enormous band of his men, to invade the tents which had been pitched out there beyond the walls, to destroy them and to harry the Turks from them, once beaten in battle. But the Turks swarmed out to meet the duke and defend the tents. Battle was joined there for a long time and there was very great suffering, until the forces of the duke and his men were exhausted and, weary of warfare, they were put to flight and only just escaped, returning through the gate by which they had come out. Many others, about two hundred, who did not make it through the narrow gate, were lost, either killed or wounded or captured. After the duke was put to flight and repulsed in this way, and very many of his men were destroyed in the gateway, the Turks charged from the fortress and the gate of the fortress, because they had prevailed over the duke, and, approaching by way of footpaths known to them and by the valley slope, they attacked stray Christians in the middle of the city with a sudden outcry, inflicting arrow wounds as they charged and straight away racing back to the citadel and mountains. While the Turks were leaping out from the mountains and valley like this, morning, noon and night, and attacking the Christians, Bohemond and Raymond, who were enraged, decided on a place to become a defence for their men, and without delay they caused an enormous fortification to be built, which is called a rampart, positioned below and in between the mountains and the town and defended by a fortress with a walled building on top, so that if the enemy burst forth suddenly from the mountains they would be unable to cut down pilgrim soldiers who were wandering carelessly through open areas in the city by attacking them with weapons and arrows.[35] The Turks who were occupying the fortress in the mountains still frequently burst forth against Bohemond's new fortress and made assaults, greatly and gravely tormenting and killing the guards and defenders of the new fortress with their hail of arrows and strength of weapons. The Christian knights who were guards and masters of the new fortress, Walbric, Ivo, Ralph of La Fontanelle, Everard of Le Puiset, Raimbold Croton, Peter son of Gisla, and their men were fighting back against the Turks just as hard, with lances and all sorts of weaponry, and they denied them access to the valley, meanwhile dying here and there from the great slaughter or from wounds.

31. Bohemond is attacked fiercely, but with the support of his brothers he comes out on top; and why it was necessary for the infidels to move their camp further away

While these constant attacks by the Turks against the new fortress were going on, and the Turks were being repulsed fiercely by the Gauls, Karbugha's soldiers formed an infantry column and marched through the impregnable gate of the fortress, down through the mountains and out-of-the-way places, and, having ascertained that Bohemond was in the new fortress, they attacked him vigorously. A heavy battle began there and very many were killed. And Bohemond would have been defeated, and his men, except that Christians flocked from the whole city: Count Robert of Flanders and Duke Godfrey (even though he was defeated in the first attack) and Robert prince of the Normans and the rest of the splendid leaders had brought reinforcements and assistance and had forced back the Turks from the city and the new fortress by the strength of their armoured men. Therefore the Turks who had been forced back with their prince Karbugha decided to stay in the mountains outside the gates and walls for two more days, still thinking to harm the Christians. But since there was not enough grass to be found in the hills as fodder for their horses, they moved camp and, crossing the shallows of the river Orontes, they pitched their tents and took up position at a distance of half a mile from the city. Another day Karbugha, on his men's advice, divided his numerous army, which was thus encircling the town in many thousands, to blockade all the gates, so that the pilgrims were shut inside and there would be no entry from any direction, neither from right nor from left, nor any exit for them.

[35] The building of this wall is also described by RC (pp. 97–8). See France, *Victory*, p. 276.

32. Where Karbugha distributes these men and those to individual gates; and Tancred attacks those who are assailing the walls

Thus the blockade was in place on all sides, and a few days passed, then one very clear dawn some Turkish soldiers left the camp and galloped up to the walls of Antioch, challenging the Gauls with crossbow and arrows, hoping to achieve the same success as previously when they triumphed in Roger's beheading, and to excel in Karbugha's camp by a remarkable deed. For this reason they exerted themselves further and more fiercely in the attack on the walls, and they dismounted so that they could fight more freely and without damage to their horses while standing on the wall, and so that, now they had become footsoldiers, they might more easily throw their javelins at the pilgrims. However, Tancred, a very fierce knight who could never have enough of Turkish bloodshed but was always eager for their slaughter, saw their madness, their raging and rashness, and, with his limbs clad in iron as usual, he put on his hauberk, took with him ten comrades who were very experienced with horse and lance, and sneaked out of the gate which Bohemond had guarded when the siege was still happening, between the city walls and the outer rampart, which is commonly called the barbican, and he fell with a sudden shout upon the Turks who were intent on battle, attacked them boldly and pierced and destroyed the unsuspecting soldiers. Although they saw their lives were in danger, there was not at first any opportunity for the Turks to get back to their horses and six who were hit were executed in front of the walls, and in revenge for Roger's head they lost their heads by the sword. Tancred returned in great triumph and happiness to his comrades in the city, taking back with him the Turks' heads as evidence of victory.

33. The Christians despair of being able to hold the new fortress, and they destroy it with fire

Then on another day, after Karbugha and his assembled army had organized their camp, and after blockading on all sides the ways in and out, it was decided by common advice of the gentiles that some two thousand Turkish soldiers should be chosen to storm and overthrow the fortress which Duke Godfrey and the other fellow leaders had established in strength and with great victory, as you have heard, when the beaten Turks were drowned in the waters of the river Orontes, under that same bridge which stretches across the river from the city and on which, when the fortress was set up, Raymond stood guard until the city was captured by the Christians.[36] Now indeed, since it was neglected and empty, on hearing of the gentiles' approach, Count Robert of Flanders summoned five hundred warlike men and positioned them to protect the way into that same fortress so that the Turkish force would not suddenly occupy it and be a great nuisance to the pilgrims

---

[36] See above, 3. 55.

when they wanted to cross the bridge and water. And so the two thousand Turks already mentioned who were intended for the ruin of the fortress converged in great strength and clash of arms, rushing from all sides to the place of the fortress and attacking with javelins and bows. At length, indeed, they became footsoldiers and endeavoured to run across the rampart, roaring with a great blare of bugles and with their accustomed outcry, and they severely harried the fortress's defenders from morning right up to the end of the day. But Robert and his fellow soldiers, seeing that they were getting into difficulties from the enemy, and knowing they would suffer cruel tortures if they were defeated and subjected to their power, courageously fought for their lives against their opponents, attacking the enemy boldly with lances and crossbows and keeping them away from the rampart by force. It is reported that on that day they were severely wounded here and there. The Turks saw they were making no progress, but all their efforts were squandered to no purpose; they abandoned those in the fortress practically undefended and returned to Karbugha, prince of the great army, seeking urgently for him to increase their resources of men and saying that with these additions they would be able to destroy the fortress and its protectors on the following day. However, when Robert and those with him saw the Turks had withdrawn, they were aware that they had gone to get more allies as reinforcements. So they made a plan, and in the darkness of night they left the protection of the fortress, since it was seen to be inadequate against the forces of so many thousands, and they set on fire the entire fortress. They demolished its rampart as they left, and they were taken back into the city of Antioch by their brothers.

34. Concerning the severity of the famine among God's people; and how dearly were sold the cheapest things

Then, after sunrise the next day, two thousand gentiles were added to the original two thousand on Karbugha's orders, and they arrived at the fortress as a strong force, with trumpets and bugles, hoping to overthrow it with a sudden charge and to destroy with swift death those within who were tired out by the previous day's defence. But they found the rampart demolished and the defences of the fortress burnt down, and they retraced their steps to their tents, tricked and frustrated. With the city thus blockaded on all sides, and the gentiles' forces increasing from day to day and barring their way out all round, famine grew so great among the Christians that in the absence of bread they did not shrink from eating camels, donkeys, horses, and mules, but even chewed pieces of leather found in the homes which had hardened and putrefied for three or six years, this as well as leather recently torn from cattle, cooked with pepper, cumin, or some other spice. They were tortured by this great famine. I know that my listeners will tremble when they hear the evils and torments of the incredible famine which oppressed God's people shut in Antioch. For one single hen's egg, if it could have been found, six Luccan pennies[37] were paid. For ten beans, a penny; for the head of one donkey, horse, cow, or camel one bezant was given, for foot or ear sixpence; in return for the entrails of any one of these animals ten shillings were accepted. Then the crowds of non-combatants and ordinary people were forced to devour their leather shoes because of the pressure of hunger. Some, indeed, filled their wretched bellies with roots of stinging nettles and other sorts of woodland plants, cooked and softened on the fire, and so they became ill and every day their numbers were lessened by death.[38] Duke Godfrey, as they say who were there, paid out fifteen marks of silver for the flesh of a miserable camel; for a she-goat it is testified beyond doubt that his steward Baldric gave three marks to the seller.[39]

35. Turks who were wanting to regain the city by stealth were discovered, and after a long struggle they were driven from the wall and died wretchedly

Then, some days afterwards, after Karbugha had established the siege around Antioch, and had closed all ways in and out of the city, and harried God's people with different attacks, and banned food from being brought in from any part, the Christians were distressed and tired from disaster and long abstinence and warlike effort, and began to be less watchful in the defence of the city and ramparts. It reached the point where a certain tower towards the mountains was left unguarded, that is to say in that place where the defence work was founded on a mixture of friable mud, and so there was no one to drive back the enemy who were coming out through the mountains from the gate which was not besieged, and pursuing the scattered pilgrims. It was here that the young man was captured by the Provençals, and a certain tower demanded for his return, but his relatives and friends refused and he was put to death.[40] Some of the Turks' boldest soldiers realized that this tower was empty of inhabitants and they leaned their ladders and siege engines secretly against the wall, hoping to bring some gentiles inside through the tower at dead of night, and so to recover the lost city. Meanwhile, a certain Christian who was out and about in the city on his necessary business lifted his gaze and saw the Turks carelessly taking a walk in the middle of the high point of that same tower. At once he shouted in a loud voice, disturbing his fellows who were stationed in a neighbouring tower, and he claimed the Turks had invaded the city and so he stirred up a great commotion among the people. At this, Henry of the castle of

---

[37] See 3. 52 and n.

[38] Cf. RC: 'Obsessi lethiferis cibis utuntur' ('The besieged eat deadly foods', p. 102). His list resembles AA's, including leather and some plant-names.

[39] The famine is also graphically described in *GF* (p. 62) and by other eye-witnesses, RA (pp. 76–7) and Peter Tudebode (PT), *Historia de Hierosolymitano itinere*, (ed.) John H. Hill and Laurita L. Hill (Paris, 1977), p. 104.

[40] See above, 3. 56.

Esch, a knight always very celebrated in his own land, son of Fredelo, one of Duke Godfrey's counsellors, heard the noise and din, seized his shield and sword, and went with great haste to the high point of the tower, having with him two excellent young knights (namely Franco and Sigemar, related by blood, inhabitants of the town called Mechelen on the river Meuse) in order to repulse the enemy who had invaded from the tower, thinking they had been sold along with the city by some brothers who had been bribed with gold or silver. When the Turks realized they had been discovered and could not escape the hands of the pilgrims by any clever idea, they ran to the threshold of the tower as their only hope of defence and fought back with deadly sword blows. They applied a great deal of pressure to Franco and struck him on the head with a very severe and almost incurable wound. When Sigemar wanted to come to his kinsman's aid they pierced him through the belly with a sword up to its hilt[41] and they kept Christ's faithful away from the threshold with a marvellous and incredible struggle. Eventually the resources of the faithful increased on all sides and their forces were augmented; the Turks were weary and worn out in spirit by the very great effort, and they began to falter in defence, to slacken their weapons and arms. Four of them died by the sword, others were cast down from the height and died with heads, legs and arms broken.

36. Concerning some Christians seeking victuals outside the walls; and about the slaughter of sailors who were selling food to those under siege

After this the pilgrims were constrained by the torment of great famine, as you have heard, and much more, and, finding no access to bring in or acquire food on account of the blockade set up on all sides, some of the humble crowd risked their lives by going secretly in great uncertainty and dread from the city under cover of darkness down to the port of St Symeon (once a hermit in the mountains there), where for a price they would receive supplies from the sailors and merchants, and then they would retrace their route through the thorn bushes and scrub in the darkness before dawn. When they brought corn they sold the eighth part of a Liège measure for three marks, a Flemish cheese for five shillings; a little wine or oil, or whatever would support life, however insignificant, was purchased at a great and incredible rate of exchange in gold or silver. Some of these pilgrims one day lingered more than usual, and because the night was short they were shown up in the sudden light of day, and it is reported that they were slaughtered and plundered by the Turks. A few hiding in the thorn bushes and scrub only just escaped and were restored to the city. Seizing the opportunity of this affair, some two thousand Turks gathered and set out for the aforesaid port and threw into disorder with a sudden attack all the sailors they found there, piercing them through with arrows. They burned the ships by throwing fire on them, seized by force the food and everything brought in by sea and carried it off. And thus they frightened away

[41] Vergil, *Aen.* ii. 553; x. 536.

those selling and buying from the port from then on, and there was no longer any sustenance of food to be found in that place for the Christians. Therefore, as this most cruel news came to the ears of the Christians who were struggling under the weight of the incredible famine, the various Turkish attacks now began to be a burden to them, and the minds of many turned to different things, how they could escape from this siege and from the dangers which threatened them. And so very many stole away from the army by night, looking for a way out by any effort or opportunity whatsoever.

37. How certain of the leaders, despairing of their lives, secretly fled from the city

Then, while such fear and despair of living grew more widespread, and thoughts of escape sprang up in the hearts of many because of the burden of daily suffering, certain chief men of the army, William the Carpenter and the other William who was once the favourite and familiar of the emperor of Constantinople, who also had taken as wife the sister of Bohemond prince of Sicily, were so much struck by great terrors that they agreed a plan and at dead of night they stole away from their fellows towards the mountains and met, and were let down on ropes from the ramparts and wall. Once down, they travelled without rest through out-of-the-way places in the mountains because of Turkish ambushes, until they struck out for Alexandria the Less. Stephen of Blois, who had withdrawn from the siege of Antioch on account of illness, was staying there to hear in that place the outcome of the affair and the fate of his comrades. In that same place Stephen learnt from these men that the dangers to his brothers had grown greater from day to day – the unbearable famine, the Turks' boasting and attacks, the destruction of men and horses – so he despaired of his life and, believing he was not at all safe in that place and not daring to make the journey on land, he prepared to make his return and escape with the aforesaid princes by sea. When the rumour got about the city of Antioch that such eminent nobles had left the city on account of fear of Turkish attacks, very many likewise considered flight, and the hearts of the strong failed from fear, and so they were not so ready in defence as they used to be, and they defended the new fortress they had established in the middle of the city, opposite the citadel which is in the mountains, rather sluggishly, being desperate and intent on escape.

38. Comforting words to the people from a certain cleric

At this point a certain most faithful brother, a Lombard by race, a cleric by rank and profession, who was positioned next to the aforesaid new fortress, held out great comfort to all the desolate soldiers of Christ who were in that place, clerics, laypeople, noble and lesser men; he lifted everyone's hearts which were hesitating and wavering with fear, saying: 'All of you, my brothers, who are oppressed by famine and pestilence, who expect to meet death in this world surrounded by the hordes of Turks and gentiles, do not believe you are undergoing this hardship for nothing, but hear and think of the reward which Lord Jesus will give back to all of those who will die for his love and favour on this journey. For at the outset of this journey a certain priest, a man of good repute and excellent conversation who lived in Italian parts, known to me from boyhood, one day, according to his custom, took the road alone across a certain little field to the parish church which was his responsibility, where he would celebrate mass. A certain pilgrim approached him in courteous respect and asked him earnestly about this journey: what he had heard about it, or what seemed to him most important about it, since so many kingdoms, so many princes and every kind of Christian were flocking to the sepulchre of Lord Jesus Christ and the holy city of Jerusalem with one purpose and desire. The priest replied: "Different people think different things about this journey. Some say this desire has been aroused in all the pilgrims by God and Lord Jesus Christ, others that the Frankish leaders and the very great common crowd are going on the journey for reasons of frivolity, and on this account so many pilgrims have met obstacles in the kingdom of Hungary and in other kingdoms, and so cannot manage to carry out their intention. And so my mind is still wavering, though for a long time affected by desire for this journey and taken up wholly by that same intention." The aforesaid pilgrim said to him immediately: "You should not believe that the commencement of this journey was frivolous or for nothing, but that it was ordered by God, to whom nothing is impossible, and you should know that any who shall be taken by death on this journey, who became exiles in Jesus' name and persevered with pure and blameless heart in God's love, and abstained from avarice, theft, adultery, and fornication, shall beyond doubt be numbered, written down, and joyfully crowned among Christ's martyrs in the court of heaven." The priest wondered at the words and promise of the pilgrim, and asked who he was, or from what region he originated, or from where he had learnt for sure that those who gave up their lives on this expedition were to be crowned in heavenly glory with the saints. Directly, the pilgrim revealed the truth of the whole affair to the inquisitive priest in this way, saying: "I am Ambrose, bishop of Milan,[42] servant of Christ, and let this be a sign to you and to all Catholic peoples making this journey, that I am not mistaken in all the things which you have heard from my lips. When three years have passed from this date, know that the Christians who are still alive will obtain after many hardships the holy city of Jerusalem and, happily, victory over all the barbarous nations." He vanished at once after saying these things and was no longer seen after this.' The same eminent

[42] Ambrose (CE339–97) was fearless, eloquent and accessible to all: see Paulinus, *Vita Sancti Ambrosii Mediolanensis Episcopi* (*PL* xiv). His dressing as a pilgrim in this vision identifies him with the suffering of the crusaders, according to A. Dupront, 'La spiritualité des croisés et des pèlerins d'après les sources de la première croisade', *Convegni del Centro di Studi sulla spiritualità medievale*, 4 (1963), pp. 451–83, at 461.

priest reported with complete truth that he had seen and heard these things from God's holy bishop. And now from the time that vision and promise were made two years had been completed; it was determined by all that the third still remained. After this, just as blessed Ambrose the bishop of Milan foretold, in the third year Christ's soldiers, the pilgrims, and their princes obtained Jerusalem and cleansed the holy places there, with the Saracens put to flight and destroyed.[43]

39. Similarly, a speech of encouragement from the most important leaders; and how the deserter princes began to sail to Constantinople

When they heard of this vision and promise from the truthful account of their brother, everyone who was up to now wavering through fear of losing this present life, and was distressed by the defection of the deserter princes, was inspired by hope and desire for heavenly life and from then on became steady; people no longer said they would withdraw from their brothers and the city out of any fear of death, but that they would live and die with them, and endure all things for Christ. Duke Godfrey, likewise, and Robert of Flanders won back with this wonderful comfort almost all of the princes who had been so stricken with fear that they were already conspiring to flee, unknown to the common crowd, and made them steadfast again in the face of all danger, speaking in this way: 'Why do you despair, distrusting God's help in the many difficulties which have happened, and why have you decided through your failure of faith to desert your brothers, that is to say the lowly crowd of foot soldiers, and make an escape? Stand firm and endure with manly spirit all your difficulties for Christ's name, and do not desert your brothers at all in this time of trouble, and incur God's wrath, whose favour and mercy do not lack for those who trust in him.' While they were speaking these words to their despairing colleagues with tears and great sighs, everyone's spirits revived, and from that time they remained steadfast with them in all hardship, no longer considering escape. William and the other William, Stephen and their fearful and fleeing comrades prepared ships, both rowing and sailing vessels, and embarked on the high seas, planning to travel to Constantinople, leaving their brothers besieged, and thinking they would never be rescued from Karbugha's hands.[44]

---

[43] Clearly AA wrote this part of his history after the battle of Ascalon, 1099.

[44] FC confirms AA in saying that Stephen took the sea route (p. 228). AK says they arrived at Philomelion by way of Tarsus, implying a land journey (p. 312). R.-J. Lilie points out that the land journey is more likely if Stephen was still accompanied by 4,000 men (AA 4. 13); however, AK says only that William of Grandmesnil and Peter of Alifa were with him: Lilie, p. 38, n. 161.

40. How the aforesaid men dissuaded the Greek emperor from helping their brothers

At length, when they had sailed for some time, while they were spending the night quartered on some islands belonging to the Greek kingdom, or staying there on account of the motion of the sea, they heard that the Christian emperor of the Greeks had arrived at the city of Philomelium with a great company of men and much equipment to assist the pilgrims, as he had promised faithfully when they were joined to him in friendship by an oath and agreed treaty. He had brought together some four hundred thousand Turcopoles, Pechenegs, Cumans, Bulgars, and Greeks skilled with bow and arrow, Danes excellent at fighting with the battleaxe, Gaulish exiles, also an army of mercenaries of different sorts from desert places and mountains, from shores and islands, that is to say from all his very extensive kingdom. The princes mentioned above found the emperor with this strength of weapons, men, and horses, and with supplies of food, tents, mules, and camels, and found with him a new army of Gauls, around forty thousand, which had been assembled through the long winter, also Tatikios with the cut-off nose who, terror-stricken as they were, had withdrawn in false faith from the allies to that same emperor, to carry a message about the promised relief, which he had not done faithfully at all, since he did not return to Antioch again.[45] As the emperor recognized the princes coming into his presence he wondered greatly how they came to be there without their allies, and he questioned them closely about the situation of their faithful fellow soldiers of Christ, about the health of Duke Godfrey, Count Raymond, the bishop of Le Puy, whether things were going well or badly for them. The princes replied that they were not at all in a state of well-being or safety, but were besieged by Karbugha prince of Khurasan and the gentile nations in such a way that not a single way in or out of the very extensive city was open, and that no one could ever escape the Turks' hands unless by stealth. They also reported the great famine by which the pilgrims were distressed, and how the Turks had destroyed merchants and ships for hatred of them. They declared that no one at all from the army could be alive in the face of so great a multitude; that they themselves had only just escaped by their own wits, suggesting to the emperor that he turned back and did not put his army through the torment to no purpose.

[45] Similar accusations of cowardice and treachery are to be found in RA (pp. 55f.); *GF* (pp. 34–5), and PT (pp. 69–70): cf. AK, who accuses Bohemond of scaring Tatikios away (p. 307). Lilie, however, claims all these accusations are groundless and Tatikios left because of a genuine need for supplies (pp. 34–5).

41. Some other princes who are thinking of flight are held back by the encouragement of good men

When the emperor heard about these dangers to the Christians and was informed about the gentiles' forces he took counsel with his nobility, and then, trembling and terrified, he ordered the entire army to turn back immediately. Further, he laid waste with fire and plunder the land of Rūm which had formerly been wickedly stolen from him by Suleyman but was now restored by the strength of the pilgrims, and he overthrew the cities and all the fortifications, so that if they should happen to be recovered by Suleyman they would not be of any use in his service.[46] The terrible news of the emperor turning back and his army dispersing sped across the ramparts of Antioch and afflicted the pilgrims' hearts with great grief and shook much of the boldness from their spirits. And so the leaders of Christ's army constantly discussed together a plan that if at all possible they would withdraw secretly from the city and leave the crowd of ordinary people there in danger. When Duke Godfrey, Robert of Flanders, and the bishop of Le Puy realized this they began once more to strengthen them, speaking thus to them all: 'Do not be distressed and let not your hearts be troubled[47] about this news of the emperor's turning back. God is powerful enough to free us from the hands of the enemy. Be very steadfast in Christ's love, and never practise this deceit on your brothers, stealing away from them and fleeing. For it is certain that if you flee from fear of the enemy, Karbugha and all his multitude will pursue you, and you will never escape from their hands, when the news of your flight first reaches their ears. Let us stand firm and die in the Lord's name as is the purpose of our journey.' At these words everyone became steadfast and they decided to live and die with their brothers.

42. About a Christian knight whose horse fell as he was fleeing

Karbugha and all the legions of the gentiles greatly intensified their attack when they heard of the emperor's retreat, and they were sallying forth from the camp in gangs and ambushing anyone who came out of the city and whom they could behead according to their custom. On one particular day the Christians saw from the city walls certain Turks leaving the quarters of their tents for this purpose with a gang of forty horsemen. Even though they were dejected, and terrified of things going against them, some armed men met them straight away across the Orontes.

---

46 According to AK, the emperor was keen to bring reinforcements to the crusaders, but he heard of Karbugha's approach and realized that he did not have the forces to defeat him, so he turned back to save Constantinople (pp. 312–13). This is also the tenor of the *Gesta Francorum expugnantium Iherusalem* attributed to Bartolf of Nangis (*RHC Occ* iii. 491–543, at 501–2).

47 Cf. John 14: 27.

But they were at once repulsed by the Turks; they fled across the shallows and took up position on the other bank, for they saw that their starved horses could not compare for speed. At length, after a great hail of arrows, a certain stout-hearted[48] knight, who still trusted in the strength of his horse and thought the strength of his comrades was following behind, pursued at breakneck pace the Turks who were turning back far from the river. But none of the comrades dared to follow to assist him, and two dreadful horsemen from the gang flung back their horses at a gallop towards the pilgrim, and they bore down with their horses' lightning speed on the man as he fled, travelling back across the fields by the same route to his comrades. His horse caught its foot in the charge and fell down with him to the ground, and so he decided he was almost at the last moment of his life. When the killers had already come near to slay the thus fallen and completely helpless knight, their horses stopped dead, heedless of spurs as if they had been struck in the face and forced to back away, until the pilgrim knight could mount his horse as it scrambled to its feet, and by the favour of God and Lord Jesus Christ he fled again to his comrades' position. All the people standing on the bank and ramparts to watch wept for joy when they got back their brother unharmed in this way, and they clearly experienced God's hand in his escape.

43. Concerning the discovery of the Holy Lance

At this time of the affliction of famine, of which you have heard, and of fear of siege and concern over ambushes and attacks which the Turks were constantly inflicting from without, when God's army was humbled and hopeless, a certain cleric from the land of Provence claimed that the lance with which Lord Jesus was pierced in the side had been revealed to him in a vision.[49] And indeed this cleric reported to Lord Bishop Adhémar of Le Puy and to Count Raymond the place where they would find the precious treasure of the lance, that is to say in the church of blessed Peter, prince of apostles, affirming his vision with every protestation of

[48] Iuvenc., iii. 672; *Carm. de Laud.*, 367 (*HL* vol. 4, p. 533).

[49] The cleric is named in other sources as Peter Bartholomew. Extreme hunger and the unfamiliar plants the crusaders were eating may help to explain the dreams and hallucinations reported at this juncture. The discovery of the Lance was pivotal for the crusaders, the boost to morale which enabled them to defeat the massed armies under Karbughā, so it is reported by all the western sources: *Kreuzzugsbriefe*, pp. 160, 163, 166, 178; *GF* pp. 59–60; FC pp. 236–41; RA pp. 68–75; *ChA* pp. 271–2. RA is at one extreme of veneration for the Lance and may be contrasted with RC, who reports the discovery as a cynical political move on the part of the Provençals (pp. 118–21). AA writes with relative impartiality. For the Lance in general, see S. Runciman, 'The Holy Lance found at Antioch', *Analecta Bollandiana*, 88 (1950), pp. 197–205; C. Morris, 'Policy and visions: The case of the Holy Lance found at Antioch', in J. Gillingham and J. C. Holt (eds), *War and Government in the Middle Ages: Essays in Honour of J. O. Prestwich* (Woodbridge, 1984), pp. 33–45.

truth he could. They believed his words and came by common decree to the place which the cleric claimed was the site. Digging there, they found the lance just as they had learnt from the cleric. They displayed the find to all the assembled princes of the Christians in that same chapel, spreading news of it widely and wrapping it in precious purple cloth. Then there was hope and great happiness among the Christian people in the discovery and display of the lance, and they venerated it with no small solemnity and by offering countless quantities of gold and silver.

44. Where Peter carries out a legation to Karbugha, the prince of the besieging force

Then, after some days had passed, while all the officers and leaders of the Christian army were still hesitating and fearing for their lives with so many problems and the pestilence of famine, and they were afraid to join battle with so many nations, because they were exhausted in terms of the strength of the men and the condition of the horses, they made a plan and decided to send a legation to Karbugha the master and chief of the army and the siege, but they did not find anyone who would dare to speak to such a very fierce and proud man until Peter, who was the origin of this journey, took care of the matter and unhesitatingly offered to go and deliver messages to that magnificent man. At once this Peter, small in size but great in worth, was charged with the legation by Duke Godfrey, Bohemond, and other princes, and undertook the journey to Karbugha's tent in the middle of the gentiles, arriving alone save for God's protection. He delivered the Christians' messages to him through interpreters in this way: 'Karbugha, most renowned and glorious prince in your kingdom, I am the messenger of Duke Godfrey, Bohemond, and the princes of the entire Christian multitude: do not scorn to listen to their decisions and advice which I am carrying. The leaders of the Christian army have decided that if you will consent to believe in Lord Christ who is the true God and son of God, and will renounce gentile superstitions, they will become your soldiers and, restoring the estate of Antioch into your hands, they are prepared to serve you as lord and prince.' Karbugha scorned to listen to this, much less to do it. Indeed he instructed Peter the Hermit in his sacrilegious rites and the doctrines of the gentiles, declaring that he would never give them up.[50]

[50] This encounter is also reported in *GF* (pp. 66–7). The gist is the same, but there are some differences in detail, for example the author of *GF* says Peter was accompanied by an interpreter, Herluin, and he does not have Peter offer conversion to Karbugha. The embassy is also mentioned in Anselm of Ribemont's letter (*Kreuzzugsbriefe*, p. 159); RA (pp. 79, 81); FC (p. 248).

45. More about the same; and how boastfully the prince received the words of his legation

When Peter heard that Karbugha received his mention and preaching of the Christian faith with derision, he revealed other messages to him: 'It still seems,' he said, 'to the Christian princes, that since you are reluctant to have such eminent men put under you, and you refuse to become a Christian, you should choose twenty young knights from your multitude, and the Christians should do the same, and, with hostages given on both sides, and an oath sworn on both sides – you in your god, they in theirs – they should join in single combat in the middle. And if the Christians do not obtain victory they will return to their own lands peacefully and without injury, restoring Antioch to you. If, though, your men are unable to triumph, you and yours will withdraw peacefully from the siege, leaving the city and land to us, and you will not allow so great an army to perish in fighting one another. Moreover, if you despise this decree from the Christians be assured that tomorrow morning everyone will join battle with you.' When Karbugha heard these things he replied to Peter very arrogantly: 'Know one thing, Peter, that the Christians should choose, namely to send all their unbearded youth to us, as slaves to me and my lord the king of Khurasan, and we shall bestow on them great favours and gifts. Similarly girls who are still virgins shall have access to us, and permission to live. But men with beards or any grey hair are for beheading, with the married women. Otherwise I shall spare no one on grounds of age, but shall destroy them all by the sword, whom moreover I shall wrap in chains and iron fetters.' And when he had said this he showed Peter a countless and infinite abundance of every kind of chain and fetter.

46. Peter returns; the reply is revealed to the leaders, and there is a discussion as to what should be done for the common good

After this Peter received from Karbugha permission to return, and entered the city of Antioch, where he was to relate the boasting he had heard from Karbugha. There all the princes gathered round Peter in a circle, with the rest of the Christian soldiers, wanting to hear what Karbugha had replied, and to know whether he offered war or some treaty for making peace. Peter told the crowds of faithful people pressing around him that Karbugha wanted war, and said that he had uttered nothing except in arrogance and confidence in his multitude. And when he started to report the rest of the threats which he had heard, Duke Godfrey did not allow him to go on, but drew him aside and warned him to say nothing to anyone about all the things he had heard, lest the people should fail through fear and torment and withdraw from the war. Now three weeks and three days had passed since the Christian people were besieged and began to suffer from shortage of supplies and lack of bread. They did not have the strength to suffer these things any longer, so great and small consulted together, saying it was better to die in battle than to perish from so cruel a famine and to grow weaker from day to day and die.

47. Battle is proclaimed; everyone is made ready as if they are about to die the next day; and the battle-divisions are drawn up and allocated to their commanders

When this voice of the complaining people was heard it was proclaimed that battle would be joined on the following morning, and all were ordered to spend the night in prayers, and when they had been purged of their sins by confession they would be strengthened by the sacrament of the Lord's body and blood, and so at first light they would be armed. When morning came, moreover, the Christian soldiers assembled, all with weapons, hauberks, and helmets, on the eve of the apostles Peter and Paul,[51] and drew up battle divisions while they were still inside the city. They appointed Hugh the Great, brother of the king of France, leader of the first division and standard-bearer of cavalry and infantry. Robert count of Flanders and Robert prince of Normans were put in charge of two divisions and, thus joined, the two of them stood close together on one side. The bishop of Le Puy was directing his division himself towards the mountains, and the lance which they had found was raised on high in the middle of his formation in the hands of a certain cleric. Peter of Astenois, his brother, Rainald of Toul, Warner of Grez, Henry of Esch, Reinhard of Hamersbach, and Walter of Domedart were placed in charge of their formation towards these mountains and the road which leads to the seaport of Symeon the aforesaid former hermit. Count Raimbold of Orange, Louis of Mousson, and Lambert son of Cono of Montaigu were sent to govern one battle division. Duke Godfrey made up his battle division from two thousand cavalry and infantry, with Germans, Swabians, Bavarians, Saxons, and Lotharingians, and their hand and sword was accustomed to be most fierce on the necks of the enemy.[52] Tancred drew up his battle division alone from cavalry and infantry. Hugh of Saint-Pol and his son Engelrand, Thomas of Castle Fère, Baldwin of Bourcq, Robert son of Gerard, Raymond Pilet, Rainald of Beauvais, Walo of Chaumont, Everard of Le Puiset, Drogo of Mouchy, Rothard son of Godfrey, Conan the Breton, Rodolph, also a Breton, all of these were appointed in charge of two divisions. Gaston of Béziers, Gerard of the city of Roussillon, and William of Montpellier were content with just the one. Bohemond of Sicily was named general of the last division, which was most numerous in cavalry and infantry, so that he could protect the other divisions and perhaps help with reinforcements any who needed them.[53]

---

[51] 28 June, 1098.

[52] Gen. 49: 8.

[53] The primary authorities vary as to the number of divisions: FC says four (pp. 251–8); *GF* six (p. 68); Anselm of Ribemont five (*Kreuzzugsbriefe*, p. 160); PT seven (p. 111); RA eight or thirteen (p. 82). Of other contemporary writers, OV has seven (v. 110–11);

48. Leaving Count Raymond in the city, the faithful sally forth from the gates and the infidels, who have received a signal from the chief citadel, meet them

Once all their men were organized and their positions decided, they left Count Raymond, who was suffering slightly from illness, to protect the city with a strong force of Christians, because of the Turks who were in the higher citadel with Sansadonias, son of Yaghi-Siyhan. When the plans were complete they unanimously decided to set out just as they had been organized, each prince with his battle division, through the open gate from which the stone bridge spans the Orontes, towards the legions of the barbarians, bearing a thousand different, decorated banners, and wearing hauberks and helmets. Karbugha, likewise, and Suleyman positioned their manifold battle divisions on right and left wing, in front and to the rear, holding bows of bone and horn in their hands for the fight. And they charged from the camp at speed to meet the Christians, so that they might first begin the conflict with a hail of arrows, sounding blasts of the trumpet and a dreadful blare of bugles. For they had had foreknowledge not only from Peter's legation, who had foretold to them that the battle would be on the next day, but they had daily been suspicious and anxious lest the Christians unexpectedly join battle with them. For this reason they constantly sent messengers to Sansadonias's citadel to ask that if at any time he spotted the Christians arming themselves or inciting to battle he should send word to them – because he had a view from the citadel sited on the mountain ridge of everything everywhere within the city – and then they themselves could also be ready and formed up for battle, and the Gauls would harm them the less since they were prepared. Sansadonias refused to send messages, but he promised to fly a very big cloth of a horrible black colour fixed on the end of spears on the top of his citadel, then to sound loudly the terrible trumpet blasts, and thus to inform the gentiles with certainty of the Christians' preparations for war. Therefore, erecting this dark cloth as a sign of battle being joined, he fixed it on the mountain top upon the aforesaid citadel itself, at the same hour when the Christians' preparations began to be made at very first light and their battle formations were being drawn up, so that when they saw this sign the gentiles would also take care of their weapons in order to fight back, and would order their battle formations. Straight away, warned by the sign of this cloth and the din of the horribly blaring trumpets, they massed and formed up, and set out to meet the Christian troops, about two thousand of them dismounting from their horses to deny them the bridge and its way across the river.

Gilo nine (*The* Historia Vie Hierosimitane *of Gilo of Paris*, (ed.) C. W. Grocock and J. E. Siberry [Oxford, 1997], pp. 184–5); AA, followed by WT, has twelve (WT pp. 330–31). For a discussion, see France, *Victory*, pp. 289–91.

49. Christ's people in the first division are victorious, but they are hindered by the infidels' smoke

The Christian princes, however, who were organized and assembled at that same gate, had suspected and foreseen that the Turks would oppose them with bow and arrow as they left the city, and sent forward all the archers of the common infantry from the gate across the bridge and the river Orontes, and with God's favour they took the bridge first; they attacked the Turks, who were shooting dangerously, by themselves shooting arrows, and with their chests protected by shields they were able to withstand and to move away from the place until, with Christian arrows flying overhead, they arrived at the place where the Turkish horses were stationed. The Turks, who had dismounted from their horses at the bridge and run ahead on foot, realized that they could not resist, nor drive away the Christian men from the bridge, but that their horses could perish, wounded by arrows, and they turned in flight, hurrying as quickly as they could to their horses and mounting them, and so they conceded, albeit unwillingly, an unimpeded way out to the Christians. At this, Anselm of Ribemont, who had been stationed in this front division with Hugh the Great, rejoicing at the happy outcome and first victory of the faithful, brandished his spear and swept into the middle of the Turks, unhorsing some, piercing some, overthrowing others and inflicting an enormous slaughter on them. Hugh the Great, indeed, seeing that Anselm had checked the enemy without any fear of death, charged up at once, punishing the hostile troops with a similar slaughter. Robert of Flanders, Robert the Norman, Baldwin prince of Hainaut, Eustace as well, were struggling bravely and boldly with the enemy forces, destroying them in a considerable massacre. Suleyman, duke of the Turks, most fierce of knights, and Rosseleon his associate, who was one of the four chief men of Antioch under King Yaghi-Siyhan, were cut off from the rest of the alliance with their troops, which numbered about fifteen thousand, and they hastily made their way towards these mountains and the road which leads to the port of St Symeon, so that if the Christians were by any chance defeated and considered fleeing there they might oppose them at the coast and, catching them unawares, quickly destroy them. They were avidly keen on this idea and hurried their march more than usual, and they came by chance upon the division of Count Reinard, Peter of Astenois, Walter of Domedart, Henry of Esch, Reinhard of Hamersbach (most illustrious knight), and Warner of Grez, and to hold them up they suddenly hurled fire from pots onto the surface of the ground across which they had to travel to reach the Christian alliance. As the fire stuck to the ground, and the parched grasses and dry branches of thorns caught light, it instantly gained strength in extent and size, and so a cloud was stirred up by the wind, the dark smoke thickened, obscuring the eyes only of the faithful and making it difficult for them to see.

50. The pilgrims are scattered in many directions; it is reported to Duke Godfrey that Bohemond's division has been placed in deadly peril

Thereupon, as the Turks pursued them cunningly behind the cloud of smoke, they went astray in the gloom and were separated from their companions, and the Turks slaughtered some and shot others through with arrows. Only those on horseback escaped by the speed of their horses, but they were not wholly unscathed by arrows, and indeed three hundred of the infantry were killed and some were kept back in fetters. Karageth, moreover, a Turk from the state of Karan, saw Suleyman's happy success in destroying the battle division of Reinhard, Warner, Peter and the rest, and, speeding up more confidently his circling advance, he swept down from the mountains next to the town and the river Orontes along with the prince of Damascus; Ridwan of Aleppo,[54] a Turkish city, was similarly approaching to outflank Bohemond's division, which was the last and most numerous in infantry and Franks. They attacked the division and tried to break it and scatter it with arrows and strength of numbers. Since they were overwhelmed, indeed, by the forces of so many and the cunning enemy's trick, Bohemond's surrounded troops were forced into a wretched and worried flock, like sheep about to be killed by wolves, and they could no longer resist, but were on the point of dying, surrounded on all sides by troops of infidels. But yet a single messenger ran the length of the road and in a tearful demand urged and exhorted Duke Godfrey, who was fighting fiercely with Pulagit, with Amasa, Boesas and Balduk and conquering in the name of Jesus son of the living God, to look back and realize what a difficult situation Bohemond and his company were in, and unless he quickly came to their assistance, the messenger declared, they would all be destroyed instantly by the Turks.

51. The duke chases the enemy and destroys them; he brings back his brothers from death's door

When Duke Godfrey heard about the attack from the account of Bohemond's swift messenger, and that his divisions were already almost surrounded by the Turks, he lifted his gaze and saw that Bohemond's strength and his divisions were exhausted by the weight of warfare[55] and could hardly withstand the enemies' forces. Whereupon he rapidly sped against the adversaries with the Swabians, Bavarians, Saxons, Lotharingians, Germans, and Romans who were in his division, bearing purple banners differently decorated, in order to repulse the forces of the gentiles and to assist the troops who were in difficulties. Hugh the Great, with the advance archers of the Christians, was occupying as victor part of the plain taken in the sortie of the first division from the bridge which stretched out from the city across the Orontes, the Turks having fled and been destroyed, and he saw that Duke

[54] Ridwan was not present.

[55] Poeta Saxo, i. 324; *Gesta Berengarii*, iii. 74 (*HL* vol. 4, p. 282).

Godfrey's division and banners were turning back on the road which led to the river Orontes, and he too went rapidly back on the same journey to the duke's division, taking with him his division to reinforce Godfrey's troops and weaponry, knowing that this was the place where the greatest intensity of the battle was happening. Both princes slowed down the pace of their cavalry so that the infantry could catch up. When the Turks saw them coming towards them unhesitatingly to reinforce their Christian comrades, they began one by one to withdraw from the attack and assault, and they turned tail and travelled the road back to their tents and took flight, while the duke and the young Christian knights fiercely pursued and cut them down.

52. More about the same

At length, after crossing a certain small and scanty stream which flowed down from the mountain region, while the Christian foot soldiers were somewhat held up in the valley, the Turks who were positioned for defence on the top of one of the mountains reined in their horses and tried to frighten away the Gauls with their arrows. In response the German pilgrims, who had fearless hearts, called on Christ's mercy in loud voices and unhesitatingly charged the Turks who stood against them. From then onwards they put the Turks to flight one after another, so that not one of them dared any longer to stand against them or torment them in that fight. The great prince Bohemond and Adam, son of Michael, saw the strength of Godfrey's resistance and relief of the people and saw that he and his men were inflicting great slaughter among the battle divisions of the enemy with all the troops and military strength of which he was the supreme commander, and so they broke off delays and charged through the middle of the Turkish divisions with a charge and a loud cry. They inflicted a terrible slaughter on them, and the plain was covered with bodies of the fallen like hailstones, on this side and that the troops most cruelly intermingled. But with God's help the fighting oppressed the enemy peoples and the entire weight of war was turned against them. Moreover, arrogant Karbugha, who had held back the greater part of his forces and resources and had occupied a position on the left of the Christians, had not been able to render any assistance to his fleeing and defeated comrades, for the bishop of Le Puy was fighting back strongly against him with the whole army of Provençals, and was always holding before him the Holy Lance. From this it is to be deduced that with God and Lord Jesus at work Karbugha's strength grew feeble, stricken with the fear of God, and the hearts of his men shook, because Karbugha remained motionless in this way before the obstruction and vision of the heavenly weapon, as if he found himself forgetful of the whole battle with his countless followers.

53. Karbugha's men have been defeated and he puts his hope of survival in flight; the bishop of Le Puy pursues, but loses him

So, as he was stuck there in stupor and ecstasy, by God's will, a man approached him bearing bad news and saying: 'Karbugha, most illustrious prince, why are you going to drag out longer this delay in front of this Christian battle division? Do you not see that all the army you led out has been defeated and destroyed and has slipped away in flight? Look, in your own camp and your men's the Gauls are all over the place stealing spoils and gathering up all sorts of things, and look, very soon they will arrive where you are.' Karbugha was disturbed by this sad and hard message and he lifted his gaze and saw that his battle divisions had disappeared in flight, and immediately he too, together with all his company, turned tail and fled, making for the road by which they had come to return to the kingdom of Khurasan and the river Euphrates.[56] The holy bishop pursued him with all his division, but not for long because of the lack of horses and the weariness of the foot soldiers. For the Christians had lost the horses they had brought out from Gaul through different misfortunes, so that people who were there declare truly that scarcely two hundred horses skilled in war survived on the day when they joined battle with so many nations of gentiles.

54. Where the princes are recorded who are begging as a result of poverty

Very many eminent and very noble cavalrymen indeed – their number is not known – were numbered among the foot soldiers after their horses had died and been eaten because of the shortages of the famine, and these people, who had always been used to horses from boyhood and were accustomed to go into battle[57] on horseback, learned to fight as foot soldiers. Any of these eminent men who had now been able to acquire a mule or a donkey or a worthless pack animal or a palfrey used it as a horse. Among them, princes who were very powerful and rich in their own land went into battle riding on a donkey. No wonder, for their own funds had long since run out and from need they had begged, and after their own weapons had been sold from want, they used Turkish weapons which were unaccustomed and incongruous in battle. Count Hartmann belonged to this number: he is said to have been rich and very noble and one of the most powerful people in the land of Swabia, but to have ridden a donkey to the battle and held merely a Turk's round shield and sword on the day. No wonder, for he was impoverished of all things; his hauberk, helmet, and weapons had been sold and for a long time he had begged, and he had almost reached the point where he could not live by begging. Henry

---

[56] More, legendary, detail concerning Karbughā's flight is to be found in *Les Chétifs*, (ed.) G. M. Myers (Tuscaloosa, AL, 1981), p. xxiv.

[57] 'certamen inire solebant': a hexameter ending, cf. *HL* vol. 1, p. 323 (e.g. Poeta Saxo).

of Esch, noble knight and worthy of soldierly praise, had reached that point too. And then glorious Duke Godfrey took pity on them and he allocated one loaf with a portion of meat or fish from his own funds to Hartmann. He named Henry his guest and table companion, because he served him for many years and through many dangers of battle as knight and his man.

55. About the same thing; and about the flight and slaughter of the enemy

Only those who have never heard anything like it marvel at these miseries and impoverishments of the noble leaders, and those who did not see the evils which befell such eminent men in the course of so long an exile, but those people do not marvel who bear witness that they saw Duke Godfrey himself and Robert prince of Flanders in need of provisions and horses at the last. Even Duke Godfrey was in need, and he accepted the horse on which he rode on the day of the great battle as a gift from Count Raymond, exacted by much entreaty. For he had lacked money on account of the difficulty of the famine we have spoken about, and the very great distribution of alms and of things which he paid out for beggars and impoverished soldiers. Robert was likewise in need, the very rich and powerful prince of fertile Flanders, and those who were there and saw this with their own eyes claim he often used to beg in the army,[58] and we learnt from many people's account that he obtained the very horse which he had mounted on the day of the great battle by begging. On these horses, then, which had been obtained by suffering, the eminent princes now rode into battle against the divisions of the infidels on the day; perceiving that Karbugha had turned his back with all his company they gave their horses their heads and pursued the Turks at a constant gallop as they failed and fled, giving ground and scattering, for a distance of three miles. Tancred, who was also commanding a division of Christians, saw plainly his opponents' flight, and arrived swiftly with his cavalry troop to slaughter the Turks, and he pursued them as they fled for six miles on the road. Karbugha saw his men flee and his army scatter, and he always pressed on to escape, until he arrived at the great river Euphrates and slipped away with his men by boat.

56. About the plundering of the camp, and the variety of chains

These aforesaid princes of the Christians were intent upon the slaughter and pursuit of the enemy; the company of Count Raymond and Bishop Adhémar from the land called Provence, eager for booty and Turkish spoils, did not join the pursuit but stayed in that same place where victory was given, and plundered abundant spoils of gold bezants, corn, wine, clothing, and tents. Others, indeed, who were keen

[58] RC also has a graphic description of Robert, reduced to begging for his very horse (pp. 79–80).

to fight, saw those men filling their hands with spoils and were corrupted by the same avarice; they took possession likewise of booty and abundant and infinite spoils and returned to Antioch in praise and happiness and shouting with delight, and those who had previously been poor and famished were now satisfied with all kinds of good things. They found countless volumes in that same camp of the gentiles, in which were written the sacrilegious rites of the Saracens, Turks, and all the other races, and wicked charms of prophets and soothsayers with detestable writings. Different kinds of chains, fetters, and nooses made of rope and iron and ox and horse hide were found there in the tents for binding the Christians. They had all been brought to Antioch, very many and infinite in number, with very many objects and tents and with Karbugha's own pavilion, which was constructed in the style of a town with turrets and walls of various colours and precious silks. That same wonderful pavilion had streets flowing away from it in which two thousand men are reported to have lived in comfort. Of all the women, young boys, and the many infants still being suckled whom they found in the camp, some were slaughtered, others trampled by the feet of horses, and they filled the plains with wretched and mangled remains, destitute of help from their own gentile peoples who were running away from the battle. The other deeds which were done in this battle, among the Christian people as well as the gentile, and those wonderful and unbelievable things which were done during the siege of Antioch cannot, I think, be recorded by any pen, any memory, so many and such various things are reported to have happened there.[59]

[59] See France, *Victory*, pp. 282–96 for a detailed analysis and reconstruction of the battle.

Book 5

1. About the restoration of the divine mysteries and the reinstatement of the patriarch

After this victory on the plain of Antioch, the great and royal Syrian city, the bishop of Le Puy and the other princes came back within the ramparts of the aforesaid town from the flight and their slaughter of Karbugha's army, and they cleansed from all defilement the basilica of blessed Peter the apostle, which the Turks had profaned with their sacrilegious rites, and they rebuilt with every adornment the holy altars which had been overturned, making good with utmost reverence the likeness of our Lord Jesus Christ and the figures of the saints which the Turks had covered over with cement and blinded as if they were living people, and they restored Catholic priests to carry out the divine mysteries in that place, from all the clergy, Greeks as well as Latins. Then they ordered chasubles, dalmatics, copes, and all adornment for the use of the living God's churches, to be made with purest purple cloth and precious silk and ornaments they found which had been left in Antioch, so that with these the priests and ministers would be furnished to celebrate divine services in the temple of blessed Peter, or when they walked in procession with psalms and hymns to the chapel of St Mary, mother of our Lord Jesus Christ, on Sundays or on special feast days. This same chapel was a short distance away from the church of St Paul and as yet remained intact and undamaged by those same Turks; after they had conquered the town it had been left by the Turks' gift and licence for the use among themselves of those Christians only who remained.[1] There was a patriarch of the city, a most Christian man whom the Turks, while they were still blockaded in the town by the Christians' siege, used frequently to hang alive by ropes on the ramparts in full view of all to increase the torments of the Christian people, and whose feet they had often injured by shackling him. The Christians restored him to his see with honour, and with all submissiveness and piety they gave him authority as prince of the Antiochene church.[2]

---

[1] AA shows here a surprisingly accurate and unprejudiced understanding of Islam, which on the one hand abhorred the portrayal of humans in their religious buildings, and on the other permitted Antiochene Christians to worship unmolested in their own chapel. It was the arrival of the Latin Christians which caused the persecution of the patriarch described in the following paragraph.

[2] Patriarch John IV was a Byzantine, appointed Greek patriarch of Antioch in 1091. His restoration by the papal legate has been seen as evidence that Adhémar, as Urban's representative, wanted to impose a unified ecclesiastical organization using both Eastern and Latin clergy. Adhémar's own death and the rivalry of the secular leaders ensured that any

2. The princes to whom Antioch was subjected

When these religious matters had been considered and put in order as a priority, they made Bohemond lord and advocate of Antioch, because he had laid out a great deal for the betrayal of the city and had put in a lot of hard work to place guards along the towers and ramparts against the Turkish raids. Bohemond assumed power and lordship over the city, and placed his residence and a guard of his men in the citadel which was higher up in the mountains, since there was no Turkish defence there any more to oppose him. For when they heard of the flight and ruin of their men, Sansadonias and those who had themselves been in the citadel likewise fled through the mountains, leaving the fortress empty and undefended. Raymond, count of the aforesaid region of Provence, who was always insatiable in his acquisitiveness, attacked that tower which was close to the bridge on the Orontes in the direction of the port of St Symeon and garrisoned it with his followers, and forced this part of the city to submit to his authority. The rest of the princes, Duke Godfrey, Robert of Flanders, Robert prince of Normandy, and all those who had laboured no less hard about the city, did not seek at all to rule the city or to bestow on themselves its revenues or tribute, for they did not want to violate the treaty and solemn promise they had made to the emperor of Constantinople. They had vowed to him that if Antioch were taken they would keep it for him with all the castles and cities belonging to his kingdom, because it was part of his kingdom like Nicaea, and they would restore it to his sovereign power. From that time on Bohemond began to envy Count Raymond, but secretly as yet.[3]

3. Concerning the two princes sent to the emperor, one of whom perished while the other only just escaped

Shortly after the victory God granted to them, the above princes – those whose concern was to keep the treaty and oath – sent Baldwin count of Hainaut together with Hugh the Great, the king of France's brother, in a legation to that same emperor of the Greeks, to find out from him the reason why he had acted so wickedly

---

such plan came to nothing: B. Hamilton, *The Latin Church in the Crusader States* (London, 1980), p. 7; J. Brundage, 'Adhémar of Puy and his critics', *Speculum*, 34 (1959), pp. 201–10. WT – himself a dignitary of the Latin Church – records that John retired voluntarily to Constantinople some two years later, because he realized that a Greek could not effectively govern Latins (pp. 339–40). The letter sent by the princes to Urban following Adhémar's death hints that they too perceived problems in the situation (*Kreuzzugsbriefe*, p. 164).

[3] Raymond's thinking at this time is equivocal. AA implies he was making a bid for Antioch, while RA naturally makes him an ally of Godfrey and Robert of Flanders, outmanoeuvred by Bohemond (pp. 83–4). There is no doubt of Bohemond's ambitions: already in July 1098 he was granting privileges in the city to the Genoese (*Kreuzzugsbriefe*, pp. 155–6).

towards the people of God, and why when they were in such great difficulty the emperor had failed to produce the assistance he had promised, since he could not find the princes deceitful or misleading in anything so far. They were also instructed to point out to that same emperor that the princes of the army were released from any promise or oath because at the prompting of fearful and fugitive men he lied about all the things he had promised.[4] These two princes accepted the legation of their brothers and made their way to that same emperor through the middle of Rūm, where they fell by chance into a Turcopole ambush in the neighbourhood of Nicaea, being unable to turn away to left or right. The Turcopoles, a wicked race and Christian in name not in deed, who were born of Turkish fathers and Greek mothers, saw the men falling into their hands and suddenly charged down on them, and they shot Baldwin, who was travelling slightly in front of Hugh, so they say, full of arrows. Some declare it is true that they led him away alive and captive, but it is not known to this very day what death so very noble and Christian prince suffered.[5] Hugh the Great, who was making his way a short distance behind Baldwin, saw the torments of that man's soul and retraced his journey at a gallop to a wood next to the mountains, where he took refuge and escaped the hands of the wicked Turcopoles.

4. Concerning the fatal pestilence which occurred among God's people

After this, while many ships plentifully laden with supplies sailed into the port of St Symeon from all directions, and the pilgrims who had been set free from the barbarians' siege by God's victory were enjoying a happy abundance of food and all necessary supplies, a plague of most severe mortality happened in the city of Antioch, by which a very great and countless multitude of the Christian army, as many noble leaders as of the common crowd, were taken. In this fatal scourge the reverend bishop of Le Puy was the first to be struck down and ended his life on the first of August. Nobles and lesser people wept over him with overwhelming grief and brought him for burial in the basilica of St Peter itself, in the same place where the Lord's lance was found.[6] After the venerable priest was buried this

---

[4] AA goes further than the author of *GF*, who says only that Hugh was sent to ask the emperor to take over the city and fulfil his obligations ('He went and he never came back', p. 72). WT is more temperate than AA, making it clear that the princes considered that their agreement with Alexios was contractual, and if he did not come to their assistance then they did not consider themselves bound by it. He dwells at some length on Hugh's disgraceful desertion (p. 343).

[5] FC, like *GF*, notes only Hugh's departure to Constantinople (not Baldwin's) and thence to France (p. 258). GN can throw no light on Baldwin's fate: 'we are still not sure what misfortune befell him', while he is reluctant to think ill of Hugh, who redeemed himself by a martyr's death in 1101 (p. 243).

[6] For Adhémar's death and something of its impact, see *GF* p. 74; FC p. 258; RA p. 84, and the letter from the princes to the pope (*Kreuzzugsbriefe*, pp. 161–5).

severe plague grew more widespread and serious, and death began to diminish the Christian army to such an extent that for six months scarcely a day dawned but a hundred, or fifty, or thirty at least, gave up the ghost, as many nobles as lesser people. In the harshness of this scourge Henry of Esch, a knight of noble birth, fell sick and died in the castle of Turbessel and was given a Christian burial there. Reinhard of Hamersbach, a very famous knight in deeds and birth, likewise lost his life and was buried in the entrance of the basilica of Peter the prince of apostles. Many more – cavalry and infantry alike, nobles and lesser people, monks and clerics, great and small, even the feminine sex – over one hundred thousand were laid waste by death, without a weapon being wielded.

5. Concerning Turkish ambushes; and about a certain Folbert and his wife

Meanwhile many rejoiced in peace and victory and they avoided the fatal scourge, and while they were making their frequent journeys to Edessa for supplies, hoping to get something from Baldwin's hand, they suffered very many ambushes and attacks from the Turks who lived in the fortress of Azaz, and quite often some were taken away as prisoners. One day a certain Folbert, an outstanding knight from the castle at Bouillon, fell into the hands of Turkish raiders while he was making the journey to Edessa with his wife, who was of graceful appearance, and the other brothers. He was overcome there and beheaded with the rest after putting up no great resistance. His wife, because she was greatly pleasing to their eyes[7] on account of her beautiful face, was taken prisoner and led away into the fortress of Azaz. The prince and lord of the fortress[8] ordered her to be treated honourably while he found out if she might be worth some great sum of money in ransom. Not long after, a renowned Turkish knight, who had come to the lord of the fortress of Azaz as a mercenary, saw Folbert's wife and was inflamed with excessive love and eager desire, and he entreated the lord of the fortress very earnestly for her, asking that he might be rewarded by receiving her in marriage as the lord's gift in place of wages. This was done.

6. Concerning hostilities between Ridwan of Aleppo and the prince of Azaz

This same Turkish knight, happy at his marriage, inflicted ambushes and warfare much more than he used to on the enemies of the lord of Azaz, and he frequently plundered Aleppo, a great city belonging to one Ridwan, a Turkish prince, and he would often take prisoner those who pursued him to seize the spoils, or he would defeat and behead them. For between Ridwan of Aleppo and the prince of Azaz there were on both sides hatred and bitter hostility. Then, when some

7 Biblical, e.g. 1 Kgs. (1 Sam.) 18: 26; 24: 5.

8 His name was Omar, according to Kemal al-Din: *RHC Or*, iii, p. 595.

days had passed, Ridwan was angry because this knight and his band of soldiers from Azaz were often opposing him, and he collected from all parts of the city of Aleppo Turks who acknowledged his authority, intending that on an agreed day they would besiege Azaz in a strong force and conquer it. When he found this out, the prince of Azaz was anxiously concerned how he might summon auxiliary forces to enable him to meet the many thousands assembled by Ridwan.

7. Advice of the Turkish husband of the Christian woman to seek an alliance with the Christians

At this point, among the various plans which they were making, the Turkish knight who had married a Christian wife urged on the prince of Azaz at her prompting, saying: 'Surely you see that Ridwan is bringing together an army and forces of Turks from everywhere, and has decided to blockade and conquer with many thousands you and the fortress you hold? Now if you will trust my advice you will waste no time before pledging friendship by giving your right hand to Godfrey, duke of the Christian army, who powerfully took Antioch when Karbugha had fled, and in this way you may be sure that you will acquire the whole assistance and alliance of the Christians in this emergency. For you know that this Christian race excels all others in military performance and courage, and none may be compared to them for loyalty and honour. So do not scorn this advice, but embrace his friendship without delay, and so, with him allied to you, you will know that all the Christians will be volunteers for every assistance.' The prince knew that this was sensible advice and that in this way he would be able to withstand Ridwan and his many forces, so he sent a messenger of the Christian faith, a Syrian by race, a wonderfully eloquent man, to Duke Godfrey at Antioch, speaking in these words:

8. The message of the prince of Azaz to Duke Godfrey, and how the duke hesitates to enter into a treaty with Turks

'The prince of Azaz sends greeting to Godfrey the great prince and duke of the Christians, and everything he may desire. On the advice of our men we are sending to you to arrange peace and friendship between us, to establish loyalty and love, and for our weapons to be shared in any emergency of war. For we have discovered that you are a man and a prince powerful in military strength, and that you are able to offer assistance to those allied by treaty to you, and you cannot be released from the bond of your loyalty by any inconstancy. For these reasons we choose you before all others, we are speaking to you, we request assistance of you, we are making a treaty with this assurance, by which you may be certain of having our trust always. Ridwan of the state of Aleppo has become our enemy, he has assembled Turkish reinforcements from everywhere and he will shortly come in great strength and with a numerous army to our fortress at Azaz. And I have decided not to meet and resist him with any assistance of the Turkish princes, but to put our defence in your hands, if you do not refuse to trust me and to help.' After Duke Godfrey had heard this legation he took his men's advice, asking them about their confidence in the proposed peace, since he was doubtful lest it might be Turkish treachery which would harm him and his men with some wicked device, and the treaty might be broken on some evil pretext.

9. Mahumeth the prince's son is given as hostage to Duke Godfrey; pigeons are sent out bearing news of the treaty

The prince of Azaz heard from his messenger's account that the duke and his men were doubtful about this agreement and did not greatly trust the Turks' promises, so he sent his own son, Mahumeth by name, whom he dearly loved, as hostage, so that from this time onwards he would be more confident about agreeing the peace and treaty between them. The duke received his son as hostage and agreed on trust and friendship with him, and promised with an enduring vow that he would assist him against all opposition and would never fail. When these promises were made they agreed a certain day on which Godfrey would lead out the Christian army as reinforcements against Ridwan and would put to flight the Turkish legions from the siege of Azaz, with the help of their Lord God Jesus Christ. When the duke promised these things faithfully the envoys from the fortress of Azaz were very joyful and happy, and without delay they took from their garments two pigeons, nice tame birds which they had brought with them. They wrote the duke's replies and faithful promises on paper and tied them to the birds' tails with thread, and sent them forth from their hands to carry the good news. The duke and everyone who was with him wondered at this sending out of birds, but the reply came at once as to why the messages were sent by way of birds: 'Our lord duke and his supporters should not wonder at these birds we have sent, for we haven't done it childishly or frivolously. They were sent for this reason, so that they may hasten with rapid and unceasing flight the message of trust which you hold towards the lord of Azaz, and they may bear assurances concerning your assistance and whatever good luck or hindrance has befallen us. There is yet another reason why these birds were sent ahead with letters: if they were found in our garments by any of our brother Turks then they would be our death sentence.' The birds had already flown away with the letters entrusted to them, and they faithfully returned to the palace and home of the lord of Azaz. The prince of Azaz welcomed the tame birds affectionately, as was his custom, released the written papers from their tails, opened them and read Duke Godfrey's secrets. He thus knew all about the day of his arrival to support Azaz, and in how many thousands the Christian armies would relieve him.[9]

[9] The tenor of AA's description makes it apparent that his audience would find the use of carrier pigeons novel. This episode and the subsequent use of pigeons in the east, and their adoption, or re-introduction, into western Europe, is examined in S. B. Edgington,

10. Ridwan besieges Azaz; a Christian army arrives on the scene

When he had thoroughly read and understood the letters, and was sure of Godfrey's friendship and loyalty, he garrisoned the fortress at Azaz with very many soldiers and their weapons and summoned the forces of his Turkish allies from different places. And Ridwan was there with a strong force numbering forty thousand Turks, coming down onto the plains of Azaz, and he pitched tents and took up position around its walls, attacking the ramparts and towers day after day with a heavy assault. He had been there just five days when Godfrey appeared, marching out of Antioch in great strength with banners of wonderful beauty, the army wearing hauberks and helmets, bringing archers both mounted and on foot, and completing the journey in three days. After one day's journey Baldwin his brother, setting out from Edessa with three thousand warriors, met him with banners fluttering in the breeze, summoned by the duke's messenger. But Bohemond and Raymond were very envious and angry, because the prince of Azaz himself had sent first to Godfrey and entered into an alliance, and given his own son to him as hostage for their mutual loyalty, and so they utterly refused to set out on this the duke's expedition.

11. Bohemond and Raymond are reconciled with Duke Godfrey; the siege is lifted, but some of the Christians are killed in ambushes

When the duke had travelled for one day and he realized that these princes had remained behind because of envy, and they could not be prevailed upon to come by coaxings, threats or humble entreaty, he sent a legation to them once again, which spoke in this way: 'It is not fitting for you who are pillars and leaders of the army to leave us, your fellow Christian brothers, without your assistance, asserting a false pretext against us, since we have never failed you yet in any difficulty or emergency, but have always been prepared even to die for you on this journey. Believe absolutely that if you stay behind today and do not bring us help in this enterprise we shall be your enemies, and we shall not lift a finger for any difficulty you get into.' When Bohemond and Raymond saw that the entire Christian army had answered Duke Godfrey's call and was making its way to Azaz, and that the duke and the other brothers spoke to them in anger, they realized that they had acted unfairly towards their brothers and, conscience-stricken, they called up around four thousand of their comrades, as many cavalry as infantry, and they followed Godfrey on the royal way and joined up with him in the region of Azaz. So the number of the assembled princes and their army was thirty thousand warriors. Ridwan and those who had come with him to besiege Azaz, knowing that the Christians' divisions had arrived on the neighbouring plains, seeing from a distance the fires from their camp glowing in the darkness and the cloud of smoke

'The doves of war: the part played by carrier pigeons in the crusades', in M. Balard (ed.), *Autour de la Première Croisade* (Paris, 1996), pp. 167–75.

going up, consulted and, as they were of like mind, they moved camp away from the blockade, knowing that they could not withstand so many thousands. Some ten thousand of them were marching in a wide circle on a route through known footpaths and mountainous country and from the rear they attacked with arrows the pilgrims who were lagging and following after the army, and, unknown to the duke and his men who were well ahead by two miles, they overcame and terrorized six hundred and put them to the sword.

12. Duke Godfrey is received with great gratitude by the prince of Azaz; the treaty is renewed

When the duke and his men heard this cruel news, they rode swiftly and hastened to meet the Turks as they were returning from this massacre in a mountain valley in the region of Azaz, inflicting no small slaughter on them there with lances and swords. When they were destroyed and fleeing through the mountain slopes and thickets of thorns, the duke and his other fellow leaders made for the fortress of Azaz, and its prince came out to meet them with three hundred wearing helmets and shining hauberks, giving many thanks to the duke for everything which had happened victoriously for him with the duke's assistance against the forces of his enemies. He was joined to the duke in that place in a renewed treaty and unbreakable friendship, in full view of all the people who were there, promising that he would stand firm and never be estranged from the company of that same duke and from friendship and love of the Christians. The duke, who made a treaty with the prince on his men's advice, bestowed on him a helmet marvellously inlaid with gold and silver and a hauberk of great beauty, which Herbrand of Bouillon, a noble knight and distinguished in warlike performance, always used to wear when fighting battles. With Ridwan fled from besieging Azaz, and the prince of that fortress graciously commended by the duke and all his fellow leaders and peacefully restored to his own, the army retraced its steps to Antioch and all the princes settled there together in victory and great peace.[10]

---

[10] The truce with A'zāz was significant because it was the first with a Moslem leader and the ensuing successful campaign showed the Christian leaders how dissension among the Turks could be exploited. AA's story of Folbert's widow and her part in the agreement is not substantiated even by WT, who says only that the amir despatched a loyal Christian to Godfrey (p. 347). AA may have introduced or embellished that part of the tale to please his audience in Lotharingia. However, the rest of the narrative is so circumstantial and AA's information about Turkish politics so well informed, that it is convincing (see Beaumont, p. 118). RA has a brief account, agreeing in essentials though suppressing any reluctance on the part of Raymond to take part in the expedition (p. 88). Most interestingly, Kemal al-Din (writing in the thirteenth century) describes the revolt of Omar, the summoning of Frankish allies, the retreat of the Aleppan army and the giving of Omar's son as hostage (*RHC Or* iii. 595). However, he calls the Frankish leader Saint-Gilles.

13. As the pestilence worsens, the duke is forced by the urgency of the situation to withdraw from Antioch

After this the aforesaid plague epidemic was growing more widespread and more severe, with many of the princes dying alongside the common people, and Duke Godfrey left Antioch, fearing that this was the same illness which he remembered had afflicted Rome long ago with a very similar disaster when he was on an expedition with King Henry IV, third emperor of the Romans, in which five hundred of the strongest soldiers and many nobles had died during the plague-bearing month of August, and many had been terrified and had left the city along with the emperor himself.[11] Duke Godfrey withdrew towards the mountainous regions of Pakrad and Kogh Vasil, and lived in the cities of Ravendel and Turbessel, which had been subdued by his brother Baldwin before the siege of Antioch and after his removal to Edessa had been handed on to his brother the duke.[12]

14. The duke himself, with a few men, overthrows fortresses hostile to the Christians

In those very same fortresses there were certain Armenian brothers who served God devoutly in monastic habit and had suffered many insults from Pakrad's soldiers who lived in a fortress neighbouring the above places Ravendel and Turbessel, and they saw in the duke a peace-loving man and one devoted to justice, so they came to him, making complaint about the injuries inflicted on them and about Pakrad's citadel, about those same castles and their occupants. The Christian duke was moved by the complaints of Christ's paupers, and had not forgotten those injuries which that same Pakrad had done to him when there was still a Christian siege around the walls of Antioch, and he was vexed and planned to take revenge for all these things. For this same Pakrad had robbed legates of Baldwin, the duke's brother, of great and magnificent gifts, of money as well as other things, while they were travelling through his country and homeland, all of which things he had no qualms about sending to Prince Bohemond with the intention of making an agreement with him. Since the duke was now troubled by these injuries and the poor brothers' complaints he chose fifty soldiers from his followers and they set out in hauberks, with shields and lances, with ballistas and Armenian archers, to the neighbouring citadel, in which Pakrad's guilty robbers

---

[11] In 1084. The siege and epidemic are described by Frutolf, though he gives no details about numbers: Frutolf and Ekkehard, p. 96.

[12] Kogh Vasil was Pakrad's brother: see 3. 17 above. RA says only that Godfrey went in the direction of Edessa (p. 84). FC was still with Baldwin in Edessa, but does not mention Godfrey's visit. The episode which follows, therefore, is reported only by AA; it would appear to be in character for Pakrad, given his earlier behaviour, though Kogh Vasil usually remained on good terms with the Franks.

were living. When he was there in strength he attacked the citadel with a sudden assault and overcame it by flame and fire and brought it down to the ground; on his orders twenty of the soldiers they found there were blinded, in retribution and revenge for the arrogance and injuries which Pakrad had dared to inflict on him and Christ's paupers. In the same way there were complaints about Kogh Vasil's citadel and fortress, so the duke attacked it and razed it to the ground with an assault and military show of strength, because of the various insults and injuries which he had inflicted on Christians.

15. Baldwin rewards the Christians who are flocking to join him with many gifts; and he subdues the Turks

After Duke Godfrey returned to Antioch from Azaz, and after he set out for Turbessel and Ravendel, leaving his hostage Mahumeth in the hands and guardianship of his faithful people of Antioch, and after Baldwin returned from Azaz with his men to Edessa, there arrived in the city of Edessa very many from the army, noble and lesser men: Drogo of Nesle, Rainald of Toul, Gaston of Béziers, Fulcher of Chartres, and other leaders and fellow soldiers in hundreds and fifties, some on horseback, some on foot, to earn rewards for military service from Baldwin, who had been made duke and prince in the city and region, by spending some time with him. For they had suffered the utmost difficulty and become impoverished of necessities by the long expedition. They flocked there and increased in numbers and strength day after day, until almost the whole city was besieged by Gauls and taken up by their hospitality. From day to day Baldwin made them individually many gifts of golden bezants, silver talents, and vessels; he overcame the regions and every opposition to him by warlike attacks, subdued the Turks and all peoples in the area, until the nobles and powerful men in the land struck a treaty with him.

16. Baldwin outlaws men conspiring against him and imprisons them under guard

When the twelve princes and the natives of the city of Rohas, or Edessa, realized that the Frankish people were swarming in from all over the place and distinguishing themselves in every deed and skill, and their advice was being preferred to their own, and Baldwin was dealing with every matter and business of the country with them and was ignoring the Edessans and their decisions more than usual, they burned with violent indignation against him and his men, and since they thought they would be entirely driven out by the Franks it displeased them very much that Baldwin had been made duke and lord over the city. So by a secret conspiracy and a legation sent to the Turks they plotted Baldwin's betrayal and how he could either be killed or expelled from the city with his men. While they were preparing this with frequent and secret meetings among themselves, one of them, Enzhu by name, who stayed loyal to Baldwin from a pure heart and mind, revealed to Baldwin in detail the instigators and conspirators in the treachery, and that it was therefore necessary to protect him and his men and the entrances to the city night and day from their betrayal, lest the strength and stratagems of the Turks might find them unprepared and careless. When Baldwin heard and understood that they were plotting this great betrayal, both from the truthful account and from the change of expression on their disagreeable faces, he sent a band of Gaulish servants who were devoted to him and he commanded that all of the conspirators were to be detained and delivered into the confinement of prison, and all their property and vast funds carried into his palace, which he then paid out generously to his followers for military service.

17. Baldwin is impoverished by too much gift-giving, so he accepts gifts to ransom the captives, certain of whom he tortures and expels from the city

Then after some days had passed, and while the conspirators were earnestly pleading for their lives and the safety of their limbs and making many excuses, and indeed offering quite large gifts for their own ransom by way of suppliants, Baldwin was always striving on his men's advice to do greater things, knowing from the mouths of spies that throughout the neighbouring castles and fortifications they had hidden great treasures and things they held precious from the eyes of the Christian army. Finally Baldwin was impoverished by excessive giving and hiring mercenaries and by the great size of the presents he had bestowed not only upon the leaders of the Gauls but also on lesser men, and he agreed to accept gifts as ransom for the prisoners. He refused the gifts of only two, whom he ordered to be blinded as overwhelmingly blameworthy and guilty of treachery. Several of the crowd who were accomplices he ordered to be banished from the city as criminals with noses, hands or feet cut off. From each man ransomed no fewer than twenty thousand bezants or thirty or sixty were taken into Duke Baldwin's treasury, in addition to mules and horses, silver vases, and very many precious ornaments. From that day on Duke Baldwin became a man to be feared in the city of Edessa, and his name was spread among the people right to the limits of his land.[13]

18. Concerning Baldwin's father-in-law and about Balak's treachery in the fortress at Amacha

Baldwin's father-in-law, called Taphnuz, seeing that Baldwin had taken revenge in this way for the men's treachery and had punished them with loss of possessions

[13] GN refers to the same conspiracy, which he says was at Christmas. However, AA provides a logical reason for the disaffection: envy of the western incomers. The mutilations were more severe according to Guibert (pp. 164–5).

and torture of their limbs, was very frightened and took an opportunity to escape to his fortifications in the mountains, and he could not be brought back, because he feared he would undergo the death sentence for money which he still owed. Balak of the city of Sororgia, frustrated in his hope of recovering the city from Baldwin's hands or of receiving anything at all because of the influx of Gauls, and knowing that Baldwin's heart was entirely set on them, began deep in his own heart to prepare deceits by which he might lead Baldwin to destruction by cunning advice. At length he found a way of wicked deceit by which he calculated to deceive and destroy him, and on a certain day he came to him as if in complete loyalty and said: 'I know that you are a man of great power and industry, and you reward in no mean way those who volunteer for military service with you. For this reason I have vowed secretly in my heart that I shall commend into your hands not only myself and my sons and my wife, but shall also hand over to you my fortress of Amacha, from which you will be able to subdue a very great deal of land, on a day which you shall choose as most suitable to take it over.' Baldwin rejoiced at taking over the fortress and totally believed the man who spoke to him so graciously and loyally, and he fixed a day on which, according to Balak's word, the handing over of the fortress would be achieved without any difficulty.

19. How certain sensible men protect Baldwin from the treachery of the Turks

Now the day drew near and Balak, mindful of his own deceit, led into the castle at Amacha a hundred Turks protected with weapons and hauberks and shut them in rooms here and there throughout the fortress in ambush, so that they might take Baldwin alive when he came in with his men, and make him submit to Balak's authority. Baldwin, who was unaware of this deception, set out on the same day to the fortress at Amacha, taking with him two hundred soldiers who were ready for any military engagement. He found Balak ready to deliver up the fortress in accordance with what he had promised, Balak asking him insistently, and fawning on him in deceit with honeyed words, to enter and take over the fortress with some men chosen from his company, and to arrange to leave any he wished of his faithful followers in Balak's charge. Baldwin heard the fawning man and almost believed him, and he was ready now to take with him some men to ascend and enter, and he decided who would remain outside. But there were some sensible men among the Gauls who did not trust the man's words and promises and they took Baldwin aside and put the case convincingly against believing the words of this gentile Turk so readily and agreeing to enter his fortress with a small group without any security or hostage.

20. How Baldwin experiences the treachery of the Turks when his men are captured

At last, after a long time undecided about it, and taking much advice, and entirely preventing Baldwin from entering the fortress, it was decided on both sides that Baldwin should wait with his companions in the valley, and he would send ahead twelve of them whom he trusted to take over the citadel, and they would effectively bring it under his authority by taking over the keys and bars, and they would shut out Balak's men. At once the twelve men chosen to take over the citadel, bearing weapons and hauberks, entered the fortress and tower of Amacha. They soon found themselves in the middle of ambushes as a hundred Turks leapt out in a rush from the rooms, surrounded the men with weapons and arrows and, the Christians being able to do little to defend themselves against so many, they seized them. Only two out of the twelve managed to extricate themselves from the enemy's hands by a great and spirited fight; they suddenly escaped into an upper room with windows which looked down onto the valley; they drew their swords and defended themselves valiantly from the pursuing enemy while they put their heads out of the windows and shouted to Baldwin, who was standing at the foot of the mountain with his men, to save himself from treacheries, declaring that ten had been captured in false faith and they were obviously in danger of death.

21. Baldwin suffers great torment over the capture of his knights

When Baldwin understood from their anxious shouting that the entire affair had gone against them and Balak's deceptions were exposed, he was tormented by great sorrow at the capture of his men. But he could not form any plan as to what he should do or what efforts to make to secure his men's release. For the fortress was sited on the top of cliffs, unconquerable by human artifice or strength. At length Baldwin, who was suffering greatly concerning the disaster which had befallen such outstanding men, confronted Balak bitterly with his wicked deceit, reminded him of his oath and told him that if he gave up his prisoners he would receive a weight of gold and bezants for their ransom. But Balak refused everything: he wanted only the city of Sororgia. Baldwin vowed by Lord God that he would never surrender the city to him, even if Balak cut the limbs one by one off all those whom he had captured in full view of Baldwin. So, as Balak refused to listen to Baldwin's pleadings and warnings, and cared nothing for his gifts except for Sororgia, Baldwin returned to Edessa, sorrowful and complaining greatly about his men who were prisoners, and from that day he began to hold in bitter hatred the Turks and their advice and help and constant presence.

22. Balduk is beheaded; six of Baldwin's comrades are restored

It was not many days after this that Balduk of Samosata, who was supposed to give Baldwin his wife and sons as hostages but had put it off for many days deceitfully, came fawningly into Baldwin's palace and he was detained on Baldwin's orders and had his head cut off. Baldwin stationed Folbert of Chartres[14] in the city of Sororgia with a hundred soldiers well tried and experienced in warfare, so that they might torment Amacha with constant attacks and try to pay back Balak a suitable return in revenge for the captured brothers. Therefore one day Folbert set out with his men to seize plunder in the lands of Amacha. They sent some comrades on ahead and lured the Turks out of the citadel to the place where Folbert's ambush was, until battle was joined and six of the Turks who were Balak's soldiers were captured and led away. For these who were captured and led away Balak restored six of Baldwin's comrades as their ransom; he kept back six in his charge up till the day of Baldwin's departure for Jerusalem. After this four escaped by the negligence and on account of the long weariness of Balak's guards. Then he ordered Gerard, Baldwin's confidant and secretary, to be beheaded along with Pisellus son of the sister of Udelard, the celebrated and noble knight of Wissant.

23. A great number of Germans arrives and is destroyed by the aforesaid pestilence

While Godfrey was spending time in Ravendel and Turbessel because of the widespread devastation caused by the severe mortality throughout Antioch, at that same plague-stricken time fifteen hundred men of German race, who had combined and collected from the city of Regensburg on the river Danube and from other cities on the river Rhine, arrived at the city of Antioch by sea and sailed into the port of St Symeon to swell the numbers of Christians who were going to Jerusalem for comfort and assistance. But when this company mingled with the recently victorious pilgrims in August it was destroyed and devastated by that same fatal scourge, so that of the fifteen hundred not even one seems to have survived.

24. Sansadonias ransoms his mother and sons. Winemer is brought back; the hostage Mahumeth is guarded carefully; ships are received again

At that same time after the Christians' victory Sansadonias, son of Yaghi-Siyhan king of Antioch, ransomed his mother, with two sons, at a price of three thousand

[14] This is probably, but not certainly, a mistake for Fulcher, whose arrival at Edessa was noted above (5. 15).

bezants, from the hand of William,[15] a noble man, fellow soldier and fellow countryman of Count Raymond of Provence, who had captured them in the first attack and entry into Antioch at first light when they were still asleep. Also at that time Winemer of the land of Boulogne, who was taken prisoner at Latakia by the Greek king's Turcopoles, was set free at Duke Godfrey's request after a long time in fetters and spending a long period in prison, but he suffered from severe pain when he was brought back to Antioch. Moreover, the boy Mahumeth, son of the prince of Azaz, who was given to Godfrey as hostage, remained in Antioch in the assiduous guardianship both of his own twelve slaves and under the expert care of Godfrey's followers, and he lacked nothing of necessary provisions from the duke's household at any time. And so indeed, when they saw the duke and the other powerful men moving away from Antioch to other places because of the imminent plague, some claiming this mortality arose from the unhealthiness of the place, others from the plague-bearing month of August, as many as possible set out at the beginning of September for the above port of St Symeon to make a stay, for the sailors were once more bringing in supplies there by ship, after the slaughter of the Turks and Karbugha's flight, and selling everything in abundance to those in need.

25. About a marvel displayed in the sky and different interpretations put upon it

Then after the middle of the month, in the silence of one night when all things are accustomed to be refreshed by sleep's relaxation, a marvellous vision was displayed high in the sky[16] to everyone who was there on the night watch. As if the stars had been collected together from every region of the sky and closely massed in a space the width of one *atrium*[17] containing three acres, they shone with the brilliance of fire, like live coals burning in a forge and heaped together, and as they died down after this long and terrible blaze they circled the heavens in the style of a crown, beneath the course of a walled city, and they lasted like this continuously in a circle until in the end they were rent and showed an entrance and way in on one side of their circle. The Christians' watchmen were terrified by the showing of this sign and shouted loudly to rouse everyone who was sunk in sleep, to see and discuss the meaning of this portent. They all wondered at it and put forward different opinions as to what it meant. Some claimed it meant the city of Jerusalem crowded by the hordes of gentiles, and that it would die down and be weakened in this way by their own forces and numbers, so that at last it would appear to offer an entry to its Christian sons. Others asserted it was the Christian army still gathered in strength and blazing with the ardour of divine devotion, and at length, divided in the lands

15 William of Montpellier.

16 Common phrase in hexameter poetry: *HL* vol. 1, p. 228.

17 An agrarian measure: cf. Du Cange, s.v. *atrium* (2).

and cities unjustly seized by the peoples, they would powerfully prevail and have dominion around Jerusalem and Antioch. Some, indeed, said it signified this present mortality and the abundant people of the pilgrims both massed together in one like a cloud and lessened in numbers. And thus they argued their different meanings. But by God's will, as they say, the meaning of the vision was changed into a better one. For when Duke Godfrey and all his Christian companions were summoned from places everywhere and returned to Antioch in the month of October, after August's heat was moderated, Count Raymond, Robert of Flanders, Robert prince of Normandy, Bohemond, and the other princes, who were still gathered in that same Antioch and staying there, spread out of one accord and travelled through the lands and cities situated around Antioch, blockaded those who resisted and rebelled, and subdued them to their authority.

26. About the deeds of the princes; and Bohemond's lordship in Antioch

Therefore they went down first with their armed divisions to the town of Albara, which was very rich in resources. They conquered it without much difficulty and occupied it, putting to the sword the Turks and Saracens they found within. Then with victory theirs, Count Raymond, Robert prince of Normans, Eustace Duke Godfrey's brother, Robert of Flanders, Bohemond now become prince of Antioch, and Duke Godfrey descended on the town of Ma'arra, which was full of arms and strength.[18] But Godfrey, Bohemond, and Robert of Flanders stayed there at the siege only fifteen days, then these three returned to Antioch. They left Count Raymond and Robert prince of Normans, Eustace, and Tancred around the city of Ma'arra with their thousands of men.[19] Then after several days Duke Godfrey, taking with him forty comrades, well armed and mounted, set out towards the city of Edessa, which is seven days' journey distant from Antioch, and there he met his brother Baldwin, who held that same city with all its dependencies, at a halfway point across the great river Euphrates to hold a conference with each other. Bohemond, whose heart was consumed by very great envy and anger towards Count Raymond, seeing the opportunity of Duke Godfrey's departure and Raymond's absence, summoned and assembled his comrades with a blast of the bugle and attacked in great strength the tower which commanded the Ferna bridge, and overcame with battle and archers Count Raymond's soldiers who had stayed

[18] The phrase 'armis et robore foetam' scans as a hexameter and uses Vergilian diction (*Aen.* ii. 238): it may quote a lost post-classical source.

[19] According to AA, all the leaders were at Ma'arra, though not all the time. RA says Raymond and Robert of Flanders attacked the city and were later joined by Bohemond (pp. 94–8). The author of *GF*, who was probably present at the siege, mentions only Raymond and Bohemond by name (pp. 77–81), as does FC (p. 266). RC adds Tancred and Robert of Normandy (pp. 114–15).

in the tower and threw them out of the citadel and the city, and in this way he gained sole lordship over Antioch.[20]

27. The way Duke Godfrey took Turkish ambushes by surprise and he overthrew many with a few

After these things Duke Godfrey, having held the talks with his brother and said goodbye to him, made a swift journey with the same forty companions to return to his brother princes in Antioch, being made welcome in peace and prosperity by Turbessel and Ravendel and other places en route. Then, as he hastened along he came into the region called Episcopate, where one day he lay down to breakfast with his companions next to a certain spring in a place of grassy meadowland; he set down full wineskins and other necessary provisions which he had brought with him on mules and horses. While he was safely breakfasting in that place with his men he learnt from the boys he had sent out to watch for Turkish ambushes that a hundred Turks were hiding below the mountains in a rushy and marshy place by a big lake full of fish, five miles from the city of Antioch, waiting in concealment there for that same duke's return. After their ambush was revealed to the duke, he soon put off his picnic and at once mounted horses with his young companions, and they seized weapons, put on hauberks, and rode out to meet the enemy. However, the Turks were no slower to turn their horses against the Christians and they joined battle boldly with bows and arrows. But the victorious outcome was granted to the duke and his men, few in number but fighting for their lives. And indeed, as the duke and his men were winning at last, they pierced the fleeing Turks with their lances and they beheaded some and took back their heads to the city of Antioch with them, hanging from their saddles, with their spoils and horses. When that same duke found that Bohemond had become prince of the entire city, he recounted to him and the rest of the co-leaders and brothers all the things which God had done for him on the journey, and how so many Turks had been defeated and destroyed by a band of few men.[21]

28. About the grumbling of the Christians and a discussion among the leaders

Some time after Duke Godfrey's return in triumph, however, the Christian people began as one to mutter that there was nothing but delay for them in this city of Antioch and they were not getting on at all with the journey to Jerusalem, for desire

---

[20] The rift between Raymond and Bohemond, which AA dismisses quite briefly, was serious enough to find a place in FC's account (p. 268). Both *GF* and RA have considerably more detail (*GF* pp. 80–81; RA pp. 98–100).

[21] AA might appear to be exaggerating the odds here at 40: 100, but RA puts them at 12: 150 and GN at 20: 120 (RA pp. 92–3; GN p. 338).

of which they had left their native shores and borne so many difficulties. And there was great discord among the people[22] and many withdrew from following Duke Godfrey, Robert of Flanders, and Bohemond, having no faith from their replies and words that they would travel to Jerusalem before very long. At last these three princes, realizing that already the people were growing weary and gradually slipping away, forbade anyone else to prepare to sail for home, and they placed a guard everywhere in the seaports. They decided to hold a meeting and discussion about this complaint from the people on the Purification of St Mary.[23] Therefore, having assembled together and held a discussion there in Antioch, all of them, great and small, decided that on the first of March they would come together again in Latakia, which was under Christian authority, and there they would gather strength from all around and after this they would pay no attention to the danger of death and they would put off no longer making the journey to Jerusalem.

29. About the dreadful torment of famine during the siege of Ma'arra

Meanwhile Count Raymond was troubled by the long siege of five weeks around the town of Ma'arra, as were all those who were staying there in his company. Stationed a long time around the city, and strongly repulsed by the Turks, they suffered the torments of a great famine. No wonder, since very many regions round about were impoverished of supplies on account of the long siege of Antioch and now of these towns, and the majority of the inhabitants had made their escape into the mountains with their possessions and herds. For there were ten thousand in Count Raymond's army and that of his fellow leaders. It is extraordinary to relate and horrifying to the ears: these same torments of famine grew so great around these cities that – it is wicked to tell, let alone to do – the Christians did not shrink from eating not only killed Turks or Saracens, but even dogs whom they snatched and cooked with fire, on account of the scarcity of which you have heard. But why marvel? There is no sharper sword than long-drawn-out hunger.[24]

30. How Count Raymond overthrew a castle and captured Ma'arra

When Count Raymond saw the affliction and grief of his people who were growing weak from hunger, he took a force of cavalry and set out into the mountains, and from time to time he brought back vast supplies of booty and provisions, with which the people of God were often refreshed. In that same place throughout

22 Cf. John 7: 43; Acts 15: 39, 23: 10.

23 2 February 1099.

24 Cannibalism at Ma'arra is reported by participants as well as later historians (*GF* p. 80; RA p. 101; FC p. 267). The sentence 'non est acutior …' appears to be a well known saying, but has not proved traceable.

the mountains and deserts of Lebanon many Christians who were compelled by the aforesaid necessity to go out looking for food were found slaughtered by the Turks. There were frequent raids then out of Damascus, which was a particular stronghold of the Turks, and they rode down the Christians who were scattered and wandering about away from the army and the siege, slaughtering some, piercing others with fatal arrows. When Count Raymond realized what difficulties his men stationed around the city were suffering from the Turkish raids, he was annoyed and he considered all ways of putting an end to this evil. And so he arrived at Talamria, a castle situated in the mountainous region, which he conquered and destroyed with a band of brave men, along with the Turks found inside, and he took wooden materials from that same castle from which he made a siege engine to overcome the aforesaid city of Ma'arra, which was strongly fortified with walls and ramparts. Once the engine was made, moreover, and devices were put in place, the city was overcome quite soon; it was captured and overthrown by the count and the other princes, Robert and Tancred and Eustace. Christian soldiers carrying shields and wearing hauberks occupied the middle of the city in great strength; they fought back fiercely against the Turks and defended themselves, and put them to the sword. They pursued some who were fleeing to the citadel and burnt them, and they remained there peacefully for three weeks, finding little food except for an abundance of oil. Engelrand son of Count Hugh, a young man of wonderful bravery, had to stay in this city because of illness and he lost his life, and his body was buried in the basilica of blessed Andrew the apostle.

31. How, after fortresses of the Turks and Saracens had been taken, Raymond besieged the fortress of Arqa; and about the difficulty of that same siege

After the aforesaid town of Ma'arra was conquered and destroyed the army of the aforesaid princes went down to a certain valley which they named 'Joy'. There they found plenty of necessary provisions and they refreshed their bodies, weary and weakened by hunger, for eight days. In that same place they took by assault two fortresses in the mountains in which lived Turks and Saracens.[25] Then when the town called Tortosa[26] was conquered and captured without much difficulty, and placed in the hands of Count Raymond and his guard, they continued their journey and entered the valley called 'of Camels'. There they seized booty and great quantities of food and set out for a certain fortress which was unconquerable by artifice and human forces, called Arqa. They pitched their tents there and announced that they would stay there for some time, until that same citadel was captured and its defenders defeated. At length they made engines and apparatus of

---

[25] Raymond marched his army south down the Orontes valley. One of the fortresses he occupied was Ḥiṣn al-Akrād, later Krak des Chevaliers (RA pp. 105–6; *GF* pp. 81–2).

[26] According to *GF* the town was captured by Raymond Pilet and Raymond of Turenne (p. 83).

mangonels there, and a pile of stones for an attack by throwers on the towers and ancient wall works, intending thereby to terrify the soldiers shut up inside that same fortress and put them to flight. But they found those defenders indefatigable and unconquerable. They fought back from inside with a similar barrage of mangonels and bombardment with stones, and wrought damage on the Christian people with arrows as well as stones. While Anselm of Ribemont, a very noble and warlike man, was bringing a great deal of force to bear on the defenders of the citadel, they hit him with a flying rock from that same citadel and broke his skull. The princes grieved and were troubled by the death of their brother and fellow soldier Anselm, a most celebrated man, and by the resistance of the besieged Saracens, and they decided to use their skill in mining to hollow out the mountains beneath the foundation of the castle walls, so that when the foundation fell down with the ramparts and walls, the gentiles who were on the ramparts, walls, and citadel would at the same time be buried in the ruin of the stones and buildings and they would perish. But this labour was in vain. For those who were inside were digging and hollowing from their side and they opposed the Christians' apparatus with their own devices and did not allow their work to arrive at a successful conclusion.

32. How there was an ordeal about the lance of the Lord; and how the boy hostage Mahumeth died and was returned to his father with honour by the duke

During that same siege a dispute arose in that place, and an investigation of the Holy Lance: whether it was that with which the Lord's side was opened, or not. For many people were in doubt and there was a split among them. On this account the instigator and betrayer of its discovery passed through the fire; he came out unharmed, so they say, and Count Raymond of Provence himself and Raymond Pilet rescued him from the hands and hustling of envious people, and they revered the lance from that day, along with all their company. It is related by some people that after this the same cleric grew so much more ill as a result of the trial's conflagration that in a short while he died and was buried. Because of this the faithful began to hold the lance in less veneration, believing its discovery to owe more to Raymond's greed and activity than to any divine truth.[27] While these sieges around Ma'arra, Tortosa, and Arqa were happening, the boy Mahumeth, who had been sent as hostage to Antioch by his father the prince of Azaz and had been commended to the trust and guardianship of Duke Godfrey, was seized by illness and died. The duke wrapped him in precious purple cloth according to the

[27] AA is quite even-handed in his reporting of Peter Bartholomew's ordeal (8 Apr. 1099), as is FC (pp. 238–41). Surprisingly, the *GF* writer does not mention it, although GN (a sceptic) does (p. 332). As might be expected, RA writes at length and with conviction about the lance's authenticity (pp. 120–23), while the most vigorous condemnation is to be found in RC (pp. 126–7).

gentile custom and sent him back to his father, absolving himself from blame, since he had acted in complete good faith and the boy had not died because of his negligence, and claiming that he was also grieving at his death no less than if it had been his own brother Baldwin's. The prince graciously accepted the duke's apologies, and, having ascertained the truth from those whom he had sent from his own household as guardians for the boy, he did not in the least change from the loyalty he promised, but remained steadfast in all the treaty and peace he had made with the duke himself and his brother Baldwin.

33. How Duke Godfrey and Robert of Flanders besieged the city of Jabala; and how Count Raymond was bribed by a treacherous legation to recall those same princes from the siege

Meanwhile in due course the first of March arrived, and Duke Godfrey, Robert of Flanders, Bohemond, and all the princes still staying in Antioch assembled their army – some twenty thousand cavalry and infantry – at Latakia, as they had promised, and pitched camp at the town of Jabala, which is situated on the seashore and well endowed with riches, imposing a blockade around it in order to be able to attack and drive out the Saracens and all the gentiles who were stationed in the town for its defence. But Bohemond, who was always wary and suspicious lest he lose the city of Antioch – which was unconquerable by human forces – by some trick or act of ill-will, went back to Latakia and retraced his journey with his men to Antioch. Soon afterwards, when they heard of the destruction of Albara and Ma'arra and the killing of their Turkish inhabitants, and now of the long siege of Arqa and the assault on it, the Saracen soldiers took counsel with the citizens and offered an enormous sum of money to Duke Godfrey and Robert of Flanders, in return for which the city of Jabala would remain untouched by them, with its citizens, its vines and all fruits, and their army would move on elsewhere. This was flatly refused by the Christian princes, unless the town was surrendered to their power with its keys. Therefore the townspeople and the magistracy realized that the aforesaid princes could not be bribed to move away their camp by offers of money or by other precious gifts, and they sent messages secretly to Count Raymond at Arqa, because he was notorious among the gentiles' leaders for his deeds and power, to ask him to accept the money the duke and the rest had refused, in return for persuading the Christian princes, by pleading or by any means, to withdraw from the siege. So Count Raymond, always greedy for gold and silver, thought over tricks and ideas,[28] how he might recall those same leaders from the siege of Jabala and free the townspeople and their vines and fruit trees so as to receive the money, for from the beginning he absolutely distrusted their turning down the requests. So he contrived this pretext, namely that the Turks, whose forces were many in Damascus, had consulted with the Saracens, Arabs, and other

[28] Vergil, *Aen.* iv. 563.

gentiles and had decided they would next wage war against him at Arqa, and now they had all arrived with a great quantity of equipment in his lands. Having fashioned this invention, he sent messengers to the aforesaid princes, who had now been settled around Jabala for a week, asking them to hasten to his assistance at Arqa, otherwise he and his brothers who were with him could not escape danger of death from the gentiles, and then they could expect a similar martyrdom.[29]

34. How the princes moved their camp away from the siege of Jabala and hurried to Raymond's assistance

When they heard Count Raymond's messengers and the danger and fear which was said to be coming upon him from the multitude of gentiles, the duke and the rest of the nobles unanimously rushed to discuss the matter, and the hearts and tongues of all were lifted in this opinion: 'The great army of Christians only just defended itself from the countless nations and weapons of the gentiles when it was still both whole and undivided at Antioch. Now, however, part is left at Antioch, part in this siege of Jabala, part has been taken away and has moved to Arqa to conquer the enemies' fortresses and cities, and thus the strength of our men was diminished and they could not now manage to stand against so many thousands of gentiles, as has become clear to us from this message from Count Raymond. But if by ill-fortune the strength of our men should be destroyed at Arqa, doubtless we can expect the same fate. Since we cannot strike and conquer Jabala so quickly, it is necessary for us to leave it intact at this time, and for us to take the camp and army to the relief of our men at Arqa, and to meet the peoples in battle together with our comrades. As heaven wills, so let it be done.' As everyone perceived this plan to be a good and useful one and supported it, the camp was moved away from the siege of Jabala, and Duke Godfrey and Robert of Flanders and all the rest made their way, bearing arms and all equipment of war, and arrived around three days later at Arqa to increase the forces and resources of their Christian fellows. They learnt the truth from Tancred and many others, that no forces or threats were imminent from the gentiles, but that Count Raymond had falsely claimed this assembly of enemies and had called them up now to his assistance for no other reason than to receive the money which the inhabitants of Jabala promised for their freedom, to ensure that the Christians would move away from the blockade of their walls.

---

[29] According to RA and *GF*, Raymond genuinely believed that the Turks were going to attack (RA pp. 110-11; *GF* p. 84). FC merely says that the expected attack did not materialize (p. 263).

35. The aforesaid princes, who had been deceived by the false message, withdraw from Raymond's company, but he brings them back to harmony by means of wheedling and gifts

When the aforesaid princes realized that Count Raymond had deceived them with this trick and false message they were seriously annoyed. Because of the affair they withdrew themselves from Raymond's society and from communication with him; they separated from him the distance of two miles and pitched their tents, giving him no assistance at all in the attack on Arqa nor having any friendly intercourse with him. There was also, there at Arqa, serious enmity which arose between Count Raymond and Tancred, concerning a sum of money and bezants which the count owed to Tancred for military service but was not paying in proportion to the effort and effectiveness of the soldiers who were maintained and led by that same Tancred.[30] Then from that same day on which Duke Godfrey took himself there with the rest of the leaders, Tancred, who had often reminded the count of their agreement but received no reply from him offering any hope, stayed with the duke, bound faithfully to him in all military obedience and he renounced the count completely, and from then on, in revenge for the injuries the count had inflicted on him, he spared no effort to harm by stratagems and by all means the comrades and friends of that same count. When Count Raymond saw that the duke and Robert of Flanders and all who were with them were bearing a grudge against him, because he misled them with a false message when he was corrupted by greed, he began to soften the duke's anger by his coaxing and the cunning in which he was expert and was instructed from the age of boyhood. And so in the end he soothed the wrath of everyone, except Tancred. Then the count sent a horse of great price and beautiful physique to the duke, so he might thus more perfectly please his mind and by these gifts recall him to the assault on Arqa with him, since he knew him to be a man of great forbearance and love, and he knew that if he was reconciled and placated the rest would return to goodwill and amity. From then on the princes who were so recently reconciled, all except Tancred, applied force equally in an attack and blockade around the fortress of Arqa; they took up positions for four weeks from that day on which the duke came down there.

36. The way a muttering grew among the duke's people because the journey to Jerusalem was delayed so long

Eventually all those besieging the fortress became weary and lost interest in undermining the mountain because of the intolerable effort and because of the incalculable defence from within, and the shortage of things necessary to life,

[30] Nicholson suggests that Tancred had spread rumours to discredit Raymond (p. 84). He bases this on RA who describes Tancred as making trouble in order to change his allegiance (p. 112).

and a muttering grew among the people of the duke and Robert of Flanders, with everyone claiming that they could no longer hold out there in that siege, and that this fortress was unconquerable by skill or strength and could hardly be captured in a year, even if then it could be overcome by the sword of hunger. So they all, small and great, urged the duke quite insistently to move the camp away from the siege and press on with the journey to Jerusalem as they had vowed, since it was for desire of Jerusalem and in order to see the sepulchre of Lord Jesus Christ that they had travelled from their native shores. On the other hand, Count Raymond was resisting, using all means and promises to persuade them to delay yet some time longer with him in that place, until by some feat of strength or skill the citadel and the gentiles who were shut up within it might be captured, and he recounted how Anselm of Ribemont had fallen and died there, and how many of their comrades had been destroyed there by those same Saracens, some by death, some by very severe wounds. But although Raymond was unable to hold them back from their desire and purpose by any attempt at coaxings or any promise, he said that he and his men would stay in that same place until the enemy citadel was reduced to ruins in revenge for his destroyed men.

37. The siege of Arqa is lifted; the princes pitch their tents at a distance from the city of Tripoli; the people suck honeyed canes they find all over the plains

While the count was persevering in this intention and postponing the brothers' departure with much skill, one day Duke Godfrey, Robert of Flanders, and Tancred and all their followers set fire to their camp and set out from the siege of Arqa, joined by many from Raymond's company. They were also tired of the long-drawn-out tediousness and were unwilling to remain at Arqa, particularly because of their constant desire to go to Jerusalem. For they had been blockading the fortress of Arqa with Count Raymond for two and a half months from the start. When the count saw that all his army was going after the duke, and his company had disappeared, and few had remained with him for his assistance, he had to follow at once in the footsteps of the duke and the rest whether he liked it or not, and he worked his passage with the rest into the territory of the town of Tripoli or Tripla, which was situated on the seashore. There everyone put up their tents at a distance from the town, so that so great an army would not harm the fruits of the earth and the vines belonging to the city's inhabitants. For mediators and messengers had frequently come down from that same city to the aforesaid princes in Arqa, bearing very many gifts and promising greater ones if they would spare the city and its possessions and would not do here as they had at Albara and Ma'arra and other towns. Because of this the army and all the leadership settled far from the city until they saw what sort of agreement and treaty or offering of gifts there might be to placate them, and until they confirmed friendship on both sides. In that place the people sucked little honeyed reeds, found in plenty throughout the plains, which they call 'zucra'; they enjoyed this reed's wholesome sap, and because of its sweetness once they had tasted it they could scarcely get enough of it. This kind of grass is cultivated every year by extremely hard work on the part of the farmers. Then at harvest time the natives crush the ripe crop in little mortars, putting the filtered sap into their utensils until it curdles and hardens with the appearance of snow or white salt. They shave pieces off and mix them with bread or with water and take them as a relish, and it seems to those who taste it sweeter and more wholesome even than a comb of honey.[31] Some say that it is a sort of that honey which Jonathan, son of King Saul, found on the face of the earth and disobediently dared to taste.[32] The people, who were troubled by a dreadful hunger, were greatly refreshed by these little honey-flavoured reeds during the sieges of Albara, Ma'arra, and Arqa.

38. Having made a truce, the ruler of the city of Tripoli grants to the people of God a guide; and they cross through very difficult terrain with his leadership

The ruler of the town of glorious and wealthy Tripoli, realizing that the legions of the faithful had been stationed in front of the town walls and gates for a long time, sent to ask the chiefs of the army, Duke Godfrey, Count Raymond, Robert of Flanders, and Robert prince of Normandy, to accept gifts from him so that he might peacefully preserve his land from them, and the town of Jubayl and the fortress of Arqa. At length, having made a treaty, the ruler proceeded in great friendship to the tents of the nobles. He satisfied them with gifts and peaceful words and granted them an elderly man as guide on the journey, since the whereabouts of paths through the mountain regions next to the seashore were intricate and unknown. He led them from the seashore on a winding route through difficult mountain passes, on a path so narrow that a man could scarcely march after a man, an animal after an animal. This mountain stretched out from the range an outstanding length right to the sea. On its top a tower, projecting over a certain gate, had been built across the road, and in its living space six men could be stationed, whose defence could deny the road to all who lived under the heavens. But, faced by the army and

[31] 1 Kgs. (1 Sam.) 14: 27; Ps. 18: 11; Prov: 24. 13. Evidently sugar was a new commodity to AA, though there was by this time sugar production in southern Europe and it was being imported by Venice: see W. D. Phillips, 'Sugar production and trade in the Mediterranean at the time of the crusades', in V. P. Goss (ed.), *The Meeting of Two Worlds: Cultural Exchange between East and West during the Period of the Crusades* (Kalamazoo, MI, 1986), pp. 393–406. FC also mentions sugar, but without the detail about its manufacture, which may reflect the two authors' different audiences (p. 329).

[32] 1 Kgs. (1 Sam.) 14: 26, 27, 43.

the ruler of Tripoli's guide, no one now resisted those passing through.[33] When these narrow and very difficult passes had been successfully negotiated using the knowledge of their Saracen guide and fellow traveller, they took the road to the seashore again, and arrived at the town of Jubayl, for which the ruler of the city of Tripoli had interceded. The army left Jubayl alone according to their promise not to harm it and went only a mile away and spent the night on a certain river of fresh water.[34] They stayed there the following day as well, waiting for the crowd of weak people who were worn out by the weariness of the journey through the steep rocky places.

39. Concerning the difficulty of the journey; and how they made a treaty with the inhabitants of the city of Beirut

Then on the third day they struck camp and moved on their way once more along the seashore and they were brought back onto a certain mountain path of amazing and incredible narrowness. It is said that this had suffered undermining from a sudden downpour of rain flowing down on top of it, and that the way for travellers there was through this hollowing out. And this mountain is constantly pounded by the waves of the sea which were so close that it was strictly forbidden to turn aside to right or left, in case someone stumbled and fell straight into the depths of the sea. When this journey through the defiles was completed, and once more a certain fortress tower was bypassed through the mountains, as unassailable as the above-mentioned tower, both of them remaining empty of any defender – fear of God not of man being inspired in the Saracen guards – towards evening they drew near the city of Baurim or Beirut to take up quarters, always with the Saracen, their companion and fellow traveller, going first and leading them. Moreover, when the inhabitants of Beirut knew about the Christians' arrival and that the army was already quartered on the plains of the town, they sent worthy gifts with peaceful words to the aforesaid princes, speaking in this way: 'We entreat you to pass through peacefully without laying waste our trees, vines, and crops. And if by good fortune you fulfil your purpose of capturing Jerusalem, we shall serve you with all our possessions.' The princes were pleased by these entreaties and promises and gifts from the inhabitants of Beirut, so they struck camp with all the Christian army and once more made their way along the seashore, through those same passes and the rough ground of rocky places, which are always dashed by seastorms.

---

33 This tower was probably on the narrowest part of the route between the shore and the foothills of the Lebanese range. The modern coastal road passes through a tunnel in the cliff. See also RA for difficulties of the coastal path (pp. 105–7, 130).

34 In *GF* the army is said to have rested by Nahr Ibrāhīm ('Braym'), which is, however, considerably more than a mile from Jubayl (p. 86).

40. How many perished because of snakes in the region of Sidon; and about the loss of a certain Walter

They emerged from these passes and descended onto the plain which contains the city called Sagitta (Sidon), where they stayed in quarters on the bank of a certain fresh-water river.[35] There they found very many heaps of stones. Among these an innumerable group of weak and poor people, who were tired, rested and slept, and while they did so some were bitten by snakes, which are called 'tarenta', and they died, their limbs cracking because they swelled and blew up incredibly on account of unbearable thirst. There also the Saracens were confident of their strength and they rode out from the city of Sidon and dared to challenge the army, killing pilgrims who were looking for supplies and provisions in the region of this city. But they were severely repulsed by the Christian cavalry; some died from weapons, some hoped to seek safety from weapons among the waves, and they were submerged and drowned by the waters. Of course the Christians applied pressure on this town in revenge for their own men, but they were turned away from the desire to go to Jerusalem. In this region of Sidon, while many were in danger from the fiery snakes mentioned above, and there was great weeping and wailing over those dying, they were taught this medicine by the natives: that anyone who was bitten by a snake should go up to one of the more noble and eminent people in the army, and if the wound of the sting was touched and embraced by that man's right hand the poison spread through the limbs would be seen to do no more harm. In the same way they were taught another medicine, that a man who was bitten should lie at once with a woman, a woman with a man, and thus they would be released from all the swelling and heat of the poison. The Christian people also learnt from the inhabitants to clash stones together with constant blows or to make a noise by frequent banging on their shields, and thus the comrades could sleep in safety from the snakes, which were terrified by this noise and clamour.[36] Then another day dawned, and a certain Christian brother, a man and knight born of noble parentage, called Walter of the castle at Verva, took with him certain close friends from the company and set out into the mountainous regions. There he seized enormous quantities of plunder which he put together and sent back to the army by way of squires and some of his fellows. Walter longed for greater explorations in a place enclosed on all sides by mountains, which gave him entry through a narrow and difficult access to very many herds and Saracen possessions. There he was surrounded by the Saracens and it is not known to this day how he died.

---

[35] The largest river on the plain is Nahr al-Awwali.

[36] The snakes were probably soft-scaled vipers, which are exceedingly poisonous and still found in Lebanon. Neither of the native therapies was likely to be much use (were the Syrians having a joke at the crusaders' expense?), but setting up vibrations in the way described would be effective in warding off the snakes.

41. How they bypassed the towns of Tyre, Acre, Haifa, and Caesarea. And so they celebrated holy Pentecost

However, the aforesaid princes and all their company, not knowing why the outstanding knight was held up beyond the frontier, still remained on the third day in the region of the city of Sidon, to see if the honourable knight might return from the mountain regions, or if they could find out anything about his approach. But when they heard nothing about him on the first nor on the second day, they moved on from their position by the city. Keeping to the level plains from here on, they went down to Tyre, which is now called Sur, with their guide, pitching camp there to stay on the level plains of the fields. For a spring flows there which is raised up on a walled and arched structure in such a way that it produces so much water by the rush and abundance in the source of its flow that the whole army could not exhaust the supply.[37] On the following day Tyre was left behind and they arrived at the town named Ptolomaida, which these days is called Acre because the city was God's Accaron. They left Acre on their right on the seashore and spent two nights on a river of fresh water which flows into the sea there.[38] There two routes divide: the one on the left leads through Damascus and the river Jordan to Jerusalem; the other always keeps to the right next to the said seashore to Jerusalem.[39] Since out of fifty thousand men scarcely twenty thousand could be found who were fit for battle, they decided they would certainly not go through Damascus, because of the numbers of Turks who lived there and because of the open plains where they could be seen for a long way on every side and attacked by the enemy. For this reason they settled on the road between the sea and the mountains where they could travel confidently, protected by the sea on the right and by the impassable height of the mountains on the left, and they passed by the town of Caiphas, so called from Caiphas who was once chief priest of the Jews.[40] And that same day they pitched camp and were quartered in the territory of Caesarea, which was formerly the city of Herod Strato who afterwards called the rebuilt city Caesarea in honour of Caesar. A spring wells up at the foot of the mountains which flows into that same city across the open plains of fields where Duke Godfrey and Robert of Flanders had sited their tents and were quartered. Count Raymond and Robert prince of the Normans placed their camp on the same river but far from them, because an extensive marsh caused by that same spring was behind them and in

---

[37] A Roman aqueduct. WT gives a more detailed description of the city's water supply from his own knowledge (p. 589).

[38] The river Na'āman.

[39] It is difficult to make sense of this, as Damascus is north-east of Acre and nowhere near the route to Jerusalem. It would be possible to strike inland *towards* Damascus from Acre then take the road south to Jerusalem and perhaps this is what AA intended to write.

[40] John 11: 49, 18: 14; Acts 4: 6.

between.[41] They stayed there four days and very devoutly celebrated the Sunday of holy Pentecost, and that same day of the advent of the Holy Spirit.[42]

42. How they found the city of Ramla empty and they were able to install a bishop there

And so, passing by the aforementioned cities and leaving them untouched, they continued their journey on Monday, Tuesday, and Wednesday in the territory and wide plains of Caesarea Cornelii, named above, in the region of the Palestinians, and on the Thursday[43] they pitched camp at the river of the town of Ramla or Ramnes,[44] and on the bank of the channel of that river they placed their tents and decided to stay the night. Robert of Flanders and Gaston, the military man of Béziers, were sent on ahead, taking with them five hundred young knights from the company, to reconnoitre the gates and walls. As these were open and unlocked they went through, finding no one in the city because, when they heard about the distress and misfortune which befell the gentiles in the siege and capture of Antioch all the townspeople together fled from the Christians through the mountains and deserts with their children, wives, herds, and treasures. Therefore, finding the town of Ramla empty of townspeople and weapons like this, they speedily sent back a messenger to the Catholic army which was camped on the riverbank, to fetch everyone to enter and take possession of the city, and to rest their limbs which they had punished by great and long endeavours. When the pilgrims heard this, they set out for the city at once and rested themselves within it for three days, refreshed by the wine and much corn and oil they found. They appointed a certain Robert as bishop there,[45] leaving Christian inhabitants in the city who would cultivate the lands, and make judgments, and restore the fruitfulness of the fields and vineyards.[46]

---

41 The Crocodile River (Nahal ha-Tanninim) still has marshes near its mouth, today a nature reserve.

42 29 May 1099.

43 2 June 1099.

44 Ramla is some 50 miles south of Caesarea. However, it is famously not on any river: its name means 'sandy' and, being without springs, huge cisterns were built there to store water. Probably AA confused Ramla and Lydda in this passage, as Lydda is situated near the river Ayyalon.

45 Robert of Rouen was appointed bishop of adjacent Lydda, where St George's principal shrine was a cult-centre (*GF* p. 87; RA p. 136; FC p. 277). For the thinking which lay behind the appointment of a Latin bishop, see Hamilton, pp. 11–12.

46 According to J. Prawer, at Ramla 'a system of colonization was perfected which … created a model': J. Prawer, *Crusader Institutions* (Oxford, 1980), pp. 112–14. H. E. Mayer modifies this judgment somewhat, but he does point out that AA's testimony in this regard is good: whatever his sources of information, he describes Bishop Robert doing exactly as he must have done in using the labour of native Christians. See H. E. Mayer, 'The origins

43. While the army is marching towards the mountains, an eclipse of the moon appears at night

When the fourth day dawned after this, the pilgrims who were travelling on the road to the left departed from the town of Ramla and they likewise decided to set out for and stay at that place where the mountain regions began which surround the city of Jerusalem on all sides so that it is sited in the middle, but in that place they found a very great shortage of water. Consequently a large contingent of squires was sent to the castle at Emmaus two miles away, where there were known to be cisterns and springs full of water from the account of their Saracen fellow traveller and guide. They brought back not only a quantity of water but also a great deal of fodder for the horses. In that place an eclipse of the moon, which was the fifteenth, happened that same night, such that it totally lost its brightness and was entirely changed into the colour of blood up till the middle of the night, bringing to all who saw this no little fear, except that comfort was offered by certain who understood the knowledge of stars. These people said that this portent would not be a bad omen for the Christians, but they were certain that the absence of the moon and its being shrouded by blood showed the annihilation of the Saracens. They claimed that an eclipse of the sun, indeed, would be an evil portent for the Christians.[47]

44. How the Christian inhabitants of the city of Bethlehem send messengers to Duke Godfrey, asking him to hasten to their assistance; and about the joyful reception of the allies

Then when the Christians were quartered in the above-mentioned place next to the mountains of Jerusalem with the entire army, and as day was already drawing towards evening, Duke Godfrey learnt of a legation from the Catholic inhabitants of the city of Bethlehem, and especially from those whom the Saracens had thrown out of Jerusalem on suspicion of treachery and were still threatening with death, and the legation asked that the Christians should hasten their journey with no slackening to help them in the name of Jesus Christ. For the gentiles had swarmed to Jerusalem from every part of the Egyptian kingdom when they heard of the pilgrims' approach, to defend the city and to kill the Christians. After the duke heard the legation with its entreaties and he understood the Christians' danger, in that same night he sent ahead about a hundred armoured cavalry chosen from the camp and his own company to help the abandoned faithful of Christ who were congregated in Bethlehem. They rode with haste, in accordance with the command of the most devout and Christian duke, and covered six miles by riding all night,

---

of the lordships of Ramla and Lydda in the Latin Kingdom of Jerusalem', *Speculum*, 60 (1985), pp. 537–52, at 539.

[47] 5 June 1099. The eclipse is also described and interpreted by ME (p. 172).

arriving in Bethlehem at first light of day. When they knew of their arrival, the Christian townspeople came in procession to meet them with hymns and praises and sprinkling of holy water and welcomed those same Christian riders joyfully, kissing their eyes and hands and reporting these things to them: 'Thanks be to God that we see now in our own time those things which were always our desire, namely you, our Christian brothers, arriving to cast off the yoke of our slavery,[48] and to restore the holy places of Jerusalem, and to take away the rites of the gentiles and their impurities from the holy place.'[49]

45. The way the army hastened to Jerusalem; the messages from Bethlehem are discovered; and about the booty brought from the region around Jerusalem; and how they stood before the walls of Jerusalem singing praises and hymns

The cavalry sent out had only just left the camp when the news reached the ears of the leaders and everyone in the army that a legation had been brought to the duke from Bethlehem. For this reason it was scarcely halfway through the night when everyone, small and great, struck camp directly and went on their way through the difficulties of the roads and the narrow hill passes. From then on all the cavalry were keen to go ahead and hurry their journey, lest the crowd of infantry overflowing on the narrow defiles of the paths might be a great hindrance to the horsemen. Indeed, great and small hastened their journey to Jerusalem with equal determination. The hundred riders sent ahead and now returning from Bethlehem joined them on the road, at that time when the dew on the grass is dried by the first heat of the early morning sun. Gaston of the city of Béziers, knowing that the strength of the approaching pilgrims was still unknown to the townspeople and soldiers of Jerusalem, as was prudent secretly withdrew from the army with thirty men who were skilful in battle and ambushes, and he galloped through the boundaries of that same city with his men, seizing booty everywhere and carrying it off. But when the townspeople and Saracen soldiers realized his boldness the booty was seized from him. They pursued Gaston and his companions to the slope of a certain cliff face. However, from that same cliff Gaston met Tancred descending towards him, as he himself had ridden ahead of the army to look for supplies. He explained the Saracens' sortie from the city and their snatching of his booty, and kindled a violent desire in Tancred's mind to pursue those same enemies. So they both joined the forces of their comrades and galloped bravely after the enemies, putting them to flight all the way to the city gates of Jerusalem. They regained the booty, though, and took it back to the army of Christians which was following. When they saw the flocks of plunder, and their brothers returning, everyone asked

---

[48] Cf. Gen. 27: 40; Gal. 5: 1.

[49] AA underplays the part played by Tancred and Baldwin of Bourcq in the capture of Bethlehem, cf. FC pp. 278–80.

where they had brought these supplies of booty from. They declared that they had seized them and carried them off from the plain of Jerusalem. Hearing Jerusalem named, all the people burst into floods of tears of happiness, because they were so close to the holy place of the longed-for city, for which they had suffered so many hardships, so many dangers, so many kinds of death and famine. Soon, for desire of the city they heard named and longing to see the holy city, forgetful of hardships and their weariness, they hastened their journey more than usual. And it was not long before about sixty thousand of both sexes stood before the walls of Jerusalem in praises and singing of hymns, crying for joy.[50]

46. How and by which of the princes the city was besieged

As the most Christian army gathered in these places with different signs and weapons, the city gates were closed by the soldiers of the king of Egypt, the Tower of David[51] was protected by an armed guard, and all the townspeople were spread out on the ramparts to bar the way and resist the Catholic army. For the king of Egypt had violated the treaty which his legates sent to Antioch had agreed with the Christian princes, having no just cause against them, except that Count Raymond had seized the town of Tortosa and besieged the fortress of Arqa for many days. The Christians, seeing the king's military strength, the defence of the city, and the resistance of the gentiles, blockaded and surrounded the walls. They stationed Duke Godfrey, because he was powerful in counsels and forces, with the Germans, who were very fierce in battle, on the side of the Tower of David, where the greater strength of the defence was concentrated, and Tancred along with him; they appointed Count Raymond to take up position with two bishops from Italy before the doorway of the same tower with his company. Then Robert of Flanders and the aged Hugh of Saint-Pol with their fellows were told to position themselves to keep watch on the town walls in the sloping part of the plains. Robert prince of Normandy and Conan the Breton pitched their tents in the due order of their comrades next to the walls where there is the chapel of the blessed protomartyr Stephen. Count Raimbold of Orange, Louis of Mousson, Cono of Montaigu, his son Lambert, Gaston of Béziers, Gerard of Roussillon, Baldwin of Bourcq, Thomas of the castle of La Fère settled on all sides around the city. Count Raymond, seeing that he could do better elsewhere, moved his camp away from the blockade of the gates of the Tower of David, leaving certain comrades to guard the gates, and set out to besiege the city by pitching tents upon Mount Sion. Once this siege was put in place all around by the leaders of the Gauls, and places had been reconnoitred so that none would be left empty or vulnerable to ambushes, they went to the Mount of Olives. There too they placed strong men as guards, so

---

[50] According to RA, whose estimate must be preferred, there were 12,000 troops, of which (he says earlier) 1,500 were knights (pp. 136 and 148).

[51] Jerusalem's citadel, by the western, or Jaffa, Gate.

that there would not be any unexpected attack from this side, and ambushes from gentiles coming down over the ridge would not entrap unwary Christians. But the valley of Jehosaphat, above which the city and its buildings towered, remained unblockaded, because of the difficulties of the terrain and the depth of the valleys. Nevertheless there were keen Christian watchmen and guards in that place night and day.[52]

---

[52] For the disposition of the armies during the siege of Jerusalem see J. Prawer, 'The Jerusalem the crusaders captured: a contribution to the medieval topography of the city', in P. W. Edbury (ed.), *Crusade and Settlement* (Cardiff, 1985), pp. 1–16 and cf. France, *Victory*, pp. 337–45. France refers to AA's 'rather curious order of siege' and his 'deep topographical confusion', and suggests that he has confused the citadel with the 'Quadrangular Tower' which occupied the north-west angle of the city walls.

Book 6

1. On the first day of the blockade different people suffer various afflictions

Once the holy city was blockaded on all sides in this way, on the fifth day of the siege,[1] on the orders and advice of the aforesaid princes, the Christians put on hauberks and helmets, made a shield roof, and attacked the walls and ramparts, bravely provoking the Saracen men to battle with hurled stones, slings, and with arrows flying over the walls, and they fought inside and out all day long. Many of the faithful were wounded and crushed by stones and destroyed; some lost their eyes when arrows pierced them. But by God's gift none of the leaders was struck down that day. Indeed the Christians were vexed by the damage to their army and they intensified the effort and the battle, attacking strongly the exterior walls of the city, which are called barbicans, and partly breaching them with iron hammers and mattocks. But nevertheless they were unable to get very far on this day.

2. A council of the leaders to discuss how the city could be taken

At length, when this tumult of battle had subsided, since the duke and the foremost in the army saw that the city was unconquerable by force of arms and attack, they returned from the assault to the camp and reached a common conclusion, that unless the city was taken by siege engines and mangonels it could never be conquered by any other strength of weapons. Everyone realized it was a good plan for engines and mangonels and battering rams to be constructed. But they lacked the timbers, of which there was a great shortage in those regions. At this point a certain brother Christian, a Syrian by birth, told the pilgrims of a place where timbers could be found for building siege engines, that is to say in certain mountains towards the region of Arabia. When the location of timber was disclosed, Robert of Flanders and Robert lord of the Normans, also Gerard of Quierzy, took a group of cavalry and infantry and set out on the four-mile journey. There they put the wood they found on the backs of camels and returned without injury to their comrades' position.[2]

---

1 Saturday 11 June 1099. (The chapter title is in error.)

2 RC also describes the search for wood, led by Tancred who was suffering from dysentery and discovered the timbers entirely by chance (or by a miracle, as Radulf says), hidden in a cave. They were revealed to be 400 ready-hewn timbers which had been left there by the Saracens after their successful assault on Jerusalem the previous year (pp. 136–7).

3. Concerning siege machines built for the conquest of the city

At first light on the following day all the master craftsmen set about the making of an engine, mangonels, and a battering ram, some with axes, some with gimlets, until within four weeks the work on the engine, ram, and mangonels was brought to perfection in front of the Tower of David, in full view of all those who were quartered in that same fortress. Then young men, old men, boys, girls, and women[3] were told to go together into the valley of Bethlehem[4] and all to bring back on mules or donkeys or on their own shoulders withies from which panels could be plaited, and when the engine was protected with these it would make light of the Saracens' projectiles. This was done. Very many osiers and withies were brought, from which panels were woven and then covered with the skins of horses, cattle, or camels, so the engine would not easily be burnt by enemy fire.

4. Certain from the people meet their deaths while they are seeking food at some distance

Meanwhile, during this lengthy siege and the long-drawn-out and painstaking construction of the engines, shortage of provisions compelled certain men to sally forth from the army in search of supplies.[5] But when they happened to enter the territory of the aforementioned city of Ramla, and they collected booty and drove together flocks, they were destroyed by ambushes of Saracens who had ridden down from Ascalon, the king of Egypt's town, and the booty was kept by them. Gilbert of Traves and Achard of Montmerle, brave leaders of Christians and noble men, were maimed and fell in that place after a great deal of fighting. The rest of their comrades were put to flight and made their way at speed through the mountain regions to Jerusalem. At this point, as he was going along, Baldwin of Bourcq, who was about the same business of gathering food with Thomas of Castle La Fère, taking a group of cavalry, met their brothers who had been thrown into flight and disorder. When Baldwin realized what was the matter and what had happened to them, he comforted them all with the suggestion that they return with

---

[3] The part played by old men and by women in the capture of Jerusalem is also recorded in an anonymous account, published by J. France, 'The text of the account of the capture of Jerusalem in the Ripoll Manuscript, Bibliothèque Nationale (Latin) 5132', *English Historical Review*, 103 (1988), pp. 641–57, at 645, 646. The much later *Chanson de Jérusalem* gives the women their own battalion and also describes their bringing water to the warriors ((ed.) N. R. Thorp [Tuscaloosa, AL, 1992], pp. 108–9, 112).

[4] Bethlehem is about 6 miles south of Jerusalem.

[5] This expedition is described in *GF* as a hundred knights from the army of Raymond of Saint-Gilles, including Raymond Pilet, Achard of Montmerle and William of Sabran (pp. 88–9). RA says it was led by Galdemar Carpenel (pp. 141–2). Both authors agree that the sortie was a response to a plea for help from Jaffa, where a Christian fleet had put in.

him to avenge their injuries. The pilgrim brothers were immediately revived by the comfort of the brave men and returned wholeheartedly and with renewed vigour to the pursuit of their enemies, joining battle with them for a long time. On this side and that many were killed and wounded. Baldwin of Bourcq was wounded in the chest by a blow from the front.

5. Where a renowned man from the infidels and two nobles from the Christians are slain

At length, as the Christians prevailed and put the Saracens to flight, they held captive one of them, a noble knight, a bald-headed man, of outstanding stature, elderly and corpulent. They brought him back to Jerusalem and bound him in fetters in the tent of the aforesaid Baldwin. But this man sat down in state on Baldwin's couch, which was covered with very precious purple cloth. Moreover, the Christian princes, who saw that this same Saracen was a wise, noble and vigorous man, frequently enquired about and discussed his life and customs, and tried to convert him to the faith of Christianity. But as he scorned this faith in every way he was brought out in front of the Tower of David to frighten the guards of the citadel, and was beheaded by Baldwin's squire in full view of all.[6] The two princes named above, Gilbert and Achard, who were slaughtered in gentile ambushes, were brought back with great lamentation to the place of the siege. Christian priests carried out the funeral rites for them and placed their bones in the sepulchre of their Christian brothers which was outside the town.

6. When the city was besieged; and about the scarcity of water to drink

The holy city and our mother Jerusalem, which her bastard sons had assaulted and denied to her legitimate sons, was besieged on the Tuesday in the second week in July[7] when the heat and burning of the sun is said to be unbearable, and especially in these eastern regions, when not only do the streams lack water, but even the small springs are only to be found three miles away.[8] In this siege the Christian army was severely tormented by the heat of the blazing sun, by the unbearable lack of water and the incredibly arid landscape. When some comrades were sent to track down and draw on the springs scattered here and there, sometimes they

[6] In *GF* one of the enemy is spared so that he could give them information (p. 89) and in BD intelligence is extracted from the prisoner of war (p. 98), but neither gives so circumstantial an account as AA. Both the *GF* author and BD, on the other hand, give very precisely the number of horses captured: 103.

[7] The date should be Tuesday 7 June 1099: cf. *GF* p. 87; RA p. 134.

[8] The Christians' sufferings from lack of water were exacerbated by the defenders' having blocked the wells and springs in the vicinity of Jerusalem: see RA p. 139.

returned unharmed, having drawn water, and at other times they were in danger of having their heads cut off in gentile ambushes. The water they brought back in goatskin bags was stirred up and muddied because so many were competing in their efforts to draw it and it had in it slippery worms of leeches. From this, as much as a person could take in his mouth from the narrow opening of the skin was sold for twopence, although it might be old and putrid, or taken from filthy marshes or ancient cisterns. Very many of the non-combatant crowd who were tormented by unbearable thirst took this opportunity of drinking, and while they did so they swallowed down the slippery water worms and so were killed by swollen throat or stomach.[9] Only the tiniest streamlet flowed from Mount Sion, and its subterranean channel runs an arrow flight away from the palace of Solomon to that place where there is a building walled and squared like a cloister, in the middle of which the streamlet collected in a pool through the night. The citizens used it during the day and watered their herds.[10]

7. The advice of one of the besieged about the enterprise they have begun

The army was sometimes refreshed from the constant drawing of water, although this part of the city was not blockaded and the citizens often hurled missiles and tried hard to frighten the Christians off their watering altogether. There was always a good supply of grapes and an abundance of wine for the leaders and those who could afford them, but for the poor and the destitute there was even a very great lack of water, as you have heard. For this reason, as this problem of thirst grew worse and the Catholic people suffered long in this siege, the foremost of them, on the advice of the bishops and clergy who were there, thought it a good idea to consult a certain man of God who was a hermit in an ancient and tall tower on the Mount of Olives,[11] as to what they should do, what should be their first purpose, revealing to him how they were burning with desire to enter the city and see the Sepulchre of the Lord, and how many dangers they had undergone on the journey for this faith and their vow. When the man of God heard their purpose and desire he offered the advice that first they should devoutly stand firm in the suffering of fasting and constant prayer, and after this they would more surely with God's aid carry out an attack on the walls and the Saracens.

---

9 Cf. the remark by G. Cansdale: 'Leeches normally fasten on the skin but some can invade the throat and nasal passages after being taken into the mouth with water, and this may have fatal results': *Animals of Bible Lands* (Exeter, 1970), pp. 233–4.

10 This was the spring and pool of Siloam. According to RA it was unreliable and soon contaminated by the bodies of animals. He describes the agonies of thirst suffered by the Christian armies (pp. 139–40), as does the *GF* author, who also refers to the use of animal-skins to carry water and how foul the contents were (p. 89).

11 A short distance outside the eastern wall of the city. (The title implies the hermit is within the besieged city.)

8. About the procession announced, which was then carried out

Now a three-day fast was announced by the bishops and clergy on the man of God's advice, and on the Friday all the Christians made a procession around the city,[12] then came to the Mount of Olives, in the place where Lord Jesus rose into heaven, and going in procession from there they halted in complete devotion and humility in another place where he taught his disciples to pray 'Our Father'. There in that same place on the Mount, Peter the Hermit and Arnulf of Chocques,[13] a castle in Flanders, a cleric of great knowledge and eloquence, preached a sermon to the people and laid to rest the very great discord which had grown up among the pilgrims from different causes. Indeed, since both princes felt remorseful after the spiritual admonition, Count Raymond and Tancred soothed with harmonious love the dissension which had long prevailed between them on account of the sum of money which had been agreed but which the count had unjustly refused to pay Tancred. When these two were reconciled, moreover, and brought back to friendship with the many other Christian brothers, that entire procession of Christians came down from the aforesaid place, the Mount of Olives, and assembled on the next mountain, Sion, in the church of the holy mother of God.[14] There the clerics, wearing albs and reverently bearing relics of the saints, and many worthy laymen were hit by arrows from the Saracens who were watching their movements on the city ramparts. For the town is very close to this church of Sion, just the distance of an arrow flight. In this place, as well, to arouse the Christians' anger, they fixed crosses in mockery and abuse, upon which they either spat, or they did not shrink from urinating in full view of everyone.[15]

9. The siege engines are brought up to the wall; opposing engines fight each other

Then, when the fast, with the holy procession and litany, was finished, once darkness was covering the sky, at dead of night the siege engine was carried off, and all the heaps of stones for the mangonels, through the districts to that same part of the town where the chapel of the protomartyr Stephen is situated,

---

[12] 8 July 1099. The procession and fast are mentioned in *GF*, though not the hermit (p. 90); RA says the instructions were given by Adhémar of Le Puy in a vision (p. 144).

[13] For Arnulf's career, see below and Appendix 1: People.

[14] To the south of the city. The church was in ruins in 1099; later rebuilt by the crusaders, it no longer stands.

[15] RA also describes the Turks insulting crosses by putting them on gallows and mocking them with blows and insults (p. 145). PT has the Turks beating and shattering a cross against the walls (p. 137).

towards the valley of Jehosaphat,[16] since on the day of the sabbath tents had been moved away from this position and had been placed around the engine. There the construction of the siege engine and of all the apparatus of mangonels and of the ram was brought to completion. In fact, by majority decision the apparatus for three mangonels was arranged and put up, so that the Christians could use their first assault and attack to frighten off the Saracen citizens who were preventing them from approaching the walls and ramparts, and they could breach the wall works with a sudden bombardment and stone attack. At length, when the Saracens realized the walls were being seriously struck and destroyed by this assault and bombardment, they brought out sacks of straw and chaff and ships' ropes of great size and closely packed, and fixed them against the walls and ramparts, so that they would cushion the attack and blows of the mangonels, and not harm the walls and ramparts at all. The duke, therefore, seeing this hindrance made of ropes and sacks put in the way of his siege engines, took burning arrows out of the fire and twisted them into his crossbow on the spot, and thus the arrow with fire affixed was shot out onto the dry stuff, and a slender flame was kindled by a gentle breeze, and it gathered strength until it consumed the sacks and ropes and once more the attack was dashing to pieces the walls and ramparts.

10. Those under siege strive to break up the ram breaching the walls

While all this was going on, the aforementioned battering ram was brought up to increase the ruin and destruction of the walls; it was of horrendous weight and craftsmanship, clad in wickerwork panels. It was driven on by the strength and sheer numbers of men, and with a heavy charge it weakened and overthrew in a moment the barbicans, that is to say the outer walls standing against the walls, the city rampart having been levelled by the men driving the ram, and it prepared a way to the inner and ancient walls for the engine and, as it now passed through an enormous and horrendous breach into the city, it damaged the town walls. When the city's defenders saw the breach through the walls they could no longer endure that risk and they set fire to the ram, which was too close to the walls, with fire kindled from sulphur, pitch, and wax, so that afterwards it would not drive at the walls with its iron-clad forehead[17] and enlarge the breach. Then God's people were stirred up by a sudden shouting; on all sides from tents and huts they were calling for water, bringing water, with which at length the fire on the battering ram was quenched.

---

[16] St Stephen's church stood north of the city, outside St Stephen's Gate, now the Damascus Gate. The valley of Jehosaphat runs north-south outside the eastern wall.

[17] Cf. Claudian, *In Rufinum*, ii. 361, where, however, the forehead belongs to a horse.

11. Those who are to be in charge of the siege engine are appointed from all sides

Meanwhile, while the ram was being extinguished, the bombardment and attack of the mangonels was constantly breaking down the walls; the guards and defenders were keeping them from the ramparts. At once, while this was going on, the siege engine was erected with all its fittings; its walls, upper storeys, and panels were covered with the skins of cattle, horses, and camels, and in it were positioned the soldiers who would attack the city and more easily harass and fight those who withstood them. Moreover, they had sweated over the work and construction of this engine from the day of the sabbath to the Thursday[18] and finished the long-drawn-out task in the evening, and they appointed Duke Godfrey and his brother Eustace along with two brothers Lithold and Engilbert, who were born in the town of Tournai, to protect the engine and to incite the city to battle. They decided Duke Godfrey and his men should stay in the upper storey; Lithold with his brother and the rest of their followers in the middle storey; in the lower, of course, were those who were pushing the engine and would bring it up to the city. So when these men were positioned in the fortress of the engine and its storeys, the Christians set fire with their own flame to the ram behind the destroyed barbicans and levelled rampart, because it was such a difficult and wearisome burden to move it out of the way, and so that its great size and strength would not be in the way of the machine being brought up.

12. How forcefully the citizens are worn down by the siege engines

Then, when morning arrived on the Saturday, the Saracen soldiers and those who were citizens of the town saw the tower erected and the armoured men occupying it, and they were stunned and trembling with fear, amazed that the soldiers appeared so early in the morning and ready for battle in the siege engine, and all of them went through the city to shoot with bow and arrows, and to press hard with javelins and rocks in constant battle anyone whom they saw from anywhere in the city on the engine which was towering above the walls. And so the gentiles who were assembled within the city were of one mind in trying to harm and resist the duke with flying arrows. And those spread out along the ramparts were injuring the pilgrims; the pilgrims were bravely fighting back. Then, from the engine which rose above both the city and the ramparts by the height of an ashen spear shaft, into this struggle to and fro, inside and out, the men and soldiers were hurling really enormous rocks to damage the walls and frighten off the citizens from the defence of the ramparts, striking with arrows and stones all who were ranging through the city. On another side of the city upon Mount Sion Count Raymond's soldiers were hurling stones and missiles from one engine, damaging the walls and those who

[18] 2–7 July 1099.

were along the ramparts and seeking in vain to harm this engine of the count's, which had been erected and put against the walls on the same night and at the same time as the duke's.[19]

13. Where a watch is assigned to the gate which allowed a way through for Egyptian messengers

When this siege of the holy city was becoming wearisome, and they were striving eagerly by all ways and means for its capture, and they were finding out much more about the threats and strength of the king of Egypt, it came to the ears of the princes of the army, by way of those same spies who told brother Tancred about the money and ornament of the Lord's Temple before the capture of the city, that from the city of Jerusalem through that gate on the Mount of Olives and valley of Jehosaphat which was not blockaded, a constant communication was sent to the king of Egypt about everything which happened, and the king's messages and advice were sent back again by the city's defenders frequently and secretly through that same gate, and this could easily become a great hindrance to the Christians.[20] On this account the Christian princes held a careful council about these things, and they secretly placed ambushes at dead of night in the valley and way out of that same mountain, protecting the footpaths before and behind with a watchful guard, so if anyone should come down from Ascalon or Egypt, or from any other part of this kingdom, or come out of the unblockaded gate to carry messages as was their custom, he would fall into an ambush and be captured unexpectedly, and would not slip away from the hands of those keeping watch and make an escape.

14. Concerning two messengers of the Egyptian king perishing by different kinds of death

At length, after men had been organized in this way to guard the roads and positioned in the aforesaid place on the Mount of Olives, two Saracens who were making haste from Ascalon and bringing down messages from the king of Egypt to the city's defenders arrived in the midst of the guards just as night was falling silent, hoping to enter the city without any hindrance. But they were unexpectedly caught and held by the soldiers and guards of the unblockaded gate. One of them

---

19 RA describes in much more detail the construction of mantlets and towers under the direction of Gaston of Béarn for Godfrey and the two Roberts; William Embriacus was overseer for Raymond of Saint-Gilles (pp. 145–6).

20 The Saracens had expelled the Christian inhabitants of Jerusalem as the crusaders approached, and these were probably the 'spies' who provided intelligence about the insecurity of the Gate of Jehosaphat. For the eviction of Christians see above, 5. 44; WT claims only men were expelled (p. 375).

was speared by an over-eager young soldier and soon breathed his last. The other, though, was brought alive and unharmed into the presence of the Christian princes so that they might extract from him by threats or by promise of his life what was the substance of the messages they had brought, so that in this way the Christians would be less liable to be harmed because the missiles were foreseen. This man, indeed, was greatly concerned and worried for his life, so he revealed a great deal of the king of Egypt's advice and message, and how already through the messengers he had warned the soldiers who were faithful to him, along with the citizens, not to be worn down by any fear or oppression and fall short, but to comfort one another and stand firm in defence, knowing that in fifteen days' time he had decided to come to Jerusalem in great strength to assist them to exterminate the Gauls and liberate their own people. After this and other reports the messenger was handed back to the soldiers, and he was put into the throwing arm of one of the mangonels with hands and feet bound, so that he would be thrown over the walls after the first and second charge. But the skin of the mangonel was too heavily weighed down by the weight of his body and did not throw the wretch far. He soon fell onto sharp stones near the walls, broke his neck, his sinews and bones, and is reported to have died instantly.[21]

15. About the apparatus used by the impious against the engines of the faithful

However, when the citizens and the king of Egypt's soldiers saw the king's legation destroyed in this way, and that the Christians were attacking the city more boldly, and that on this side and that the engines were turned against the city in a very dangerous manner, they decided they themselves would also erect the apparatus of fourteen mangonels, so that by their strength and force stones would constantly be thrown onto the towers, and by their frequent blows the engines would be thunderously shattered and destroyed, and those who were stationed inside them would at the same time be endangered by their ruin.[22] Nine of these fourteen mangonels were placed opposite Count Raymond's engine with a countless number and strength of citizens. The tower was severely shaken and weakened by their frequent and unbearable attack and its joints were loosened. Indeed, all the warlike men in the engine were very much crushed and stunned and they only just escaped with their lives. And so, because they could not withstand so many very rapid blows from the stones, and there was no protection for the tower, it was taken back far from the ramparts and no one would volunteer to climb it again and harm the citizens by attacking them. The five remaining mangonels were erected

---

[21] PT also has the story of the captured spy, though in his account only the one was sent. His fate, however, was the same (p. 139).

[22] Cf. RA, who says that for each of the crusaders' machines the Saracens had nine or ten (p. 149).

against the duke's tower in order to strike and weaken it with a comparable attack and bombardment. But with God's help, although it was hit by the frequent blows and shaken and threatened to collapse, it remained whole and unconquered, and because it was protected by the wicker panels it sustained and was cushioned against the amazing attack of stones.

16. About the crucifix which the frenzy of the infidels was unable to harm

There was a cross shining brightly with gold on top of that same engine, containing a statue of Lord Jesus. The Saracens were striving keenly to destroy this by the bombardment of mangonels, but they were given no opportunity of hitting or displacing it. While, indeed, they were hurling frequent attacks of stones against this cross, a stone flying randomly hit a certain soldier who was standing at the duke's side hard on the head. His skull was broken and his neck shattered and he was killed instantly. The duke, who narrowly missed so sudden a blow, fought back fiercely with his crossbow against the citizens and those manning the mangonels, and whenever the panels were torn away from the engine in the attack he repaired them and fastened them with ropes.

17. More about different machines of the infidels

The Saracen soldiers saw that the mangonels' attack could not penetrate the wicker panels, so from time to time they hurled pots vomiting flames onto the panels protecting the engine, so that the live coals or sparks would stick to the dry stuff and, being kindled by a light breeze, would grow in strength and burn up the engine. But the Gauls' diligence met artifice with artifice. For the engine and panels were covered with slippery skins and did not hold the flames or live coals thrown onto them, but at once the fire slipped from the skins, fell to the ground and went out. At length the duke and his men were oppressed and in difficulties from the constant blows of these five mangonels, and they used the strength of Christians to place the engine close in to the ramparts and walls, so in this way it might withstand the mangonels more safely and, as the mangonels could not be brought into a large space because of the buildings of houses and towers, they were less able to throw and to batter the engine. Once the tower had been brought up next to the walls, and the five mangonels could not find a sufficient distance to withdraw from it, a stone loaded and ejected by force from them flew over the too-close engine or sometimes, being too short in flight, fell next to the walls and crushed Saracens. At length the Saracens realized that the men in the engine were undaunted, and that they could not be harmed by use of the mangonels, so they protected one of the towers which was quite close to the engine against the Christians' mangonels by cladding it with sacks filled with straw, hay, or chaff, and also wicker panels, also the thickness of ships' rope on all sides around it, stationing warriors in it who would constantly hurl piles of stones onto the engine with slings or small mangonels, and terrorize its occupants with different kinds of weapons. But when Duke Godfrey's engine did not withdraw, and its guards were not forced back from the assault, but prevailed more strongly and fiercely, the master craftsmen of the Saracens prepared another device, by which the engine and its occupants would be destroyed beyond recovery.

18. Where fire is quenched by vinegar, and a chain is wrenched from the infidels by force

They brought up a tree trunk which was really enormous and very heavy, and fixed iron nails and hooks all over it, and covered the nails with tow soaked and impregnated with pitch, wax, and oil and all kinds of things for kindling fire.[23] They also fixed a heavy iron chain in the middle of the trunk so that it could not easily be taken off and removed by the pilgrims' curved iron hooks while this timber was being hurled over the walls and ramparts to burn up the engine. When this tree-trunk device was prepared and perfected, one day all the citizens and the king of Egypt's soldiers gathered inside the city and assembled around this creation. Using their ladders and spears and equipment they set alight the great timber with a fire which could not be put out with water, and instantly sent it over the walls with great strength, throwing it between the walls and the engine so that the posts on which the entire engine rested would catch light from the very intense heat and be burnt up, and thus its occupants would be destroyed, and so fierce a fire would not be put out by any water, until the entire engine was reduced to ashes along with the said tree trunk, and it fell down. But in the event native fellow Christians had explained to the Christians how this fire, which could not be put out using water, could only be extinguished with vinegar.[24] So vinegar which had fortunately been placed in wineskins inside the engine was thrown onto the trunk and poured out and in this way the great fire was put out and could not harm the engine any longer. Then there was a great rush of pilgrims to this quenching of the tree trunk. They seized the chain and embarked on a tug-of-war with all their might, those outside the walls pulling, those inside holding it back. But the strength of the Christians prevailed, by God's grace and so the chain was snatched from the Saracens and kept by the faithful.

---

[23] This device seems to be the one described in the short anonymous source, see France, 'The text', p. 646.

[24] The idea that Greek fire could be extinguished using vinegar is found as early as Aeneas (*c.*360BCE), *Polyorkeitikon*, xxxiii–xxxv (quoted in J. R. Partington, *A History of Greek Fire and Gunpowder* [Cambridge, 1960], p. 1).

19. Who were the first to occupy the holy city

While this struggle for the chain was going on inside and outside, and during the failure of the five mangonels which were throwing in vain from within, the duke, who had taken possession of the room at the top of the towering upper storey, was hurling all kinds of missiles and rocks into the midst of the dense crowd with his men, and was keeping those standing on the wall away from the ramparts without letting up. Three mangonels of the Christians were letting fly at once over the ramparts without a pause in an unceasing bombardment, and were keeping the guards on this side and that a long way back from the ramparts. At this point the brothers named above, Lithold and Engilbert, seeing that the Saracens were flagging and withholding their hands from the defence, and that on both sides of the ramparts they were withdrawing a long way because of the attack of the mangonels outside, at once, since they were quite close to the wall, stretched out beams and pushed them over the ramparts from the second storey where they were, and climbed down, the first into the city in strength of arms, putting all the guards of the walls to flight. When the duke and his brother Eustace realized that these men had already entered the city they came down at once from the upper storey and soon they were also standing on the ramparts and assisting them. When all the army saw these things and that the princes were already in possession of the town, they shouted with an incredible din, put ladders against the wall on all sides and hastened to climb in and enter.

20. Concerning the scattering and destruction of the degenerate enemy

When the citizens and the city's defenders observed that the ramparts and walls were captured, and Christian men were present in the middle of the city, and the entire town was awash with the Gauls' weapons, they were seized by terror and dullness of mind, and, quickly making their escape, a very great multitude fled to the palace of King Solomon in the hope of protection, since it was large and very solid.[25] The Gauls pursued them bravely with lances and swords and went into the gates of the palace with the fugitives themselves, and they kept up a very great slaughter of the gentiles. Some cavalry, indeed, about four hundred, had been sent by the king of Egypt and were constantly riding all over the city to alert the citizens to defence and to reinforce them, and when they saw the difficulties and flight of their men they galloped from different directions to the fortress of the Tower of David. But the Gauls were close behind them in pursuit and they only just got inside the gate of the tower, and of one accord they dismounted in front of the gate and left their horses, which the Christians seized and took away with their bridles and saddles.

---

[25] The Temple Mount, which occupies the south-eastern corner of the city.

21. What happened when the people burst in through the gates

Meanwhile certain of the pilgrims were making for the city gates where they drew back bolts and iron bars and admitted the entire common crowd to reinforce them, but it is reported that the pressure and anxiety of those entering this gate was so great that even the horses themselves, vexed by the excessive pressure, attacked very many with their teeth, opening their mouths to bite even though their riders did not want them to, and they were sweating incredibly. Moreover, about sixteen men were trampled under the feet of horses, mules, and men; they were mangled and suffocated and gave up the ghost. Very many thousands of men and women were also admitted by way of the breach in the walls which the battering ram had made with its iron-clad forehead. All of these gathered and rushed to the aforesaid palace with shouting and loud clamour, taking assistance to their brothers who had been sent ahead, striking down the Saracens with cruel death throughout the building, which was large. There was such great bloodshed that streams even flowed out across the very floors of the royal court, and the stream of spilt blood was ankle-deep.[26] The Saracens now and then recovered spirit and strength and rallied to the defence in vain, but nevertheless they pierced many unwary among the faithful in repayment for the slaughter.

22. About the cistern of the royal palace

Moreover, many Saracens fled together into the royal cistern – which was in front of the entrance of that same palace and held water in its cavern the extent and great capacity of a lake, having over it a roof of arched construction, supported on all sides by marble pillars – by way of the steps which led down to allow those who entered to draw water. Some of them were drowned in the water; others were killed by the pursuing Christians on those same steps which were the way down. And through those openings which there were in the roof in the manner of wells, as many Christians as Saracens fell headlong in the flight and blind rush, and were not only in danger of drowning, but also died of broken necks and limbs or ruptured entrails. Throughout all the siege of the city the water of this royal cistern used to be measured out to needy citizens and soldiers to water horses, flocks, and all their herds, and for every necessary use. Every time rain fell this cistern was filled with water flowing from the roofs of the palace and from gutters and from the arched roof of the Lord's Temple[27] and from the roofs of many buildings,

---

[26] Similar images are found in all the accounts, though worded differently. They are probably drawn from the Book of Revelation, which speaks of blood 'up to the horses' bridles' (Rev. 14: 20. Cf. *GF* p. 91; RA p. 150; FC p. 301; *Kreuzzugsbriefe*, p. 171, and EA p. 154).

[27] Vergil, *Aen.* i. 505.

serving all the inhabitants plentifully through all the seasons of the year with cold and wholesome water.[28]

23. More about the universal slaughter of the citizens and the plundering of the Temple of the Lord

Moreover, as the Christian victors came back out of the palace after the very great and cruel slaughter of Saracens, of whom ten thousand fell in that same place, they put to the sword great numbers of gentiles who were running about through the quarters of the city, fleeing in all directions on account of their fear of death: they were piercing through with the sword's point women who had fled into the turreted palaces and dwellings; seizing by the soles of their feet from their mothers' laps or their cradles infants who were still suckling and dashing them against the walls or lintels of the doors and breaking their necks; they were slaughtering some with weapons, or striking them down with stones; they were sparing absolutely no gentile of any age or kind. Whoever was first to invade a house or palace occupied it peacefully with all its furniture, corn, barley, wine, and oil, money or clothing, or whatever there was, and in this way they became the possessors of the entire city.[29] After the Christians were admitted to the town and while they were raging through palace and city in the long massacre, and gazing in amazement at the spoils and riches of the Saracens, Tancred, who ran quickly ahead to the Temple of the Lord in the first invasion of the city, pulled back the bolts and entered it, and tore off an incomparable quantity of gold and silver from the walls, which were gilded about with columns and pillars, with the strength and assistance of his escort, exerting himself for two days in the seizure of this treasure, which had been brought together by the Turks to decorate the chapel. It is reported that two Saracens who had left the city during the siege had revealed this to this same Tancred in order to find favour in his eyes and save their own lives. After the aforesaid passage of time he opened the doors of the Temple and took out with him the riches, and he faithfully shared them with Duke Godfrey, whose knight he was, and, so they say who know the entire amount, six camels or mules could scarcely carry them.

24. An account of the Temple of the Lord

Truly this temple which is called the Lord's is not to be understood as that ancient and wonderful masterwork of King Solomon, since the entire city of Jerusalem was

---

[28] On Jerusalem's cisterns, cf. FC pp. 282–3.

[29] J. Prawer traced the origin of burgage tenure in Jerusalem to this occupation, which is also described by FC (Prawer, *Crusader Institutions*, pp. 253–4; FC p. 304; WT pp. 412–13).

destroyed many years before the Lord's incarnation by King Nebuchadnezzar,[30] then by King Antiochus,[31] and the temple of Solomon was razed to the ground and its ornaments and sacred vessels were pillaged. Once again, after the incarnation, in accordance with the prediction of Lord Jesus, it was utterly destroyed with its occupants by the Roman princes Titus and Vespasian in such a way that, in accordance with the Lord's pronouncement, there would not be left one stone upon another.[32] In fact many confirm that this temple was afterwards rebuilt by modern people and Christian worshippers,[33] that is to say in that place where Solomon the peaceful placed the former tabernacle of God made of cedar wood and Parian marble,[34] and in it the Holy of Holies. Moreover, in the middle of this modern tabernacle a stone mountain of natural rock sticks up, comprising almost the third part of an acre in area, two cubits in height, on one side of which there are positioned steps leading down to cavernous places; on another side, indeed, there is something which in truth those who observed it call a little door of stone, but always sealed. And in that place certain holies of holies are said still to be kept in the opinion of some people. In the middle of the arched roof of this same modern temple, which now with wonderful carpentry of timbers encloses overhead a round shape all around the verticals of the walls, they declare a chain is fixed on which a vessel of shining gold and craftsmanship, weighing about two hundred marks, is always accustomed to hang. Some declare it is the golden pot,[35] some say the blood of the Lord is concealed in it, others manna, and in this way they are encouraged by different ideas to varying opinions.[36]

25. About the chapels of the holy city, and how devoutly the duke visited the Lord's Sepulchre

Therefore this vessel and the little promontory which, as we have said, stuck out in the middle of the Temple remained untouched by Tancred; moreover the Turks venerated them with complete piety and kept them both inviolate, and they

---

[30] 4 Kgs. (2 Kgs.) 24 and 25.

[31] 1 Macc. 1: 20–40.

[32] Matt. 24: 2; Mark 13: 2; Luke 19: 44, 21: 6.

[33] AA is mistaken in his belief that Christians rebuilt the Temple, but it is an error shared by Acard of Arrouaise, the prior of the Temple 1112–36, and expressed in his poem dedicated to King Baldwin: P. Lehmann, 'Die mittellateinischen Dichtungen der Prioren des Tempels von Jerusalem Acardus und Gaufridus', *Corona Quernea: Festgabe Karl Strecker*, Schriften des MGH, 6 (Stuttgart, 1941), pp. 296–330, at 302–3). Acard was not sure whether the rebuilding was the work of Justinian, of Helena mother of Constantine, or of Heraclius: J. Wilkinson, *Jerusalem Pilgrimage, 1099–1185* (London, 1988), p. 12.

[34] 1 Chr. 29: 2.

[35] Heb. 9: 4.

[36] AA is describing the Dome of the Rock, sacred to Jews, Christians and Moslems as the place of Abraham's sacrifice (Gen. 22: 2).

also treasured the tabernacle with much ornament and decoration, only leaving it empty of all the rest of the gentiles who were shut out during the observation of their ceremonies. In this way, venerating this very Temple with greatest reverence and care for performing the rites of their mistaken religion, they also spared only the Temple of the Lord's Sepulchre and its Christian worshippers, on account of the tribute which they used to pay them regularly from the offerings of the faithful, along with the little church of St Mary of the Latins,[37] which was also tributary to them. In the rest of the chapels of the holy city Turks and Saracens alike exercised their very great tyranny by slaughter, especially driving out the Catholic worshippers from them. Then, as Tancred turned aside to this Temple of the Lord, as has been said, for the sake of greed for the wealth revealed to him, while others were swiftly pursuing fugitives to the fortress of the Tower of David, and while all the princes were gazing open-mouthed at the possessions and the turreted buildings, and all the common crowd was making for Solomon's palace and inflicting a massacre with excessive cruelty on the Saracens, Duke Godfrey soon abstained from all slaughter, and, keeping only three of his men with him, Baldric, Adelolf, and Stabelo, he took off his hauberk and linen clothes, went out of the walls with bare feet and made a humble procession around the outside of the city; then, entering through that gate which looks out on the Mount of Olives, he presented himself at the sepulchre of Lord Jesus Christ, son of the living God, keeping up steadfastly tears, prayers, and divine praises, and giving thanks to God because he had earned the sight of that which had always been his greatest desire.

26. A certain man's dream concerning the duke

When this pious desire of the duke had been satisfied, the vision in this dream was proved to be perfectly true. Before the beginning of this journey when this same duke would often sigh deeply, and when before all things his heart's desire was to visit the holy town of Jerusalem and to see Lord Jesus' sepulchre, and often he would secretly reveal the purpose of his mind to his attendants, a vision was shown to one of his servants, namely Stabelo, in this way. He saw a golden ladder, extremely long, stretching all the way from heaven to earth, which the duke himself, burning with very intense desire, tried to climb with a certain steward of his, Rothard by name, who carried a lamp in his hand. But when the steward was standing just halfway up the ladder, the lamp which he bore in his hand was put out, and the middle rung of the ladder by which he was climbing to the throne of heaven on high was seriously damaged and worn away. And so the steward went back down below and because of his fear he could no longer arrive and knock with the duke on the heavenly door. At this point Stabelo, whose dream this is, rekindled the quenched lamp and confidently mounted the ladder by which the

[37] Also known as St Mary Minor, established by Amalfitan merchants in 1047 in the Muristan (later to be the Hospitallers' quarter), close to the church of the Holy Sepulchre.

steward was unworthy to be raised up, and, bearing the lamp which still did not fail, he penetrated the court of heaven with the duke himself. There a table was made ready for them and was covered with all kinds of heaped up sweetness of delicious things.[38] Then the duke reclined at this table with the chosen ones and those worthy of it, and he shared in all the sweetness which was there.

27. The interpretation of the dream

What is signified by this ladder leading to the palace of heaven, unless the journey which the duke undertook with the entire purpose of his mind to the city of Jerusalem, which is the gate of the heavenly homeland? For the ladder was of purest gold, because one must come to this journey and the gate of heaven with pure heart and perfect free will. Moreover, halfway up the ladder the steward's lamp was put out and the damaged rung failed and denied his ascent, for he deserted the work and weariness of the holy journey, which of good and pure free will he had vowed along with the duke, in the middle of the undertaking with very many others, as you have heard. Because of his lack of faith and the pressing hardships he withdrew from the duke and from Antioch and thus became an apostate and returned to the plough of afflictions,[39] and he was no longer worthy to enter the gate of heaven with the duke by way of the ladder and to eat at the table of the saints. Stabelo, though, the duke's chamberlain, took the lamp from his hand and rekindled it, because he retained the good free will of this journey which he had when he undertook it, and when the lamp of good will was relit amidst the different waverings of mind, and his vow was rekindled, he stuck to it steadfastly. And so he climbed to the top of the ladder on an indestructible rung with the duke and, remaining his steadfast ally and faithful servant through all the difficulties, he arrived with him in Jerusalem, and he was worthy to enter and pray at the Lord's Sepulchre, which is the table and the desire of all sweetness of the saints.

28. About the greed of Raymond and Tancred; and about the slaughter of certain infidels

After these things the duke returned from the sanctuary of the Lord's Sepulchre in heartfelt happiness and exultation after finishing praying there, and he refused entertainment in favour of resting, for now the whole army was settling down from the killing of gentiles, and because of the hard work night was weighing down everyone's eyes on that same night of the Saturday on which Jerusalem, city of the living God, and our mother, was restored to her sons in great victory, on the solemn

---

38 Ps. 22 (23):5.

39 Cf. Isa. 17: 9.

day of the division of the apostles.[40] Count Raymond, corrupted by greed, allowed the Saracen soldiers whom he had besieged when they fled into the Tower of David to go away unharmed after he had received a huge amount of money.[41] Moreover, he kept back all the weapons, food, and things looted from them along with that same fortress. As the next day, which was the sabbath, grew brighter, certain of the Saracens who had escaped the weapons, about three hundred, fled together onto the top of the roof of the very high Temple of Solomon in the hope of saving their lives. They were pleading with much prayer for their lives, being in danger of death, and they dared not descend on anyone's word or promise until they received Tancred's banner as a token of protection and survival. But it did the poor wretches no good at all. For many people were angry about this, and the Christians were incensed with rage, so not a single one of them escaped with his life.[42]

29. Where Tancred's anger is calmed by the advice of the leaders

Tancred, glorious knight, was fired with violent anger about this insult to him[43] and his anger would not have quietened down without discord and great vengeance, except for the advice and opinion of greater and wiser men who soothed his pride with these words: 'Jerusalem, city of God on high, has been recovered, as you all know, with great difficulty and not without harm to our men, and today she has been restored to her own sons and delivered from the hands of the king of Egypt and the yoke of the Turks. But now we must be careful lest we lose it through avarice or sloth or the pity we have for our enemies, sparing prisoners and gentiles still left in the city. For if we were to be attacked in great strength by the king of Egypt we should be suddenly overcome from inside and outside the city, and in this way carried away into eternal exile. And so the most important and trustworthy advice seems to us that all the Saracens and gentiles who are held prisoner for ransoming with money, or already redeemed, should be put to the sword without delay, so that we shall not meet with any problem from their trickery or machinations.'

---

40 15 July 1099.

41 According to *GF* Count Raymond ordered the amir who had surrendered the Tower of David to him, and those with him, to be taken to Ascalon, safe and sound (p. 92).

42 This event is recorded by FC, who says that many were shot with arrows and, in all, nearly 10,000 were beheaded in the Temple (p. 301). ME reports 65,000 killed, not counting the rest of the city (p. 173). Arab historians have as many as 70,000 killed in the same place, the Masjid al-Aqṣā (IA p. 21). AA's figures appear to be more realistic.

43 Tancred's angry reaction is also mentioned in *GF* (p. 92). The episode is not dealt with in the *Gesta Tancredi* of RC, perhaps because it would have thrown a bad light on the hero. PT goes so far as to say the massacre was on Tancred's orders (pp. 141–2). See Nicholson, p. 94, n. 3.

30. The massacre of surviving infidels

After they heard this advice, on the third day after the victory[44] judgment was pronounced by the leaders and everyone seized weapons and surged forth for a wretched massacre of all the crowd of gentiles which was still left, bringing some out from fetters and beheading them, slaughtering others who were found throughout the city streets and districts, whom they had previously spared for the sake of money or human pity; they were beheading or striking down with stones girls, women, noble ladies, even pregnant women, and very young children, paying attention to no one's age. By contrast, girls, women, ladies, tormented by fear of imminent death and horror-struck by the violent slaughter, were embracing the Christians in their midst even as they were raving and venting their rage on the throats of both sexes, in the hope of saving their lives. Some were wound about the Christians' feet, begging them with piteous weeping and wailing for their lives and safety. When children of five or three years old saw the cruel fate of their mothers and fathers, of one accord they intensified the weeping and wretched clamour. But they were making these signals for pity and mercy in vain. For the Christians gave over their whole hearts to the slaughter, so that not a suckling little male child or female, not even an infant of one year would escape alive the hand of the murderer. And so the streets of the whole city of Jerusalem are reported to have been so strewn and covered with the dead bodies of men and women and the mangled limbs of infants, that not only in the streets, houses, and palaces, but even in places of desert solitude numbers of slain were to be found.

31. Concerning the previous lordship of the Turks in the city of Jerusalem

Moreover, from the day on which the holy city was besieged and was protected and defended by the Saracens up to this day, when the city was conquered and restored to its own, none of the Turks was found in it who had invaded the city some little time before and taken possession for a long time, and who used to exact heavy tributes from Saracens as well as pilgrims of Christ and the poor faithful. There were three hundred Turks who had captured the holy city; they ruled there for a long time, making very many cities around in the region of Syria and Palestine tributary to them, which the king of Egypt was formerly accustomed powerfully to possess along with Jerusalem, as subject to him and dependencies of his kingdom. Now, as you have heard, when the Christians' army was organized for the siege of Antioch after Nicaea had been captured, that same king of Egypt, having heard of the glory, strength, and victory of the Christian princes and the humiliation of the Turks, besieged with equipment and a numerous army the three hundred Turks in the city of Jerusalem which he had lost, and he overcame them and wore them

---

[44] This renewed massacre on the third day is not mentioned in other sources.

down by a very great assault and attack with mangonels, while the Turks withstood him and fought back fiercely, but not without great loss to their side.[45]

32. How the Turks were cast out; and about the false promise of the Egyptian king

Moreover, Sokman was prince and chief of these Turks, a very bold warrior and always opposed to the king of Egypt and his kingdom. At length the Turks and their prince, seeing that their small band could not sustain the weight of war and an attack by so many thousands, gave right hands and exchanged pledges concerning their lives and safety and they obtained leave to return to the city and to leave it peacefully, and received the king's safe conduct to Damascus, where a magnificent prince, brother of Sokman, is reported to rule, who was now thrown out of the city of Jerusalem with these Turks.[46] When they were thrown out and had the king's safe conduct to Damascus, the king entered Jerusalem and approached the Temple of the Lord with utmost reverence and humility in accordance with the ritual of the gentiles, then he entered the temple of the Lord's Sepulchre with all the observance of the gentile religion, going through all things peacefully and not turning any of the Christians away from the faith and regular observance of his own ritual.[47] Then when he returned he entrusted the town to loyal guardianship, garrisoned the Tower of David with his own followers, and took into his own jurisdiction the palace of Solomon and the other royal buildings and defensive works. He rejoiced exceedingly to have this town back under his rule after throwing out the Turks. But he was still afraid that the Turks would oppose him from Damascus, and he sent legates to the Christian princes who were positioned around the city of Antioch, reporting how he had thrown the Turks out of the city of Jerusalem and his kingdom, and that he wanted to satisfy their will concerning the holy city in all things, and to yield to their advice concerning Christ's faith and the religion of Christianity. But he lied in all things and spoke deceitfully, for with every sort of defence of weapons and strength of soldiers he could he denied entry to the city to pilgrims, until they were now admitted, once the Saracens had been cruelly killed with the help of the Heavenly King, as you have heard.

---

[45] AA shows an impressive understanding of Muslim politics: see Szklenar, pp. 193–5 and R. C. Schwinges, *Kreuzzugsideologie und Toleranz* (Stuttgart, 1977), pp. 158–65. The Turks had captured Jerusalem from the Fatimids of Egypt in 1071, but al-Afḍal ibn Amīr al-Juyūsh, vizier of Egypt (1094–1121), recaptured the city in August 1098.

[46] At the time of the capture of Jerusalem the ruler of Damascus was the Saljūq, Duqāq (1095–1104), who was not Suqmān's brother.

[47] AA acknowledges that the Egyptian ruler of Jerusalem treated Christians justly and fairly: see R. M. Hill, 'The Christian view of the Muslims at the time of the First Crusade', in P. M. Holt (ed.), *The Eastern Mediterranean Lands in the Period of the Crusades* (Warminster, 1977), pp. 1–8.

33. The advancement of the glorious duke in Jerusalem

When this pitiable slaughter of Saracens was finished, on the next day, Sunday,[48] the faithful and the leaders of the Christians took counsel and decided to give Count Raymond lordship of the city and guardianship of the Lord's Sepulchre. As he refused, and so did all the rest of the chiefs who were chosen for this office, Duke Godfrey, although reluctant, was at last put forward to hold the principate of the city.[49] Once promoted, on the advice of all the Christians and with their goodwill, he asked for the tower of King David, which Raymond himself had seized after letting the Saracens escape. But Raymond absolutely refused to give it up, until he was forced to relinquish it by threats from the duke himself and the Christians. The election and promotion of this duke is believed not to have been the result of human will at all, but done entirely by God's arrangement and favour, since we have learnt beyond doubt from the vision of a certain good and truthful knight ten years before this journey that Godfrey was chosen by God and appointed leader and prince and commander of the Christian army, and before all the officers he was more blessed in deed, victory and counsel, more perfect in faith and truth.

34. The dream of one of the duke's knights

One night the aforesaid knight, called Hecelo, from Kenzvillare, an estate which is in the Ripuarian district, was with that same duke in a certain wood called Ketena. He was tired from hunting and was easily overcome by sleep, and at once he was transported in spirit to Mount Sinai, where Moses the Lord's servant, after he had fasted for forty days, was worthy to see the splendour of God's glory and receive the law from the hand of the Most High.[50] Then upon the peak of this mountain he could see the aforesaid duke being raised up with awe and gentleness in an easy ascent, and two men hurrying to meet him in white clothes and the insignia of bishops. As they came up to him there they offered him their blessing in these words: 'May you be filled with the blessings of the living God who conferred blessing and favour on

48 Sunday 17 July was probably the day the process of electing a ruler began, with the rulership offered to Raymond. Godfrey accepted on Friday 22 July according to *GF*: 'a week after the city was taken' (pp. 92–3). See A. V. Murray, *The Crusader Kingdom of Jerusalem: A Dynastic History 1099–1125* (Oxford, 2000), pp. 66–8.

49 In spite of AA's partisan attitude to Godfrey, he appears to be reporting the sequence of events accurately. Cf. *GF*. pp. 92–3, where the offering of the post elsewhere is not recorded; RA p. 152; FC pp. 307–9. The title adopted by Godfrey was probably 'princeps': see J. Riley-Smith, 'The title of Godfrey of Bouillon', *Bulletin of the Institute of Historical Research*, 52 (1979), pp. 83–6. Murray argues for 'princeps et defensor': *Crusader Kingdom*, pp. 68–77.

50 Exod. 24: 18; Deut. 9: 9.

His servant and faithful follower Moses and may you find favour in His eyes. May you be appointed duke and commander of His Christian people in all faith and truth.' After this was said the knight woke up and the vision disappeared.

35. The explanation of the dream

What else is to be perceived in this vision, except that in the spirit and gentleness of Moses there may arise a spiritual leader of Israel, preordained by God and appointed prince of the people? And so, truly, we know this vision and blessing to have been clearly fulfilled in him, since in reality when very many princes and potentates, bishops and counts and sons of kings made this journey before him and after him, and became leaders of the Christian army, God did not make the journey go at all well for them, nor did they obtain their desire, but many difficulties were inflicted on them and all their army by kings and barbarous nations because they were not those people through whom deliverance came in Israel.[51] Truly, when Duke Godfrey made the journey after all those who had been sent ahead, and he was leader and prince of the despairing army, all the adverse conditions were turned into favourable ones. And there was nothing to stand in their way, no difficulty to harm them, except where wickedness was found in criminals and lawbreakers. And when wickedness was found, vengeance was pursued in accordance with the true justice of God, by which the great army was also sanctified, and after the sons were punished in this way, now by hunger, now by the sword, at last they were happy and cleansed of filth, and, fulfilling their blessed desire with their leader and prince, they were worthy to enter the city of Jerusalem, they worshipped at the Lord's Sepulchre and, taking possession of the ramparts by God's favour and will, they made Godfrey ruler of the city and commander of the people.

36. Similarly, the vision of a certain cleric in Aachen concerning the duke himself

Besides this, it was revealed to a certain Catholic brother and canon of St Mary's in Aachen, called Giselbert,[52] in the seventh month of this same duke's departure and pilgrimage, that he would be chief of all and prince in Jerusalem, preordained and appointed by God. Indeed, it appeared to that same brother while he was still dreaming that the aforesaid duke powerfully took a seat in the sun, and a countless number of birds of all the kinds under heaven flocked around him. A part of them began little by little to diminish by flying away, but the greater part remained fixed and motionless to right and left. After this the sun was for the most part obscured

[51] 1 Macc. 5: 62.

[52] AA is believed also to have been a canon of St Mary's in Aachen and so this is likely to have been heard first-hand from his brother canon.

by the rays of its brightness, and the duke's seat was utterly blotted out for a short period, and almost all the multitude of birds which had remained flew away.

37. Explanation of the vision

The duke took a seat in the sun, as he was promoted to the throne of the kingdom of Jerusalem, which exceeds all the towns in the world in name and holiness, just as the sun exceeds all the stars in the sky with its brilliance. Christ Jesus, son of the living God who is the true sun of justice,[53] illuminated Jerusalem and raised it up with His deity when He was crucified there and suffered, died and was buried and on the third day He rose again[54] and appeared alive to His friends. The birds of heaven were gathered round the seated duke, like those from all Christian lands, great and small, noble and lesser people, who were joined with him and subject to him. The birds flew away, just as a very great number of pilgrims returned to the land of their birth with the duke's consent and permission. But very many birds remained fixed and motionless, as many were attached to him by dutiful love, and having delighted in his intimate and comforting speech they vowed to stay longer with him. A short while after this the sun was obscured while the duke's seat was blotted out, just as Jerusalem was bereft after a very short time, with so magnificent a prince dead, and it was greatly darkened from his fame and glory and diminished by many soldiers and warriors at his death.

38. The way in which a portion of the Rood of Salvation was found

In accordance with God's command, presignified by these dreams, and in accordance with the goodwill of the Christian people, Godfrey was raised up to be prince and ruler of his brothers on the throne of the kingdom of Jerusalem. Then a certain faithful Christian native of the city, fully instructed in Christ's law, revealed that he had hidden a certain cross – half a cubit high and clad in gold, with a little bit of the Lord's rood inserted in the middle, but devoid of skilled workmanship and bare – in a humble and dusty place in an abandoned house, because of his fear of the Saracens and that in the turmoil of the siege the cross would be found and stripped of its gold, and the Lord's rood treated shamefully by them. All the faithful who were there rejoiced at this holy revelation of the Lord's Cross, and after complete, pure abstinence and instruction, on the Friday, which is the day of the Lord's suffering, clergy and people came together in a holy

---

[53] Mal. 4: 2. See also Fulbertus Carnotensis, 'In Nativitate Beatae Virginis', in *Enchiridion Euchologicum Fontium Liturgicorum* (Rome, 1979), p. 884, no. 1964.

[54] Cf. Nicene creed: G. L. Dossetti, *Il simbolo di Nicea e di Costantinopoli* (Rome, 1967), p. 186.

procession to the place where the venerated Cross had been hidden.[55] They took it up with care and reverence and decided to carry it to and place it in the temple of the Lord's Sepulchre with all prayer and singing of hymns.[56]

39. About the death of the patriarch of Jerusalem

After this it was pleasing to the whole company of the faithful, and seemed advantageous and acceptable in the eyes of God, once all the gentile race was expelled from the holy city and their sacrilegious ritual, and after Godfrey had been raised up on the throne of Jerusalem as prince of Christians to protect the city and its inhabitants, that its shepherd and patriarch should also be restored, who would be in charge of the flock of the faithful and of the holy church. For it had been bereft of its shepherd the patriarch, a very holy man, who left this life on the island of Cyprus at the time of the siege of Jerusalem.[57] That same patriarch had journeyed from Jerusalem and the Lord's Sepulchre when he heard of the Christians' arrival and siege around the ramparts of Antioch, setting out for the island of Cyprus on account of the Turks' threats and the Saracens' insolence. He was, in fact, an elderly man, a faithful servant of Christ, who sent from the island very many gifts of love to that same Duke Godfrey and the other leaders at the start of the siege of Jerusalem, sometimes the tree fruit which is called pomegranate, sometimes precious fruits of the cedars of Lebanon, on occasion fat bacons, or praiseworthy wine, or whatever good and costly things he could manage according to his means, hoping yet to serve and be in charge at the Sepulchre of our Lord Jesus Christ, son of the living God, under those same princes when the holy church was peacefully and securely restored. But when the city of Jerusalem had been recovered by the faithful, and its holy church renewed, the most Christian patriarch left this life, and so the holy church remained bereft of its shepherd. Because of this a council was held among the princes of the Christians and it was frequently debated, as was said before, who should succeed so great a man, and no one was found worthy of so great an honour and divine governance. And therefore it was delayed until such a man might be found who would be worthy of this pontifical office. But they only appointed Arnulf of Chocques, a cleric of wonderful wisdom

---

[55] 'venerabile lignum': cf. Vergil, *Aen.* xii. 767, but also Christian poets (*HL* vol. 5, p. 524).

[56] The finding of the relic of the True Cross is not reported in *GF*, but it is recounted by FC, who says a Syrian had concealed it and describes it as partly covered with gold and silver (pp. 309–10). RA says the relic was found on Arnulf's initiative (p. 154). See also A. Frolow, *La Relique de la Vraie Croix* (Paris, 1961), pp. 286–7.

[57] According to Hamilton it is not certain that the crusaders were aware of Patriarch Symeon's death at this point. In his view there was no doubt in their minds that the patriarch of Jerusalem should be a Latin: he points out that they did not consult the Orthodox canons of the Holy Sepulchre then in Cyprus (p. 12).

and eloquence, as chancellor of the holy church of Jerusalem, procurator of the holy relics, and keeper of the alms of the faithful.[58]

40. About the clerics and the signals of bells installed in the Lord's Sepulchre

When Arnulf had been promoted to this office in the holy and new church until a patriarch acceptable to God and the people was elected, it seemed a good idea to Duke Godfrey, the highest prince of Jerusalem, and likewise to all the rest, that twenty brothers in Christ should be appointed to observe the divine office in the Temple of the Lord's Sepulchre, who at every hour would sing praises and hymns to the living Lord God, would piously offer up the sacrifice of Jesus Christ's body and blood, then would undertake the daily upkeep arranged from the offering of the faithful. When divine observance had thus been honourably restored by the Catholic duke and Christian princes, they ordered bells to be made from bronze and other metals, and soon when the brothers heard the signal and sound of these they would hurry to the church to celebrate the praises of the psalms and the prayers of masses, and the faithful people would as one make haste to hear these things. For there were no sounds or signals of this sort seen or heard in Jerusalem before these days.

41. How the duke met the hordes of the enemy

Then, after five weeks had passed, Duke Godfrey, hearing the rumour of an army of gentiles, garrisoned the city and the Tower of David with a loyal guard and, taking with him certain comrades, likewise Robert of Flanders and Tancred, set out for the plains of Ascalon to hear and find out about the affairs and plans of the gentiles. There by chance a messenger met him, reporting that Meraius, second to the king of Egypt, and the entire multitude of gentiles, innumerable as the

[58] Arnulf was a very controversial figure. RA was opposed to him and referred to his being the son of a priest and having a bad reputation (p. 154). RC, formerly his pupil, attests his learning (pp. 20–21). There is general agreement that he was a charismatic preacher. In addition, Arnulf's crusading career made him the obvious candidate for patriarch in 1099: there is evidence that he was appointed ancillary legate by Urban II himself in 1096, and after Adhémar's death at Antioch he was the only legate left. RC goes so far as to say that Adhémar commended the crusaders to Arnulf's care as he lay dying (pp. 113–14). Nevertheless it should be noted that AA is explicit that Arnulf was not made patriarch at this point. This may reflect AA's knowledge of later disputes or an ambiguity at the time: Hamilton suggests he was patriarch-elect awaiting papal ratification (pp. 12–14). The *Chronicle of Saint-Pierre-le-Vif* says that in 1102 Arnulf was *scriniarius* in charge of Baldwin I's treasury: see J. Richard, 'Quelques textes sur les premiers temps de l'église latine de Jérusalem', *Recueil Clovis Brunel*, 2 (1955), pp. 420–30, at 420–23.

sands as the sea,[59] were already sailing to Ascalon on the king's orders, bringing weapons, food, and countless herds, and plenty of all the apparatus of war, and that they had decided to besiege the city of Jerusalem and the Christian exiles. The race of Publicans[60] and the race with very black skin from the land of Ethiopia, commonly called Azoparth,[61] and all the barbarous nations which belonged to the kingdom of Egypt had decided to hold an assembly there at the city of Ascalon. Moreover, when Duke Godfrey and those with him – Robert of Flanders, Tancred, and Eustace the duke's brother – heard the news of the advancing hordes and the weapons of the gentiles, they took up quarters next to the mountain regions which lead to Jerusalem and they sent a legation to Jerusalem to Raymond and Robert, prince of Normans, ordering that all things were to be disclosed to them: the size of the assembly of gentiles which occupied Ascalon, and that they had taken up position to hold the road leading to Jerusalem. And as a result they summoned those same princes to resist the infidels with the whole army of cavalry and infantry. They commanded Peter the Hermit and Arnulf, whom they had appointed chancellor and keeper of the Lord's Sepulchre, to attend with the Lord's Cross to meet the infidel troops at Ascalon without any delay.[62] They decreed that few, but nevertheless loyal people should stay for the protection and defence of the city.

42. The people, who have been warned not to take plunder from the infidels, abstain

When these things had been arranged, and after the army which was scattered all over the city had been warned by the legation of the duke and his co-leaders, they retrieved the horses and the weapons they had briefly laid aside and took them up again, and made the journey through the mountain regions with trumpets and bugles, bagpipes and stringed instruments, and all singing in exultation and happiness, and they joined up with Duke Godfrey, who was settled in the territory of Ascalon, where they were quartered throughout the meadows and plains. Only Count Raymond, who was still feeling the goad of envy against Duke Godfrey

59 An Old Testament simile, e.g. 2 Kgs. (2 Sam.) 17: 11.

60 The Publicans, or Paulicians, were, strictly speaking, Manichaean heretics, but the word seems to have been used by AA to denote a people from Africa or Arabia. Other writers, following *GF*, use the term much earlier in the campaign and probably more accurately: see *GF* p. 20 and note: 'Unexplained, but possibly the Caucasian Albanians (Aghovanians), for whom see Runciman, *The Medieval Manichee*, pp. 59–60.' See also Du Cange, *s. v. Populicani*; *GF* pp. 26, 49, 83; PT pp. 54, 61, 84, 89, 128; RM pp. 763, 770, 808; GN p. 208.

61 The Ethiopian troops are also referred to by FC (pp. 311–12), by PT (p. 147) and by BD (p. 108).

62 While *GF* assigns Peter a rôle in Jerusalem during the battle (p. 94), AA and the *Chanson de Jérusalem* stress his importance as a warrior: *ChA* lines 8947, 9389 (pp. 234, 246) and *passim*.

because he had lost the Tower of David, was summoned and refused to come with all the army of his followers, while once again he was pushed and incited to action by threats from the duke and all the princes, until at length, on the advice of his own people and in response to persuasion from loyal men, he got up and marched on the royal way through the mountains with a huge army and was united with the duke and the aforesaid princes on the plains of Ascalon. Herds, camels, oxen, wild cattle, and every kind of domestic beast had been sent out and scattered on those plains in a great multitude as a trick, so that the Christian army would covet them and seize and drive them, and would be distracted by booty so that, encumbered by plunder in this way, they would more easily be overcome by the enemy. But a certain most noble man from among the Saracens, once prefect of the city of Ramla, who had entered a peace and treaty with the duke when Jerusalem was conquered, now came to the assistance of that duke, being faithful in purpose although he was a gentile, and explained the Egyptians' tricks, saying that the Saracens, Arabs, and other gentiles had sent out the herds for this reason only: to hinder the pilgrims, who were much keener on plunder than defence. The duke and all the rulers of the Christian army were put on their guard by this warning from the gentile prince and they pronounced an edict in all the Catholic army that any of the pilgrims who touched booty before battle would be punished by having ears and nose cut off.[63] In accordance with that pronouncement and edict the whole army held back from the forbidden deed and otherwise they only seized sufficient provisions for the night.

43. The duke explains to the infidel prefect why the people march gladly into battle

On the second day as dawn broke the whole people of the living God[64] was armed for war, rejoicing in songs of exultation and all sweet music, with stringed instruments and bagpipes, as happy as if they were going to a feast; they were protected and signed with the sign of the holy cross by Arnulf, Peter and the other priests and strengthened with the purity of confession. Once again plunder and any looting before the combat were forbidden under threat of excommunication from the priests. Moreover, the prefect of Ramla, when he saw the people rejoicing and singing psalms with flutes, stringed instruments, the sounds of bagpipes, and the voice of exultation,[65] just as if they had been invited to a banquet of all kinds of

---

[63] RA and, more briefly, the *GF* also describe the herds on the plains of Ascalon and the leaders' warnings against looting. However, in these accounts the penalty for disobedience was to be excommunication. Furthermore they do not present it as a Saracen trick (RA pp. 156–7; *GF* pp. 94–5).

[64] Frequent in the Bible, though in OT 'Dei uiuentis', e.g. in a martial context 1 Kgs. (1 Sam.) 17: 26, 36; in NT 'Dei uiui', e.g. Matt. 16: 16.

[65] Ps. 41 (42): 5.

delights, was greatly amazed, and questioned the duke about these things, saying: 'I wonder, and I cannot wonder enough, why this people glories in such great happiness and with a voice of exultation as if going to a party, when today death is close at hand for them and instant martyrdom waits for them all and the outcome of war may go either way and a great and insufferable force of opponents is now assembled and has pitched camp not far from here.' The duke, full of Christ's faith and instructed in spiritual response, responded to the man's enquiry by discoursing wisely about these things: why the Christian people delighted with great joy and sweet music in expectation of death this very day and of the imminent battle. For he said: 'Know that these people, whom you see and hear singing in exultation as they hurry towards their enemies and join battle in the name of Lord Jesus Christ their God, are certain today of the crown of the kingdom of heaven, and know that they will pass on to a better life, in which they shall begin to live more happily for the first time, if they are found worthy to die in this battle for his name and favour. For this reason our hearts are lifted to joy and jubilation, that if we should chance to fall into the hands of the enemy, Lord Jesus our God has the power to place our souls in the paradise of His glory, and because of this we do not fear death or the charge of the enemy, since we are sure of His eternal reward after death in this world. Indeed, this sign of the holy cross by which we are protected and sanctified is beyond doubt a spiritual shield against all the enemies' missiles, and putting our hope in that same sign we venture to stand more firmly against all dangers. And assuredly we have been redeemed by this wood of the Holy Cross from the hand of death and hell[66] and by angelic power from harm and we have been cleansed in the blood of Lord Jesus, son of the living God, from all the filth of former error[67] and we have confidence in eternal life.'

44. The common crusaders from among the Christians march to meet fully armed men

When he heard the duke's reply and his instruction concerning eternal life, the above-mentioned gentile entreated that as he too was going to fight on the side of the most Christian duke and the Catholic people against his own race and brothers, he might be protected and sanctified by that same sign of the holy cross, so that he might be kept unharmed from the weapons and stratagems of the enemy by the faith and hope of that same holy cross and crucifix. However, we are not sure whether he received baptism at once or after the battle, only that some claim that after he had seen the strength and triumph of the Christians he received the favour of baptism. Once the whole company of Christians, along with the gentile prince, had been sanctified with the sign of this holy cross by Arnulf's hand, it was everyone's work and purpose to take up weapons, put on hauberks, organize the

[66] Ps. 48 (49): 16; 88 (89): 49; Rev. 20: 13, 14.

[67] Cf. 2 Cor. 7: 1.

battle lines and raise up banners on their spears. There was no coveting or seizing of herds or of forbidden flocks, but the flocks and herds which had been sent out to deceive Christ's faithful grew astonished at the glitter of weapons, helmets, and shields, and the flocks were thunderstruck and amazed by the loud din and shouting of the army. And so, stupefied, their ears pricked up,[68] they stood still for a long time, then at length they joined the cavalry and infantry, and, mingled in this way with the armed formations, they went forward when they went forward, they stood still when they stood still, and by increasing the cloud of dust they excited fear in the Saracens, who were unaware of what had happened, by their great numbers in the distance.[69]

45. The way their battle line was drawn up

Then, when the Christians had come out of the mountains and were positioned in the valley and on the plain where the tents of the Saracens, Arabs, Moors, and Publicans had been pitched and their battle lines drawn up, the flocks and all the herds which no one could count separated themselves of their own accord and made their way without guides and masters to a place of pasture fairly nearby as if, forewarned and commanded by divine instruction, they would, without being asked, give way to the Catholic formations in order not to be a hindrance to them, but so that, standing firm there in the place of pasture, they could be found by the Christians after the victory. Immediately, when the herds had moved aside and they had seen the infidel hordes, the Gauls' battle formations, as they had been drawn up – these to fight in front, these to right and left, others in the rear – joined battle. All the cavalry and infantry were gathered company by company around their banners and standards. Godfrey, the duke and after God the highest ruler in Jerusalem, besieged the gate of Ascalon with two thousand cavalry and three thousand infantry, fully equipped with hauberks, helmets and shields, lances and arrows, so that no force of inhabitants would sally forth from the city on this side and attack the Gauls unexpectedly from the rear. Count Raymond, with an enormous number of his men, directed his division to the right, towards extensive and very thick orchards which were outside the walls, so that as the battle became fierce he could use his forces and resources to strengthen the allies and raise their spirits when they faltered from fear in the present torment. Robert prince of the Normans and Robert of Flanders, Oliver of Jussey, Gerard of Quierzy, and Rainald of Toul organized their troops on the plain with a closely packed front line on the left to join battle against the Moors and all kinds of gentiles, and all the infantry

---

[68] Vergil, *Aen.* ii. 303, but also a hexameter comonplace (*HL* i. 134).

[69] The 'miracle' of the marching herds is widely reported, though the other accounts say these were animals which had been seized and released, while AA still insists that no plundering took place until after the battle (*Kreuzzugsbriefe*, pp. 172–3; RA p. 158; EA p. 156).

and cavalry of the Christians were likewise assembled and positioned there to resist under their banners and standards.

46. After crises on both sides, the enemy side takes flight

In this way cruel war shook those who were standing face to face on the two sides. For the Ethiopians, whose custom was to wage war in their own fashion on bended knee, were sent ahead in front of the battle and attacked the Gauls fiercely with a hail of arrows, making a thunderous noise with trumpets and drummers in order to frighten off the terrified horses and men with such a horrible din from the battle and the plains. Those same Ethiopians, dreadful and hideous men, also had iron-tipped and savage whips, which they used to penetrate hauberks and shields with a severe blow, strike horses on the face, and make a terrible noise throughout all the army of the faithful. The Arab and Saracen and Publican peoples, fighting in their thousands, now with lances, now with arrows, now slings and every sort of weapon, were engaged in combat against the Christian troops, intensifying the battles and taking up the greater part of the day. On the other hand, the Christian army, slight in contrast with so many and countless thousands, was enveloped in the midst of the strife, joining battle ceaselessly, diminishing and destroying the enemy troops. When at length the battle became fiercer, and with God's assistance the gentile forces were weakened, the entire army of the king of Egypt took flight and was scattered, fleeing before the striking and pursuing enemy across the fields of the plain towards the coast.

47. Concerning the slaughter and the spoils of the slain

Duke Godfrey, Count Raymond, Eustace, Tancred, Cono of Montaigu, and his son Lambert, seeing that the strength of the army of the gentiles was failing, and it was withdrawing, charged on horseback into the midst of the enemy with a violent rush and clamour of the infantry and by inflicting a very great slaughter upon them they brought very great assistance to their brothers. The Arabs and the other peoples saw that they could no longer sustain the battle, and they were scattered and destroyed all over the fields and narrow paths and took flight, but on all sides they were killed here and there like wretched cattle by the pursuing and victorious soldiers. An infinite number of them, as they withdrew defeated, overwhelmed by the Christians' pursuit, made for ships and shore in the hope of safety and to escape, and there Count Raymond chanced to meet them; he struck at them cruelly and pursued them, and as they fled to the depths of the sea he forced some three thousand by constant weapon blows to be drowned. Moreover, while the cohorts of the Saracens were terrified in this way by the dreadful slaughter, and some were contemplating only flight to the sea, others to the orchards, and very many, indeed, were seeking to enter the gates of Ascalon, all the Christian victors spread out through the tents and camps of the gentiles, and, as if they were famished and weakened by long abstinence, they were now entirely forgetful of war and they took possession, some seizing precious purple, others clothes and silver vases and a very great heap of both precious metals, others mules, camels, horses, dromedaries, with very hardy donkeys and all sorts of booty.

48. The people intent on plunder is destroyed; the army, which controls itself, comes out better

At this point the gentiles, whose irresistible forces were still plentiful on the seashore and the plains, seeing that the entire people of Gaul was intent upon plunder and prey and had ceased pursuit, drew allies together again from all over the place and reassembled their forces by a signal of trumpets and bugles, and they charged fiercely on the men who were concentrating on plunder, forgetful of war, and destroyed the unsuspecting Christians with a severe slaughter, and they would have paid back the whole cruel victory of the Christians, except that Duke Godfrey, highest prince of Jerusalem, who was commanding the furthest lines towards the mountains, realized the Christians' danger and that they were blinded by greed, and charged at once in the face of the enemy, forbade plunder and railed at them all, urging them to defence in this way, saying: 'Oh, rebellious and incorrigible men, who has bewitched you, that your hand is turned to forbidden and illicit plunder, before our enemy, with God's help, has fallen to the sword? Alas! Leave off looting, resist the enemy, and do not give way now to those who are rising up and looking for bitter vengeance from you.' This said, they broke through the middle of the lines, and with drawn swords in the hands of his followers Godfrey visited severe destruction on the enemy and then spurred on all those with him who had been called back from looting to the task of renewed battle, until the gentiles were overcome a second time and turned tail from the constant blows of weapons, making good their escape to the city of Ascalon.

49. More about the slaughter of the degenerate enemy

The duke and those who were pursuing the fleeing gentiles with him, as many infantry as cavalry, were not far from the rear of the enemy, but were keeping up the most severe slaughter as they pursued them right up to the gate of Ascalon. Those who were taken in at the gate or could be admitted were fortunate. For it is reported that the Saracens suffered so great a crush and lack of space for fleeing and entering through those same doors of the city that two thousand and more of them fell dead in the gateway and in front of the gates, killed and suffocated under the feet of men entering and of horses and mules. The very last and those slower to escape, seeing here and there the dangers to their lives and the difficult entry of the gates, and that they were shut out of the city by closed gates in this horror of weapons, hurried to climb palm trees, and some the branches of olives or figs, so that they could at least hide and be saved by the thickness of the branches and leaves. But the Christian foot-soldiers were too close and saw the wretched men in the trees and, once discovered, they suddenly shot them with arrows, and like birds struck by a flying bolt they fell dying to earth from those same tree branches, and gathered closely to cover the ground.[70]

50. When this battle was joined, and about deeds done there

This battle was fought on a Friday in August, on the birthday of the martyr Euplius,[71] by twenty thousand Christians against three hundred thousand gentiles, Saracens, Arabs, Publicans, and Moors from the land of Ethiopia. It was reported to us by people who were present in that same conflict that thirty thousand of the gentiles fell on the open plains, besides two thousand who were suffocated and killed in the gateway of the city, and not counting those who reckoned to escape the danger of weapons and sank in the waves of the bottomless sea and died without number. No celebrated men on the Christian side fell in that place, only a few of the crowd of foot soldiers, as was revealed to us by truthful brothers as beyond doubt. In this flight and destruction of the gentiles and victory of the Christians a very long spear entirely covered with silver, which they call a *standard*,[72] and which was carried as the sign of the king of Egypt before his army, and around which a particular strength was amassed, and to which the conquered and scattered troops rallied, was captured by Robert prince of the Normans and sent to the temple of the Lord's Sepulchre; and right up to this present day it is dedicated in memory of the Christians' victory. Moreover, now this storm of battles had settled, and Meraius, who was second to the king in all decision-making and counsel, had been conquered with all his people, permission was granted to the Christians to plunder – as many tents as herds, camels, wild cattle, and donkeys, sheep, goats, and oxen and all possessions and resources – and very many of them returned to Jerusalem laden and refreshed with these things, travelling all night in heartfelt joy and singing in exultation, bringing back before the Holy Sepulchre praises and thanks to God for all things which had turned out happily and triumphantly for them.

---

[70] *GF* records this (p. 96), as does PT who has the same image of the falling birds (pp. 146–7).

[71] The battle of Ascalon, 12 Aug. 1099.

[72] The standard is described in *GF* as having a golden apple on top of a silver-clad pole (p. 95).

51. Count Raymond sets his sights on Ascalon and Arsuf for his own interests against the Christians

When Duke Godfrey had brought together again about two thousand comrades, infantry and cavalry, he besieged the gates of the city of Ascalon on all sides, so that the citizens and soldiers, stunned and quaking from the fresh slaughter and recent victory, would surrender, despairing of any further assistance from the king of Egypt since the strength of his whole kingdom now assembled had been severely weakened and scattered. Truly, when the greater part of the night had passed, and they had consulted about the surrender of the city of Ascalon and about surety for life, Count Raymond, envious of all Duke Godfrey's glory on account of the Tower of David which he had lost, sent a secret legation to the Saracen citizens in this way: 'Be men of great courage, and do not be frightened by Duke Godfrey's threats into surrendering the city into his hands, since all our princes have decided to return to the land of their birth after the war is over, and you may be confident that a very small band of warriors remains with him around the city tonight.'[73] The citizens and soldiers were encouraged by this legation and comfort from the count and they rejected the idea of surrendering the city and pledging friendship, so when the sun rose they were stationed on the ramparts for defence, holding off the duke and his men from the siege with arrows, slings, and all sorts of weapons. When the duke saw their boldness and resistance, and that of all his men no more than seven hundred cavalry had stayed with him, and that all the princes had left at the prompting and persuasion of Count Raymond and were continuing their journey on the seashore, he moved his camp away from the siege, even he himself, and followed his peers who had gone before on the royal road along the coast all the way to the town of Assur or Arsuf. There Raymond had carried out a siege around the town of Arsuf for the period of one day and night, thinking that the townspeople would be alarmed by the fresh and recent victory and would surrender the town into his hands. He was bringing very many threats and fears to bear on the townspeople, and at the same time he was promising life and safety and that all favour would be granted by him if they surrendered the city. But when he heard of Duke Godfrey's approach, conscious of the trick he had played on him through envy, he withdrew with all his company from the siege of the Arsufians, having urged the townspeople not to fear Godfrey greatly, and not to open up the city to him whatever threats were made or warlike attack, arguing strongly that none of the princes who had gone before would come back to assist the duke.

---

[73] Raymond of Saint-Gilles' biographers defend him against AA's accusations and suggest that AA was trying to cover up Godfrey's failures: J. H. and L. L. Hill, *Raymond IV, Count of Toulouse* (Syracuse, NY, 1962), pp. 123, 137–8. However, there is no eyewitness account of events, which they reconstruct from a variant in BD (pp. 110–11), from AA and from RC (pp. 154–5). The strategic importance of Ascalon cannot be disputed: it was a forward base for forces sent by land and sea from Egypt and it posed a threat to the kingdom of Jerusalem until its capture in 1153.

52. The duke and Count Raymond are reconciled

Having urged on the townspeople in such a way to hinder the duke, Raymond hastened his journey and joined up with Robert of Flanders and his namesake Robert count of the Normans and the other co-leaders in the region which is between Caesarea and the city of Haifa, next to a certain river of fresh water.[74] Godfrey arrived at Arsuf and besieged the town for a day to see if by any chance, or fear on the part of the Arsufians, it might be delivered into his hands. But finding that these people, just like the Ascalonites, were ready for war and ready to resist him because of Raymond's persuasion and testimony, he turned aside from the city with sorrowful heart. And he told his comrades to seek out Raymond immediately in the camp and return on his head all the injustice he had enacted against him. At once, after telling his comrades, he put on his hauberk and raised the banners; while he arranged to go into the count's camp in an angry mood, Raymond had likewise had the foresight to arm for defence and decided to attack him. Robert of Flanders and the other splendid men came between them, reproved the men severely, and at length with much endeavour they soothed both sides and brought them back into agreement.

53. The duke bids farewell to the princes who want to go home; and the citizens of Arsuf make a treaty with the duke

Once these two were brought back into agreement, with the approval of God and our Lord Jesus Christ, Robert of Flanders, Robert prince of the Normans, Raymond likewise of Provence and all the princes revealed to the duke their intention of returning home and, after humble and gentle consultation, they found him agreeable to all the things which they had in mind. The duke, fulfilling in all things the will of his brothers, decided to remain in Jerusalem, because the power of the city was granted to his protection and defence, and, embracing his comrades' necks for a long time and graciously kissing them, he beseeched them tearfully with all his strength, while wishing them well, that they should be mindful, and should impress on their Christian brothers that they should not hesitate to come to the Lord's Sepulchre, but should flock daily to assist him and the other comrades who were staying in exile to oppose so many barbarous peoples.[75] When the men and townspeople of Arsuf heard that the duke was staying and had returned to agreement with Raymond and the rest, they struck a treaty with the duke

[74] There are many small rivers on the coastal strip between Caesarea and Haifa and this one cannot be identified.

[75] The same concern to attract reinforcements is expressed in the crusaders' letter of April 1100 (*Kreuzzugsbriefe*, pp. 176–7). In a well known passage FC says that in 1101 there were no more than 300 knights and a similar number of infantry to defend the kingdom (pp. 388–9).

concerning the safety and peace of the city, sending him a hostage for the tributes and the town, and at the same time they received from that same duke, as hostage for the security of the treaty and peace, Gerard, a faithful knight of Godfrey, who came from the castle at Avesnes.

54. About the rest of the faithful who go home

And so, with so many battles won, so many endeavours never before imaginable brought to victory and a good conclusion, commended by the duke and all their allies alike, great and small, leaders and followers prepared their return from long exile to the land of their birth. They carried palms of victory in their hands, and because of their great devotion they poured out tears for their brothers left in exile. They bade them farewell with a loving kiss, and retraced their way through those same towns and difficulties of the mountain terrain next to the sea of Palestine by which they had also come to Jerusalem, and there they were granted licence to sell and buy necessary provisions from all the aforementioned towns: Acre, Tyre and Sidon, Tripoli and Beirut, and other towns. Then the people desisted before them from any attack or ambush, and their cities were terrified and trembling because of the destruction of the king of Egypt and the victory which was granted to his faithful people by the living God. Thus they traversed this and that place in peace and security, having few weapons but carrying palms in their hands as a token of victory, and they came down into the region of the town of Jubayl, which was rich in fruits and vines. There they spread out their tents far from the city ramparts because there were suitable places with streams and pastures on the open plains, and for two days they enjoyed the abundant goods of that land.

55. Bohemond besieges Latakia, a city belonging to Christians

While they were staying in these places a message reached them that Bohemond, his greed for aggrandizement and acquisition unsatisfied, after a long siege had seized Latakia, a city inhabited by Greek Christians, with support and a naval attack from the Pisans and Genoese,[76] and he had captured and entered two towers of the town situated on the seashore, citadels which exacted dues from sailors, and he had slaughtered some of the Catholic guards, had blinded others, and had thrown them from the top of the towers. But the Pisans and Genoese were not greatly to blame for these injuries, for they had understood from Bohemond's lips something quite other than the truth. And so with his lying encouragement they had

---

[76] AA may be mistaken about the presence of the Genoese, since their annalist Caffaro does not mention this campaign. It is mentioned in the *Gesta Triumphalia per Pisanos facta de captione Hierusalem*, along with the blockade of Jubayl: *Rerum Italicarum Scriptores*, vi.2 (Bologna, 1930), p. 89.

surrounded the towers with two hundred ships, and with their ships' masts which touched the clouds with their great length and had wicker baskets fixed to the tops, they bore down heavily upon the guards of the fortresses, attacking towers and men with a constant bombardment of stones and arrows from the towering timber. For indeed, when he heard of the Pisans' and Genoese approach, Bohemond, cunning prince and greedy brother, met them near Latakia, about six miles from Antioch, and told them that the Latakians were entirely bad and really evil, and that they were criminal opponents of the Christians, so that with this prompting he could more easily stir up the minds of them all to hatred of the townspeople and to a blockade of the town. And thus it was done, so that the men who were taken in by his words first besieged the towers and forced their guards to surrender, and then, once the towers were overwhelmed by their skill or strength, they encircled the city. They were tormenting the townspeople with a severe and long attack; already they had placed two bridges strategically across the rampart of the defences, by way of which they would gain easy access to the ramparts and thus the tormented city would surrender to Bohemond in a short while. For indeed the next thing was that the city would be captured by engines of this sort brought up to it, the citizens would be punished, and all things would unfairly be surrendered to Bohemond. Unfairly indeed, for this same Latakia and these same towers had been overcome and captured during the siege of Antioch by a naval siege and attack by Winemer of Boulogne, master of pirates, and certain Christians. These people assembled ships drawn from different kingdoms and lands, namely from Antwerp, Tiel, Frisia, and Flanders, and they joined by sea the Provençals in the land of Saint-Gilles who were subject to Count Raymond and sailed around the world to that same city of Latakia. They took possession of it and conquered it, putting to the sword those Turks and Saracens they found there as unjust lords and, seizing the city and its ramparts, they conveyed it with those same towers to Count and Prince Raymond after the siege of Antioch. Winemer, master and leader of the pirates, was captured after this by Turcopoles and soldiers of the king of the Greeks, and was sent to prison, but by Duke Godfrey's intervention he was brought out of prison and from fetters after some considerable time. After the capture of Antioch Count Raymond, having decided to journey with the others to Jerusalem, restored to the emperor of Constantinople the town of Latakia which had been seized from the Turks and gentiles, so that he would in this way keep his oath to him unbroken. For Raymond had vowed and made a treaty with him, along with Duke Godfrey and the other princes, that they would not keep any at all of the cities, lands, and castles belonging to his kingdom, nor would they deceive him. For this reason, when the princes returned from Jerusalem and were quartered in the territory of the town of Jubayl, and they realized Bohemond had unfairly besieged Latakia, and had wronged the emperor and Count Raymond, they appointed messengers on the instruction and request of the Christian brothers returning victoriously from Jerusalem, who addressed Bohemond in friendly and peaceful fashion and asked him to withdraw from the siege of the city and not to inflict any further injustice on Christians.[77]

56. The bishop of Pisa humbly greets the returning pilgrims

Meanwhile, until the messengers were chosen for this purpose, the bishop of the Pisans, called Daibert, who had heard about the arrival and return of the pilgrims from Jerusalem – where there had been no news or record of them for a considerable time to this day – hurried to hear and see the brothers, taking with him some eminent men from his company. When he found them in the aforesaid region he could not restrain himself at all from weeping for joy, but fell on the necks of everyone, great and small, and began to kiss them all with tears, saying: 'Truly and unequivocally I acknowledge you as sons and friends of the living God, for you did not only renounce your possessions, cities and castles and estates, wives and sons and daughters, but you did not even grudge your lives, since you did not hesitate to make this expedition of God and Lord Jesus Christ into such distant and barbarous nations, and you suffered so many difficulties, as we have heard, for the sake of our Redeemer. What we now hear concerning your glory and power is unheard of since Christ's nativity: that any army of Christians, travelling through so many kingdoms and dangers, should take Jerusalem in power and strength, having conquered and thrown out its bastard sons and inhabitants, and should cleanse the holy places, and raise up Godfrey, magnificent prince of Christians, to protect the defences in the city after the victory. Rejoicing because of this, we decided to come here in the desire of seeing you, greeting you and talking with you.'

57. Discussion between the bishop and the pilgrims

The faithful pilgrims replied to the venerable bishop in this way: 'If you are glad and pleased at the good fortune and deliverance of Christians, why have you unfairly exerted force against Christian citizens, namely those of Latakia, why have you captured their towers, slaughtered their guards and why do you still surround the city by a siege?' When he heard these things the bishop absolved himself courteously and patiently, and claimed that he and his men had done wrong in complete ignorance, saying: 'We are innocent of this bloodshed,[78] for when we sailed to these parts, in ignorance and unaware of your entire undertaking, Bohemond met us from Antioch, and he declared that the citizens of Latakia were false Christians, and always opposed to the Christian brothers, and he reported that they had been in an extreme degree traitors of the pilgrims among the Turks and Saracens. He beseeched our assistance and strength to revenge this. We, indeed,

---

77 For the complex history of Latakia, see Lilie, Appendix 1, pp. 259–76.

78 Cf. Dan.13: 46 (Sus. 46).

believed his words and declaration and thought these citizens most wicked; we brought our forces and assistance to him to besiege the city and its occupants, and thought we were performing a service to God in killing them. But now we know the truth from your lips, that Bohemond pursued these people from envy and avarice and not for God's sake, and that he wretchedly deceived us into besieging and killing Christians. And so we shall go back at once to our people and reveal the matter to them, and so we shall hold them back from the city and from any attack.'

58. Bohemond refuses to lift the siege and is deserted by all

After he said this, messengers from the Jerusalemite army set out with the Pisan bishop, but they found Bohemond persevering exceedingly in his greed. They revealed the legation of the brothers and fellow leaders to him courteously, asking that he move his weapons and forces away from the city of Latakia, so that they would not bely their promised faith towards the emperor of the Greeks and suffer severe hindrance to their return through his kingdom. Bohemond, when he heard the messengers' words, utterly scorned the request and advice of the faithful, and declared that he would never retreat from the walls and ramparts of Latakia until the city and citizens were delivered into his power. The messengers took back all Bohemond's replies and harsh words and his impatience to the army, and made them known to the leaders, and they excited everyone's anger fiercely, stirring up their feelings so that everyone, great and small, was minded to take arms and prepare for war. At this point, the bishop went down to the camp and the fleet of his men, knowing Bohemond's purpose and reply, and he informed all who were in his company of the matter and of the advice of the Christians' army, and so he withdrew from the siege of the city and from Bohemond's assistance all the Pisans and Genoese, who were conscience-stricken by the Lord God, so that they would no longer venture to raise a hand towards the citizens except to help them. Therefore, seeing he was destitute of help and his forces were greatly weakened, and that Christ's faithful and the princes had conspired to move him away from battle and force of arms, as evening was shadowing the heavens and earth Bohemond withdrew far from the siege of the walls with all his company, and, I know not whether from love or fear, he was forced to comply with the will of his brothers, whether he liked it or not.

59. Christians arrive at Latakia under arms and find that Bohemond has fled

When the next day dawned through all the world, the entire multitude of pilgrims put on weapons and hauberks and went on their way, and when much of the day had passed they arrived at Latakia with purple banners and a clamour of trumpets. But finding no opposition or resistance from the people, they entered peacefully the town gates which were opened to them voluntarily by the citizens and received a completely genuine welcome. They were told that Bohemond had in fact withdrawn to a distance and was positioned as much as half a mile from there. Therefore Count Raymond entered the city defences with five hundred brothers of his company and erected his banner, which was very well known, on top of the highest tower, placing a guard of his men throughout all Latakia's towers. The other brothers and fellow leaders were divided among all the buildings inside and outside for the sake of finding quarters. The number of Jerusalemites was about twenty thousand when they entered Latakian territory on the way back from Jerusalem and a plentiful supply of all the necessities of life was brought together for them by the merchants. For it was the month of September and the season of autumn when they arrived at Latakia, and they rejoiced in an especial abundance of corn, grapes, new wine, oil, and barley, and they happily spent a period of fifteen days with the citizens and pilgrims, the Pisans and Genoese, displaying every favour of friendship and courtesy to one another.

60. Bohemond is reconciled with the Latakians; and about some other people

Amidst these joys of mutual love on all sides they were mindful of their Christian name and of the trouble they had undergone together, of their suffering and former love, and they appointed intermediaries to speak to Bohemond about friendship and to reprove him for his injustice, so that he would be remorseful and not refuse to be reconciled to his brothers, and the brothers would graciously accept him, if he fulfilled this condition, into friendship and love. When Bohemond heard these messengers, he was remorseful about everything and hastily returned to unity and love. And on an appointed day talks were held on the plains of Latakia, especially between Count Raymond and Bohemond, and then peace and friendship were established among the others, and all the old hatred shut out, and so for three days Bohemond stayed with them in the observance of love while he enquired about the victory at Jerusalem, and after this he returned to Antioch with his men. After some days Robert of Flanders, likewise Robert prince of the Normans, Gaston of Béziers, Cono of Montaigu, and the other fellow nobles arranged their return by ship to the lands of their birth. But Count Raymond, fearing he might lose Latakia, Tortosa, and the cities which he had conquered by hard work to Bohemond's avarice and unreliability, stayed on with a very great company of his followers.[79]

[79] For the continuing suspicions between Raymond and Bohemond, see also FC (pp. 320–21; 342–3).

Appendix 1: People

NB The name is as in the English translation and the reference is to first appearance. The following abbreviations are used for reference works:
Jamison – E. Jamison, 'Some notes on the *Anonymi Gesta Francorum*, with special reference to the Norman contingent from South Italy and Sicily in the first crusade,' *Studies in French Language and Mediaeval Literature presented to Professor Mildred K. Pope* (Manchester, 1939), pp. 183–208.
Murray – A. V. Murray, *The Crusader Kingdom of Jerusalem: A Dynastic History 1099–1125*, Occasional Publications of the Linacre Unit for Prosopographical Research 4 (Oxford, 2000).
R-S – J. Riley-Smith, *The First Crusaders, 1095–1131* (Cambridge, 1997).

Achard of Montmerle, 2. 23: castellan of Montmerle (dép. Ain, Fr.). See J. Riley-Smith, *The First Crusade and the Idea of Crusading* (London, 1986), pp. 40, 46 for charter evidence from Cluny recording his preparations for the expedition; *Recueil des chartes de l'abbaye de Cluny*, (ed.) A. Bernard and A. Bruel (6 vols, Paris, 1876–1903), vol. 5, pp. 51–3.

Adelbero, 3. 46: son of Count Conrad of Luxembourg and archdeacon of Metz. Murray observes that the name Adelbero had been considered auspicious for bishops since the time of Adelbero, bishop of Augsburg (d. 909) and was apt to be given to younger sons destined for the Church by the families of Ardenne-Verdun, Bar and Luxembourg. Adelbero, bishop of Metz 1047–72, was the archdeacon's uncle. This supports Albert's picture of a rather worldly career churchman: Murray, pp. 178–9.

Adam son of Michael, 3. 36: not identified, but in the *ChA*'s 'twelve couplets', 'Adan le fil Michiel' precedes Tancred and Bohemond in the list of barons (*ChA* p. 324).

Adelolf, 6. 25: nothing known.

Adhémar, bishop of Le Puy, 2. 20: Adhémar of Monteil, bishop of Le Puy, appointed by Urban II to be his legate on the expedition; †1098: J. H. and L. L. Hill, 'Contemporary accounts and the later reputation of Adhémar, bishop of Puy', *Medievalia et Humanistica*, 9 (1955), pp. 30–38.

Adorsonius, 3. 36: Turkish amir; nothing known.

Alan surnamed Fergant, 3. 23: duke of Brittany. According to charter evidence Alan was absent from Brittany between 27 July 1096 and 9 Oct. 1101: C. W. David, *Robert Curthose, Duke of Normandy* (Cambridge, MA, 1920), p. 221; R-S, p. 198; *ChA* p. 133.

Alexios, 1. 6: Alexios I Komnenos, Byzantine emperor 1081–1118.

Amasa of Curzh, 4. 8: fabulous Turkish leader.

Amasa of Niz, 4. 8: fabulous Turkish leader.

Anselm of Ribemont, 2. 22: dép. Aisne, Fr. Anselm led his own detachment on the expedition. He sent two letters to Archbishop Manasses of Reims, which are extant (*Kreuzzugsbriefe*, pp. 144–6; 156–60). †during the siege of Arqa *c.*25 Feb. 1099 (5. 36).

Arnulf of Chocques, 6. 8: poss. ancillary legate of Urban II; candidate for patriarchate of Jerusalem, 1099. For the controversy over his election see note to 6. 39.

Arnulf of Tirs, 2. 23: nothing known; †in battle 1097 (3. 47). Not otherwise known.

Balak, 3. 25: Balak ibn Bahrām, cadet of the Artuqid dynasty.

Balas of Amacha and of Sororgia, 4. 8: fabulous Turkish leader.

Baldric, 2. 2: Godfrey's seneschal.

Balduk of Samosart, 4. 8: fabulous Turkish leader.

Balduk, 3. 21: amir of Samosata (prob. same as previous entry).

Baldwin Calderun, 2. 22: Anselm calls him *Chalderuns*. Beyond the reports in Anselm's letter and the *ChA*, where he is called Bauduins Cauderon, nothing is known of him (*Kreuzzugsbriefe*, p. 145; *ChA passim*).

Baldwin of Bourcq, 2. 1: Baldwin's surname derives from Bourcq (dép. Ardennes, Fr.). He was the son of Count Hugh I of Rethel and Melisende of Montlhéry and Godfrey's kinsman. He was to succeed Godfrey's brother Baldwin both as count of Edessa (1100) and king of Jerusalem (1118); †1131 (Murray, pp. 185–6).

Baldwin of Ghent (Baldwin of the castle of Lant), 2. 22: advocate of St Peter's Abbey (Sint-Pietersabdij, Blandijnberg); count of Ghent (prov. Oost-Vlaanderen, Be.) and lord of Aalst. *Annalista Saxo* lists him among the leaders: *MGH SS* vi. 730. Also in the *ChA* (p. 133 and *passim*) and mentioned by Anselm of Ribemont (*Kreuzzugsbriefe*, p. 145).

Baldwin of Hainaut, 2. 8: Baldwin II of Mons, count of Hainaut (Murray, pp. 186–7).

Baldwin of Lant, 2. 22: Baldwin of Ghent

Baldwin, 2. 1: 3rd s. of Eustace II, count of Boulogne. Count of Edessa 1097–1100; king of Jerusalem 1100–18.

Barkyārūq, 4. 2: son of Malik-Shāh and Saljūq sultan 1094–1105.

Bernard, 2. 23: Bernard of Saint-Valéry (dép. Somme, Fr.). Son of Walter of Domedart (Saint-Valéry), *q.v.*

Boesas, 2. 8: fabulous Turkish leader.

Bohemond, 2. 14: eldest s. of Robert Guiscard, duke of Apulia and Calabria 1059–85; count of Antioch 1098; †1111.

Bohemond, 3. 61: convert to Christianity; also found in RA (pp. 158–9) and RM (p. 207). See also 4. 15–16.

Buldagis, 4. 2: Yāghisiyān's second son (Muḥammad).

Cazcornuz, 3. 36: Turkish amir; nothing known.
Clarembald, 1. 28: Clarembald of Vendeuil (dép. Aisne, Fr.). Also found in *ChA* as 'Clarembaus de Venduel' (p. 133 and *passim*).
Coloman, 1. 6: king of Hungary (1095–1116). Coloman had succeeded László I (St Ladislaus) who had firmly re-established Christianity in his lands.
Conan, 2. 23: 2nd son of Geoffrey I, count of Lamballe (dép. Côtes-d'Armor, Fr.). See David, p. 222; *ChA* (p. 133); OV v. 54, 58; RC p. 82.
Cono, count of Montaigu, 2. 11: eldest son of Gozelo, count of Behogne. Montaigu (prov. Luxembourg, Be.) was a castle on the left bank of the river Ourthe near Marcourt in the Ardennes. Cono was accompanied on crusade by his sons Gozelo and Lambert. See also OV, v. 110, 166–8; Murray, pp. 189–91.
Constantine, 3. 22: Armenian ruler of Gargar.
Copatrix, 3. 36: Turkish amir; nothing known.

Daibert, 6. 56: had been appointed by Urban II to succeed Adhémar as papal legate. He had become bishop of Pisa in 1088 and, in 1092, the see became an archbishopric in his honour. He had taken the cross at Clermont and preached the crusade, but did not leave for the east until 1099 (Hamilton, pp. 14–15). For his later career see especially Book 7 of Albert's history. See M. Matzke, *Daibert von Pisa: Zwischen Pisa, Papst und erstem Kreuzzug* (Sigmaringen, 1998).
Dodo of Cons, 2. 1: Dodo, lord of Cons-la-Grandville (dép. Meurthe-et-Moselle, Fr.) in the Ardennes. It is known from charter evidence that his wife Hadwida accompanied him on crusade: *Chartes de l'abbaye de Saint-Hubert en Ardenne*, (ed.) G. Kurth (2 vols, Brussels, 1903), vol. 1, pp. 80–82, 89 (Murray, pp. 191–2).
Don Walker of the castle of Chappes, 2. 23: see Walker.
Drogo of Mouchy, 4. 47: Mouchy-le-Châtel (dép. Oise, Fr.). Drogo's departure on crusade is reported by Orderic Vitalis (v. 30; vi. 192) and in *ChA* his presence at Nicaea is mentioned, as well as at Antioch. After his return from the crusade, he married Edithua, widow of Gerard of Gournay (see 2. 23).
Drogo of Nesle, 2. 1: Probably a relation of Ralph, lord of Soissons (dép. Somme, Fr.) and his son Ivo II, lord of Nesle and count of Soissons. Another son of Ralph was called Drogo, but he is known to have been in France between 1115 and 1157, while the crusading Drogo is attested in Palestine up to 1126: R. Röhricht, *Regesta Regni Hierosolymitani* (Innsbruck, 1893; *Additamentum* 1904), nos. 76a and 115; Murray, p. 191. Drogo is also a hero of the *ChA* (*passim*) and features in the Latin epic of Gilo of Paris (pp. 148–9, 190–93).
Duqāq ibn Tutush, 4. 8: ruler of Damascus 1095–1104.

Emicho, 1. 27: Emicho of Flonheim (Kreis Alzey-Worms, Ger.). Traditionally identified as count of Leiningen on the evidence of the very late German source known as the chronicle of Zimmern, but more recently it has been argued convincingly that he was Emicho of Flonheim on the middle Rhine. See *Die*

Chronik der Grafen von Zimmern. Handschriften 580 und 581 der Fürstlich Fürstenbergischen Bibliothek Donaueschingen, (ed.) H. Decker-Hauff (3 vols, Stuttgart, 1964), vol. 1, p. 75; I. Toussaint, *Die Grafen von Leiningen. Studien zur leiningischen Genealogie und Territorialgeschichte bis zur Teilung von 1317/18* (Sigmaringen, 1982), cited in A. V. Murray, 'The Army of Godfrey of Bouillon, 1096–1099: structure and dynamics of a contingent on the First Crusade', *Revue belge de philologie et d'histoire*, 70 (1992), pp. 301–29, at 320–21; H. Möhring, 'Graf Emicho und die Judenverfolgungen von 1096', *Rheinische Vierteljahrsblätter*, 56 (1992), pp. 97–111.

Engelrand, 2. 22: s. of Hugh of Saint-Pol. Engelrand and Hugh are prominent figures in the *ChA*: see discussion in the introduction to the translation to the *ChA*, esp. pp. 20–24.

Engilbert of Tournai, 6. 11: brother of Lithold and with him the first into Jerusalem in 1099. Little is known of the brothers, other than their birthplace (prov. Hainaut, Be.).

Enzhu, 5. 16: Armenian; no more known.

Eustace, 2. 21: Eustace III of Boulogne; eldest br. of Godfrey and Baldwin. Although Eustace travelled to Constantinople with Robert of Normandy and with his lord, Robert of Flanders, he was later closely associated with his brother Godfrey: Murray, p. 193.

Everard of Le Puiset, 3. 33: Everard III, son of Hugh I of Le Puiset (dép. Eure-et-Loir, Fr.). See J. La Monte, 'The lords of Le Puiset on the Crusades', *Speculum*, 17 (1942), pp. 100–118, at 100–101.

Fer, commander of Turbessel, 3. 18: nothing known.

Florina, 3. 54: poss. dau. of Eudes I and Sibyl of Burgundy. Florina is not recorded in WT or elsewhere. Riley-Smith surmises that she was the daughter of Eudes I and Sibyl of Burgundy (R-S, pp. 95, 247), while J. M. Jensen has suggested tentatively that the tale might be a garbled record of the participation of the bishop of Funen (Fiona), one of the two mentioned by the 'Annalista Saxo': 'Danmark og den hellige krig. En undersøgelse af korstogsbevægelsens indflydelse på Danmark ca. 1070–1169', *Historisk Tidsskrift*, 100 (2000), pp. 285–328 at 295–6. Florina's erstwhile husband remains unidentified (as does his provenance 'Philippi').

Folbert of Bouillon, 5. 5: nothing known: Murray, pp. 195–6. Riley-Smith believes him to be another Fulcher (R-S, pp. 204, 206).

Folbert of Chartres, 5. 22: prob. a mistake for Fulcher.

Folcher of Orléans (or Chartres), 1. 12: see nn. to 1. 12 and 1. 21.

Franco of Mechelen, 4. 35: Franco and his brother Sigemar were from Maasmechelen, north of Maastricht, Be. They were related to the Esch brothers and hence to Duke Godfrey. See Murray, pp. 196, 228.

Fredelo of the castle of Esch, 3. 44: while not himself a crusader, Fredelo figures in the background not only as father of Henry and Godfrey, but also as accomplice of Giselbert of Clermont in the depredations which upset the prince-bishop of Liège and indirectly led to Giselbert's participation in the expedition: see below *s.v.* Giselbert, and Murray, p. 48.

Fulcher of Chartres, 3. 25: count of Sororgia (dist. from Folcher of Orléans/Chartres and from historian FC).

Gaston of Béziers (*Bederz*), 2. 23: dép. Hérault, Fr. Sandwiched at the siege of Nicaea between two south-French nobles, Gaston's provenance is surely Béziers (dép. Hérault, Fr.). He has been identified with Gaston IV, vicomte of Béarn, although WT makes them two different people (pp. 331, 377–8, 410). See R-S, pp. 206, 234.

Gerard of Avesnes, 6. 53: Avesnes-sur-Helpe (dép. Pas-de-Calais, Fr.). Gerard had originally been a vassal of Baldwin of Hainaut who disappeared (5. 3) and had then transferred his allegiance to Godfrey. See Murray, p. 199.

Gerard of Gournay, 2. 23: Gournay-en-Bray (dép. Seine-et-Maritime, Fr.). Son of Hugh Flaitel; accompanied on crusade by his wife Edith: he died, while she returned and was married to Drogo of Monchy. See David, pp. 222–3; William of Jumièges, *Gesta Normannorum ducum*, (ed.) E. M. C. van Houts (2 vols, OMT, 1992–95), vol. 2, pp. 214–15; OV v. 34, 58; *ChA*, pp. 144, 311.

Gerard of Quierzy, 2. 22: dép. Aisne, Fr. See also the *ChA* where he is Gerars de Cerisgi (pp. 144, 311).

Gerard of Roussillon, 2. 23: s. of Gilbert, count of Roussillon. Gerard succeeded his father Gilbert as count of Roussillon: *RHC Occ* iv. 316, note (k); R-S, p. 208. He is poss. the *ChA*'s Girart.

Gerard, 4. 9: later identified as Baldwin's secretary and confidant (5. 22): see Murray, p. 199.

Gilbert of Traves, 2. 23: as noted in *RHC Occ* iv there was a castle at Traves (dép. Haute-Saône, Fr.), but no records of the names of its lords (p. 316, note l).

Giselbert of Clermont, 3. 16: Clermont-sur-Meuse (Clermont-sous-Huy, prov. Liège, Be.). Murray suggests, plausibly, that Giselbert had been dispossessed of Clermont by Otbert, the prince-bishop of Liège, and went on crusade with Godfrey in 1095 as an avenue of escape (p. 202).

Giselbert, 6. 36: canon of St Mary's, Aachen: not in the surviving records: E. Meuthen, *Aachener Urkunden 1101–1250* (Bonn, 1972).

Godevere, 3. 27: or Godechilde, Baldwin's wife, was the daughter of the Norman lord Ralph of Tosny (Murray, p. 203).

Godfrey Burel, 1. 7: 'born in the city of Etampes'; nothing known.

Godfrey, duke of Lotharingia, 2. 1: Godfrey, the future ruler of Jerusalem, is the hero of Albert's narrative. He was born *c.*1060, the second son of Eustace II, count of Boulogne and Ida of Bouillon, daughter of Godfrey the Bearded, duke of Lower Lotharingia and count of Verdun. In spite of being the second son, Godfrey succeeded to the duchy of Lower Lotharingia in 1087 as heir to his maternal uncle, Godfrey the Hunchback. There is no more satisfactory biography of Godfrey than J. C. Andressohn, *The Ancestry and Life of Godfrey of Bouillon* (Bloomington, IN, 1947), but Godfrey's preparations for departure in 1096 are described in detail by Murray, 'The Army of Godfrey of Bouillon, 1096–1099: structure and dynamics of a contingent on the First Crusade', *Revue belge de philologie et d'histoire*, 70 (1992), pp. 301–29, at 325–7. Ruler of Jerusalem 1099; †1100.

Godfrey, 2. 1: He and his brother Henry belonged to the family which held the castle of Esch-sur-Sûre (G-D Luxembourg) in the Ardennes (Murray, pp. 205, 209).

Gottschalk, 1. 23: German leader of the 'Peasants' Crusade'; his followers were massacred in Hungary. There is a Godeschalk in *ChA*, but he was apparently a Basque (p. 133).

Gozelo, 2. 23: s. of Cono of Montaigu. †(of disease) at Artah (3. 29). According to *ChA* Gozelo ('Gosson') was killed in battle at Artah (pp. 166–7).

Guy of Possesse, 2. 22: nr. Vitry (dép. Marne, Fr.). Guy's short career is also celebrated in the *ChA* and by Anselm in his first letter (*Kreuzzugsbriefe*, p. 145).

Guz, 2. 7: Hungarian noble, governor of Zemun.

Hartmann, 2. 1: s. of Hupold III, count of Dillingen in Swabia (Kr. Dillingen, Ger.). In 1095 Hartmann founded the monastery of Neresheim; its first abbot, Ernest, is known to have gone on the first crusade. Although his name is not mentioned in Book 1, Hartmann apparently accompanied the expedition of Emicho, this being his 'misfortune'. †1121. See Murray, pp. 208–9 and idem, 'Army', p. 321: here Murray points out that Hartmann's is the only name in the late German source, *The Chronicle of Zimmern*, which can be confirmed from other sources: H. Decker-Hauff (ed.), vol 1, p. 79; Bernold of St Blasien, *Chronicon*, *MGH SS* v. 466 where he is cited as one of six leaders of the crusade.

Hecelo, 6. 34: nothing known.

Henry of Esch, 2. 1: Henry and his brother Godfrey belonged to the family which held the castle of Esch-sur-Sûre (G-D Luxembourg) in the Ardennes (Murray, pp. 205, 209).

Henry IV, emperor (1056–1106), 1. 6: Henry's imperial coronation was in 1084. Albert also calls him Henry III later (5. 13) and numbers his son the fifth king and fourth emperor (11. 48).

Herbrand of Bouillon, 2. 23: castellan of Bouillon and an important member of Godfrey's household: see Murray, pp. 209–10.

Hugh of Saint-Pol, 2. 22: Saint-Pol-sur-Ternoise (dép. Pas de Calais, Fr.). Hugh and his son Engelrand are prominent figures in the *ChA*; see also OV v. 34, 54, 58.

Hugh the Great, 2. 7: Hugh of Vermandois, brother of Philip, king of France. (Philip was excommunicate at the time so there was no question of his taking the cross.) Hugh's cognomen seems not to have been earned, but a corruption or mistranslation of *mainsné* (or *moins né*), meaning 'the Younger': *Histoire Anonyme de la Première Croisade*, (ed.) L. Bréhier (Paris, 1924), p. 14, n. 3.

Husechin, 3. 4: nothing known.

Ivo, 4. 13: Ivo of Grandmesnil, near Lisieux (dép. Calvados, Fr.). Also sheriff of Leicester, England (R-S, 214).
Ivo, 4. 30: prob. Ivo of Grandmesnil (4. 13).

John of Nijmegen, 2. 23: possibly identical with *Jonas de la Mehca* in the *Canso d'Antioca*, otherwise not known: *The* Canso d'Antioca: *An Occitan Epic Chronicle of the First Crusade*, (ed.) C. Sweetenham and L. M. Paterson (Aldershot, 2003), pp. 232 (line 629), 345.
John, 2. 15: s. of Alexios and ruled as emperor John II Komnenos 1118–43.

Karageth of the town of Karan, 4. 8: fabulous Turkish leader; his name may incorporate the Turkish element 'Kara-', meaning 'black'.
Karbugha, 4. 2: Karbughā al-Mawṣilī, atabeg of Mosul (1095–1102).

Lambert, 1. 10: not otherwise known.
Lambert, 2. 23: s. of Cono of Montaigu. After the crusade Lambert returned home with his father: Alberic of Troisfontaines, p. 815. See also A. V. Murray, 'The origins of the Frankish nobility of the kingdom of Jerusalem, 1100–1118', *Mediterranean Historical Review*, 4 (1989), pp. 281–300, at 297, n. 25.
Lithold of Tournai, 6. 11: brother of Engilbert and with him the first into Jerusalem in 1099. Little is known of the brothers, other than their birthplace (prov. Hainaut, Be.). See Murray, p. 216 (as Letold).
Louis of Mousson, 2. 23: count of Mousson (dép. Meurthe-et-Moselle, Fr.), representing his father, Count Thierry I of Bar and Montbéliard: *ChA*; Alberic of Troisfontaines, *Chronica*, *MGH SS* xxiii. 804 (Murray, pp. 216–7).
Louis, 3. 53: archdeacon of Toul. Louis is known only from this story, although, as Murray says, it is likely he travelled with Rainald of Toul (*q.v.*): Murray, p. 217.

Mahumeth, 5. 9: son of amir of 'Azaz.
Meraius, 6. 41: prob. al-Afḍal, vizier of Egypt 1094–1121.
Milo Louez, 2. 23: nothing known.

Nichita, 1. 7: Byzantine 'dux', governor of Belgrade [Niketas].
Nicusus, 3. 18: Armenian landowner; nothing else known.

Odo count of Champagne, 2. 23: father of Stephen of Aumale.
Oliver of the castle of Jussey, 2. 23: Probably Jussey, dép. Haute-Saône, Fr.. In *ChA*: pp. 143, 145, 176; R-S, p. 215.
Omar of Azaz, 5. 5. The name is given by Kemal al-Din: *RHC Or* iii, p. 595.

Pakrad, 3. 17: Pakrad (or Bagrat) was brother of Kogh Vasil (Basil the Robber) who held several castles east of Marash at Kesoun and Raban: see the detailed note in E. Dulaurier's edition of Matthew of Edessa, *RHC Arm* i. 35–6; WT pp. 348–9.

patriarch of Antioch, 5. 1: John IV, a Byzantine Greek, appointed patriarch of Antioch in 1091. See Hamilton, *Latin Church*, p. 7. WT records that John retired voluntarily to Constantinople following the crusader capture of Antioch because he realized that a Greek could not effectively govern Latins (pp. 339–40).

Payen of Garlande, 2. 27: WT has *Guido de Garlanda* (p. 139) and *Galterus de Garlanda* (p. 201). He is mentioned in the *ChA* as Paiens de Garlande, in the *Chanson de Jérusalem* as Paien de Guillant (p. 243), and in the Chronicles of St Bertin as 'Guido de Garlandia Senescallus Franciae' (*RHGF* xiii. 459), but he seems to have no history besides his crusading career. R-S lists him as Gilbert Payen of Garlande (p. 208).

Peter Bartholomew, 4. 43: not named in AA. The Provençal peasant who discovered the Holy Lance.

Peter, son of Gisla, 4. 30: also mentioned by WT (p. 310), but otherwise not known.

Peter 'the Hermit', 1. 2: Peter participated in the First Crusade to its conclusion in 1099. In 1100 he returned to Europe and founded an Augustinian monastery at Neufmoutier near Huy (prov. Liège, Be.), himself becoming prior. He died in 1115. AA is generally thought to have been mistaken in making Peter the instigator of the expedition, but for a review of the evidence and a reassessment of his rôle see E. O. Blake and C. Morris, 'A hermit goes to war: Peter and the origins of the first crusade', *Studies in Church History*, 23 (Oxford, 1985), 79–107; J. Flori, *Pierre l'Ermite et la Première Croisade* (Paris, 1999).

Peter, 2. 1: Peter, count of Astenois (Champagne), younger brother of Rainald of Toul (*q.v.*); also known as *Petrus de Dunperrun* from Dampierre-le-Château (dép. Marne, Fr.) (Murray, p. 219).

Pisellus, 5. 22: nephew of Udelard of Wissant (*q.v.*); beheaded by Balak. Murray, p. 221.

prince of Damascus, 4. 8: see Duqāq.

Pulagit, 4. 2: not identified.

Raimbold, count of Orange, 2. 23: Count Raimbold II of Orange (dép. Vaucluse, Fr.). See *ChA* (p. 311); R-S, p. 218.

Raimbold Croton, 4. 30: from Chartres. Raimbold survived to play a distinguished part at Antioch and Jerusalem, see *ChA* pp. 133, 195–7, 248, 311 and OV v. 168–9; other refs R-S, p. 218. Raimbold returned to Chartres after the crusade and a dispute with Bishop Ivo is described by R-S, pp. 155–6.

Rainald count of Toul, 2. 1: Rainald III, episcopal count of Toul (dép. Meurthe-et-Moselle, Fr.) in Upper Lotharingia. He and Peter of Astenois (*q.v.*) were sons of Frederick, count of Astenois and Gertrude, daughter of Count Rainald II of

Toul, and kinsmen of Godfrey. Their participation in the crusade is confirmed by Laurence of Liège: *MGH SS* x, p. 494 (and see Murray, p. 221).

Rainald of Beauvais, 2. 23: Probably Beauvais in dép. Oise, Fr.: see Walo of Chaumont. Also in the *ChA* pp. 133, 311, 325; the *Chanson de Jérusalem*, pp. 223–4 and Gilo, p. 190.

Ralph of La Fontanelle, 4. 30: Probably La Fontanelle, near Vendôme (dép. Loir-et-Cher, Fr.): see RC p. 101; BD p. 65 (variant reading); Murray, pp. 222–3.

Raymond Pilet, 2. 23: lord of Alès (dép. Gard, Fr.), a follower of Raymond of Saint-Gilles. See *GF* pp. 73, 83, 87; RA pp. 122–3, 141–2. The poet Gilo celebrates his career: pp. 196, 222, 226, 238. See also Riley-Smith, *First Crusade*, p. 71.

Raymond, count of Saint-Gilles, 2. 20: Raymond IV of Saint-Gilles, count of Toulouse and marquis of Provence, was the first of the magnates to respond to Pope Urban's appeal: in fact, he enlisted so rapidly that it is believed that he had been primed by the pope. When he set out Raymond was in his mid-fifties; he had left his son Bertrand to govern his lands in Provence and did not expect to return to the west: J. H. and L. L. Hill, *Raymond IV of Saint-Gilles 1041 (or 1042)–1105* (Syracuse, NY, 1962). †1105.

Reinhard of Hamersbach, 4. 47: Murray suggests Hemmersbach (Kr. Bergheim, Nordrhein-Westfalen, Ger.) as Reinhard's probable place of origin (p. 224).

Reinold of Broyes, 1. 7: (identified as Broyes in *RHC Occ* iv. 277): see R-S, p. 218.

Richard of Salerno, 3. 15: Richard of Salerno (Campania, It.) was son of Robert Guiscard's brother William, therefore Bohemond's cousin and (probably) second cousin to Tancred. See Jamison, pp. 197–8.

Ridwan, 4. 2: Riḍwān ibn Tutush, Saljūq ruler of Aleppo 1095–1113.

Robert of Anzi, 3. 16: prov. Potenza, It. Robert was later granted the revenues of the port of Arsuf (7. 12). See Jamison, pp. 202–3.

Robert of Flanders, 2. 19: Robert II, count of Flanders, was the son of Robert I 'the Frisian' who had travelled as a pilgrim to Jerusalem between 1087 and 1089. While returning he met Alexios Komnenos and he promised to send five hundred knights to assist him against the Turks and Pechenegs. These knights fought for Alexios in Asia Minor in 1090 (AK pp. 109, 202). This precedent may have influenced Alexios in appealing for help from the west, and Robert II in responding to it: M. M. Knappen, 'Robert II of Flanders in the first crusade', *The Crusades and other Historical Essays presented to Dana C. Munro*, (ed.) L. J. Paetow (New York, 1928), pp. 79–100.

Robert of Paris, 2. 39: also mentioned in Anselm of Ribemont's letter to Manasses, archbishop of Reims (*Kreuzzugsbriefe*, p. 145). Nothing more is known about him, though tradition, sanctified by Sir Walter Scott in his novel *Robert of Paris* (1831), identifies Robert with the nobleman who sat on Emperor Alexios's throne: AK pp. 291–2.

Robert, son of Gerard, 2. 23: second son of Gerard, count of Buonalbergo (prov. Benevento, It.). Served Bohemond as constable and standard-bearer, returning to Italy before 1112. He is widely mentioned in the sources, e.g. *GF* p. 36; OV v. 78; RC p. 108. See Jamison, pp. 201–2; Murray, p. 226.

Robert, count of Normandy, 2. 21: Robert was born in the early 1050s, the eldest son of William, duke of Normandy and Matilda, daughter of Count Baldwin V of Flanders. To finance his expedition he pawned Normandy to his brother King William II (William Rufus) of England. The biography by C. W. David, *Robert Curthose, Duke of Normandy* (Cambridge, MA, 1920), has been superseded by W. M. Aird, *Robert 'Curthose', Duke of Normandy (c.1050–1134)* (Woodbridge, 2008).

Robert, 5. 43: Robert of Rouen, bishop of Lydda. See Murray, pp. 226–7.

Rodolph Peeldelau, 2. 9: Frank in Byzantine emperor's service.

Rodolph, a Breton, 4. 47: Ralph I of Gaël: BD pp. 28, 33; OV ii. 318, v. 34, 54, 58; *Gesta Normannorum Ducum*, (ed.) E. M. C. van Houts (2 vols, OMT, 1992–95), vol. 2, pp. 146, 226. Ralph had formerly held Norwich, but had been expropriated and exiled. He was accompanied on crusade by his wife, daughter of William Fitz Osbern and Adeliza, daughter of Roger of Tosny. R-S, pp. 91, 219.

Rodolph, 2. 23: identity uncertain. R-S suggests Rodolph is Rudolf of Sarrewerden (p. 222), mentioned in the *Chronicle of Zimmern*, but see Alan V. Murray, who argues convincingly that Rudolf and his brother Ulrich must be regarded as pure fiction: 'The Chronicle of Zimmern as a source for the First Crusade', *The First Crusade: Origins and Impact*, (ed.) J. P. Phillips (Manchester, 1997), pp. 78–106. Duparc-Quioc proposes more tentatively that he may be Count 'Rotols del Perce' (line 1174), i.e. Rotrou du Perche, vassal of the king of France and of the duke of Normandy for the counties of Perche and Mortagne, later lord of Tudela and Saragossa (Spain): *Chanson d'Antioche*: *Edition*, pp. 73, 566.

Roger of Barneville, 2. 27: almost certainly Barneville-sur-Mer, now Barneville-Carteret (dép. Manche, Fr.). Roger is also mentioned by eye-witnesses: in *GF* (pp. 15–16); RA (p. 55) and Anselm of Ribemont's second letter to Manasses of Reims (*Kreuzzugsbriefe*, p. 159). He was a baron of Count Roger of Sicily and appears in witness lists in Sicily in 1086, 1094 and 1095. He probably joined Robert of Normandy as he overwintered in Calabria: Jamison, pp. 207–8.

Roger of Rozoy, 3. 28: Rozoy-sur-Serre (dép. Aisne, Fr.). See Murray, p. 227. Roger was to make a career in the Latin Kingdom of Jerusalem, but also to become a hero of the fourteenth-century *Godefroid* chanson, where he is described as lame (line 6873): F. de Reiffenberg, *Le Chevalier au Cygne et Godefroid de Bouillon* (3 vols, Brussels, 1846–54), vol. 3, p. clvii.

Roger, son of Dagobert, 2. 9: Frank in Byzantine emperor's service; 'Roger, son of Dagobert' and 'Hubert, son of Raoul' witnessed the treaty of Devol, 1108, as members of the imperial court (AK p. 395).

Rosseleon, 3. 36: Turkish amir; may be the *ChA*'s 'Rouge Lion'.

Rothard, son of Godfrey, 2. 23: nothing known.

Rothard, 6. 26: Godfrey's steward (appears in a dream). It appears from the interpretation of the dream, 6. 27, that he had deserted the crusading army at Antioch. For Rothard and other officers of Godfrey's household, see Murray, p. 80, n. 77.

ruler of Tripoli, 5. 38: Abū 'Alī b. 'Ammār (*RHC Occ* iv. 457, note b).

Ruthard, 1. 27: Ruthard II, archbishop of Mainz (1089–1109).

Sansadonias, 3. 36: Shams al-Dawla, son of Yaghi-Siyan, the amir of Antioch.

Sigemar of Mechelen, 4. 35: Maasmechelen, north of Maastricht, Be. He and his brother Franco were related to the Esch brothers and hence to Duke Godfrey. See Murray, pp. 196, 228.

Sokman, 6. 32: Suqmān ibn Artuq, d. 1104.

Stabelo, 2. 2: Godfrey's chamberlain. (Only named in AA.)

Stephen of Aumale, 2. 23: Aumale on the river Bresle (dép. Seine-et-Maritime, Fr.). Stephen's mother was William the Conqueror's sister Adelaide and his father her third husband Odo of Champagne. Although Stephen had opposed his cousin Robert of Normandy previously, siding with William Rufus, they were evidently reconciled in 1096, for he travelled with Robert. See David, *Robert Curthose*, p. 228; also in *ChA* p. 178.

Stephen of Blois, 2. 21: count of Blois, son of Theobald III. Stephen was married to the redoubtable Adela, daughter of William I of England. Two of Stephen's letters written to Adela during the expedition have survived: *Kreuzzugsbriefe*, pp. 138–40; 149–52.

Suleyman, 1. 16: Qilij Arslan I, sultan of Rūm 1092–1107.

sultan of Khurasan, 4. 2: see Barkyārūq.

Svend, 3. 54: Danish prince. The romantic story of Svend is told only by AA (and, following him, WT). It has therefore sometimes been labelled a fiction, but the prince has been identified as one of the many sons of the Danish king Svend II Estridson (1047–*c*.1074) and the story of his crusade accepted: *Danmarks Riges Historie*, (ed.) J. C. H. Steenstrup et al. (6 vols, Copenhagen, 1904–07), vol. 1, pp. 473, 505. See also 'Annalista Saxo', *MGH SS* vi. 730: 'preterque hos frater regis Danorum cum duobus episcopis aliique perplures tocius Europe principes'.

Symeon II, 1. 2: orthodox patriarch of Jerusalem, died 1099.

Tancred, 2. 19: Tancred, son of Robert Guiscard's daughter Emma (i.e. Bohemond's nephew); the youngest of the leaders, being not yet twenty. †1111. The standard biography is R. L. Nicholson, *Tancred* (Chicago, 1940).

Taphnuz, 3. 31: Armenian prince whose dau. m. Baldwin.

Tatikios, 2. 22: Byzantine general. According to Greek sources Tatikios was of servile origin, the son of a Saracen prisoner-of-war, but he rose to hold high military rank under Alexios. He and the emperor had a relationship of loyalty and trust which is documented from 1078–99. Only the Latin sources describe him as having a cut-off nose, Guibert adding that he wore a gold prosthesis: RA

p. 54; GN p. 182. See B. Skoulatos, *Les personnages byzantins de l'Alexiade* (Louvain, 1980), pp. 287–92; A. G. C. Savvides, 'Varia Byzantinoturcica II: Taticius the Turcople', *Journal of Oriental and African Studies* 3–4 (1991–92), 235–8.

Thierry, count of Montbéliard, 2. 23: Count Thierry I of Bar and Montbéliard (father of Louis of Mousson).

Thomas of La Fère, 2. 22: Thomas of Marle (below).

Thomas of Marle, 1. 28: or La Fère, lord of Coucy, count of Amiens; killed 1130 in a punitive expedition conducted against him by Louis VI of France. Thomas features in *ChA* as 'Thumas de le Fere', but he was also a major hero of the *Chanson de Jérusalem*. For his lurid career before and after the crusade, R-S pp. 156–7.

Thoros (or T'oros), 3. 20: governor of Edessa; see J. Laurent, 'Des Grecs aux croisés: Étude sur l'histoire d'Edesse', *Byzantion*, 1 (1924), 404–34.

Udelard of Wissant, 3. 27: dép. Pas-de-Calais, Fr. Udelard had been in Eustace of Boulogne's contingent: Murray, p. 231.

Urban II, 1. 6: pope 1088–99. His former name was Odo, or Eudes. He was born *c.*1035 at Châtillon-sur-Marne, became canon and archdeacon at Reims, then monk and prior at Cluny. Under the patronage of Gregory VII he became cardinal bishop of Ostia *c.*1080 and served as legate in Germany 1084–85. Then, and later when he was pope, he and Henry IV were implacable opponents in the dispute over lay investiture of bishops.

Walbric, 4. 30: poss. Alberic of Grandmesnil; see RC p. 101.

Walker of Chappes, 2. 23: probably Chappes near Bar-sur-Seine (dép. Aube, Fr.): R-S, p. 223.

Walo of Chaumont, 2. 23: Chaumont-en-Vexin (dép. Oise, Fr.). Probably, but not certainly, the same as Walo, constable of the king of France, who was killed at Antioch (3. 35; cf. Anselm of Ribemont's letter, *Kreuzzugsbriefe*, p. 159) – notably AA puts him in the company of Rainald of Beauvais at Nicaea and at Antioch. According to RM, Walo's wife also went on crusade (p. 140); Gilo gives her name, Humberge of Le Puiset, and describes her grief at Walo's death in affecting terms (p. 126–7 and n. 6).

Walo of the 'isle of Flanders', 2. 29: Walo of Lille (or L'Isle) is also mentioned by WT (p. 203), but his brief crusading career is not otherwise recorded.

Walo, steward of the king of France, 3. 35: prob. Walo of Chaumont (above).

Walter 'Sansavoir', 1. 6: his cognomen has misled generations of historians into thinking he was impoverished, but the family probably came from Boissy-Sans-Avoir (dép. Yvelines, Fr.). R-S identifies Walter as a member of the Poissy family from the same region (pp. 93, 100). See also Murray, 'Army', p. 323.

Walter of Domedart, 2. 23: Walter of Saint-Valéry (dép. Somme, Fr.). Listed by OV as departing on crusade in the company of Robert of Normandy; OV cites him as 'great-grandson of Richard III duke of Normandy by his daughter Papia' (v. 34). In *ChA*, as Gautiers de Donmeart, p. 133 and *passim*.

Walter of Verva (Verna, Verra and Werra in later mss), 5. 40: poss. Walter of Verveis (below).

Walter of Verveis, 2. 23: poss. from Verviers (prov. Liège, Be.). Not otherwise recorded.

Walter, son of Waleran of the castle of Breteuil which is near Beauvais, 1. 7: only in AA. He was part of the influential crusading Montlhéry/Le Puiset clan, a nephew of Hugh I and Alice of Montlhéry: see R-S, pp. 224, 249.

Warner of Grez, 2. 1: Warner, count of Grez-Doiceau (prov. Brabant Wallon, Be.). He is mentioned once in the *ChA* and in cartularies in west and east, notably Röhricht, *Regesta* nos. 80, 134, 291. He died shortly after Godfrey in 1100 (7. 21). See Murray, pp. 234–5.

Welf of Burgundy, 3. 10: Welf's provenance is unknown. WT, following AA, calls him 'Guelfo, natione Burgundione' (pp. 196, 224). According to RC (pp. 63–5), an Armenian called Ursinus was master of Adana when Tancred arrived. Hagenmeyer suggested that AA had made a nonsense by changing RC's 'bear' ('Ursinus') into a 'wolf' ('Welfo'), but the change in nationality adds to the improbability of this: *Gesta Francorum*, (ed.) H. Hagenmeyer (Heidelberg, 1890), p. 224, n. 66; cf. J. Laurent, 'Les Arméniens de Cilicie', *Mélanges Schlumberger*, i (Paris, 1924), 159–68, at pp.165–6. Runciman's solution to the problem was to write that Ursinus (Oshin) captured part of Adana in 1097 and Welf subsequently captured the citadel, but there does not appear to be any contemporary evidence for this (Runciman, *History of the Crusades*, vol. 1, pp. 196, 199).

William of Forez, 2. 22: William III, count of Forez and Lyon (dép. Rhône). There is a charter confirmed 10 Dec. 1096: 'Willelmus comes forensis volens cum aliis christianis zelo Dei ductis contra paganos ire Ierusalem' (*Chartes de Forez*, (ed.) G. Guichard et al (24 vols, Mâcon, 1933–70), vol. 1, no 1, p. 1). In the *ChA* he is Gautier de Forois (p.133). R-S, p. 225.

William of Grandmesnil, 4. 37: mentioned by all the major sources, save FC. He was married to Robert Guiscard's daughter Mabel (June 1095) and had taken refuge at the Byzantine court following an unsuccessful rebellion in Apulia. See Jamison, pp. 199–200.

William of Montpellier, 2. 23: Count William V of Montpellier (dép. Hérault, Fr.). One of Raymond of Saint-Gilles' most important followers and as such mentioned in most of the sources. He stayed after Raymond's departure from Palestine in Aug. 1099, but was back in the Languedoc by 1103: R-S, p. 226.

William, 1. 28: William 'the Carpenter', viscount of Melun (dép. Seine-et-Marne, Fr.). In *ChA* 'Li carpentiers Guilelme' (p. 133).

William, 2. 39: son of Bohemond's sister Emma. According to *GF* (p. 5), William had travelled to the East with Hugh the Great. See Jamison, pp. 192–3.

William, 4. 37: William of Grandmesnil; see above.

William, 5. 24: William of Montpellier; see above.

Winemer of Boulogne, 3. 14: pirate leader. His role is described by AA and, following him, by WT (pp. 228; 362–3; 371). He is not otherwise known. See also 3. 59, 6. 55.

Yaghi-Siyan, 3. 35: Yāghisiyān, amir of Antioch, appointed by the Saljūq sultan Malik-Shāh. In the political fragmentation following Malik-Shāh's death in 1092 he achieved a large degree of practical autonomy: P. Holt, *The Age of the Crusades* (London, 1986), pp. 14–15.

Appendix 2: Places

(Form is that used in translation and reference is to first appearance.)

Acre, 5. 41: ‘Akkā (Arabic); ‘Akko (Hebrew). Fulcher of Chartres says some crusaders mistakenly called it Acharon, which was a Philistine city near Ascalon (FC pp. 274–5).
Adana, 3. 10: provincial capital, Adana, Tu.
Adrianople, 1. 6: Edirne (prov. Edirne, Tu.).
Albara, 5. 26: al-Bāra (prov. Idlib, Syr.). One of the ‘dead cities’ which had been prosperous under the Byzantines and occupied by Arabs after their departure.
Aleppo, 2. 39: Ḥalab (provincial capital, Syr.).
Alexandria the Lesser, 3. 26: Iskenderun (Alexandretta), prov. Hatay, Tu.
Altalon, 3. 37: near Antioch; not identified.
Amacha, 4. 8: not identified.
Amiens, 1. 2: dép. Somme, Fr.
Antioch the Less, 3. 3: (Antioch in Pisidia); now lost, site west of Yalvaç (prov. Isparta, Tu.).
Antioch, 2. 39: Antakya (provincial capital, Hatay, Tu.).
Antwerp, 3. 14: Antwerpen, Be.
Anzi, 3. 16: prov. Potenza, It.
Apulia, 2. 14: Puglia; region in S. It.
Armenia, 3. 17: principality in Caucasus region.
Arqa, 5. 31: ‘Arqa, N. Lebanon, near the modern border with Syria.
Arsuf, 6. 51: Arsūf (Arabic); Tel Arshaf (Hebrew); classical Apollonia.
Artah, 3. 28: near Reyhanlı (prov. Hatay, Tu.); a well fortified town in the twelfth century but deserted today (Cahen, *La Syrie du Nord*, p. 134).
Ascalon, 6. 4: Al-‘Asqalān (Arabic); Ashqelon (Hebrew).
Ascanian Lake, 2. 24: İznik Gölü, on the western side of Nicaea.
Astenois, 2. 23: a district of Champagne.
Aumale, 2. 23: dép. Seine-et-Maritime, Fr.
Avesnes, 6. 53: Avesnes-sur-Helpe (Pas-de-Calais, Fr.).
Avlona, 2. 18: modern Vlorë, Albania.
Azaz, 5. 5: A‘zāz (prov. Ḥalab, Syr.).

Bari, 2. 5: capital of Bari province and of Puglia region, It.
Barneville, 2. 27: prob. Barneville-Carteret (dép. Manche, Fr.).
Beauvais, 1. 9: dép. Oise, Fr.
Beirut, 5. 39: Bayrūt, capital of Lebanon.
Belgrade, 1. 6: Beograd, capital of Serbia-Montenegro.

Berry, 1. 2: former province in central Fr.
Bethlehem, 5. 44: Bayt Laḥm (Arabic).
Béziers, 2. 23: dép. Hérault, Fr.
Black Mountains, 3. 1: the Amanus range (Gävur Dağlari, Tu.), but used by AA for a range in Asia Minor.
Blois, 2. 21: dép. Loir-et-Cher, Fr.
Bouillon, 2. 22: Luxembourg province, Be.
Bourcq, 2. 1: dép. Ardennes, Fr.
Breteuil, 1. 9: dép. Oise, Fr.
Brittany, 2. 23: region in north-west Fr.
Broyes, 1. 7: near Epernay (dép. Marne, Fr.).
Burgundy, 2. 23: former duchy and province, now Fr.
Butentrot, 3. 5: Pozanti (prov. Adana, Tu.).

Caesarea, 5. 41: Qayṣariyya (Arabic); Qesari (Hebrew). Albert refers to it as Caesarea Cornelii in 5. 42, perhaps to distinguish it from other Caesareas, especially Caesarea Philippi. See Acts 10.
Caiphas, 5. 41: Ḥayfā (Arabic); Haifa (Hebrew).
Calabria, 2. 14: region in southern It.
Camels (valley of), 5. 31: there has been much discussion about the identification of this valley, for 'Camela' was the popular name for Ḥimṣ. However, from the context it must be al-Buqay'a (the plain of 'Akkār in N. Lebanon). Possibly, as Deschamps suggested, it was named for the camels bred there: P. Deschamps, *Les Châteaux des Croisés en Terre Sainte I: le Crac des Chevaliers* (Paris, 1934), p. 110.
Cappadocia, 1. 15: Kapadokya, region in central Anatolia.
Carinthia, 1. 29: state, now in southern Austria.
Castle of the Maidens, 3. 26: according to C. Cahen (pp. 148–9), in the foothills of the Amanus near the Sakaltoutan pass (the Syrian Gates) there is an Ottoman castle Kiz-Kalesi, which is a translation into Turkish of AA's 'Castrum Puellarum' (which AA places further north at Payas).
Castle of the Shepherds, 3. 26: not identified, but Cahen believed it preserved the memory of a real fortress: *La Syrie du Nord*, pp. 148–9.
Castle of the Young Men, 3. 26: A. W. Lawrence claimed 'de Bakelers' was a corruption of Baghras (now Bakras, prov. Hatay, Tu.), a castle which guarded the Belen pass north of Antioch: 'The castle of Baghras', *The Cilician Kingdom of Armenia*, (ed.) T. S. R. Boase (Edinburgh, 1978), pp. 34–83, at 41.
Champagne, 3. 23: historic province in north-east Fr.
Chappes, 2. 23: nr Bar-sur-Seine (dép. Aube, Fr.).
Chartres, 2. 35: dép. Eure-et-Loir, Fr.
Chaumont, 2. 23: Chaumont-en-Vexin (dép. Oise, Fr.).
Choques, 6. 8: village near Thérouanne (dép. Pas-de-Calais, Fr.).
Civitot, 1. 15: Hersek (prov. Kocaeli, Tu.).
Clermont, 1. 5: modern Clermont-Ferrand (dép. Puy-de-Dôme, Fr.).

Clermont, 3. 16: Clermont-sous-Huy (prov. Liège, Be.).
Cologne, 1. 26: city in Nordrhein-Westfalen, Ger.
Combrus, 3. 38: north of Antioch; not identified.
Cons, 2. 1: Cons-la-Grandville (dép. Meurthe-et-Moselle, Fr.).
Constantinople, 1. 6: İstanbul, Turkey.
Curzh, 4. 8: not identified.

Damascus, 3. 33: Dimashq, capital of Syria.
Dandronuch, 4. 6: not identified.
Degorganhi (valley), 2. 38: see Orellis.
Domedart, 2. 23: prob. Domart-en-Ponthieu (dép. Somme, Fr.).
Drava (river), 2. 6: or Drau; flows into the Danube east of Osijek (Croatia).
Dyrachium, 2. 18: Durrës, Albania (Durazzo).

Edessa, 3. 19: Şanliurfa, provincial capital in south-east Anatolia, Tu.
Egypt, 3. 59: translates 'Babylonia'.
Emmaus, 5. 43: 'Amwās (Arabic), some 15 miles west of Jerusalem. Ancient Nichopolis according to WT (p. 376). See R. D. Pringle, *The Churches of the Crusader Kingdom of Jerusalem* (4 vols, Cambridge, 1993-2009–), vol. 1, pp. 52–3.
Episcopate, 5. 27: not identified.
Esch, 2. 1: Esch-sur-Sûre (G-D Luxembourg).
Etampes, 1. 7: dép. Essonne, Fr.
Fère, La, 2. 22: dép. Aisne, Fr.
Ferna, 3. 54: in Asia Minor; not identified.
Foloroca, 4. 6: not identified.
Forez, 2. 22: former province in central Fr.
Francavilla, 2. 6: Modern Slankamen, north-west of Belgrade (Serbia-Montenegro).
Frisia, 3. 14: coastal region on North Sea.

Garlande, 2. 27: not identified.
Gorgania, 2. 43: see Orellis.
Gournay, 2. 23: Gournay-en-Bray (dép. Seine-et-Maritime, Fr.).
Grez, 2. 1: Grez-Doiceau (prov. Brabant-Wallon, Be.).

Hainaut, 2. 8: province of Wallonia, Be.
Hamersbach, 4. 47: Hemmersbach (Kr. Bergheim, Nordrhein-Westfalen, Ger.).
Hantax (river), 2. 6: in Hungary; not identified.
Harim, 3. 60: Ḥārim (prov. Idlib, Syria).
Haruni, 4. 6: not identified.
Heraclea, 3. 3: Ereğli (prov. Konya, Tu.).

Iconium, 3. 3: Konya (provincial capital, Tu.).

Isle of Flanders, 2. 29: Lille (or L'Isle), dép. Nord, Fr.

Jabala, 5. 33: prov. al-Lādhiqiyyah, Syr.
Jehosaphat (valley of), 5. 46: runs north-south outside the eastern wall of Jerusalem.
Jubayl, 5. 38: ancient Byblos, Lebanon.
Judas (gate), 3. 5: the Cilician Gates, a pass through the mountains.
Jussey, 2. 23: dép. Haute-Saône, Fr.

Karan, 4. 8: possibly Harran (prov. Şanliurfa, Tu.).
Kenzvillare, 6. 34: prob. Kinzweiler (Kr. Aachen, Nordrhein-Westfalen), a hamlet some 7 miles north-east of Aachen.
Ketena, 6. 34: poss. Ketelwald, 'silva Ketela', the old name of the royal forest, near Kleve, Nordrhein-Westfalen, about 70 miles north of Aachen: M. Gysseling, *Toponymisch woordenboek van Belgie, Nederland, Luxembourg, Noord-Frankrijk en West-Duitsland, vóór 1226* (2 vols, Brussels, 1960), vol. 1, p. 561, s.v. *Ketelwald.*
Khurasan, 1. 17: Khurāsān, Iran. Khurāsān had been one of the first lands to be conquered by the Saljūq Turks after their migration from their original homeland and continued to form the most easterly part of the Saljūq empire. Albert may have used the name to emphasise the vastness of the Turkish possessions. See A. V. Murray, '*Coroscane:* homeland of the Saracens in the *chansons de geste* and the historiography of the crusades', *Aspects de l'épopée romane: Mentalités – Idéologies – Intertextualités*, (ed.) Hans van Dik and Willem Noomen (Groningen, 1995), pp. 177–84.

Lant, 2. 22: Ghent (prov. Oost-Vlaanderen, Be.).
Latakia, 3. 59: al-Lādhiqiyyah (provincial capital, Syr.); classical Laodicia.
Le Puiset, 3. 33: dép. Eure-et-Loir, Fr.
Le Puy, 1. 5: dép. Haute-Loire, Fr.
Leukai, 2. 38n.: now Orhaneli (prov. Bursa, Tu.).
Leitha (river), 1. 28: not identified.
Lotharingia, 1. 5: duchy in north-west Europe; considerably larger than the modern Fr. region of Lorraine.
Lydda, 5. 42n: Ludd (Arabic); Lod (Hebrew).

Ma'arra, 5. 26: Ma'arrat-an-Nu'mān (prov. Idlib, Syr.).
Mainz, 1. 27: capital city of Rheinland-Pfalz, Ger.
Malabrunias, 3. 1: not identified.
Malavilla, see Zemun.
Mamistra, 3. 15: Mopsuestia (classical), now Misis (prov. Adana, Tu.).
Marash, 3. 27: Kahramanmaraş (provincial capital, Tu.) situated on a cross-roads in the foothills of the Taurus mountains: Cahen, *La Syrie du Nord*, pp. 137–8.
Mechelen, 4. 35: Maasmechelen, north of Maastricht, Be.

Melitene, 4. 6: Malatya (provincial capital, Tu.).
Mesopotamia, 3. 19: area of Tigris-Euphrates river system.
Metz, 3. 46: capital city (dép. Moselle, Fr.).
Meuse (river), 4. 35: Maas (Flemish).
Mons, 2. 22: dép. Nord, Fr.
Montaigu, 2. 11: prov. Luxembourg, Be.
Montbéliard, 2. 23: dép. Doubs, Fr.
Montmerle, 2. 23: dép. Ain, Fr.
Montpellier, 2. 23: dép. Hérault, Fr.
Mosony, 1. 23: Mosonmagyaróvár (co. Györ-Moson-Sopron, Hu.); former German name Wieselburg.
Mouchy, 4. 47: Mouchy-le-Châtel (dép. Oise, Fr.).
Mount of Olives, 5. 46: outside the walls of Jerusalem to the east.
Mount Sinai, 6. 34: in the Egyptian desert.
Mount Sion, 6. 6: south of Jerusalem.
Mousson, 2. 23: dép. Meurthe-et-Moselle, Fr.

Nesle, 2. 1: dép. Somme, Fr.
Neuss, 1. 26: Nordrhein-Westfalen, Ger.
Nicaea, 1. 15: İznik (prov. Bursa, Tu.).
Nicomedia, 1. 15: İzmit (prov. Kocaeli, Tu.).
Nijmegen, 2. 23: Gelderland, east Neths.
Niš, 1. 6: Serbia-Montenegro.
Niz, 4. 8: not identified.

Orange, 2. 23: dép. Vaucluse, Fr.
Orellis (valleys), 3. 3: the name given in AA 2. 38, 40, to the valley 'de Gorghani'; site of battle of Dorylaeum (prov. Eskişehir, Tu.).
Orléans, 1. 12: dép. Loiret, Fr.
Orontes (river), 3. 31: the Orontes (al-'Āṣī) rises in modern Lebanon and flows through Syria and Turkey, reaching the sea south-west of Antioch at the crusaders' Port of St Symeon.

Pannonhalma, 2. 3: co. Györ-Moson-Sopron, Hu.; religious centre.
Philippi, 3. 54: in western Europe(?); not identified.
Philippopolis, 1. 6: Plovdiv, Bulgaria.
Philomelium, 3. 3: Akşehir (prov. Konya, Tu.).
Possesse, 2. 22: dép. Marne, Fr.

Quierzy, 2. 22: dép. Aisne, Fr.

Ramla, 5. 42: Al-Ramla (Arabic); Ramla (Hebrew).

Ravendel, 3. 17: Revanda kale, Tu. Turbessel and Ravendel are discussed in R. Gardiner, 'Crusader Turkey: the fortifications of Edessa', *Fortress*, 2 (1989), pp. 23–35.
Regensburg, 5. 23: Oberpfalz, Ger. (formerly Ratisbon).
Ribemont, 2. 22: dép. Aisne, Fr.
Rossa, 4. 13: poss. the Rūj valley. (See also 8. 2; 12. 19).
Roussillon, 2. 23: dép. Isère, Fr.
Rozoy, 3. 28: Rozoy-sur-Serre (dép. Aisne, Fr.).
Rufinel, 2. 20: poss. Nicomedia (İzmit, prov. Kocaeli, Tu.).
Rūm, 1. 17: used for 'Romania', Turkish possessions formerly part of the Byzantine empire, to avoid confusion with the modern country.

St Argent, 2. 13: nr palace of Blachernae, Constantinople.
St George (Arm of), 1. 6: straits between Europe and Asia, Constantinople.
Saint-Gilles, 2. 20: dép. Gard, Fr.
St John, 3. 21: fortress near Samosata; not identified.
St Martin's oratory, 1. 24: in Pannonhalma (co. Györ-Moson-Sopron, Hu.).
St Mary at the Granaries (convent), 2. 37: in the Oeren (Euren) district of Trier.
St Mary of the Latins (church), 6. 25: also known as St Mary Minor, in the Muristan close to the church of the Holy Sepulchre, Jerusalem.
St Paul's Gate, 3. 38: northern gate of Antioch, identified by WT (p. 251).
Saint-Pol, 2. 22: Saint-Pol-sur-Ternoise (dép. Pas de Calais, Fr.).
St Stephen's (church), 6. 9: to the north of Jerusalem.
St Symeon (port), 3. 42: al-Suwaydīyya (Ancient Seleucia Pieria), near Çevlik (prov. Hatay, Tu.); south-west of Antioch on the coast.
Sakarya, river, 3. 2: in Asia Minor (identification not certain).
Salabria, 2. 8: Silivri, on the Sea of Marmora near Constantinople (prov. İstanbul, Turkey).
Salerno, 3. 15: prov. Campania, It.
Samarthan, 4. 3: city in Khurāsān. Meyer identified Samarthan as Samarkand (*RHC Occ* iv. 390), but it is more likely to be a version of *Sormasane*, found in *Les Chétifs*. Myers suggested this was Hamadhān, the sultan's capital: *Les Chétifs*, p. xxiv, or Albert may be reflecting the fabled wealth of Is̱fahān which had been the magnificent capital of Malik-Shāh, though contested by his sons and not in Barkyārūq's possession at this point. None of these cities is within historical Khurāsān, but, as before, Albert seems to use the word to refer to the greater Saljūq empire. PT lists 'Gorbandus impius de Samarzana' as one of the 75 legendary kings of Antioch (p. 120).
Samosart, 4. 8: prob. Samosata.
Samosata, 3. 21: site now submerged beneath the lake made by the building of the Atatürk dam, near Samsat (prov. Malatya, Tu.).
Sarus (river – classical name) or Seyhan (Turkish): flows through Adana (not named by AA: 3. 10).

Sava (river), 1. 6: The Sava flows into the Danube near Belgrade. AA's geography in Book 1 is mistaken; he calls the river the Morava, but it is the Sava that separates Belgrade and Zemun. William of Tyre copies his mistake (p. 141). AA names the Sava correctly in Book 2.

Sea of Palestine (Palestine sea), 6. 54: eastern Mediterranean.

Sidon, 5. 40: Ṣaydā, Lebanon.

Sofiya, 1. 6: capital of Bulgaria.

Sooch, 4. 10: Cahen conjectured that 'Castle Sooch' was 'un Tell ach-Chaïkh entre Mardin et Hiçn Kaïfa qui fut au XIIe siècle un fréquent lieu de rendez-vous', at or near Diyarbakır (Tu.), north-east of Edessa on the river Tigris: *Syrie du Nord*, p. 215 n. 35. In *ChA* the meeting place is 'Soces', which Duparc-Quioc tentatively identifies as Ra's al-'Ain (Tu. Resūlayn), further south and now on the Syrian-Turkish border, approximately equidistant from Aleppo and Mosul (*Edition*, p. 276).

Sopron, 1. 7: co. Györ-Moson-Sopron, Hu.; on the north-west border of Hungary, some 40 miles south of Vienna.

Sororgia, 3. 25: Suruç (prov. Şanliurfa, Tu.).

Swabia, 1. 23: region in southwestern Ger.

Talamria, 5. 30: poss. Tell-Mannas (prov. Idlib, Syr.); although Tell-Mannas is much closer to Ma'arra than Albert's account suggests. Furthermore, it is recorded in the *Gesta Francorum* that 'Talamania' was taken earlier by Raymond Pilet (pp. 73–4). According to Kemal al-Din, the crusaders made their siege-tower from timber cut down in the neighbourhood of Ma'arra (p. 587).

Tarsus, 2. 39: prov. Içel, Tu.

Temple (palace) of King Solomon, 6. 13: the Temple Mount, Jerusalem.

Tiel, 6. 55: Tiel, Gelderland, Neths. Riant translated *Tila* as Thule and asserted that there were Danes in Winemer's fleet: P. Riant, *Expéditions et pèlerinages des Scandinaves en Terre Sainte* (Paris, 1865), p. 134.

Tirs, 2. 23: not identified.

Tortosa, 5. 31: Tarṭūs (provincial capital, Syr.).

Toul, 2. 1: dép. Meurthe-et-Moselle, Fr.

Tournai, 6. 11, prov. Hainaut, Be.

Tower of David, 3. 59: citadel of Jerusalem.

Traves, 2. 23: dép. Haute-Saône, Fr.

Trier, 2. 37: city in Rheinland-Pfalz, Ger.

Tripoli, 5. 37: Ṭarābulus, port in N. Lebanon.

Tulln, 2. 1: Niederösterreich, Austria; some 25 miles (40km) west of Vienna on the river Danube. As the residence of the Babenberg dynasty 1042–1113, Tulln was effectively the capital of Austria at the time of the expedition.

Turbessel, 3. 17: Tilbaşir, Tu. Turbessel and Ravendel are discussed in R. Gardiner, 'Crusader Turkey: the fortifications of Edessa', *Fortress*, 2 (1989), pp. 23–35.

Tyre, 5. 41: Ṣūr: city in S. Lebanon.

valley of Joy, 5. 31: poss. part of Orontes valley.
Vendeuil, 2. 1: dép. Aisne, Fr.
Verva, 5. 40: poss. Verveis.
Verveis, 2. 23: poss. Verviers (prov. Liège, Be.).
Verzellaus, 1. 5: probably Vercelli (prov. Vercelli, It.). Urban is known to have been in Lombardy in the summer of 1095: F. Duncalf, 'The Councils of Piacenza and Clermont', *Wisconsin History* i. 230. However, William of Tyre has *Vigiliacum* (WT p. 130) and this seems to be the source of later accounts which place Urban in Vézelay. It must be acknowledged that Albert's geography becomes more unreliable the further he ventures from Aachen, which may explain the ambiguity as to whether Urban crossed the Alps before or after 'Verzellaus'.

Waiferii (gate), 3. 39: also called the Dog Gate (WT, p. 252). The name is possibly a corruption of 'Farfari', from the colloquial name for the river, or a mishearing of (a version of) line 2910 in the *ChA* (p. 175): 'vers pont de Fer'.
Wissant, 3. 27: dép. Pas-de-Calais, Fr.

Zemun, 1. 6: Semlin, Serbia-Montenegro. Whether Zemun acquired its sinister Latin name, 'Mala villa', as a result of the events described in Book 1, or at an earlier time, has not been established (*Enciklopedija Jugoslavije* 8 [Zagreb, 1971], s.v. *Zemun*).

Bibliography

See also **Abbreviations** for works frequently cited.

Primary

Acard of Arrouaise: Paul Lehmann, 'Die mittellateinischen Dichtungen der Prioren des Tempels von Jerusalem Acardus und Gaufridus', *Corona Quernea: Festgabe Karl Strecker*, *Schriften des MGH*, 6 *(Leipzig: K. W. Hiersemann, 1941).*

Alberic of Troisfontaines, *Chronica*, *MGH SS* 23.

Anna Komnene, *The Alexiad*, trans. Edgar R. A. Sewter, rev. edn Peter Frankopan (London: Penguin, 2009).

Annalista Saxo, MGH SS 6.

Bernold of St Blasien, *Chronicon*, *MGH SS* 5.

Caffaro, *Annales Ianuenses*, (ed.) Luigi T. Belgrano, *Annali Genovesi*, 1 (*Fonti per la storia d'Italia*, 11, Genoa, 1890): 3–75.

Caffaro, *Regni Iherosolimitani Brevis Historia, Annali Genovesi*, 1: 127–46.

Caffaro, *De liberatio civitatum Orientis liber, Annali Genovesi*, 1: 99–124.

The Canso d'Antioca: *An Occitan Epic Chronicle of the First Crusade*, (ed.) Carol Sweetenham and Linda M. Paterson (Aldershot: Ashgate, 2003).

La Chanson d'Antioche, (ed.) Suzanne Duparc-Quioc (2 vols, Paris: Paul Geuthner, 1976), vol. 1: *Edition.*

The Chanson d'Antioche, (trans.) Susan B. Edgington and Carol Sweetenham (Farnham: Ashgate, 2011).

La Chanson de Jérusalem, (ed.) Nigel R. Thorp (Tuscaloosa, AL: University of Alabama, 1992).

La Chanson de Roland, (ed.) Gerard J. Brault (2 vols, London: Pennsylvania University Press, 1978); (ed.) Robert Fawtier (Paris: E. de Boccard, 1933).

Chartes de Forez, (ed.) Georges Guichard et al (24 vols, Mâcon: Protat, 1933–70).

Chartes de l'abbaye de Saint-Hubert en Ardenne, (ed.) Godefroid Kurth (2 vols, Brussels: n. pub., 1903).

Le Chevalier au Cygne et Godefroid de Bouillon, (ed.) Frédéric de Reiffenberg and Adolphe Borgnet (3 vols, Brussels: M. Hayez, 1846–59).

Les Chétifs, (ed.) Geoffrey M. Myers (Tuscaloosa, AL: University of Alabama, 1981).

Chronicles of St Bertin, RHGF 13.

Chronicon pictum Vindobonense, SSRH 1.

Chronicon S. Andreae, MGH SS 7.

Die Chronik der Grafen von Zimmern. Handschriften 580 und 581 der Fürstlich Fürstenbergischen Bibliothek Donaueschingen, (ed.) Hansmartin Decker-Hauff (Stuttgart: J. Thorbecke, 1964).

Cosmas of Prague, *Die Chronik der Böhmen des Cosmas von Prague*, (ed.) Bertold Bretholz (Berlin: Weidmannsche Verlagsbuchhandlung, 1923).

Danmarks Riges Historie, (ed.) Johannes C. H. Steenstrup et al. (6 vols, Copenhagen: n. pub., 1904–07).

Diplomata Hungariae Antiquissima, (ed.) György Györffy (2 vols, Budapest: Academia Scientarum Hungarica, 1992).

Enchiridion Euchologicum Fontium Liturgicorum (Rome: C. L. V.-Edizioni liturgiche, 1979).

S. Eusebii Hieronymi, *Liber de viris illustribus, PL* 23.

S. Eusebii Hieronymi, *Commentarium in Epistolam ad Galatos, PL* 23.

Ekkehard: *Frutolfs und Ekkehards Chroniken und die anonyme Kaiserchronik*, (ed. and trans.) Franz-Josef Schmale and Irene Schmale-Ott (Darmstadt: Wissenschaftliche Buchgesellschaft, 1972).

Fulcher of Chartres, *Fulcheri Carnotensis Historia Hierosolymitana (1095–1127)*, (ed.) Heinrich Hagenmeyer (Heidelberg: Carl Winter's Universitätsbuchhandlung, 1913).

Gesta Francorum, (ed.) Heinrich Hagenmeyer (Heidelberg: Carl Winter's Universitätsbuchhandlung, 1890); *Histoire Anonyme de la Première Croisade*, (ed.) Louis Bréhier (Paris: Champion, 1924).

Gesta Francorum expugnantium Iherusalem (attributed to Bartolf of Nangis) *RHC Occ* 3.

Gesta Normannorum Ducum, (ed.) Elisabeth M. C. van Houts (2 vols, Oxford: OMT, 1992–95).

Gesta Triumphalia per Pisanos facta de captione Hierusalem, (ed.) Ludovico Muratori, *Rerum Italicarum Scriptores*, 6. 2 (Bologna: Zanichelli, 1930).

Gilo of Paris, *The* Historia Vie Hierosimitane *of Gilo of Paris*, (ed.) Christopher W. Grocock and J. Elizabeth Siberry (Oxford: OMT, 1997).

Guibert of Nogent, *Dei gesta per Francos*, (ed.) Robert B. C. Huygens, *CCCM*, 127A (Turnhout, 1996).

Historia belli sacri, RHC Occ 3.

Kemal al-Din, 'Ta'rīḳḥ Halab' *RHC Or* 3.

Laurence of Liège, *MGH SS* 10.

Matthew of Edessa, *Chronicle*, trans. as *Armenia and the Crusades*, Ara E. Dostourian (New York: University Press of America, 1993).

Michael Psellus, *Fourteen Byzantine Rulers*, (trans.) Edgar R. A. Sewter (Harmondsworth: Penguin, 1966).

Paulinus, *Vita Sancti Ambrosii Mediolanensis Episcopi, PL* 14.

Peter Tudebode, *Historia de Hierosolymitano itinere*, (ed.) John H. Hill and Laurita L. Hill, Documents relatifs à l'histoire des croisades, 12 (Paris: Paul Geuthner, 1977); (trans.) J. H. and L. L. Hill, Memoirs of the American Philosophical Society, 101 (Philadelphia: American Philosophical Society, 1974).

Pseudo-Turpin: *Historia Karoli Magni et Rotholandi ou Chronique du Pseudo-Turpin*, (ed.) Cyril Meredith-Jones (Paris: E. Droz, 1936); *An Anonymous Old French Translation of the Pseudo-Turpin Chronicle*, (ed.) Ronald N. Walpole (Cambridge, MA: Mediaeval Academy of America, 1979).

Recueil des chartes de l'abbaye de Cluny, (ed.) Auguste Bernard and Louis A. Bruel (6 vols, Paris: n. pub., 1876–1903).

Rosenfeld Annals, *MGH SS* 16.

William of Jumièges, *Gesta Normannorum ducum*, (ed.) Elisabeth M. C. van Houts (2 vols, Oxford: OMT, 1992–95).

Secondary

Aird, William M., *Robert `Curthose', Duke of Normandy (c.1050–1134)* (Woodbridge: Boydell, 2008).

Andressohn, John C., *The Ancestry and Life of Godfrey of Bouillon* (Bloomington, IN: University of Indiana, 1947).

Aubé, Pierre, *Godefroy de Bouillon* (Paris: Fayard, 1985).

Beaumont, André A., 'Albert of Aachen and the County of Edessa', *The Crusades and other Historical Essays presented to D. C. Munro*, (ed.) Louis J. Paetow (New York: F. S. Crofts, 1928): 101–38.

Blake, Ernest O. and Colin Morris, 'A hermit goes to war: Peter and the origins of the first crusade', *Studies in Church History*, 22 (1985): 79–107.

Brundage, James A., 'Adhémar of Puy and his critics', *Speculum*, 34 (1959): 201–10.

———, 'An errant crusader: Stephen of Blois', *Traditio*, 16 (1960): 380–95.

Bruylants, Placide, *Les Oraisons du Missel Romain: Texte et Histoire* (2 vols, Louvain: Centre de Documentation et d'Information Liturgiques, 1952).

Cahen, Claude, *La Syrie du nord à l'époque des croisades et la principauté Franque d'Antioche* (Paris: Paul Geuthner, 1940).

Cansdale, George, *Animals of Bible Lands* (Exeter: Paternoster Press, 1970).

Chabot, Jean-Baptiste, 'Edesse pendant la première croisade', *Comptes rendues de l'Académie des inscriptions et belles lettres* (Paris, 1918): 431–42.

Charanis, Peter, 'The Byzantine Empire in the eleventh century', *Wisconsin History*, 1: 177–219.

Chazan, Robert, *European Jewry and the First Crusade* (London: University of California Press, 1987).

Cohen, Jeremy, 'The Hebrew crusade chronicles in their Christian cultural context', *Juden und Christen zur Zeit der Kreuzzüge*, (ed.) Alfred Haverkamp (Sigmaringen: J. Thorbecke, 1999): 17–34.

Cook, Robert F., *'Chanson d'Antioche', chanson de geste: le cycle de la croisade est-il epique?* (Amsterdam: Benjamins, 1980).

Cottineau, Laurent H. (ed.), *Répertoire topo-bibliographique des abbayes et prieurés* (2 vols, Mâcon: Protat frères, 1935–37).

Daniel, Norman, *The Arabs and Medieval Europe* (2nd edn, London: Longman, 1979).

David, Charles W., *Robert Curthose, Duke of Normandy* (Cambridge, MA: Harvard University Press, 1920).

Deschamps, Paul, *Les Châteaux des Croisés en Terre Sainte I: le Crac des Chevaliers* (Paris: Paul Geuthner, 1934).

Dossetti, Giuseppe L., *Il simbolo di Nicea e di Costantinopoli* (Rome: Herder, 1967).

Du Cange, Charles, *Glossarium mediae et infimae Latinitatis: conditum a Carolo du Fresne, domino Du Cange; cum supplementis integris D. P. Carpenterii, Adelungii, aliorum, susque digessit G. A. L. Henschel* (10 vols, Niort: Favre, 1883–87).

Duncalf, Frederic, 'The Councils of Piacenza and Clermont', *Wisconsin History* 1: 220–52.

Duparc-Quioc, Suzanne (ed.), *La Chanson d'Antioche*, (2 vols, Paris, 1976): vol. 1 *Edition*; vol. 2 *Etude*.

Dupront, Alphonse, 'La spiritualité des croisés et des pèlerins d'après les sources de la première croisade', *Convegni del Centro di Studi sulla spiritualità medievale*, 4 (1963): 451–83.

Ebels-Hoving, Bunna, *Byzantium in westerse ogen 1096–1204* (Assen: Gorcum, 1971).

Edgington, Susan B., 'The *Historia Iherosolimitana* of Albert of Aachen: A Critical Edition', Ph.D. thesis (London, 1991).

———, 'The doves of war: the part played by carrier pigeons in the crusades', *Autour de la Première Croisade*, (ed.) Michel Balard (Paris: Publications de la Sorbonne, 1996): 167–75.

———, 'The First Crusade: reviewing the evidence', *The First Crusade: Origins and Impact*, (ed.) Jonathan Phillips (Manchester: Manchester University Press, 1997): 57–77.

———, 'Albert of Aachen and the *chansons de geste*', *The Crusades and their Sources: Essays Presented to Bernard Hamilton*, (ed.) John. France and William G. Zajac (Aldershot: Ashgate, 1998): 23–37.

Flori, Jean, *Pierre l'Ermite et la Première Croisade* (Paris: Fayard, 1999).

France, John, 'The text of the account of the capture of Jerusalem in the Ripoll Manuscript, Bibliothèque Nationale (Latin) 5132', *English Historical Review*, 103 (1988): 641–57.

———, *Victory in the East: A Military History of the First Crusade* (Cambridge: Cambridge University Press, 1994).

Frolow, Anatole, *La Relique de la Vraie Croix* (Paris: Institut français d'études byzantines, 1961).

Gardiner, Robert, 'Crusader Turkey: the fortifications of Edessa', *Fortress*, 2 (1989): 23–35.

Green, Dennis H., *The Millstätter Exodus* (Cambridge: Cambridge University Press, 1966).

Grierson, Philip, *Byzantine Coins* (London: Methuen, 1982).

Hamilton, Bernard, *The Latin Church in the Crusader States: The Secular Church* (London: Variorum, 1980).

Hatem, Anouar, *Les Poèmes épiques des croisades: genèse – historicité – localisation* (Paris: Paul Geuthner, 1932).

Hill, John H. and Laurita L., 'Contemporary accounts and the later reputation of Adhémar, bishop of Puy', *Medievalia et Humanistica*, 9 (1955): 30–38.

———, *Raymond IV de Saint-Gilles 1041 (ou 1042)–1105* (Toulouse: Privat, 1959).

———, *Raymond IV, Count of Toulouse* (Syracuse, NY: Syracuse University Press, 1962).

Hill, Rosalind M., 'The Christian view of the Muslims at the time of the First Crusade', *The Eastern Mediterranean Lands in the Period of the Crusades*, (ed.) Peter M. Holt (Warminster: Aris and Phillips, 1977): 1–8.

Holt, Peter M., *The Age of the Crusades: The Near East from the 11th Century to 1517* (London: Longman, 1986).

Jamison, Evelyn M, 'Some notes on the *Anonymi Gesta Francorum*, with special reference to the Norman contingent from South Italy and Sicily in the first crusade,' *Studies in French Language and Mediaeval Literature presented to Professor Mildred K. Pope* (Manchester: Manchester University Press, 1939): 183–208.

Jensen, Janus M., 'Danmark og den hellige krig. En undersøgelse af korstogsbevægelsens indflydelse på Danmark ca. 1070–1169', *Historisk Tidsskrift*, 100 (2000): 285–328.

Kalić, Jovanka, 'Les données d'Albert d'Aix sur l'histoire des relations Byzantino-Hongroises vers la fin du XIe siècle' [in Serbo-Croat], *Recueil de travaux de la Faculté de philosophie*, 10 (1968): 189–90.

Kedar, Benjamin Z., *Crusade and Mission: European Approaches toward the Muslims* (Princeton, NJ: Princeton University Press, 1984).

Knappen, Marshall M., 'Robert II of Flanders in the first crusade', *The Crusades and other Historical Essays presented to Dana C. Munro*, (ed.) Louis J. Paetow (New York: F. S. Crofts, 1928): 79–100.

Knoch, Peter, *Studien zu Albert von Aachen* (Stuttgart: Klett, 1966).

Krey, August C., 'A neglected passage in the *Gesta* and its bearing on the literature of the first crusade', *The Crusades and other Historical Essays presented to Dana C. Munro*, (ed.) Louis J. Paetow (New York: F. S. Crofts, 1928): 57–78.

Kriszt, Gyorgy, *Medieval Churches of Hungary* (Budapest: Hungarian News Agency, 1990).

Kugler, Bernhard, 'Peter der Eremite und Albert von Aachen', *Historische Zeitschrift*, 44 (1880): 22–42.

———, *Eine Neue Handschrift der Chronik Alberts von Aachen* (Tübingen: n. pub., 1893).

———, *Die Deutschen Codices Alberts von Aachen* (Tübingen: n. pub., 1894).

Kuhn, Fritz, 'Zur Kritik Alberts von Aachen', *Neues Archiv der Gesellschaft für ältere deutsche Geschichtskunde*, 12 (1887): 545–58.

La Monte, John, 'The lords of Le Puiset on the Crusades', *Speculum*, 17 (1942): 100–18.

Laurent, Joseph, 'Les Arméniens de Cilicie', *Mélanges Schlumberger*, 1 (Paris, 1924): 159–68.

———, 'Des Grecs aux croisés: Étude sur l'histoire d'Edesse', *Byzantion*, 1 (1924): 404–34.

Lawrence, Arnold W., 'The castle of Baghras', *The Cilician Kingdom of Armenia*, (ed.) T. S. R. Boase (Edinburgh: Scottish Academic Press, 1978): 34–83.

Leyser, Karl, 'Money and supplies on the first crusade', *Communications and Power in Medieval Europe: The Gregorian Revolution and Beyond*, (ed.) Timothy Reuter (London: Hambledon, 1994): 77–95.

Lilie, Ralph-Johannes, *Byzantium and the Crusader States, 1096–1204* (Oxford: Clarendon Press, 1993).

Matzke, Michael, *Daibert von Pisa: Zwischen Pisa, Papst und erstem Kreuzzug* (Sigmaringen: Thorbecke, 1998).

Mayer, Hans E., 'The origins of the lordships of Ramla and Lydda in the Latin Kingdom of Jerusalem', *Speculum*, 60 (1985): 537–52.

———, *The Crusades* (2nd edn, Oxford, 1988).

Metcalf, David M., *Coinage of the Crusades and the Latin East in the Ashmolean Museum Oxford* (London: Royal Numismatic Society, 1995).

Meuthen, Erich, *Aachener Urkunden 1101–1250* (Bonn: P. Hanstein, 1972).

Minis, Cola, 'Stilelemente in der Kreuzzugschronik des Albert von Aachen und in der volksprachigen Epik, besonders in der "Chanson de Roland"', *Literatur und Sprache im europäischen Mittelalter: Festschrift für Karl Langosch* (ed.) A. Önnersfors, J. Rathofer and F. Wagner (Darmstadt: Wissenschaftliche Buchgesellschaft, 1973): 356–63.

Möhring, Hannes, 'Graf Emicho und die Judenverfolgungen von 1096', *Rheinische Vierteljahrsblätter*, 56 (1992): 97–111.

Morris, Colin, 'Policy and visions: The case of the Holy Lance found at Antioch', *War and Government in the Middle Ages: Essays in Honour of J. O. Prestwich*, (ed.) J. Gillingham and J. C. Holt (Woodbridge, 1984): 33–45.

Murray, Alan V., 'The Army of Godfrey of Bouillon, 1096–1099: structure and dynamics of a contingent on the First Crusade', *Revue belge de philologie et d'histoire*, 70 (1992), 301–29.

———, '*Coroscane:* homeland of the Saracens in the *chansons de geste* and the historiography of the crusades', *Aspects de l'épopée romane: Mentalités – Idéologies – Intertextualités*, (ed.) Hans van Dik and Willem Noomen (Groningen: E. Forsten, 1995): 177–84.

———, 'The Chronicle of Zimmern as a source for the First Crusade', *The First Crusade: Origins and Impact*, (ed.) J. P. Phillips (Manchester: Manchester University Press, 1997): 78–106.

———, *The Crusader Kingdom of Jerusalem: A Dynastic History 1099–1125*, Occasional Publications of the Linacre Unit for Prosopographical Research, vol. 4 (Oxford, 2000).

Nicholson, Robert L., *Tancred: Crusading Leader and Lord of Galilee and Antioch* (Chicago, IL: Chicago University Press, 1940).

Nicolle, David, *Arms and Armour of the Crusading Era, 1050–1350* (2 vols, New York: Greenhill, 1988).

Paris, Paulin, *Nouvelle étude sur la Chanson d'Antioche* (Paris: L. Techener, 1878).

Partington, James R., *A History of Greek Fire and Gunpowder* (Cambridge: W. Heffer, 1960).

Phillips, William D., 'Sugar production and trade in the Mediterranean at the time of the crusades', *The Meeting of Two Worlds: Cultural Exchange between East and West during the Period of the Crusades*, (ed.) Vladimir P. Goss (Kalamazoo, MI: Medieval Institute Publications, 1986): 393–406.

Poliakov, Léon, *The History of Anti-Semitism* (2 vols, London: Routledge & Kegan Paul, 1974–85).

Prawer, Joshua, *Crusader Institutions* (Oxford: Clarendon Press, 1980).

———, 'The Jerusalem the crusaders captured: a contribution to the medieval topography of the city', *Crusade and Settlement*, (ed.) Peter W. Edbury (Cardiff: University College Cardiff Press, 1985): 1–16.

Pringle, Denys, *The Churches of the Crusader Kingdom of Jerusalem* (4 vols, Cambridge: Cambridge University Press, 1993–2009).

Pryor, John H., 'The oath of the leaders of the first crusade to Emperor Alexius I Comnenus', *Parergon*, n.s., 2 (1984): 111–41.

Rassow, Peter, 'Der Text der Kreuzzugsbulle Eugens III', *Neues Archiv*, 45 (1924): 302–5.

Riant, Paul, *Expéditions et pèlerinages des Scandinaves en Terre Sainte* (Paris: Imprimerie de A. D. Lainé et J. Havard, 1865).

Richard, Jean, 'Quelques textes sur les premiers temps de l'église latine de Jérusalem', *Recueil Clovis Brunel*, 2 (1955): 420–30.

Riley-Smith, Jonathan, 'The title of Godfrey of Bouillon', *Bulletin of the Institute of Historical Research*, 52 (1979): 83–6.

———, *The First Crusade and the Idea of Crusading* (London: Athlone, 1986).

———, *The First Crusaders, 1095–1131* (Cambridge: Cambridge University Press, 1997).

Riley-Smith, Louise and Jonathan, *The Crusades: Idea and Reality, 1095–1274* (London: Edward Arnold, 1981).

Röhricht, Reinhold, *Regesta Regni Hierosolymitani* (Innsbruck: Libraria Academica Wageriana, 1893; *Additamentum* 1904).

Rousset, Paul, *Les origines et les caractères de la première croisade* (Neuchâtel: Ed. de la Baconnière, 1945).

Runciman, Steven, 'The Holy Lance found at Antioch', *Analecta Bollandiana*, 88 (1950): 197–205.

———, *A History of the Crusades* (3 vols, Cambridge: Cambridge University Press, 1951–54).

Savvides, Alexes G. C., 'Varia Byzantinoturcica II: Taticius the Turcople', *Journal of Oriental and African Studies*, 3–4 (1991–92): 235–8.

———, 'Late Byzantine and western historiographers on Turkish mercenaries in Greek and Latin armies: the Turcoples/Tourkopoloi', *The Making of Byzantine History: Studies dedicated to Donald M. Nicol*, (ed.) R. Beaton and C. Roueché (Aldershot: Ashgate, 1993): 122–36.

Schwinges, Rainer C., *Kreuzzugsideologie und Toleranz* (Stuttgart: Hiersemann, 1977).

Skoulatos, Basile, *Les personnages byzantins de l'Alexiade* (Louvain-la-Neuve: Bureau du recueil, Collège Érasme, 1980).

Sybel, Heinrich von, *Geschichte des ersten Kreuzzugs* (Leipzig: F. Fleischer, 1841).

———, *The History and Literature of the Crusades*, trans. Lady Duff Gordon (London: Chapman and Hall, 1861).

Szklenar, Hans, *Studien zum Bild des Orients in vorhöfischen deutschen Epen* (Göttingen: Vandenhoeck & Ruprecht, 1966).

Toussaint, Ingo, *Die Grafen von Leiningen. Studien zur leiningischen Genealogie und Territorialgeschichte bis zur Teilung von 1317/18* (Sigmaringen: Thorbecke, 1982).

Waha, Guillaume de, *Labores Herculis christiani Godefredi Bullionii* (2nd edn, Luxembourg: S. Rauch, 1690).

Wilkinson, John, *Jerusalem Pilgrimage, 1099–1185* (London: The Hakluyt Society, 1988).

Index

The chief adversaries (Christians [Latin], pilgrims vs. Saracens, Turks, pagans, infidels, gentiles) are so ubiquitous it would be unrealistic and unhelpful to index them. For more detail concerning people and places, see the two appendices.

Aachen 1, 2
St Mary's church 1, 2, 232, 255
abbots 16, 61, 66
sent as emissary to Egypt 123
Achard of Montmerle 60, 212, 213, 251
Acre 204, 245, 265
Adam, son of Michael 108, 109, 172, 251
Adana 87, 90, 137, 263, 265
Adelbero of Luxembourg 113, 251
Adelolf 226, 251
Adhémar, bishop of Le Puy 6, 58, 60, 63, 73, 74, 100, 104, 235n, 251
at siege of Antioch 106, 110, 124, 153, 163–5
in battle of Antioch 168, 172–4, 177
death 179
Adorsonius 107, 133, 251
Adrianople 12, 19, 28, 49, 53, 265
Alan Fergant of Brittany 60, 251
Albara 192, 197, 200, 201, 265
Aleppo 74, 133, 138, 171, 180–1, 259, 265
Alexandria the Lesser 99, 103, 142, 160, 265
Alexios I Komnenos 7, 19–20, 92–3, 119, 123, 134–7, 163–4, 178–9, 246, 248, 251
and Peter the Hermit 27–9, 31, 34–5
and Godfrey 47–56
and other leaders 56–7, 61
siege of Nicaea 57, 64–5, 67–8, 72–3
alms 23, 28, 66, 70, 77, 174, 235
Alps 18, 272
Altalon 108–9, 265
Amacha 139, 187–90, 252, 265
Amasa 139, 171, 252
Amasa of Curzh 139, 251
ambushes 29, 32, 74, 81, 94, 96, 98, 101, 110–12, 114–15, 120, 127–9, 130, 140, 145, 152, 160, 164, 179, 180, 183, 188–90, 193, 207, 212–13, 218, 245
Amiens 15, 262, 265
amirs 106, 107, 109, 111, 130, 135, 184n, 228n, 251–64
of Egypt 123, 230n
Anselm of Ribemont 60, 166n, 168n, 170, 196, 200, 252
Antioch 74, 92, 101, 103–5, 177–9, 184, 186, 190–3, 197, 249, 265
description 107
basilica of St Peter 153, 165–6, 177, 179, 180
chapel of St Mary 177
church of St Paul 177
citadel 109, 121, 133n, 148–51, 154, 160, 169, 178, 192–3
'Iron' or Farfar bridge 104–5, 112, 126–7
ship bridge 109, 111–12, 127
siege 108–50
battle 168–75
capture 8, 144–51
Karbugha's siege 153–64
Antioch the Less 81, 265
Antiochus 107, 225
Antwerp 90, 246, 265
Apulia 53, 265
aqueduct 204
Arabia 211, 236n
Arabs 104, 197, 237, 239, 240, 242

Armenia 83n, 92, 103, 107, 137, 140, 265
Armenians 8, 83, 85, 87, 88, 89, 92–3, 95, 101, 140–1, 142, 149, 150, 185
Arnulf of Choques 215, 234–5, 236, 237, 238, 252
Arnulf of Tirs 60, 114, 252
Arqa 195–6, 197–200, 208, 265
Arsuf 243–4, 265
Artah 100–3, 143, 265
Ascalon 212, 218, 235–6, 243, 265
  battle 236–42
Austria 43
Auvergne 18
Avlona 56, 265
Azaz 180–4, 186, 191, 196, 265
Azoparth *see* Ethiopians

Balak of Sororgia 98–9, 187–9, 252
Balas of Amacha 139, 252
Baldric, Godfrey's seneschal 44, 158, 226, 252
Balduk of Samosata 95, 97–9, 139, 171, 190, 252
Baldwin of Boulogne 6, 43, 45–6, 92–3, 98–9, 103, 180, 183, 192, 252
  at Constantinople 50, 52, 54
  at Nicaea 59
  at Tarsus 80–90
  at Mamistra 91
  at Edessa 93–7, 137, 139–42, 185–90
  Balak's treachery 187–90
  1st wife 46, 46–8, 100
  2nd wife 103
Baldwin of Bourcq 43, 51, 54, 59, 77, 84, 91, 168, 207n, 208, 212–13, 252
Baldwin Calderun 60, 63, 65, 252
Baldwin of Ghent 60, 65, 252
Baldwin of Hainaut 48–9, 59, 77, 109, 170, 178–9, 252
baptism 39, 62, 125, 238
Bari 17, 265
Bavaria 35
Bavarians 20, 22, 35, 79, 109, 168, 171
bear 81–2
Beirut 202, 245, 265
Belgrade 18–20, 22–3, 36–7, 48, 265
Bernard of Domedart 60, 252
Berry 16, 266
Bethlehem 8, 206–7, 212, 266
bishops 16, 18, 61, 66, 77, 122, 214, 215, 232
  Ambrose, bishop of Milan 161–2
  from Italy 208
  of Edessa 93
  of Mainz 38
  of Ramla (Lydda) 205
  see also Adhémar of Le Puy, Daibert of Pisa
Black Mountains 79, 266
Boesas 139, 171, 252
Bohemond of Taranto 53–4, 74, 81, 83–6, 100, 102, 106–8, 178, 183, 185, 192, 193–4, 197, 252
  at Constantinople 56–7
  at Nicaea 58–9, 62–4, 70
  battle of Dorylaeum 74–7
  siege of Antioch 108, 117–18, 122, 125, 126–30, 140, 142–3, 154–5, 163n, 166
  capture of Antioch 144–9
  battle of Antioch 168, 171–2
  and Latakia 245–9
Bohemond, Turkish convert 125, 144–5
booty 22, 23, 26, 29, 35, 39, 79, 83, 85, 89, 90, 92, 113, 117, 122, 174, 175, 194, 195, 207–8, 212, 237, 241
  see also plunder
Boutoumites 72n
Bretons 79
Buldagis 134, 136, 154, 252
Bulgaria 19, 22, 24, 47–8, 53, 56
Bulgars 18–21, 23, 24–6, 163
Burgundians 79
Butentrot 82–3, 266
Byzantines, *see* Greeks

Caesarea 204, 205, 244, 266
Caiphas (Haifa) 204, 244, 266
Calabria 53, 266
cannibalism 194
canons 1, 61, 232, 234n
Cappadocia 28, 55–8, 82n, 266
Carinthia 41, 266
carrier pigeons 182
Castle of the Maidens 99, 266
Castle of the Shepherds 99, 266

Castle of the Young Men 99, 266
Cazcornuz 107, 253
Christians, Eastern 7–8
  Armenian 8, 92, 100–1, 149
  Greek 7, 30, 34, 119, 121, 149–50, 177, 245
  Palestinian 221, 233
  Syrian 149–50, 151, 181, 211
cisterns 205n, 214
  at Emmaus 206
  in Jerusalem 223–4
Civitot 29, 32–4, 64, 65, 67, 136, 266
Clarembald of Vendeuil 39, 40, 41, 43, 48, 49, 143, 253
clergy, clerics 16, 34, 119, 122, 153, 160, 177, 180, 214, 215, 233, 235
Clermont 18, 266
coinage 70n
  bezants 27, 28, 55, 95, 97, 98, 99, 103, 140, 158, 174, 186, 187, 189, 191, 199
  of Chartres 70
  marks 113, 118, 158, 159, 225
  penny, pence 118, 158, 214
  shillings 118, 158, 159
  talents 139, 186
  tetartaron 28, 55
Cologne 37–8, 267
Coloman 253
  and Peter the Hermit 18–23
  and Gottschalk 35–7
  and Emicho 39–41
  and Godfrey 43–8
Combrus, plain 109, 267
Conan of Brittany 60, 168, 208, 253
confession 168, 237
Cono of Montaigu 51, 54, 60, 101, 102, 110, 129, 168, 208, 240, 249, 253
Constantine, Armenian leader 83n, 96, 103, 137, 253
Constantinople 19, 27–8, 31, 47, 49–56, 162, 267
Copatrix 107, 133, 253
Cumans 24, 163
Cyprus 234

Daibert, bishop of Pisa 247, 253
Damascus 105, 139, 195, 197, 204, 230, 267
Dandronuch 137, 267
Danes 18, 119–20, 163
Danube 21, 22, 39, 41, 190,
deserters 160, 162–3
disease 123, 153, 179–80, 185, 190–1
doctors 82
Dodo of Cons 43, 60, 253
Dorylaeum, battle of 74–8
Drava, river 47, 267
Drogo of Mouchy 168, 253
Drogo of Nesle 43, 48, 49, 59, 143, 186, 253
Duqaq of Damascus 107n, 139n, 230n, 253
Dyrachium 48n, 56, 86n, 267

earthquake 17–18
eclipse 206
Edessa 93–6, 99, 139–42, 180, 183, 186–7, 189, 192, 267
Egypt 206, 218, 236, 267
  king of 123, 126–7, 208, 212, 218–19, 221–2, 228, 229, 230, 235, 240–3, 245
Egyptians 8, 123n, 218, 237
Emicho 38–41, 43, 253
Emmaus 206, 267
Engelrand of Saint-Pol 60, 115, 116, 168, 195, 254
Engilbert of Tournai 217, 222, 254
England 37, 90n
English 18, 100, 124n
Enzhu 186–7, 254
Episcopate 193, 267
Etampes 21, 267
Ethiopians 236, 240, 242
Euphrates, river 94, 95, 138, 142, 173, 174, 192
Eustace of Boulogne 43n, 58, 59, 90, 143, 170, 192, 195, 217, 222, 236, 240, 254
Everard of Le Puiset 105, 108, 127, 155, 168, 254

famine 26, 118–19, 122, 123, 140, 143, 157–63, 166, 168, 173, 174, 194, 208

Fer 93, 254
Ferna 119, 267
Flanders 2, 37, 43n, 49n, 79, 90, 246, 268
Florina of Burgundy 119–20, 254
Folbert of Bouillon 180, 254
his wife 180, 181, 184n
Folbert of Chartres 190, 254
Folcher of Orléans 26, 28, 32, 33, 254
Foloroca 137, 267
Francavilla 47, 267
France 35, 37
Francia; Frankish kingdom 17, 18, 134
Franco of Mechelen 159, 254
Franks 20, 32, 49, 50, 52, 79, 102, 111, 171, 186
Fredelo of Esch 112, 159, 254
French 22, 29, 33
Frisia 90, 246, 267
Fulcher of Chartres (not the historian) 99, 186, 255

Gaston of Béarn 218n, 255
Gaston of Béziers 60, 77, 168, 186, 205, 207, 208, 249, 255
Gaul 43, 44, 54, 90, 153, 173
Gauls 21, 31, 32, 36, 40–1, 67–9, 78, 86, 93, 96–8, 101–2, 104, 111–13, 119, 124, 129–30, 135, 141, 145, 148–52, 156, 163, 169, 172, 173, 186–8, 208, 219–20, 222, 239–41
Genoese 178n, 245–6, 248–9
Gerard of Avesnes 245, 255
Gerard of Gournay 60, 253, 255
Gerard of Quierzy 59–60, 76–7, 211, 239, 255
Gerard of Roussillon 60, 168, 208, 255
Gerard, Baldwin's secretary 139–40, 190, 255
Germans 6, 22, 24, 79, 90, 102
defeated near Nicaea 29–31
Gottschalk's followers 36
attack Jews in the Rhineland 37–9
at Antioch 168, 171, 190
at Jerusalem 208
Gilbert of Traves 60, 212–13, 255
Giselbert, canon at Aachen 232–3, 255
Giselbert of Clermont 91, 255
Godevere (Godechilde), Baldwin's first wife 46, 46–8, 100
Godfrey of Bouillon 5–6, 38n, 81, 86–8, 100, 102, 106, 107, 178, 191, 197, 201, 204, 206, 226, 231–3, 243–7, 255–6
journey to Constantinople 43–53
at Constantinople 54–6
at Nicaea 58–73
battle of Dorylaeum 74–7
fights bear 81–2
at Antioch 108–67, 192
battle of Antioch 168–75
and Azaz 181–4, 196
in Edessa 185, 190, 192–3
at Arqa 198–200
siege of Jerusalem 208–224
elected ruler 233–4
battle of Ascalon 235–42
Godfrey Burel 21, 23, 26, 32, 33
Godfrey of Esch 43, 44, 51, 110, 256
Gottschalk 35–7, 43, 44, 256
Gozelo of Montaigu 60, 100, 102, 256
Greece, Greek empire 19, 50, 51, 86, 92, 134
Greek fire 68, 111, 221
Greek islands 163
Greek language 145
Greeks 7–8, 27, 29, 50, 136, 149, 150, 163, 177
see also Christians, Greek
guides 83, 201–2, 204, 206
Guy of Possesse 60, 64, 66, 256
Guz 20, 22, 256

Haifa *see* Caiphas
Hantax, river 47, 267
Harim124, 267
Hartmann of Swabia 43, 66, 173–4, 256
Haruni 137, 267
hawks 80
Hecelo 231, 256
Henry IV (or III in AA), emperor 5, 6, 18, 113, 185, 256
Henry of Esch 43, 49, 66, 73, 108, 110, 112, 158–9, 168, 170, 173–4, 180, 256
Heraclea 80–1, 267

heralds 47, 128
Herbrand of Bouillon 60, 184, 256
hermit 214–15
see also Peter the Hermit; St Symeon
Holy Lance 165–6, 168, 172, 179, 196
Holy Sepulchre 15–18, 28, 161, 200, 214, 225–7, 230–2, 234–6, 242, 244
hostages 23, 46–7, 53–5, 95, 98, 167, 182, 183, 186, 188, 190–1, 196, 245
hounds 80, 81
Hugh 'the Great' 48, 49, 60, 109, 168, 170, 171, 178, 179, 256
Hugh of Saint-Pol 60, 115, 168, 208, 256
Hungarians
and Peter the Hermit 18–24, 27
and Gottschalk 35–7
and Emicho 39–41
and Godfrey 43–7
Hungary 18, 20, 35–6, 39, 43, 44–7, 161
hunting 80, 81, 231
Husechin 82, 257

Iconium 80, 267
interpreters 86, 145–8, 166
Israel 232
Italy 18n, 41, 91, 145n, 208
Ivo of Grandmesnil 143, 155, 257

Jabala 197–8, 268
Jaffa 212n
Jerusalem xvi, 15–17, 18, 20, 25, 28, 35, 37, 39, 41, 43, 53, 90, 92, 123, 161–2, 190, 191–2, 193–4, 199–200, 202–6, 227–30, 231–5, 236, 242, 244–6, 249
chapel of St Stephen 215–16, 270
Jehosaphat, valley 209, 216, 218, 268
St Mary of the Latins 226
Temple 218, 223, 224–6, 228, 271
Tower of David 123, 208, 212, 213, 222, 226, 228, 230, 235, 237, 243, 271
see also Holy Sepulchre; Mount of Olives; Mount Sion
crusaders approach 206–8
siege and capture 208–23
Jews 9, 37–41, 204, 225n
John IV, patriarch of Antioch 177–8, 258
John Komnenos 54, 257
John of Nijmegen 60, 257
Jordan, river 204
Jubayl 201, 202, 245, 246, 268

Karageth 139, 171, 257
Karan 139, 171, 268
Karbugha 134, 136–8, 140–3, 145, 257
siege of Antioch 149, 152–8, 162–7
battle of Antioch 169, 172–5
Kenzvillare 231, 268
Ketena 231, 268
Khurasan 8, 30, 133, 134, 136, 139, 173, 268
sultan 134–5, 138, 140, 167, 261
Kogh Vasil 137, 185, 186, 258

Lambert (not identified) 24
Lambert of Montaigu 60, 168, 208, 240, 257
Latakia 90n, 123–4, 191, 194, 197, 245–9, 268
Le Puy 18
see also Adhémar
Lebanon 195, 203n, 234
leeches 214
Leitha, river 39, 41, 43, 268
letters 5, 15n, 38n, 43n, 60n, 93, 134–6, 166n, 178n, 244n
patriarch to pope 17
Godfrey to Coloman 44, 45
at Azaz 182–3
Lithold of Tournai 217, 222, 257
Lombards
siege master 70
interpreter 145
cleric 160
Lotharingia 18, 35, 37, 41n, 43, 184n, 268
Lotharingians 20, 59, 79, 109, 168, 171
Louis of Mousson 60, 168, 208, 257
Louis, archdeacon of Toul 119, 257
Lydda 205n, 206n, 268

Ma'arra 192, 194–5, 196, 197, 200, 201, 268
magicians 138
Mahumeth of Azaz 182, 186, 190, 191, 196, 257

Mainz 38, 268
Malabrunias, valleys 79, 268
Mamistra 90, 99, 110, 123, 137, 268
Marash 100, 268
martyrdom 25, 33, 37, 44, 62, 63, 116, 119, 127, 142n, 143, 161, 179n, 198, 238
Melitene 137, 269
Meraius, Egyptian vizier 230n, 235, 242, 257
mercenaries 34n, 163, 180, 187
merchants 29, 65, 67, 90n, 159, 163, 226n, 249
Mesopotamia 93, 269
mills 23
Milo Louez 60, 257
mines 71–2, 196, 199
money *see* coinage
monks 16, 34, 61, 77, 180
    Armenian 185–6
Moors 239, 242
Mosony 35, 39, 40, 43, 44, 269
Mount of Olives 208, 214, 215, 218, 226, 269
Mount Sinai 231, 269
Mount Sion 123, 208, 214, 217, 269

Neuss 38, 269
Nicaea xiii, 29–32, 33, 34, 57, 74, 78, 83, 92, 107, 119, 133, 134, 136, 137, 178, 179, 229, 269
    lake 61, 67–8, 265
    siege 58–72
Nichita, governor of Belgrade 20, 22, 23, 24, 27, 257
Nicomedia 28, 58n, 269
Nicusus 93, 140, 257
Niš 19, 22, 23, 24, 26, 27, 48, 269
Niz 139, 269
Normans 79, 140n

oaths 46, 55–6, 58, 65, 93, 97, 128, 144, 163, 167, 178, 179, 189, 246
Oliver of Jussey 60, 239, 257
Omar, prince of Azaz 180–2, 183, 184, 196–7
Orellis, valleys 74, 75, 80, 269, *and see* Dorylaeum
Orontes, river (Farfar) 103–6, 109, 111, 112, 113, 114, 127, 130, 152, 155, 156, 164, 169, 170, 171, 172, 178, 269

Pakrad 92–4, 137, 140, 185–6, 258
Palestine 229, 245
Pannonhalma 36n, 44, 45, 47, 269
paradise 17, 238
Payen of Garlande 64, 258
Pechenegs 22, 23, 24, 163
Peter of Astenois 43, 45, 54, 60, 84, 108, 110, 168, 170, 171, 258
Peter Bartholomew 165, 196–7, 258
Peter of Dampierre *see* Peter of Astenois
Peter, son of Gisla 155–6, 258
Peter the Hermit 5, 35, 43, 44, 48, 258
    preaching 15
    pilgrimage to Jerusalem 16–17
    and 'Peasants' Crusade' 20–35, 72–3, 106, 136–7
    and main expedition 58
    envoy to Karbugha 166–7, 169
    siege of Jerusalem 215
    battle of Ascalon 236–7
Philippopolis 19, 27, 48, 53, 269
Philomelium 80, 119, 120, 163, 269
pirates 89–90, 123, 246
Pisans 245–9
Pisellus of Wissant 190, 258
plague *see* disease
plunder 20, 29, 30, 31, 44, 48, 49, 53, 76, 83, 96, 106, 108, 117–18, 119, 122, 159, 164, 174, 180, 190, 203, 207, 237, 241, 242
popes
    Urban II 2n, 5, 6, 16–18, 43n, 179n, 262
portents 191, 206
    see also visions
priests 61, 70, 77, 138, 177, 213, 237
prisoners 24–6, 31, 35, 40, 48, 49, 63, 65, 72–3, 74, 75, 76, 78, 92, 115, 124, 125, 141, 153, 180, 187, 189, 191, 228, 246
Provençals 109, 140n, 158, 165n, 172, 246
Provence 61, 165, 174
provisions 141, 194, 195, 237

'Peasants' Crusade' 19, 27–8, 29
main expeditions 51, 65, 104
at Antioch 118, 151, 174, 191, 193
on march to Jerusalem 203
at Jerusalem 212, 245
Publicans 236, 239, 240, 242
Pulagit 133, 138, 171, 258

Qilij Arslan I *see* Suleyman

Raimbold Croton 155, 258
Raimbold of Orange 60, 168, 208, 258
Rainald of Beauvais 60, 77, 106, 168, 259
Rainald of Toul 43, 45, 60, 84, 108, 110, 143, 168, 186, 239, 258–9
Ralph of La Fontanelle 155, 259
Ramla 205, 206, 212, 237, 269
ransom 16, 42, 121, 145, 180, 187, 189, 190–1, 228
Ravendel 92–4, 103, 185, 186, 190, 193, 270
Raymond Pilet 60, 168, 196, 259
Raymond of Saint-Gilles 81, 100, 106, 108, 183–4, 196, 201, 204, 208, 259
at Constantinople 57–8, 61, 63
at Nicaea 61, 63, 66, 68, 74
at Antioch 109, 110, 120–1, 122, 126, 127, 128, 130–1, 140, 142, 143, 144, 149, 154, 156, 163, 165, 169, 174, 178
at Ma'arra 192–3, 194–5
at Arqa 195, 197–200
siege of Jerusalem 208–15, 217, 219, 228
battle of Ascalon 231, 236, 239–40
and Arsuf 243–4
and Latakia 124n, 246, 249
Regensburg 39n, 190, 270
Reinhard of Hamersbach 168, 170, 171, 180, 259
Reinold of Broyes 21, 26, 31, 33, 259
Rhine; Rhineland 1, 2, 4, 9, 10, 35, 37n, 190
Richard of Salerno 91, 259
Ridwan of Aleppo 133, 138, 171, 180–4, 259
Robert of Anzi 91, 259
Robert of Buonalbergo 60, 259–60
Robert of Flanders 43n, 49n, 57, 58, 59, 63, 64, 77, 81, 100, 102, 106, 197, 199, 200, 201, 204, 205, 235, 236, 239, 244, 249, 259
at Antioch 109, 117, 118, 125, 129, 139–40, 142, 143, 144, 145–7, 148, 155, 156–7, 162, 164, 168, 170, 174, 178, 192, 194
at Jerusalem 208, 211
Robert of Normandy 43n, 58, 59, 64, 69, 74, 100, 104, 106, 195, 201, 204, 236, 239, 242, 244, 249, 260
at Antioch 109, 125, 129, 140, 143, 155, 168, 170, 174, 178, 192, 194
at Jerusalem 208, 211
Robert of Paris 74–5, 259
Robert, bishop of Ramla (Lydda), 205, 260
Rodolph (Rotrou de Perche?) 60, 77, 260
Rodolph, a Breton (Ralph of Gael) 168, 260
Rodolph Peeldelau 49, 260
Roger of Barneville 64, 105, 108, 109, 125, 152–3, 156, 260
Roger, son of Dagobert 49, 260
Roger of Rozoy 100, 102, 106, 260
Rohas *see* Edessa
Romans 22, 29, 90, 102, 171
Rome 17, 185
Rossa 143, 270
Rosseleon 107, 170, 260
Rothard, son of Godfrey 60, 77, 168, 260
Rothard, Godfrey's steward 226, 261
royal road 38, 82, 90, 91, 108, 243
Rufinel 58, 270; *see also* Nicomedia
Rūm 8, 12, 30, 61, 73, 74, 78, 86, 100, 104, 119, 133, 134, 137, 140, 143, 164, 179, 270
Russia 40, 137
Ruthard, bishop of Mainz 38, 261

Sagitta *see* Sidon
St George, straits 20, 28, 58, 270
Saint-Gilles 246, 270
St John (place) 96, 270
St Symeon, port 111, 129, 159, 170, 178, 179, 190, 191, 270
Salabria 49, 270

Samarthan 134, 270
Samosart 139, 270
Samosata 95–6, 97–8, 190, 270
Sansadonias 107, 121, 133, 136, 154, 169, 178, 190–1, 261
Sava, river 19, 22–3, 47, 271
Saxons 109, 168, 171
sermons 35, 125–6, 215
ships 22, 29, 47, 61n, 64, 65, 67–8, 72, 89–90, 109, 127, 159, 162, 163, 179, 191, 240, 246, 249
Sidon 203, 204, 245, 271
siege engines 40, 66, 70–1, 110–11, 126, 127, 158, 195, 211–12, 215–18, 219–21, 246
  ballistas 111, 185
  battering rams 65, 68, 211, 212, 216–17, 223
  'fox' 66
  'tortoise' 67
  mangonels 66, 97, 99, 114, 196, 211, 212, 215–17, 219–21, 222, 230
  slinging machines 106, 211, 221, 240, 243
  throwing machines 65, 66, 68, 104, 196
  towers 70–2, 217–20, 222
Sigemar of Mechelen 159, 261
snakes 203
Sofiya 19, 27, 48, 271
Sokman 230, 261
Sooch 140, 271
soothsayers 138, 175
Sopron 20, 45, 46, 271
Sororgia 98–9, 139, 188–90, 271
spies 61–2, 102, 119, 127, 142, 187, 218
Stabelo 3, 44, 226–7, 261
Stephen of Aumale 60, 261
Stephen of Blois 58, 60, 74, 108, 109, 142, 160, 162, 261
sugar 200–1
Suleyman 80, 83, 107, 119–20, 133–6, 138, 139, 164, 169, 170, 171, 261
  and 'Peasants' Crusade' 29–32, 33
  siege of Nicaea 58, 61–3, 72
  battle of Dorylaeum 74–5, 76, 78
  wife and sons 72
Svend of Denmark 119–20, 261
Swabia 35, 173, 271
Swabians 20, 22–4, 30, 31, 35, 79, 106n, 109, 168
Symeon II, patriarch of Jerusalem 16–17, 234, 261
Syria 86, 92, 100, 139, 140, 177, 229
Syrians 142, 149, 150, 151, 181, 211

Talamria 195, 271
Tancred 57, 59, 64, 75, 92, 99–100, 103, 104, 108, 144, 192, 195, 198, 199, 200, 207, 261
  at Tarsus 80–7
  at Adana 87–90
  at Mamistra 90–1, 99
  at Antioch 109, 113, 115, 117, 125, 143, 149, 156, 168, 174
  at Jerusalem 208, 215, 218, 224, 225–8
  battle of Ascalon 235–6, 240
Taphnuz 103–4, 261
Tarsus 74, 82–5, 89–90, 91, 137, 271
Tatikios 59, 72, 108, 109, 163, 261
thirst 79–80, 203, 214
Thomas of Fère *see* Thomas of Marle
Thomas of Marle 39–41, 59, 77, 168, 208, 212, 262
Thoros of Edessa 83n, 94–7, 262
Tiel 246, 271
Tortosa 195, 196, 208, 249, 271
torture 62, 93, 121, 157, 187–8
tribute 15, 95, 98, 100, 101, 178, 226, 229, 245
Trier 39n, 72–3, 271
Tripoli 200–2, 245, 271
True Cross 233–4
Tulln 43–4, 45, 271
Turbessel 92–4, 103, 137, 140, 180, 185, 186, 190, 193, 271
Turcopoles 34, 51, 52, 68, 123, 163, 179, 191, 246
Tyre 204, 245, 271

Udelard of Wissant 204, 245, 271

valley 'of Camels' 195, 266
valley 'named Joy' 195, 272
Verzellaus 18, 272
visions 161–2, 165, 172, 191–2, 226, 231–2, 232–3

Walbric 155, 262
Walker of Chappes 60, 262
Walo of Chaumont 50, 77, 168, 262
Walo, steward of the king of France 106, 262
Walo of Lille 66, 262
Walter of Breteuil 23, 26, 32, 33, 263
Walter of Domedart 60, 125, 168, 170, 262–3
Walter Sansavoir 18–19, 21, 28, 31, 33, 262
Walter of Verva 203, 263
Walter of Verveis 60, 263
Warner of Grez 43, 45, 54, 59, 108, 127, 128, 168, 170, 171, 263
Welf of Boulogne (or Burgundy) 87, 90, 104, 263
William, Bohemond's nephew 75, 263
William Embriacus 218n
William of Forez 60, 263
William of Grandmesnil 160, 162, 263
William of Melun ('the Carpenter') 40, 41, 49, 160, 162, 263
William of Montpellier 60, 168, 191, 263
Winemer of Boulogne 90, 123, 190–1, 246, 264

Yaghi-Siyan 106, 107, 109, 121, 130, 133, 135, 136, 138, 139, 145, 148, 149–51, 170, 264

Zemun 18–19, 20, 21, 22, 23, 24, 27, 47, 272